PATRIOTISM AND POETRY
IN EIGHTEENTH-CENTURY BRITAIN

The poetry of the mid and late eighteenth century has long been regarded as primarily private and apolitical; in this wide-ranging study, Dustin Griffin argues that in fact the poets of the period were addressing the great issues of national life – rebellion at home, imperial wars abroad, an expanding commercial empire, an emerging new "British" national identity. Taking up the topic of patriotic verse, Griffin shows that the poets, like many contemporary essayists, sermon writers, and political journalists, were engaged in the century-long debate about the nature of "true patriotism." Griffin argues that canonical figures – James Thomson, William Collins, Thomas Gray, Christopher Smart, Oliver Goldsmith, William Cowper – along with less canonical writers such as Mark Akenside, John Dyer, and Ann Yearsley ask how poets might serve and even save their country, and take their place in a broader tradition of patriotic verse.

DUSTIN GRIFFIN is Professor of English at New York University. He is the author of a number of books on Restoration and eighteenth-century English literature, including *Satires on Man: The Poems of Rochester* (1973), *Alexander Pope: The Poet in the Poems* (1978), *Regaining Paradise: Milton and the Eighteenth Century* (1986), *Satire: A Critical Re-Introduction* (1994), and *Literary Patronage in England, 1650–1800* (Cambridge, 1996).

PATRIOTISM AND POETRY IN EIGHTEENTH-CENTURY BRITAIN

DUSTIN GRIFFIN

PUBLISHED BY THE PRESS SYNDICATE OF THE UNIVERSITY OF CAMBRIDGE
The Pitt Building, Trumpington Street, Cambridge, United Kingdom

CAMBRIDGE UNIVERSITY PRESS
The Edinburgh Building, Cambridge CB2 2RU, UK
40 West 20th Street, New York, NY 10011-4211, USA
477 Williamstown Road, Port Melbourne, VIC 3207, Australia
Ruiz de Alarcón 13, 28014 Madrid, Spain
Dock House, The Waterfront, Cape Town 8001, South Africa

http://www.cambridge.org

Publication of this book has been aided by a grant from the
Abraham and Rebecca Stein Faculty Publication Fund
of New York University, Department of English.

First published 2002

Printed in the United Kingdom at the University Press, Cambridge

Typeface Baskerville Monotype 11 / 12.5 pt.   *System* LATEX 2ε   [TB]

A catalogue record for this book is available from the British Library

Library of Congress Cataloguing in Publication data
Griffin, Dustin H.
Patriotism and poetry in eighteenth-century Britain / by Dustin Griffin.
p.   cm.
Includes bibliographical references (p. 296) and index.
ISBN 0 521 81118 X
1. English poetry – 18th century – History and criticism.   2. Politics and literature – Great
Britain – History – 18th century.   3. Patriotism – Great Britain – History – 18th century.
4. Political poetry, English – History and criticism.   5. Patriotism in literature.
I. Title: Patriotism and poetry in 18th-century Britain.   II. Title.
PR555.H5 G75   2001
821′.509358 – dc21   2001037852

ISBN 0 521 81118 X hardback

To the memory of my father
W. L. Hadley Griffin (1918–1997),
who served his country and his city

Of thee more worthy were the task, to raise
A lasting Column to thy Country's praise;
To sing the land, which yet alone can boast
That Liberty corrupted Rome has lost.
                George Lord Lyttelton, *Epistle to Mr. Pope* (1730)

Lo! patriots, heroes, sages croud to birth:
And bards to sing them in immortal verse!
                James Thomson, from *Alfred. A Masque* (1740)

            me, with Britains Glory fir'd,
Me, far from meaner Care or meaner Song,
Snatch to the Holy Hill of Spotless Bay,
My Countrys Poet, to record her Fame.
                Alexander Pope, "Fragment of Brutus, an Epic" (1743)

Contents

Illustrations

Acknowledgments

For reading chapters of this book in draft, I thank Linda Colley, Robin Dix, Roger Lonsdale, James Sambrook, Mary Waldron, Richard Wendorf, and especially Betty Rizzo. The two anonymous readers for Cambridge University Press made very helpful comments, both large and small. For listening to a paper drawn from chapter 2, thanks to the Eighteenth Century Club in the Department of English at New York University. For generously replying to inquiries, I thank Rob Hume and Kit Hume, Michael Schwartz, and Diane Dugaw, and especially Susan Goulding. For bibliographical suggestions, thanks to Manuel Schonhorn.

I also thank the staffs of the several research libraries in which I have worked: the New York Public Library, the British Library, Bobst Library at New York University, and Butler Library at Columbia University. Illustrations are reproduced with the permission of the British Library, the British Museum, and the Pierpont Morgan Library.

Abbreviations

BL	British Library
BM	British Museum
DNB	*Dictionary of National Biography*
ECS	*Eighteenth Century Studies*
ELH	*English Literary History*
Foxon	David Foxon, *English Verse, 1701–1750: a catalogue of separately printed poems with notes on collected editions* (London, 1975)
JEGP	*Journal of English and Germanic Philology*
OED	*Oxford English Dictionary*
PMLA	*Publications of the Modern Language Association*
SEL	*Studies in English Literature*

Introduction

Introduce the topic of *patriotism* to a literary audience, and the chances
are the first response will be to recall Johnson's famous apothegm:
"Patriotism is the last refuge of a scoundrel."[1] Bring up patriotic *poetry*,
and the response is likely to be similarly skeptical: what respectable poet
since Wilfred Owen – if not blinded by sentiment or hired for the purpose – would be so naive or so uncritical as to write in honor and un-
qualified praise of his native land? Narrow the focus to English patriotic
poetry of the eighteenth century, and skepticism about its interest or
its merit is likely to persist. Eighteenth-century poems celebrating contemporary Britain as the land of liberty and commercial prosperity, secure and confident, under the leadership of wise ministers and kings, of
its superior place in Europe and the world – these effusions would be
peremptorily dismissed as "Whig panegyric." The last time – until quite
recently – that such poems were given serious and sympathetic attention
by literary scholars was more than fifty years ago, in Bonamy Dobrée's
British Academy lecture on "The Theme of Patriotism in the Poetry of
the Early Eighteenth Century."[2]

As Dobrée shows, a common feature of these poems was an apostrophe to Britannia, or a "panegyric on Great Britain" as the home of
liberty, happiness, and prosperity, a nation generously prepared to offer its services abroad as defender of freedom or as global merchant.
He finds them in verses by Lewis Theobald, James Thomson, Matthew

[1] It is sometimes forgotten that Johnson's remark was uttered in the heat of conversation, and that,
in Boswell's view, "he did not mean a real and generous love of our country, but that pretended
patriotism which so many, in all ages and countries, have made a cloak for self-interest" (*Life of
Johnson*, ed. G. B. Hill, rev. L. F. Powell [Oxford: Clarendon, 1934–50], II, 348). A true patriot,
Johnson observes in *The Patriot*, "is he whose public conduct is regulated by one single motive,
the love of his country" (*Political Writings*, ed. Donald Greene [New Haven, 1977], 390).

[2] *Proceedings of the British Academy*, 35 (1949), 49–65. Earlier treatments of the topic include W. J.
Courthope's discussion in volume V of his *History of English Poetry*, 6 vols. (1895–1909), and Cecil
Moore's essay on "Whig Panegyric Verse, 1700–1760: A Phase of Sentimentalism," *PMLA*, 41
(1926), and reprinted in his *Backgrounds of English Literature, 1700–1760* (Minneapolis, 1953), 104–44.

Prior, Gilbert West, Thomas Tickell, Elijah Fenton, Samuel Croxall, and Edward Young. The fact that none of these writers (with the exception of Thomson) were then – or are now – regarded as poets of the first rank is significant. Eighteenth-century patriotic effusion has long been associated with minor or merely ceremonial poetry. Even Dobrée regarded his subject with amused condescension, but he could still be touched by the "emotion of patriotism," its "humane" and "noble" vision of an idealized British empire, "a vision of the future, of tranquillity, of plenty, and of universal brotherhood" (62). His essay was written in the aftermath of World War II, in which Britain, undefeated and rebuilding, was celebrating its heritage and, in some quarters, trying to reassume the mantle of benevolent empire. It is easy to smile at Dobrée now, especially with acute hindsight, and to dismiss the idea of patriotism as an anachronism. The British empire, Britons know now, was already fading by 1949 – India having become independent in 1947 – and Britain was rapidly sinking into the status of second-rank power.

Among literary historians and critics, the patriotic poetry of the eighteenth century was largely dismissed even at the time that Dobrée wrote.[3] Whatever claims he made for the interest of patriotic verse were not accepted by the rising New Critics. At the time his essay appeared such verse was regarded as far inferior to the poems of Pope and Swift, who looked on the spectacle of contemporary life not with patriotic ardor but with the bemusement or the contempt of a satirist firmly located in the political opposition to Walpole and his hired panegyrists.

About one matter the traditional literary historians and the New Critics agreed: eighteenth-century patriotic verse was regarded as a relatively short-lived phenomenon, overshadowed by the satiric Augustans in the first part of the century, and superseded by a new group of poets at mid century – Collins, Gray, Smart, Cowper – who, it was said, showed little poetic interest in affairs of state or national topics such as liberty and commerce, and devoted themselves instead to the state of poetry or the state of their own sensibilities.

Why take up the topic of eighteenth-century poetry and patriotism again *now?* In part because Dobrée and his predecessors did little more than scratch the surface. They largely limited themselves to the *theme* of patriotism, and regarded it in unproblematic terms, as a "universal" emotion or an aspect of a much broader but underdefined "sentimentalism," rather than as highly self-conscious and calculated deployments of what

---

[3] Moore in 1926 regarded "Whig panegyric" as "of slight intrinsic value" (*Backgrounds of English Literature*, 104).

might be called an eighteenth-century *discourse of patriotism*. In their brief discussions they did not attempt to reconstruct the dense political and literary contexts of the middle decades of the century, in which those on all sides claimed to be true patriots (and regarded their opponents as false patriots – malcontents or office-seekers). They made little effort to determine whether patriotism meant love of one's country as it is, as it once was, or as it might be.[4] They did not ask what "country" it was that the patriot claimed to love – at a time when Britain was a union of three separate nations (England, Wales, Scotland – and four if we count Ireland), and when the empire was rapidly expanding overseas. And they left unexplored what it might mean for a *poet* – as opposed to a politician or a pamphleteer – to claim to provide patriotic service to the country. Do they also serve who only stand and write verses?[5]

There is a second reason for taking up the topic of patriotism and poetry now. It is a way of correcting a still influential misreading of mid- and late-eighteenth-century poetry. For several decades, and perhaps for most of the twentieth century, that poetry has seemed to many readers to be preoccupied with meditations in lonely country churchyards, gentle twilight reveries, withdrawal to quiet rural retreats, to religious ecstasy, or imaginative flights to a medieval past. The poets after Pope are said to have turned inward and become self-conscious because of their sense of personal or cultural inadequacy in the face of the extraordinary accomplishments of their mighty predecessors, a sense that there was little left for them to do, that an age of enlightenment was somehow inimical to the production of poetry, or a kind of "ontological insecurity" that made the external world itself seem impoverished. In the early 1980s these themes were brought together in two influential books, John Sitter's *Literary Loneliness in Mid-Eighteenth-Century England* (1982) and Fredric Bogel's *Literature and Insubstantiality in Later Eighteenth-Century England* (1984). Both books argued that, by contrast to the earlier eighteenth century, when the poet was a trenchant and engaged observer of the socio-political scene or even a participant in the world of affairs, poets by about 1750 had begun to turn away from that world, became increasingly pre-occupied with private experience and with the experience of the poet, now conceived

---

4 Dobrée notes only that patriotism can take many different forms – "an intense attachment to . . . the countryside you inhabit," "the triumph of your tribe," or "the love of people and their ways," and that the "emotion" of patriotism can be "nourished by a sense of the past, or again by a vision of the future" ("Theme of Patriotism," 50).

5 Dobrée's essay became the basis for a brief discussion in his 1959 volume in the Oxford History of English Literature, where patriotic poetry figures as one of "various trends" in verse (*English Literature in the Early Eighteenth Century, 1700–1740* [Oxford, 1959], 516–20).

of as a solitary, isolated, and even alienated figure. The poet retired from society not, like Pope, *pour mieux sauter*, but to search for meditative or religious peace, and meditative or religious vision.[6] Such a retreat might be seen as a confession of failure, or as an acute awareness that literature itself had become marginalized. Writers of course did not forsake the world of public experience altogether, but a kind of division of labor is thought to have taken place: the poets (and perhaps the Gothic novelists) take up private experience, while to engage the public world writers turn to "intellectual prose" and produce great works of history (Gibbon), biography (Boswell), philosophy (Hume), critical theory (Reynolds), economics (Smith), politics (Burke), and law (Blackstone).

This view of mid- and later-eighteenth-century poetry, buttressed by the influential arguments of Walter Jackson Bate on "the burden of the past" and Harold Bloom on "the anxiety of influence," has remained largely in place, even as political and social historians of the period are re-examining the writers who took part in the development of a new "British" national identity following the 1707 Union between England and Scotland, the Jacobite rebellion of 1745 and its aftermath, and the rise of nonpartisan loyal attachment to the Hanoverians and to empire as a consequence of the century-long struggle against France.[7] My reading of eighteenth-century poetry has been colored by the work of these historians, who help direct literary scholars to the dense and tangled political issues of mid century, that, so I argue, deeply affected the poets writing at the time. It is the essentially apolitical reading of eighteenth-century poetry after Pope that I, along with other scholars, want to challenge. As I would argue, poets such as Thomson, Collins, Gray, Smart, and Cowper, along with Goldsmith, Mark Akenside, John Dyer, Ann Yearsley, and others, are acutely aware of the risks and rewards of foreign war, the attractions and the dangers of foreign trade, the loss (or the triumph) of traditional English liberties, outcries against political division, the invasion of French "effeminacy," and the consequent fears of depleted national vigor. Not only are they politically conscious; they implicitly

---

[6] See William Dowling, "Ideology and the Flight from History in Eighteenth-Century Poetry," in Leopold Damrosch, ed., *The Profession of Eighteenth-Century Literature* (Madison, 1992), 135–53.

[7] Linda Colley, *Britons: Forging the Nation, 1707–1837* (New Haven, 1992); Robert Harris, *A Patriot Press: National Politics and the London Press in the 1740s* (Oxford: Clarendon, 1994); Kathleen Wilson, *The Sense of the People: Politics, Culture and Imperialism in England, 1715–1785* (Cambridge, 1995). On the debate about the creation of a common "British" identity vs. the persistence of older identities continues, see Murray Pittock, *Inventing and Resisting Britain: Cultural Identities in Britain and Ireland, 1685–1789* (Basingstoke, 1997), Colin Kidd, *Subverting Scotland's Past: Scottish Whig Historians and the Creation of an Anglo-British Identity* (Cambridge, 1993), and *British Identities Before Nationalism: Ethnicity and Nationhood in the Atlantic World, 1600–1800* (Cambridge, 1999).

conceive a political or social function for the poet, and try to imagine what it means for a poet to play that public role. Literary historians are beginning to examine the ways in which poets of the period took up the topics of political opposition to Walpole, dynastic struggle between Stuarts and Hanoverians, commercial empire, or national identity.[8] Other books might be written on the literary engagement with the topic of moral decline, or British ambivalence about French culture. My approach here is to focus on the complex idea of "patriotism" and to consider the ways in which the poets of the middle and later decades of the century – from the 1740s through the French Revolution – set themselves up not just as Opposition "Patriots" but as "patriots" (small *p*), writers who both professed their love and admiration for their native land, and offered, at least implicitly, to provide some public *service* to the nation.

A study of patriotism and poetry in the eighteenth century does not, however, take place in a cultural vacuum, and before proceeding I wish to situate it in a larger and not purely literary or academic context at the opening of the twenty-first century. For students of literature, whether they realize it or not, are in some sense responding to the pressures of their own culture. And there may be some reasons why literary scholars find themselves thinking about eighteenth-century patriotism at the present moment. Despite the increasing globalization of economies and cultures in the 1990s, one sees everywhere a countervailing interest in ethnic and national *identity*, in *loyalty* directed toward the group, the tribe, or the nation – whether Palestine, Armenia, Kosovo, or Chechnya – that would be a sovereign state, in short, in a self-proclaimed *patriotism*. Resurgent nationalism is not restricted to sites of collapsing federations such as the USSR and Yugoslavia. It is found today in Great Britain, where a sense of Welsh and Scottish cultural distinctiveness, never absent, has reasserted itself in the form of separatist political aspirations and a governmental policy of "devolution," perhaps, as Linda Colley has suggested, because Britain is not only more culturally diverse but because it has lost its sense of national – that is, British – identity. An increasing awareness of cultural

---

[8] On the "Patriot" Opposition to Walpole, see Christine Gerrard, *The Patriot Opposition to Walpole: Politics, Poetry, and National Myth, 1725–1742* (Oxford, 1994). For poetry and the dynastic struggle, see Murray Pittock, *Poetry and Jacobite Politics in Eighteenth-Century Britain and Ireland* (Cambridge, 1994), and Howard Erskine-Hill, *The Poetry of Opposition and Revolution: Dryden to Wordsworth* (Oxford, 1996). On poetic response to overseas empire, see Suvir Kaul, *Poems of Nation, Anthems of Empire: English Verse in the Long Eighteenth Century* (Charlottesville, VA, 2000). On national identity, see Howard Weinbrot, *Britannia's Issue: The Rise of British Literature from Dryden to Ossian* (Cambridge, 1993), and Leigh Davis, *Acts of Union: Scotland and the Literary Negotiation of the British Nation, 1707–1830* (Stanford, 1998).

diversity in the US makes some observers wonder whether America can still be *one* country, toward which all patriotic citizens can feel loyalty. Is it possible or desirable in a world both global and multicultural to feel some sentiments of patriotism, of attachment to one's native country, one's Burkean "little platoon"? For many Americans, scarred or appalled by McCarthyism in the 1950s and by an unpopular war in the 1960s and 1970s, patriotism has been reduced to a crude flag-waving and a mean-spirited "Love it or leave it" taunt. At a time when "Patriot" is the name of a guided missile, a professional sports team, and a summer movie, patriotism can only with great difficulty be discussed without severe skepticism, or imagined as a proper subject for poetry.

In such a context it may help to return to the patriotism of an earlier and what seems to us – though not to those who lived through it – a less problematic era, not to the belligerent patriotic huffing of an aggressive or triumphalist British empire but to the ambivalent engagements by poets who declared an attachment to their country, worried about its fate and about the excesses of the national "spirit" or character, and wondered if there was an appropriate public role for a poet to play.

Is there a place for a public poetry today, for a poetry which engages the aspirations of an entire country, which tries somehow to speak for the nation, and can rightfully be called *patriotic*, in the best sense of the term? It is worth remembering that some great poems – like the *Aeneid* – once concerned themselves with the founding and destiny of the nation – or with a critical moment in its history – Marvell's "Horatian Ode," Milton's heroic sonnets, Dryden's witty political narratives. In later eras Shelley, Whitman, and Yeats in their various ways all sought to speak to and for the nation at times of crisis. Who speaks for it now?

CHAPTER I

The eighteenth-century debate about patriotism

It is remarkable and a little surprising to rediscover that not only minor eighteenth-century poets but many of the poets whom we regard as major figures quite explicitly put themselves forward in their poems as *patriots*, from Pope, who in an introductory fragment from his projected epic *Brutus* (1743) aspired to be "My Countrys Poet," to Cowper, who in *The Task* (1785) exclaimed "England, with all thy faults, I love thee still – / My Country!" (II, lines 206–7), and asserted that the poet "serves his country; recompenses well / The state" (VI, lines 968–69.) Between Pope and Cowper, not just the small fry quoted by Dobrée but virtually every poet whose works we consider canonical made a similar claim. Thomson aspires to "mix the Patriot's with the Poet's Flame" (*The Seasons, Autumn*, line 22), and salutes his native land: "Britannia, hail! . . . island of bliss amid the subject sea" (*Summer*, lines 1581–85). "Transported by my Country's Love," he says, "I've aimed / To sing her praises in ambitious verse" (*Summer*, lines 671–73). Even John Gay begins one of his Fables with an address "To My Native Country."

> Hail happy land, whose fertile grounds
> The liquid fence of Neptune bounds;
> By bounteous nature set apart,
> The seat of industry and art.[1]

The "design" of *Ocean. An Ode* (1730), says Edward Young, is to promote "the glory of my country and my King."[2] Akenside, in a poem written "On Leaving Holland," addresses his homeland, "where liberty to all is known" (line 26). It is there that "freedom's ample fabric" has

---

[1] Fable VIII in the second volume of his *Fables*, published posthumously in 1738 (*Poetry and Prose*, ed. Vinton Dearing, 2 vols. [Oxford: Clarendon, 1974], II, 406). The advertisement to the collection claims that the fables show Gay to have been "a man of a truly honest Heart, and a sincere Lover of his Country" (II, 380). Gay's lines were included in a 1760 print celebrating the accession of George III (see figure 1).

[2] *Poetical Works*, 2 vols. (London, 1866), II, 153.

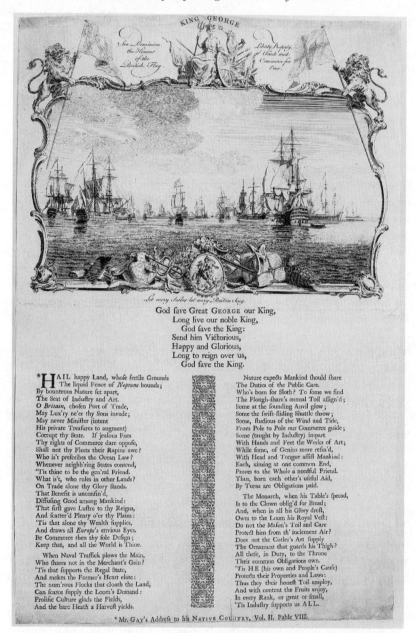

Figure 1. "God Save King George" (1760). Pierpont Morgan Library, New York. Peel Col. III, fol. 50, no. 174

long been "fix'd . . . / On Albion's happy shore" (*The Pleasures of Imagi-nation* [1744], II, lines 43–44). For Akenside, the poet has a public and patriotic role to play: "Not far beneath the hero's feet / Nor from the legislator's seat / Stands far remote the bard" ("To Townshend in the Country," lines 19–21). Included in William Collins' 1746 collection of *Odes on Several Descriptive and Allegorical Subjects* is a set of poems critics have long thought of as "patriotic odes." In the century's most famous Pindaric ode, Thomas Gray's bard confronts an invading monarch, and in a prophetic and patriotic vision unveils the future triumphs of "Britannia's issue." As he muses on Roman ruins, "High ambitious thoughts" inflame John Dyer "greatly to serve my country" (*The Ruins of Rome*, lines 128–29). Charles Churchill, though self-consciously a satirist and an adversary to the ministry, exclaims: "be England what she will, / With all her faults, she is my country still" ("The Farewell," lines 27–28).[3] Goldsmith, men-tally traveling through Europe, longs to return and settle in his native land. Even Christopher Smart, though locked up in Bedlam, celebrated Britain's military heroes, and declared with patriotic fervor that he him-self was "the Reviver of *Adoration* amongst *English-Men*" (*Jubilate Agno*, B332).

Why should poets from Pope to Cowper have put themselves forward at key moments in their poems as *patriots*? The answer is not simply to be found by examining the circumstances of each poet's life or career but in locating causal factors in their shared culture. Proceeding on the double assumption that poetry has its own internal history, and that it is written and read within a particular public world, one would expect to find that patriotic poets in eighteenth-century Britain were at once responding to the poets who came before them, and to the pressures exerted by the larger political world in which they moved. I will look first at that larger political world.

In the middle decades of the eighteenth century it would probably have been difficult for a poet *not* to have a sense that he – or she – was a pa-triotic "Briton," or at least that he was expected to be one. To begin with, the nation was more or less continuously at war from the late seventeenth century until the Congress of Vienna in 1815. The distinc-tive names assigned to particular "wars" – the Nine Years' War under

---

3 Churchill's admirers thought of him as a patriot-poet. See Percival Stockdale: "Thine is the Poet's; thine the Patriot's Crown" (*Churchill Defended, a Poem Addressed to the Minority* [London, 1765]).

William III (1689–97), the War of the Spanish Succession under Queen
Anne (1702–13), the War of the Austrian Succession (1743–48), the Seven
Years' War (1756–63), the American Revolutionary War (1776–83), the
wars against Revolutionary France (1793–1802) and against Napoleon
(1803–15) – obscure the fact that Britain's chief adversary in each of these
wars was France. Britain and France had become rivals for European –
and worldwide – hegemony.

It was not simply the presence of a threatening "other" across the
Channel that aroused British national feeling. As Linda Colley has argued, patriotic self-consciousness can be traced to domestic causes as
well. The 1707 Union of the parliaments of England and Scotland[4]
brought into being the new nation of Great Britain, comprised in fact
of three once distinct nations, England, Scotland, and Wales. Cultural
differences between the English core and the Celtic periphery did not
simply disappear after 1707. They persisted, and made it necessary, so
Colley has shown, to invent a new national identity which could enable
regional differences and loyalties to be submerged even if not forgotten. That new "Britishness," she argues, was based on the twin pillars
of Protestantism and "liberty," squarely opposed to French papistry and
absolutism.[5] If, as Benedict Anderson has written, a nation is not so much
a geographical or demographic fact as it is an "imagined community,"
there is all the more reason to assume that the work of imagining Great
Britain would be carried on – explicitly or implicitly – in significant part
by the country's poets.[6]

Other large-scale political factors contributed to a heightened national
self-awareness. Over the course of the eighteenth century Britain was
being increasingly transformed – in fact, and in imagination – from an
agricultural country to a commercial country, from a nation of yeomen
to a nation of shopkeepers, from a self-dependent island set in a silver
sea to a world-trading empire. These transformations could not but
provoke a reexamination of the nation's identity. What, for the patriotic
Briton, is "my country"? Is it a green and pleasant rural land? Or is
it a stoutly defended island? If I am one of the many Scots living in

---

[4] The crowns had been united in 1603.   [5] *Britons*, 11–54.
[6] *Imagined Communities: Reflections on the Origin and Spread of Nationalism* (rev. edn., London, 1991).
Anderson's work has prompted a vigorous literature on nationalism and national identity. Despite
a developing consensus that "nations" have no objective existence but are "imagined communities," historians still debate whether Britain in the eighteenth century was commonly regarded
as one nation – or as three or four.

London, is "my country" Scotland, or England, or Britain?[7] Is the heart and soul of the nation to be found in London, the bustling metropolis, or in the rural counties? Does my country include "the empire" across the seas? And who are my countrymen? Do they include the Scots? the Irish? the white Protestant colonists in America? the wealthy sunburned nabobs who return from India or the West Indies to buy up great estates? the dark-skinned natives of Africa and the Indies who speak their own tongues and worship their own gods but are now subjects of the British empire? The case of Tobias Smollett, a Scot who spent most of his career in London, suggests that there was no simple answer. In an early poem ("The Tears of Scotland" [1746]) "my country" refers to Scotland. He later went on to write the *History of England* (1757) and the pro-government pamphlet *The Briton* (1762–63).

Other political factors emerging about mid-century would have contributed to the rise of patriotic consciousness throughout the new nation. The Jacobite rebellion of 1745 obliged Britons to clarify their political attachments – to the House of Hanover, on the throne since 1714, or to the former ruling family, the Stuarts, whose champion had landed in Scotland and marched as far south as Derby, 125 miles from London. Was Charles Edward, as his followers claimed, the rightful heir to the throne, or was he simply the pawn of Catholic plotters in Rome and Paris? Was George II "our noble King, Great George our King" – as the new popular song hailed him during the '45 – or was he just a German prince who spoke little English and pursued Hanover's continental interests with British blood and gold? The self-division of civil war tested British loyalties, but the fears of a French invasion in the 1750s prompted most of George's subjects to rally 'round the flag and throne, at least for the duration of the Jacobite threat.

In the previous discussion I have avoided the term "nationalism," and have used the terms "patriotism" and "national feeling" interchangeably. Before going further it is probably best to clarify the meanings I assign to my master term, patriotism. Some students of political theory and international relations will perhaps object that patriotism and nationalism are distinguishable. The former is usually said to be the older term, referring to what is assumed to be a universal attachment to one's country, its

---

7 Thomson, author of a "Panegyric on Britain" in his forthcoming *Summer*, wrote to a fellow Scot in 1726 that "Britannia . . . includes our native Country, Scotland" (*Letters and Documents*, ed. A. D. McKillop [Lawrence, KS, 1958], 48).

soil, its cultural legacy, typically as embodied in its monarch. The latter is said to be the newer term (it does not appear in English dictionaries until the mid-nineteenth century), referring to "nationalist" movements for independence or nation-building in Germany, Italy, and elsewhere. For political scientists, it refers to an attachment to the nation-state, and is prompted by a sense of cultural and ethnic homogeneity, and by a conscious sense of difference from other (presumably adversarial) nations.[8]

But it is very difficult to maintain this distinction in Britain, where "nationalism" appears to have arisen by the eighteenth century, probably because of the century-long confrontation with France, against whom Britons defined themselves.[9] For my purposes, nationalism will refer primarily to the relation between Britain and its foreign enemies or rivals and to Britain's domination of global trade. Patriotism, my particular subject, focuses on the patriot's attachment to his or her country, and on the service the patriot hopes to provide.

For all its loyalty and devotion, patriotism was not simply a celebrative mode. It often involved anxiety and ambivalence about the state of the nation and its prospects. One loved one's country and feared for it, or one loved the country it once was and had perhaps ceased to be. We look back now on Britain across the whole length of the eighteenth century and see widening prosperity, political stability (especially in contrast to France), and a steady expansion of British power and empire. But for Britons of the day, the path to glory was punctuated by a series of shocks. To be sure, the "Bloodless Revolution" of 1688 and the Act of Settlement of 1701 established a firm political foundation. Marlborough's victories and the successful conclusion of peace in 1713 demonstrated that British military power was more than equal to the French challenge, and significantly expanded the empire. But the brief Jacobite rising of 1715 brought another reminder that Britain's own dynastic quarrel had not been resolved. For the next thirty years the Jacobite threat was sharp enough

---

[8] See, for example, Leonard Doob, *Patriotism and Nationalism* (New Haven, 1964). But recent commentators, including Anderson, acknowledge that nationalism is very difficult to define. See also Eric Hobsbawm, *Nations and Nationalism Since 1780: Programme, Myth, Reality* (Cambridge, 1990). Literary scholars tend to use the term nationalism more loosely. Lawrence Lipking, in "The Genius of the Shore: Lycidas, Adamastor, and the Poetics of Nationalism" (*PMLA*, 111 [1996], 205–21) refers to the "nationalism of Renaissance poets" (220n).

[9] See Gerald Newman, *The Rise of English Nationalism: A Cultural History, 1740–1830* (New York, 1987). Colley (*Britons*), drawing on Newman, makes no effective distinction between patriotism, a sense of "national identity," and nationalism. Kathleen Wilson (*The Sense of the People*) tries to maintain the distinction, finding both present in eighteenth-century Britain. Liah Greenfeld (*Nationalism: Five Roads to Modernity* [Cambridge, MA, 1992]) finds nationalism in England by the mid seventeenth century (27–87). John Cannon includes a chapter on "Johnson and Nationalism" in his *Samuel Johnson and the Politics of Hanoverian England* (Oxford, 1994).

to provoke parliamentary investigations of the Tories, who made a suspiciously generous peace with France, and the famous treason trial of Bishop Atterbury in 1723. In 1745 the landing of Charles Edward Stuart demonstrated that worries about the Jacobites were not fanciful, and although the rebellion was easily put down within eight months of the first battle, early Jacobite successes led many to wonder about the wisdom of British commanders and the valor of common British soldiers, and to fear that the Hanoverian monarchy would be overthrown.

By the same token, early French victories in the Seven Years' War seemed to confirm the dire analysis of British political, military, and cultural degeneration in John Brown's widely read *Estimate of the Manners and Principles of the Times* (1757). Brown saw in the "present State and Situation of the Country" a *"Crisis"* both "important and alarming" ("Advertisement"). "We are rolling to the Brink of a Precipice that must destroy us," not simply because of the external French threat but because of internal weakness, *"vain, luxurious,* and *selfish* EFFEMINACY."[10] He was not alone. The Scottish bard of *The Patriot, or A Call to Glory* (1757) sounded a Brownian alarm, warning Britons that they were

> Immers'd in shameful lethargy and sloth,
> In fatal pleasures and fantastic schemes,
> Delusive prospects, and ignoble care,
> Destructive of her native dignity.   (5)

As military historians have confirmed, there were limits to English willingness to make sacrifices for their country. Even in wartime, one-third to a half of all naval seamen had to be impressed. Desertion rates were very high, not just in the face of battle but from units stationed at home – 7 percent per year in the Seven Years' War, 13 percent per year in the American War. As late as 1808, one-third of draft-eligible men avoided overseas service.[11]

Even when the tide of battle turned in 1759 to favor the British, Brown's warnings were not forgotten.[12] Commentators such as Johnson and Goldsmith plainly questioned the wisdom of a war to gain territory

---

[10] *Estimate of the Manners and Principles of the Times* (London, 1757), I. 15, 27. Compare Smollett's *Complete History of England* (1757–58), which also claimed that England was in crisis: "Her debts are enormous; her taxes intolerable, her people discontented, and the sinnes [i.e., the sinews] of her government relaxed . . . She is even deserted by her wonted vigour, steadiness, and intrepidity: She grows vain, fantastical, and pusillanimous" (8 vols., 1791, III, 191–92).

[11] *An Imperial State at War: Britain from 1689 to 1815*, ed. Lawrence Stone (London, 1994), 13–14; N. A. M. Rodger, *The Wooden World: An Anatomy of the Georgian Navy* (Annapolis, 1986), 203.

[12] In some eyes Brown was discredited by British victories, but for many readers in succeeding decades – Cowper among them – his analysis was still sound.

(in Canada, for example), that at best would drain the resources of the nation and at worst would prove hostile and barren. In a *Citizen of the World* essay published in April 1760, Goldsmith's Lien Chi Altangi observes that "extending empire is often diminishing power . . . that colonies by draining away the brave and enterprizing, leave the country in the hands of the timid and the avaricious, . . . that there is a wide difference between a conquering and a flourishing empire."[13]

The Peace of Paris in 1763 brought the Seven Years' War to a triumphant close, but military victory could be as troubling as defeat. British wars in the century always led to a sharp increase in the national debt. As Colley has suggested, Britons also had to adjust to the new idea that Britain was now a global empire, ranging from Bombay in the east to Hudson's Bay in the west. It had gained not only new territory but new people who spoke other tongues and observed other customs. Would the values and traditions of the home island be preserved in the new commercial–military empire? Horace Walpole in 1773 querulously asked: "What is England now? – A sink of Indian wealth, filled by nabobs, and emptied by Maccaronies! – A senate sold and despised! . . . A gaming, robbing, wrangling, railing nation, without principles, genius, character, or allies; the overgrown shadow of what it was."[14] Junius in 1769 lamented "a nation overwhelmed with debt; her revenues wasted; her trade declining; the affections of her colonies alienated; the duty of the magistrate transferred to the soldiery; . . . the whole administration of justice become odious and suspected to the whole body of the people."[15]

Despite the arguments of Colley and others who have emphasized the growth of loyal attachment to the crown, especially after the accession of George III in 1760, evidence of political unrest and disaffection abounds, from the anti-administration Wilkesite riots in the 1760s to the anti-Catholic Gordon riots in 1780. Burke's famous *Thoughts on the Causes of the Present Discontents* (1770) suggests that a sense of crisis had invaded parliament itself:

That government is at once dreaded and contemned; that the laws are despoiled of all their respected and salutary terrours; that their inaction is a subject of ridicule, and their exertion of abhorrence; that rank, and office and title, and

---

[13] *Citizen of the World*, Letter XXVI, in *Collected Works*, ed. Arthur Friedman, 5 vols. (Oxford: Clarendon, 1966), II, 108. One of the chief arguments for peace in 1763 was that by continuing the war (and retaining all captured territory) Britain ran the danger of "draining and exhausting our mother-country" (*Patriotism! A Farce* [1763], 3).

[14] *Horace Walpole's Correspondence*, ed. Wilmarth S. Lewis, 48 vols. in 49 (New Haven, 1937–83), XXIII, 498.

[15] Letter of 21 January 1769, in *Letters of Junius*, ed. John Cannon (Oxford: Clarendon, 1978), 33.

all the solemn plausibilities of the world, have lost their reverence and effect; that our foreign politics are as much deranged as our domestic economy; that our dependencies are slackened in their affection, and loosened from their obedience; that we know neither how to yield nor how to enforce; that hardly anything above or below, abroad or at home, is sound and entire; but that disconnection and confusion, in office, in parties, in families, in Parliament, in the nation, prevail beyond the disorders of any former time; these are facts universally admitted and lamented.[16]

In the decade to follow, Burke played a central role in the divisive national debate about how to respond to the developing crisis in the American colonies. His famous motion for *Conciliation with the Colonies* (1775), although defeated, was a clear sign that many Britons did not support the war to put down the rebellious colonists. The war was to draw in the French, and Britain's resounding defeat – the only war in the century that Britain clearly lost – led, not surprisingly, to pro-found soul-searching: what national weakness had led to humiliating failure? Johnson's letters after the 1783 Peace of Paris show he was deeply disturbed:

I cannot but suffer some pain when I compare the state of this kingdom, with that in which we triumphed twenty years ago . . . To any man who extends his thoughts to national considerations, the times are dismal and gloomy . . . we have all the world for our enemies . . . the King and Parliament have lost even the titular dominion of America, and the real power of government every where else. Thus Empires are broken down when the profits of administration are so great, that ambition is satisfied with obtaining them.[17]

Cowper's *The Task* (1785) is among other things a troubled probing, on the part of a man who declares his deep love of his country, of the causes of what he saw as a grievous "loss of Empire" (V, line 457).

At century's end the Reverend Richard Price, in an ardent *Discourse on the Love of our Country* (1789), could nonetheless conclude his patriotic sermon with a troubled survey of "the state of this country."

It is too evident that the state of this country is such as renders it an object of concern and anxiety. It wants (I have shewn you) the grand security of public liberty. Increasing luxury has multiplied abuses in it. A monstrous weight of debt is crippling it. Vice and venality are bringing down upon it God's displeasure. That spirit to which it owes its distinction is declining, and some late events seem

---

[16] *Thoughts on the Causes of the Present Discontents* (1770), in *Writings and Speeches of Edmund Burke*, gen. ed. Paul Langford, 8 vols. (Oxford: Clarendon, 1980–), II, 253.

[17] *Letters*, ed. Bruce Redford (Princeton, 1992–94), IV, 62–63, 267, 277.

to prove that it is becoming every day more reconcileable to encroachments on the securities of its liberties.[18]

Worries about the "condition of Britain" prompted one writer after another to declare his own patriotic devotion. It is not surprising that poets too felt called upon to examine themselves and to stand up to be counted.

THE DISCOURSE OF PATRIOTISM

It was not only political circumstances that prompted national feeling: patriotism became the subject of intense textual discussion. Beginning in the 1730s and extending over the rest of the century, there developed what might be called a discourse of patriotism, in which participants – both the writers who supported the political Opposition and those who supported the successive ministries – laid claim to the title of "patriot" and debated the nature of true patriotism.

During the last decade of Walpole's rule, a number of his opponents, mostly disaffected Whigs, gathered under the banner of "Patriotism," and sustained a critique of Walpolean government-by-corruption in the name of traditional English "liberties." As Christine Gerrard has noted, they had roots in neo-Harringtonian "Country party" ideology, arguing for the crucial role of the Commons in maintaining the balance of government, and resisting what they saw as extensions of executive influence through the awarding of places and pensions. In foreign policy they tended to be nationalistic, invoking the glorious memory of English military might, when Edward III and Henry V defeated the French at Crécy and Agincourt, or when Elizabeth destroyed the invading Armada of Spain. But they were reluctant to engage British forces in continental wars (largely in the pursuit of the King's Hanoverian interests), preferring a blue-water policy, and championing what they saw as a genuine British interest in maritime commerce. The most prominent of the "Patriot" leaders, Bolingbroke and William Pulteney, were joined by the Earl of Chesterfield, Richard Temple Viscount Cobham, George Lyttelton, William Pitt, and others.[19] The theoretical underpinnings of the "Patriot"

---

[18] *Political Writings*, ed. D. O. Thomas (Cambridge, 1991), 194.

[19] Historians continue to disagree about the political landscape of the 1730s – whether the "Tories" survived as a party, whether there was a distinct "Country" party, whether the "Patriots" formed a distinct group, whether there were clear distinctions between "Patriots" and Jacobites. For details, see Gerrard, *Patriot Opposition*, the best account of the literary "Patriots." What matters for my purposes is that "Patriot" rhetoric was now part of the national political debate.

position were laid down beginning about 1731, first in the Opposition journal, *The Craftsman*, largely the work of Pulteney and Bolingbroke, and later in Bolingbroke's *The Idea of a Patriot King*, written in 1738 and widely circulated among the "Patriot" group, though not published until 1749 as *Letters on the Spirit of Patriotism: on the Idea of a Patriot King; and on the State of Parties, At the Accession of George I*. Bolingbroke's "Patriot King" is a limited monarch who preserves the constitution and the spirit of liberty, who espouses "no party," but rather governs "like the common father of his people," wins their affection, and reconciles them to each other. He governs by "a national concurrence instead of governing by the management of parties and factions in the state." He is animated by "real patriotism" in contrast to the "private ambition" that motivates the unnamed Walpole, then (in 1738) the still successful manager of the state. Bolingbroke's *Idea* concludes with the "whole glorious scene of a patriot reign":

concord will appear, brooding peace and prosperity on the happy land; joy sitting in every face, content in every heart; a people unoppressed, undisturbed, unalarmed; busy to improve their private property and the public stock; fleets covering the ocean, bringing home wealth by the returns of industry, carrying assistance or terror abroad by the direction of wisdom, and asserting triumphantly the right and the honor of Great Britain, as far as waters roll and as winds can waft them.[20]

This is a vision of Britain, an "imagined community," to match the panegyrics on the new nation found in the most ardently patriotic poems of the century. And the "Patriots" attracted a number of the younger writers of the 1730s, excited by the political rhetoric. They included such major figures as James Thomson, Alexander Pope, Samuel Johnson, and Henry Fielding, and such lesser lights (remembered now primarily by scholars) as Richard Glover, David Mallet, and Henry Brooke.[21] As Johnson put it, in characterizing Brooke's political tragedy, *Gustavus Vasa* (1738), their works seemed "designed to kindle in the audience a flame of

---

[20] *The Idea of a Patriot King*, in *Bolingbroke's Political Writings: The Conservative Enlightenment*, ed. Bernard Cottret (New York, 1997), 419.

[21] Joseph Warton, who in 1797 thought of these "Patriot" writers as animated by a "great Spirit of liberty," included the names of Robert Nugent (his *Ode to Mankind* and *To Mr. Pulteney*) and William King (his *Miltonis Epistola* and *Templum Libertatis*). See Warton's *Works of Pope*, 9 vols. (London, 1797), IV, 309n. Christine Gerrard adds James Hammond, William Somerville, Richard Powney, George Lillo, and (especially) Gilbert West and Aaron Hill (*Patriot Opposition*, 63–66, 76–81, 224–29).

opposition, patriotism, publick spirit, and independency."[22] Burke later declared that Walpole, who preferred a pacifist policy, was forced into war "by the most leading politicians, by the first orators, and the greatest poets of the time."[23]

Bolingbroke's vision was an attractive one, so attractive that any politician could endorse it, whether in Opposition or in the ministry. From the beginning, indeed, the ministry deployed a similar vision and the same discourse of patriotism, with invocations of England's "ancient constitution," of "Gothic" or "Saxon" (i.e., pre-Norman) "liberties," of Crécy and Agincourt, of Elizabeth (beloved queen, champion of Protestantism, who defeated Spain abroad and sedition at home), and of "Revolution principles," commerce, and the British navy. From the beginning of the "Patriot" campaign, the ministry responded by demonizing their adversaries as faction-mongers and casting themselves as the true patriots.

One attack on Bolingbroke, *The Patriot at Full Length; or, an Inscription for an Obelisk* (1735), regards him as "An Enemy to his King, To his Country, and to all Good Men." Recalling Bolingbroke's flirtation with the Jacobites in 1715, the anonymous polemicist goes so far as to declare that "the Professions of the Patriot were always urged, / To disguise the schemes of the Traytor" (2). It was a commonplace to insist that self-proclaimed patriots were hypocrites.[24] William Arnall, one of the ministry's most prolific apologists, warned that "private Passion often calls itself publick Spirit; and . . . very selfish and very foolish Men call themselves Patriots." In the no-nonsense words of his title, "Opposition" was "No Proof of [true] Patriotism." "True Patriotism" – by which he meant that exemplified by the "Men in Power" – is divested of all "Passion and of Party-Spirit."[25] Walpole himself was praised by obliging poets as the nation's "most Illustrious *Patriot*."[26]

---

[22] From Johnson's *Compleat Vindication of the Licensers of the Stage* (1739, in *Political Writings*, 64), where Johnson, adopting the voice of a government licenser, pretends to condemn Brooke's play.

[23] The first "Letter on a Regicide Peace," in *Writings and Speeches*, IX, 226.

[24] Cf. the attack on the "*seeming* Patriot" in another contemporary satire: "our worst of Foes! / Who makes, and mourns, at once, his Country's Woes" (*Modern Patriotism. A Poem* [1734], 2).

[25] *Opposition No Proof of Patriotism; with Some Observations and Advice Concerning Party-Writings* (London, 1735), 31. Cf. John Lord Hervey's *The Conduct of the Opposition, and the Tendency of Modern Patriotism* (Edinburgh, 1734), warning that steps taken by the Opposition tend not toward the "Maintenance of Liberty" but its "Destruction" (5). Other attacks include *Sedition and Defamation Display'd* (London, 1731) and *A Coalition of Patriots Delineated* (London, 1735).

[26] Thomson, dedication [to Walpole] of the "Poem Sacred to the Memory of Sir Isaac Newton" (1727). Compare Joseph Mitchell's "The Patriot" (*Poems on Several Occasions*, 2 vols. [London, 1729], II, 322–23), and verses that appeared in the *Daily Gazeteer* for 24 April 1738: "This is the Sovereign Man Compleat; / Hero; Patriot; glorious; free; / Rich, and wise; and fair, and great; / Generous

After the fall of Walpole in 1742, Pulteney's unwillingness to form a new government, his apparent abandonment of the Patriot cause, and his acceptance of a peerage as the Earl of Bath seemed only to confirm the old charge – heard at least since Dryden's days[27] – that "Patriots" were motivated not by principle but by self-seeking.[28] A contemporary print reveals "The Treacherous Patriot Unmask'd" (see figure 2). But the term possessed such political attractions that it was reclaimed by the ministry. The supporters of Henry Pelham, Prime Minister in the mid-1740s, declared that there was indeed no inconsistency between patriotism and office, that one might be a patriot "in *Place* and *Power.*"[29] Sir Hanbury Williams, who never tired of mocking "Patriots" such as Pulteney, could still hail the Duke of Cumberland as a "patriot" who fought on behalf of "liberty opprest."[30] At the height of the Jacobite rebellion in 1745–46 Fielding, who in *The Champion* (1739–41) had previously written in support of Opposition "Patriots," founded a new journal, *The True Patriot*, to distinguish between "modern" or "false" patriotism and the real thing. The false patriot – and Fielding has in mind the political Opposition – uses love of country as a cloak for "Ambition, Avarice, Revenge, Envy, Malice, every bad Passion in the Mind of Man" (no. 2).[31] He is in fact an "Incendiary," who seeks only to "blow up and inflame . . . Party-Divisions." (Note that it is now the Opposition rather than the ministry which tries to arouse factional or party distinctions.) By contrast, true patriotism is "Love of one's Country carried into Action" (117). The true patriot "will use his most ardent Endeavours . . . to extinguish a Rebellion which so greatly threatens the Destruction of . . . the present Royal Family [and] . . . THE VERY BEING OF THIS NATION" (120).

Fielding's rhetorical tactic proved to be popular with ministerial writers in succeeding decades. Pitt in the 1750s was hailed as the "Patriot

WALPOLE, Thou art He." For brief discussion, see Tone Urstal, *Sir Robert Walpole's Poets: The Use of Literature as Pro-Government Propaganda, 1721–1742* (Newark, DE, 1999), 197–99.

[27] Cf. his sneer at Achitophel (Shaftesbury) who "Usurp'd a Pattriott's all-attoning Name" (*Absalom and Achitophel*, line 179).

[28] See for example *The Patriot and the Minister Reviewed: by Way of Dialogue* (London, 1743), apparently written from the point of view not of the ministry but of a disappointed Patriot. The memory of Pulteney's "apostasy" remained vivid enough to be invoked in attacks on patriots twenty-five years later. See *An Essay on Patriotism, in the Style and Manner of Mr. Pope's Essay on Man* (n.p., 1766) and the prose *Essay on Patriotism* (London, 1768).

[29] See *Power and Patriotism: A Poetical Epistle Humbly Inscribed to the Right Honourable H. P. Esq.* (London, 1746): "*true Patriots* may be *able Politicians*, and . . . our *Polliticians* are actually *Patriots*, not in *Name* but in *Fact*" (7).

[30] *Works*, 3 vols. (London, 1822), I, 104. See also his "The Patriot Parrot: A Fable" (I, 214–15), "A New Ode" [on Pulteney's apostasy] (II, 156), and a mock epitaph (I, 171).

[31] *The True Patriot and Related Writings*, ed. W. B. Coley (Middletown, 1987), 116.

Figure 2. "The Treacherous Patriot Unmask'd" (1742). BM Cat 2538

Minister." Upon his accession to the throne in 1760, George III, grandson of George II, proclaimed that (unlike his grandfather) he was born and bred a Briton, and he offered himself to his subjects as a "Patriot King." In the opening number of a new government-financed periodical entitled *The Briton*, the editor Tobias Smollett promised to "pluck the mask of patriotism from the front of faction," and proceeded to honor the "true patriotism" of Bute, the new patriot-minister (no. 5).[32]

Despite ministerial efforts to monopolize the term, the meaning of "patriot" continued to be contested. *Ministerial Patriotism Detected* (1763) sought to refute Bute's claim to patriotism.[33] A "Patriot" opposition persisted throughout the century, always laboring under the suspicion that it was actuated not by love of country but by discontent or avarice. Wilkes raised a "Patriot" banner in the 1760s, and it was Wilkesite patriotism that Johnson had in mind both in his famous definition of "patriot" in the 1773 revision of the *Dictionary* ("a factious disturber of the government") and in his political pamphlet, *The Patriot* (1774).[34] Political writers continued to bandy the slogans of "true" and "false" patriot. The author of an *Essay on Patriotism* in 1768, for example, offers satiric observations on "the Character and Conduct of some late famous Pretenders to that Virtue, Particularly of the present Popular Gentleman." The "Popular Gentleman" is Wilkes, ridiculed as an "impostor" who has fooled a gullible public with his patriotic rhetoric:

he has only to set up for what is called a Patriot, to write, and to scribble, and to bawl out for Liberty and Independence, and all his profligacy and flagitiousness will be looked over and forgotten, nay, even reckoned a virtue. (3)[35]

Another "impostor" in patriotism is Pitt, who resigned his ministerial office in 1761 (and accepted a peerage as Earl of Chatham) when

---

32 *Poems, Plays, and "The Briton,"* intro. Byron Gassman, ed. O. M Brack, Jr. (Athens, GA, 1993), 241, 266.

33 "If the minister really had had the good of the nation at heart, . . . what a fine field we find here [peace negotiations in 1762], to display his patriotism" [the author thinks Bute concluded a "disadvantageous peace"]. The real "worthy patriots" of the day, he goes on, are Lord Temple, Pitt, and Wilkes, "men of honest views" (*Ministerial Patriotism Detected; Or the Present Opposition Proved to be founded on Truly, just and laudable Principles* [London, 1763], 11, 25, 33).

34 Johnson's essay is one of the most sustained comparisons of "true" and "false" patriotism in the period. Although suspicious of self-professed Patriots, Johnson assigned great value to patriotism, as in his meditation on the power of place to prompt emotion: "That man is little to be envied, whose patriotism would not gain force upon the plains of Marathon, or whose piety would not grow warmer among the ruins of Iona" (*Journey to the Western Isles of Scotland*, ed. Mary Lascelles [New Haven, 1971], 148).

35 In other attacks, Wilkes' vaunted "Liberty" is a cover for faction and even rebellion. Like Bolingbroke and Pulteney before him, he is accused of political ambition. It is clear from Wilkes' example, says the Pope-inspired satirist:

> That pow'r and place are Oppositions aim,
> That Patriotism and Int'rest are the same.

(Richard Bentley, *Patriotism, a Mock-Heroic* [2nd. edn., London, 1765]). As another Popean polemicist put it, in pretending to offer instruction in patriotism, "First muse unfold, one universal Thing, / To love your Country, you must hate your King" (*The Patriots Guide. A Poem Inscribed to the Earl of C—M, Junius, and John Wilkes* [London, 1773], 3).

he was unable to secure support for war against Spain. Hostile critics and former friends alike compared the "apostasy" of Pulteney some twenty years earlier.[36] One writer suspects that the "Patriot Minister" was still scheming for a return to power. In *Patriotism! A Farce* (1764) Pitt appears as "Slyboots" to explain his strategy to a political supporter: "My resignation was a master-stroke of policy: and if my schemes do not miscarry, you shall soon see me at the helm again, with more absolute authority than ever" (1). The war was popular, but the country needed peace – this is the writer's view – and Slyboots "knew it would be next to impossible for any minister to conclude a peace, without bringing upon himself an immense load of popular odium, which therefore I resolved to avoid" (2).

Given the acrimonious controversy from the 1730s into the 1780s, both in the public press and in lampoons, about "patriotism",[37] it is perhaps surprising that a mid-century poet would risk identifying himself as a "patriot." As the oft-cited examples of Pulteney and Pitt seemed to show, even the patriot had his price. But patriotism was not in fact thoroughly discredited, and writers sought to reclaim the term. John Conybeare, Bishop of Bristol, preached a sermon on *True Patriotism* (published 1749) before the House of Commons on a day of Thanksgiving at the end of the War of the Austrian Succession (see figure 3). His text was Psalm 122, a prayer for peace and prosperity in Jerusalem, in which the psalmist concludes by addressing his country: "I will seek thy good." Not surprisingly (given the audience), Conybeare avoids polemic and, while defending both the peace and the King, appeals for all sides to show "real Patriotism, . . . the just and reasonable Love of our Country." Although Conybeare avoids awkward topics such as what it might mean for a Frenchman to love *his* country, he implicitly invokes the Christian idea of the "common body" of the church, but gives it a distinctively Erastian and even secular sense, imagining the "country" to be the "Great Society we belong to; in which the several Members are united together by common Laws under One Common Head" (28).[38]

[36] *An Essay on Patriotism, in the Style and Manner of Mr. Pope's Essay on Man*, esp. 16–17, and the prose *Essay on Patriotism*.

[37] *Liberty and Patriotism: A Miscellaneous Ode* (London, 1778), mocks a new generation of pro-American "patriots," William Beckford, the Reverend John Horne (later known as John Horne Tooke), and Catharine Macaulay (along with Wilkes).

[38] Compare the popular ballad of the same year, appealing for "Patriots" to stop quarreling with each other, *A Ballad. To the Tune of Chevy Chase* (London, 1749): "God Save the King, and bless the Land, / In Plenty, Joy, and Peace; / And grant, henceforth, that foul Debates / 'Twixt Patriots may cease" (6). The "debates" may be those between Dodington and James Ralph, both members of the "Patriot" group.

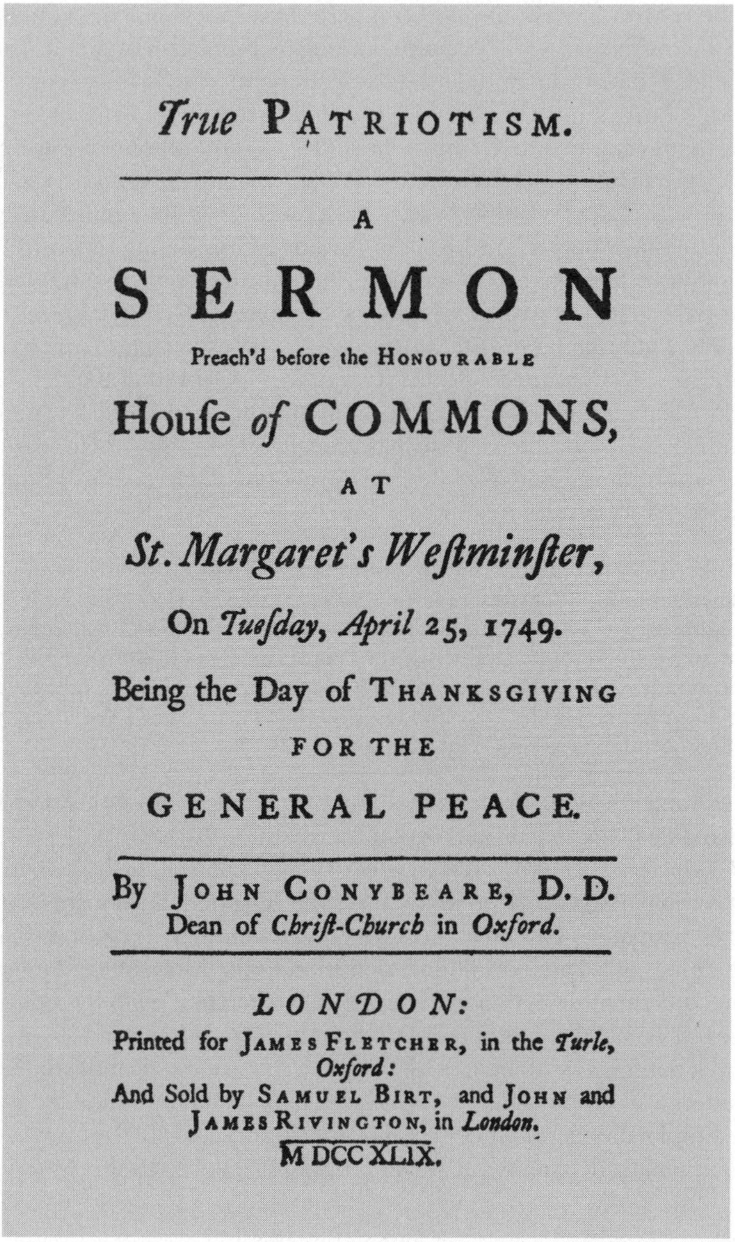

True PATRIOTISM.

A

S E R M O N

Preach'd before the HONOURABLE

Houſe *of* COMMONS,

A T

St. Margaret's Weſtminſter,

On *Tueſday, April* 25, 1749.

Being the Day of THANKSGIVING

FOR THE

GENERAL PEACE.

By JOHN CONYBEARE, D. D.
Dean of *Chriſt-Church* in *Oxford.*

L O N D O N:
Printed for JAMES FLETCHER, in the *Turle,*
Oxford:
And Sold by SAMUEL BIRT, and JOHN and
JAMES RIVINGTON, in *London.*
M DCC XLIX.

Figure 3. Title page to *True Patriotism. A Sermon* (1749). BL shelfmark 695.g.5.(6)

The controversy about patriotism also drew in less polemical writers who discoursed at essayistic length, seeking to distinguish between "true" and "false" patriotism and between a higher and a lower form. An essay "On the Love of our Country" in *The Museum* in July 1746, for example, finds that because "our Country" includes "almost all our moral Relations," the "Duty which we owe the Public" is almost the highest of our moral duties (282).[39] But in fact we have two higher obligations, to "the whole human species" and to "the Author of our Being." Thus if our country uses "unjust, treacherous, or dishonourable Methods" or pursues a vicious end, e.g., if it aims at "universal Empire" (284), then love of our country would be "a criminal Affection." The essayist perhaps has in mind the idea that just as British writers were celebrating the defeat of the Jacobites at Culloden, the French (in pursuit, so the British claimed, of "universal monarchy") were patriotically celebrating their military success at Fontenoy and elsewhere on the continent. His praise of English patriotism is discreetly qualified:

I should rejoice to find that our Love of *Old England* partook of no inhospitable Pride, of no *Gothic* Superstition, of no *French* or *Turkish* Servility. An *Englishman* should be asham'd if, by the *Love of his Country*, he be found to mean anything less than a calm, resolute Desire that the People of *England* may for ever be free, virtuous, and orderly among themselves, and for ever watchful, valiant, and glorious in protecting their Neighbours and the whole civiliz'd World, against the Encroachments of Universal Monarchy. (286–87)

What implicitly worries the essayist is that patriotism can slide into what we would call aggressive and expansionist nationalism.

The Analysis of Patriotism (1768) goes beyond exposing the imposture of Opposition "patriotism" to argue that "the Nature of Patriotism" varies as the "temporary Circumstances [of government] change." Sometimes "the Duties of a Patriot call for Opposition to the Measures of Government," but on other occasions a "hearty Concurrence" with the ministry is "as much Patriotic Duty" (viii–ix). The "principal Concern" of the true Roman patriot was "to benefit his Country" (17). In modern Britain both ministers and Opposition "patriots" seek only "the Disposal of the valuable Employments" of office (24). The specific occasion of the essay is the parliamentary debate about the appropriate response to the American

---

39 The writer adopts the Ciceronian idea that love of country includes all other attachments: "Cari sunt parentes, cari liberi propinqui familiares; sed omnes omnium caritates patria complexa est" (*De Officiis*, I, 57, "Parents are dear, and children, relatives and acquaintances are dear, but our country has on its own embraced all the affections of all of us," tr. M. T. Griffin and E. M. Atkins, in *On Duties* [Cambridge, 1991], 23).

"patriots" in Boston, and to their friends in England, who pretend loyalty to the crown and "esteem for the common good" (37), but who are in fact guilty of "factious Bickerings" (44). The essay calls on patriotic Englishmen to close ranks in support of the ministry and to take a hard line against the "black Ingratitude" of the American colonists.

By contrast, the Reverend Charles Christian Newman's poem, *The Love of our Country* (1783), insists that supporters of American independence are true British patriots. Written in the aftermath of military defeat in America at a time when many were bemoaning the loss of the colonies, Newman's poem, dedicated to the fifth Duke of Devonshire, takes its epigraph from the locus classicus on "love of country" from Cicero's *De Officiis.* By distinguishing between a "vulgar" patriotism based on "an attachment to the soil" and a "proper" patriotism founded "upon a principle of reason, duty, and affection" (vi), Newman in effect dismisses the idea that one's "country" consists of so many acres of ground, and that Britain has lost some integral part of itself. He reassures Britons that they still enjoy "with independence and security" the "blessings" of "Relations, family, connections, friends and property." He goes on to honor three kinds of patriotic hero: soldiers who "offer up their consecrated blood, / The willing victims for their country's good";[40] those public-spirited men who quit their "Ease, pleasure, fortune for the public weal"; and writers, those "talents of the mind" (like himself) who serve "the public end" by teaching morals, passing "sentence" on virtues and crimes, and warning of "rights invaded" or reminding Britons of their freedoms:

> . . . on the public mind a sense to press
> Of blessings which the free alone possess.
>
> (20)

As we shall see, identifying a patriotic service for the poet to perform is of acute concern not just to the Reverend Newman, but to most of the better-known poets of his century as well.

Just as the American Revolution prompted many writers to reconsider the nature of "true" patriotism, so too did the increasing presence of women in the nation's cultural and political life. Was it appropriate for women to offer themselves as "patriots" or for women writers to take up public and political topics? When Catharine Macaulay did so, she was greeted – in some quarters – with censure and ridicule. Her *History*

---

[40] Although Newman approves of American independence, he perhaps finds it politically tactful to praise British soldiers who did their duty. Indeed, he makes a special appeal (17–19) that the state ought to compensate its veterans.

of England (1763–83) celebrated the overthrow of what she regarded as
Stuart tyranny in the civil war, and the public spirit of the parliamentary
leaders – "the government of the country was in the hands of illustrious
patriots, and wise legislators; the glory, the welfare, the true interest
of the empire was their only care."[41] Some readers such as Cowper
enthusiastically shared her view.[42] But she also drew fire from many
conservative male critics both for her Whiggish and allegedly republican
sympathies and (implicitly) for her trespassing on the "male" territory of
history writing. Johnson's proposal that she invite her footman to join her
at dinner, perhaps the best known of the jokes at her expense, ridicules her
"levelling" principles, but other contemporary reactions suggest hostility
toward her as a female political writer.[43] When she married William
Graham in 1779, she was greeted with *The Female Patriot*, that imagines
her writing to Dr. Thomas Wilson, her former benefactor:

> How oft, ye sacred hearths, when patriot blaze
> Illum'd our souls, and into raptures rais'd,
> Instinct with bold enthusiastick rage
> We hung with transport o'er th'Historick page!
> And trac'd those heroes, whose avenging blow
> Through tyrants breasts bade liberty to flow;
> Then damn'd to infamy those venal things,
> Which earth-born flattery created Kings.

Her "patriot tongue" later sings the glories of the Whig hero, the Duke of
Marlborough, but the appearance of a new "hero," her young husband to
be, sends all ideas of political liberty out of the head of "our Republican
Heroine":

> When the bold hero to my ravish'd view
> His Godlike shape display'd so wondrous true;
> Stern Patriotism ceas'd my Soul to move,
> And all the Heroine languish'd into love.[44]

Macaulay's enthusiastic patriotism is ridiculed as a kind of displaced
eroticism, and the parodist dismisses her to woman's proper fate as

---

41 *The History of England . . .*, 3rd. edn., 8 vols. (London, 1763–83), V (1772), 364.
42 See his 1782 letters in *Letters and Prose Writings*, ed. James King and Charles Ryskamp (Oxford: Clarendon, 1979), II, 13, 17, 31.
43 Boswell, *Life of Johnson*, I, 448.
44 *The Female Patriot* (London, 1779), 7–8, 12, 28. At the time of the marriage Graham was twenty-one, Macaulay a forty-seven-year-old widow. For an account of Macaulay's second marriage, see Bridget Hill, *Republican Virago: The Life and Times of Catharine Macaulay, Historian* (Oxford: Clarendon, 1992), 105–29.

subservient and doting wife. Johnson, who crossed polemical swords with her more than once, sneers at her in his *Taxation No Tyranny* (1775) as "a female patriot."[45]

After Georgiana, Duchess of Devonshire, young, fashionable, and beautiful, actively electioneered for Charles James Fox in a 1784 Westminster election, she too was derided by cultural conservatives. But she was celebrated by Fox's supporters in his victory procession to Devonshire House, her carriage surmounted with a banner bearing the legend "Sacred to Female Patriotism."[46] A month later the clerk of Fox's election committee complimented her as a "patriot Heroine":

> By truth directed, shall my lay commend
> The patriot Heroine, and, the faithful friend,
> Who to avert her country's threatened fate,
> Deign'd to lay by her dignity and state
> And urge, with heav'n born grace, the virtuous plea
> Of injured rights, and trembling liberty.[47]

Political printmakers were divided about the efforts of the Duchess and of other female patriots. A 1784 Rowlandson engraving of "Liberty and Fame introducing Female Patriotism to Britania [*sic*]" (see figure 4) shows a fashionably dressed Duchess being presented to a plainly dressed Britannia, who reaches out to place a wreath (perhaps a Ciceronian civic crown) on the Duchess's head – already dressed with a very large feathered hat.[48] Although the Duchess's eyes are "modestly downcast" (Harriet Guest's apt description), the caption – "She smiles. –Infused with a fortitude from Heaven. Vide Shakespear Tempest" – perhaps implies barely disguised female effrontery.[49] Women who raised funds to clothe the army were likewise suspected of a kind of duplicity. In 1793 Gillray's satirical print on *Flannel–Armour; –Female-Patriotism, or Modern Heroes accoutered*

---

45 Johnson, *Political Writings*, ed. Greene, 449. Her *Address to the People of England, Scotland and Ireland, on the Present Important Crisis of Affairs* (1775) had attacked Johnson's *The Patriot* (1774).
46 Amanda Foreman, *Georgiana, Duchess of Devonshire* (London, 1998), 155, citing the *London Chronicle*, 15–18 May 1784.
47 *Georgiana: Extracts from the Correspondence of Georgiana, Duchess of Devonshire*, ed. Earl of Bessborough (London, 1955), 82.
48 On the civic crown, see below, 278. Another Rowlandson print of April 1784 (see figure 5) shows "The Two Patriotic Duchess's [of Devonshire and Portland] on their Canvass." One duchess kisses a Westminster butcher and slips money into his pocket. For other prints on the topic (BM Cat 6493, 6520, 6527, 6533, 6541), see John Brewer, *The Common People and Politics, 1750s–1790s* (Cambridge, 1986).
49 Guest, *Small Change: Women, Learning, Patriotism, 1750–1810* (Chicago, 2000), 217. The smiling Duchess is plainly no Miranda, whose smiling "fortitude" bore her up in shipwreck (*Tempest*, I. 2. 154).

Figure 4. Thomas Rowlandson, "Liberty and Fame introducing Female Patriotism to Britania," frontispiece to *History of the Westminster Election*, 2nd. edn. (1785). BL shelfmark 8135.k.6

Figure 5. Thomas Rowlandson, "The Two Patriotic Duchess's on their Canvass"
(1784). BM Cat 6494. The Duchesses of Portland and Devonshire

for the Wars laughs at female patriots eagerly pulling drawers onto the
haunches of a soldier (hinting perhaps that female patriotism, as with
Swift's Aeolists and the satirist's Mrs. Macaulay, is only a sublimated
form of more carnal enthusiasm), but also acknowledges, in the words
of its subtitle, some respect for the efforts of "the Benevolent Ladies of

Great Britain, who have so liberally supported the new system of Military Cloathing."[50]

What lay behind the controversies over Mrs. Macaulay and the Duchess was, not surprisingly, traditional assumptions that women should remember their proper place, and that politics and patriotic activity ought to be left to men. But despite lingering prejudices, women writers increasingly found ways after mid-century to make themselves heard on patriotic topics.[51] Three reasons suggest themselves for why this should have been so: first, that the regular appearance in print of books by women authors on a variety of topics gradually wore down the assumption that they could have no political opinions worth listening to; second, that in the culture at large patriotic sentiment seems to have increased rather sharply as a consequence of the successes of the Seven Years' War; third, that by the 1790s women, as Linda Colley has shown, were beginning to play an active role in public affairs, not only canvassing at elections, but signing loyal petitions, and collecting money to support the war against France. The public challenge to those assumptions, especially in the last three decades of the eighteenth century, in turn prompted a number of writers, including William Russell, William Alexander, James Fordyce, and Henry Home, Lord Kames (as Harriet Guest has recently noted), to articulate a case against female patriotism based on the nature or the history of women. Russell's 1773 translation from the French of an *Essay on the Character . . . of Women* argues that women, lacking the capacity for patriotism and public spirit, are made not for governing but for love and marriage: "A man to them is more than a nation."[52] Alexander, in his *History of Women* (1779) distinguished between male love of country (an abstraction, an idea), and female compassion for other human beings: "Patriotism is a principle seldom so strong in them as in men, and humanity is generally much stronger."[53] It was common for writers on the topic to remember that Roman and Spartan women were after all famous for their patriotism. Russell, for example, notes that the matrons of republican Rome displayed "an enthusiastic love of their country," and Kames commends the "Spartan matrons" who flocked to the temples to thank the gods "that their husbands and sons had died gloriously, fighting

[50] See Colley, *Britons*, 250, 260.

[51] See for example Elizabeth Montagu's patriotic defense of Shakespeare in response to the "misrepresentations of Mons. Voltaire" in her *Essay on the Writings and Genius of Shakespeare* (London, 1769).

[52] I cite Russell from a 1774 edition, 2 vols. (Philadelphia), II, 36. Kames, in his *Sketches of the History of Man*, 2 vols. (Edinburgh, 1774), claimed that "women . . have less patriotism than men" (I, 169).

[53] I cite Alexander from the 1779 edition of his *History of Women*, 2 vols. (London), I, 35.

for their country." But, as Guest notes, some observers did not think the example of classical antiquity appropriate for modern British women, because it was "incompatible with feminine sensibility and humanity."[54] Fordyce advised that the heroic virtues of the patriotic "Roman Matron" are "over-balanced by the loss or the diminution of that gentleness and softness, which ever were, and ever will be, the sovereign charm of the female character."[55] Taking up the cause of patriotism in effect un-sexes a woman (even as, so the examples of Macaulay and the Duchess of Devonshire show, it uncovers their sexual desire). Guest goes on to argue that a new model for female patriotism – based squarely on feminine sensibility – was developed in the last quarter of the century, as if to answer male objections, and can be observed in the writings of Anna Letitia Barbauld and Anna Seward.[56] But, as I will argue, the poems of Ann Yearsley and others demonstrate that women writers in the 1790s could still deploy the rhetoric of traditional (male) patriots.

A third factor that prompted reconsideration of the nature of patriotism was the publication of essays and sermons that sought, at a time of political ferment, to redefine the true patriot as essentially a moral or religious man. Vicesimus Knox's essay on "The Idea of a Patriot" (1784), deploring the "prostitution" of the name of patriot by selfish and hypocritical men, insisted that just as "a bad man cannot be a patriot," so "every good man is indeed a patriot, for a good man is a public good." Although he praises the patriotism of George III and of Lord North, he declares that the "truest patriotism is not to be found in public life." In words that perhaps inspired the spirit of Cowper's *Task* (1785), he added: "What can influence him who secretly serves his country in the retired and unobserved walks of private life. His motives must be pure, and he is a *patriot*."[57] The Scottish Presbyterian Archibald Bruce took up the point that the highest obligation of the Christian "patriot" is not to the state but to God, and, in a sermon on *True Patriotism* published in 1785, developed the idea of "religious patriotism," which "deserves the preference to any other; as it is employed about the best of causes, that of heaven, and the highest interests of men."[58] It is the duty of all Christians, he declares, "to appear openly and actively on the side of the cause of God, and to

---

54 *Small Change*, 245.
55 I cite Fordyce from his *Sermons to Young Women*, 14th. edn., 2 vols. (London, 1814), II, 183.
56 See *Small Change*, 220–67.
57 *Essays Moral and Literary*, 6th. edn., 2 vols. (London, 1785), I, 40, 43, 44.
58 *True Patriotism; or, a Public Spirit for God and Religion Recommended, and the Want of It Reprehended* (Edinburgh, 1785), 18. His text was Judges 5. 23, in which the inhabitants of Meroz are cursed because "they came not to the help of the Lord."

exert themselves for the public good, especially in times of great danger and opposition" (17). As we will see, this is an idea that impressed itself on both Christopher Smart and William Cowper.

The Reverend Richard Price's famous 1789 sermon on the love of our country, which provoked Burke's *Reflections on the Revolution in France* (1790), summarizes a range of eighteenth-century reflections on the true meaning of patriotism. His text was the same Psalm 122 that Bishop Conybeare had preached on forty years earlier.[59] His purpose, he says, is "to explain the duty we owe to our country, and the nature, foundation, and proper expressions of that love to it which we ought to cultivate."[60] Like several of the essayists who preceded him, Price distinguishes between true patriotism and mistaken versions of it which might easily mislead his hearers. Love of country is a passion that requires "regulation and direction."

Invoking the Christian spirit of universal benevolence, Price (like others before him) separates patriotism from the "conviction" of the superiority of our country or any preference for its laws and constitution, or any "spirit of rivalship and ambition." A true patriot is at the same time a "citizen of the world" (181). (Burke would later claim that "universal benevolence" was just a stalking horse for Price's secret preference for Revolutionary France.) Price also rejects, as Newman implicitly had, the idea that love of country means attachment to "the soil or the spot of earth on which we happen to have been born." Anticipating Anderson's idea that a nation is an "imagined community," Price declares that "by our country is meant . . . that community of which we are members, or that body of companions and friends and kindred who are associated with us under the same constitution or government, protected by the same laws, and bound together by the same civil polity" (178). It is notable that when Burke attacked Price, he did not challenge his idea of the "country" as the "community of which we are members." It was on the same attachment to the "little platoon"[61] that Burke built his own implicit theory of patriotism.

What distinguishes Price's discourse from the many that preceded his is the emphasis, at a time when nationalist and anti-Gallican feeling had built to a fever pitch, on the need to "correct and purify" the "passion" of patriotism. Even the famous love of country of the "old Romans," he says, was only "a principle holding together a band of robbers in

---

[59] Price was preaching to the Society for Commemorating the Revolution in Great Britain on 4 November 1789. He notes that "the love of our country has in all times been a subject of warm commendations" (*Political Writings*, 178).

[60] Price, *Political Writings*, 177.

[61] *Reflections on the Revolution in France*, in *Writings and Speeches*, VII, 97.

their attempts to crush all liberty but their own." Distinctive too is his preacherly focus on the "duties" of the patriotic Briton toward the country he loves and would serve: to "enlighten" and "liberalize" it, to practice virtue, to obey the laws and respect the magistrates, and to defend the country against its enemies, both internal and external. It is here that Burke was especially to attack Price, for among the country's internal enemies Price implicitly numbered those who defended what, based on a radical reading of the Revolution of 1688, he himself regarded as an "imperfect state." Burke's own *Reflections* might in fact be regarded as the last in a series of eighteenth-century reflections on patriotism, centered on "the country" not as Price's community of Protestant Dissenters but on King, church, and the "natural landed interest." Central to Burke's argument is his distinction between a "good patriot," with a "disposition to preserve, and an ability to improve," and the latest instance of the false patriot, a "man full of warm speculative benevolence" (267).

Like any patriot or nationalist, Burke and Price must invent the country they love.[62] The Price–Burke debate can serve as a summary reminder of the century's preoccupation with the meaning of patriotism and of the contested nature of the term. Like Price and Burke, the poets from Thomson to Cowper either implicitly or explicitly deployed an idea of "the country." Inclined, like Burke, to panegyric of their native land, they were inclined at the same time, like Price, to think that the spirit of British patriotism needed to be corrected and purified.

The French Revolution may serve as a useful end point for an inquiry into patriotism and poetry in eighteenth-century Britain. Debates about patriotism continued into the 1790s, deploying some of the same arguments about true and false patriotism.[63] But new elements appear: the cosmopolitan "citizen of the world" comes under suspicion as a French sympathizer, or simply as indifferent or selfish. And the entire discussion was largely focused on the conflict between British radicals and conservatives over French-inspired reform proposals at home. When poets after Cowper offered themselves as patriots, they ran the risk of being attacked by their own countrymen.

---

[62] Cf. Bolingbroke, who defines Britain as essentially a maritime trading nation: "the situation of Great Britain, the character of her people, and the nature of her government, fit her for trade and commerce. Her climate and her soil make them necessary to her well-being... Like other amphibious animals, we must come occasionally on shore: but the water is more properly our element" (*Patriot King*, in *Political Writings*, 396, 402).

[63] For details, see Evan Radcliffe, "Burke, Radical Cosmopolitanism, and the Debate on Patriotism in the 1790s," *Studies in Eighteenth-Century Culture*, 28 (1999), 311–39.

CHAPTER 2

Patriotic odes and patriot-poets

As a consequence of the intense nationalist and patriotic consciousness of the mid-eighteenth century, and the well-established discourse of patriotism which kept the idea on the pages of magazines and newspapers, and despite the opprobrium attaching to the idea of the "patriot" in many eyes, the major poets of the day found themselves considering the ways in which a poet might be a patriot. Some poets, as we have seen, engaged in the public debate about the nature of patriotism, about the difference between the true patriot and the pretender to that virtue. Some denounced or defended the ministry and its Patriot critics. Some supplied xenophobic and jingoistic ballads for the popular press. But most poets, from anonymous ode-writers to well-established figures like Thomson, Gray, and Cowper, approached the problem obliquely, sensing perhaps that the distinctive nature of poetry, as opposed to political journalism, called for something other than polemic, bellicose rant, or discursive analysis. To help them define their role, the poets of the mid-century also had before them a body of verse in which British poets had announced themselves as patriots.

A poet setting out in the 1730s or 1740s to play a patriotic role would not have been at a loss for models to emulate, to avoid, or to transform. Much of the poetry that a reader or an aspiring poet of the day encountered was frankly occasional verse. By its nature it tended to be ephemeral – many "patriotic" poems appeared in newspapers or in broadside editions and were not reprinted – but a surprising amount remained in circulation for several generations. The official New Year's and birthday odes produced by the Poet Laureate constitute another form of patriotic verse. Because most laureate verse was sneered at by Pope and Gray, modern readers tend to dismiss it as beneath their notice, but some of the laureate odes – those by William Whitehead, for example – had considerable reputations in their own day and are worth a critical look.

Classical writers also provided models. Most modern readers, assuming that eighteenth-century poets turned to Rome for exemplary figures, overlook the considerable interest in the Greek lyric poets and the ways in which Pindar and his fellows served as models for the patriotic poet.[1]

VICTORY ODES

Much of the steady stream of occasional verse of the eighteenth century, as of any period, has been effectively lost to the modern reader. Tied to events that come to seem unimportant to later generations, and rarely reprinted after its first appearance, it has sunk below the horizon of all but the curious reader in the rare book or microfilm room of a research library. Most of such poems have little of what used to be called intrinsic literary value, and are probably deservedly forgotten. But they help to establish the month-to-month literary texture of an era, and can highlight, if only by contrast, the literary practice of poets whose work deservedly endures. One such body of forgotten verse – poems that were surely in the mind of Collins as he composed his "patriotic odes" in 1745 and 1746 – might be called the victory ode in celebration of contemporary military heroes. "War," as Johnson observed in the *Life of Addison*, "is a frequent subject of Poetry."[2] And English poets, as most students of early-eighteenth-century poetry know, competed to celebrate the victories of William III at Namur and especially of Marlborough at Blenheim and Ramillies.[3] Less well known are the poetic commemorations of the battles of the 1740s, when British soldiers and sailors were engaged against the French and Spanish from the West Indies and Canada to continental Europe, and against domestic rebels from Inverness to Derby. As news of British victories at Porto Bello, Dettingen, or Culloden filtered back to London, it was greeted in daily newspapers, monthly magazines, or broadside sheets with poetic celebration. (Britain's military defeats – as at Fontenoy or Falkirk – tended to pass without acknowledgment in verse, except in elegiac lament for fallen warriors.[4]) Even if the British bards of

---

[1] In his first and fourth books, Horace wrote patriotic odes on Augustus, Lollius ("non ille pro caris amicis / aut patria timidus perire" – "not afraid to die for dear friends or country" [IV. 9]), and other public figures, but because many in the eighteenth century regarded him as a "court slave" and flatterer of a tyrant, he did not provide an unambiguous model.

[2] *Lives of the English Poets*, ed. G. B. Hill, 3 vols. (Oxford: Clarendon, 1905), II, 128.

[3] Johnson notes that "Many of our writers tried their powers upon this year of victory [i.e., 1704, the year of Blenheim]" (*Lives*, II, 128–29).

[4] But cf. *A New Satiric Ballad* (1745) on the Battle of Fontenoy, which blames the defeat on the Dutch allies, who ran away, and avows that the English and Scots showed "Cannon-Proof Courage" (stanza 8).

mid-century had no Marlborough, Wellington, or Nelson to celebrate, they found such heroes as were available, particularly Admiral Edward Vernon and George II's younger son, William, Duke of Cumberland.[5]

Vernon, little known today except to historians, was probably the most popular English admiral in the eighteenth century before Nelson.[6] Promoted to captain in 1706 at the age of twenty-one, he had no war to fight after 1714, and from 1722 to 1734 served in parliament as a Whig who made his name as an opponent of Walpole's excise taxes and pacific policy. In 1739, with Britain at war with Spain (largely at the urging of champions of Britain's maritime trade, including Vernon himself), he was promoted to vice admiral (at the age of fifty-four) and sent to the West Indies, where he succeeded in capturing the fortified Spanish town of Porto Bello (on the coast of Panama) in December with the aid of only six men-of-war. When news of the victory reached London in March of 1740, Admiral Vernon was hailed as a national hero. Medals were struck and bonfires were built in London and in the provinces, and repeated annually for several years on his birthday in November.[7] Poems celebrating Vernon as national hero and British patriot who revenged Spanish "depredations" and reestablished British naval supremacy began appearing immediately.[8]

The tone of many of the poetic celebrations tended to be boisterous and popular rather than formal and lofty, as in the broadside *A New Ballad on the Taking of Porto-Bello, by Admiral Vernon* (London, 1740):

> Come attend *British Boys*,
> I'll make you rejoice,
> I will tell you, how *Vernon* did scare,
> PORTO-BELLO the Strong,
> Lay'd it's castles along,
> And all this, with *but six Men of War*.

---

[5] Poems in praise of Marlborough (including Lyttelton's *Blenheim* [1727]) were still being reprinted in Dodsley's *Collection of Poems*, 6 vols. (London, 1748–63), vol. II (1748) and vol. V (1758), and in subsequent reprintings. By 1759 there was a new army hero to celebrate (and lament), James Wolfe, whose death at Quebec prompted a flood of odes. For a survey of them, see Alan McNairn, *Behold the Hero: General Wolfe and the Arts in the Eighteenth Century* (Montreal, 1997), 40–61, 205–33.

[6] See Gerald Jordan and Nicholas Rogers, "Admirals as Heroes: Patriotism and Liberty in Hanoverian England," *Journal of British Studies*, 28 (1989), 202. Vernon's prominence is also remarked in Rogers' *Whigs and Cities: Popular Politics in the Age of Walpole and Pitt* (Oxford, 1989), 235–40, 375–78, and in Kathleen Wilson's *The Sense of the People*.

[7] For a summary of popular celebrations, see Rogers, *Whigs and Cities*, 235–36.

[8] Rogers (*Whigs and Critics*, 237, 375) notes a poem in the *London Evening Post* for 25–27 March 1740, and a hasty collection entitled *Vernon's Glory, Containing 14 New Songs, Occasion'd by the Taking of Porto Bello and Fort Chagre* (London, 1740).

Poems continued to appear the following year. *Io! Triumphe! A POEM upon Admiral VERNON* (London, 1741), by "an undergraduate of *Jesus*-College, *Oxon.*," naively adopts epic style in solemn imitation of the *Aeneid*:

> Arms and the *Man* I sing, the first who rose,
> And rising, sought, by honourable War,
> An honourable Peace . . .
> Say for what Cause *Iberia*'s haughty Sons
> Still loud with Insults, still provoke to Arms?

The poem continues for twenty-three pages, concluding with the fall of Porto Bello and the restoration of peace and plenty, along with British "Commerce, the Child of Peace."

Other poets aimed at a discursive middle style, like the author of *The Three Politicians: or, a Dialogue in Verse Between a Patriot, a Courtier, and their Friend. Concluding with an Exhortation to Admiral Vernon* (London, 1741), writing at a time when the court favored peace, and the Opposition wanted renewed war with both Spain and France. The "Courtier" of the poem thinks England is now strong, the "Patriot" denounces continuing Spanish insults and pillaging, and blames the court for not supplying Vernon the "seasonable Aid" he needed at Cartagena (which he failed to take in 1741). The "Friend" hopes to patch up the quarrel, and (in elevated rhetoric) foresees new British victories:

> I see, methinks, as with a Prophet's View,
> Some vast Atchievements, bold, surprizing, new.
> D'Antin retires, affrighted and alarm'd:
> Begirt with Terrors, and with Thunder arm'd,[9]
> Lo, Britain's HERO follows at his Heels,
> While ev'ry Breast the Rage of Battle feels.
> STANHOPE and BYNG the great EXAMPLE gave.[10]
> Look up, immortal STANHOPE, from thy *Grave*.
> O let thy genius VERNON's Vigour guide,
> And o'er his Actions on the sea preside.
> Thy words still live in ev'ry *Briton*'s Heart:
> *Destroy their Fleet.*[11] This now be VERNON's Part.
> Strike, Noble VERNON; vindicate the sea;
> As Byng be great, nay greater far than he.

---

9   Probably Louis-Antoine de Pardaillan de Gondrin, Duke d'Antin (1665–1736).
10 Stanhope is James, first Earl of Stanhope (1673–1721), who was First Lord of the Treasury in 1718, when he negotiated the Quadruple Alliance against Spain. Byng is Admiral George (not the better-known John) Byng, who crushed the Spanish fleet at the battle of Cape Passaro in 1718.
11 Stanhope's instructions to Byng before the battle at Cape Passaro, which form the epigraph to the poem.

> *Spain's* fearful Fleet was scatter'd at his Word:
> But let *France* honour thy superiour Sword.
>
> (10–11)

Vernon himself tends to disappear in the memory of past British victories and of this politically motivated poet's eagerness for war with France. Vernon never repeated his great victory, but he continued in active service until 1746, and remained in the public eye. Shenstone's expanded *School-Mistress* (1742, and reprinted in Dodsley's *Collection*) salutes "the firm fixt breast" of Vernon's "patriot soul" (stanza 27).[12] He joined Drake and Raleigh on the roster of great English admirals, and perhaps prepared the poets and the public to rejoice in the later naval successes of Commodore Anson (the circumnavigator of 1744), Admiral Hawke (victor at Cape Finisterre in 1747 and Quiberon Bay in 1759), Admiral Pocock (who captured Havana in 1762), and Nelson.

There were also poetic celebrations for British victories on land. From 1740 to 1748 Britain took part in the War of the Austrian Succession, and although France dominated the early years of the war, the presence of King George himself at the battle of Dettingen, on German territory, in 1743, inspired British poets to make the most of what was in fact an inconclusive battle in which British forces avoided defeat, while the Duke of Cumberland himself was wounded. The most enthusiastic of the poems, *A Joyful Ode: Inscribed to the King, on the late Victory at Dettingen* (London, 1743), simply ignores reports that the battle was a stalemate, declares victory – "While *Victory* beholds the Rout, / Exulting hears the Conq'ring Shout" (7) – and compares earlier triumphs in English history at Crécy and Agincourt, or "When *Churchill* thunder'd in the smoaking Plain" (5). John Lockman more cautiously refers only to the "repulse" of the French, and acknowledges some past criticism of his young hero for devoting himself to pleasure. In his *Verses to his Royal Highness the Duke of Cumberland: on His being wounded, at the Repulse of the French near Dettingen* (London, 1743), Lockman insists that the same spirit which inspired Cumberland's "Love of Pleasure" also fires the hero "with brave Ardour" (2).

Stephen Duck, long a compliant favorite of the court, responded with *An Ode on the Battle of Dettingen* (London, 1743), but even he wonders whether poetry is suitable for the occasion:

> What Poet, with *Maeonian* Wing,
> Shall your immortal Praises sing,
> And glorious Acts record? (3)

---

[12] Dodsley's *Collection*, 2nd. edn. (London, 1748), I, 252.

The muse trembles as the King dares the thickest dangers of the field (a poetic overstatement). William is wounded, and at last the French retreat.

> Muse, whither would thy Fancy soar?
> These Subjects far surpass thy Pow'r,
>   And suit sublimer Lays:
> From GEORGE's glorious Name refrain;
> Nor with thy low ignoble Strain
>   Degrade brave William's Praise. (7)

Duck seemingly cannot commit himself to his poem, though he conventionally blames his verse rather than the subject.

Another poem in the same year, *A Poem on the Battle of DETTINGEN. Inscrib'd to the King*, hints at the controversy that underlay the battle: doubts, expressed by the political Opposition at home, about Britain's participation in a continental war.

> Thy Worth, the Plains of *DETTINGEN* will tell,
> Tho' Envy should detract[13] and Faction swell;
>   (5)

Led by the King, "Great *Cumberland*" fights gloriously, and "wounded still fought on, / Nor left the Field before the Battle won" (7). The poem concludes with assurances that "dread *Britannia's* Name" will make the French blush and (perhaps more important) will promote domestic tranquillity, will

> At Home hush Discord into friendly Peace,
> And join us all in Love of Brunswic's Race.
>   (7)

Even a friendly poet, it seems, cannot help acknowledging the loud opposition to the King.[14]

A defensive tone recurs two years later, in *A Religious Ode, Occasion'd by the Present Rebellion. Written Oct. 11, 1745. By a Clergyman*. The Jacobites had had early success in September at Prestonpans, and some alarms were being sounded that British patriots were not rallying to the defense of their

---

[13] The text in fact reads "dertact" (an obvious misprint).
[14] The author of the satiric *A Scheme for rewarding the Heroic Actions of His Royal Highness the Duke of Cumberland* wonders whether Dettingen was in fact a "Victory" or just an "Escape" from disaster, ironically proposing that Cumberland, since he was primarily fighting on behalf of Hanoverian rather than British interests, be made Elector of Hanover. A copy of the *Scheme* is collected in a British Library bound volume entitled "Jacobite Tracts," shelfmark C115.i.3(81). It is an anti-Hanoverian tract, but not clearly a Jacobite one.

King.[15] The "clergyman" addresses Jehovah, asks protection from "fell Rebellion" (9), and worries that Britain is being punished for some unspecified "Scarlet Crimes." The poem is equipped with "Notes," which deny the Jacobite claim that James III has an "indefeasible hereditary Right," and declare that "His present Majesty's title to the Crown is indisputable." One infers that the clergyman worries that some readers are listening to Jacobite claims and need to be reminded that "Obedience" is due to King George, as is "evident from Scripture, from the Nature and Ends of Government, and from the Laws of our Constitution, from the Custom of our own Country, and that of others."[16]

By this time Cumberland, leading the King's loyal troops against the rebels, had clearly displaced his father as the hero of the hour. The northward Jacobite withdrawal from Derby in December 1745 occasioned an ode addressed to Liberty "On the Retreat of the Rebels": "Hail, godlike *Liberty*, to thee / We raise the voice, we bend the knee; / To thy widestructur'd dome / Shall ev'ry free born *Briton* come."[17] After the loss at Falkirk, poets still looked to Cumberland as the savior.[18] His decisive victory at Culloden on 16 April 1746 – one day after his twenty-fifth birthday – brought forth a torrent of British verse.[19] Another round of poems appeared when Cumberland triumphantly returned to London in July.[20]

[15] In October, so a contemporary wrote, "the newspapers [are] every day full of pathetic incitements to fight for our king and our liberties; and the pamphlet shops crowded with entire new books on the same important subjects" (quoted in Harris, *A Patriot Press*, 9, quoting J. Black, *Culloden and the '45* [1990], 91).

[16] Cf. "An Ode to the People of Great Britain," published in 1746 and reprinted in Dodsley's *Collection* in 1748, in which Britain is punished at home and abroad for the moral crimes of a "monstrous age" (2nd. edn., III, 22).

[17] Printed in the *London Magazine*, 15 (Feb. 1746), 95. See also the "Hymn to Liberty. An Ode on the Success of His Royal Highness the Duke of Cumberland," advertised in the *British Magazine*, Jan.–Feb. 1746.

[18] See *An Elegy Inscribed to the Duke of Cumberland* (Edinburgh, 1746), occasioned by the battle at Falkirk, which ends with the assurance that Britain "n'er can fall" and that William "soon, rebellion's children will dismay" (13, 14).

[19] A sampling of such poems includes an "Ode in Honour of the Duke of Cumberland" in the *London Magazine*, 15 (April 1746), 205; *Liberty: An Ode, Occasion'd by the Happy Victory obtain'd by His Royal Highness the Duke of Cumberland* (Foxon L 171); *An Epistle on Liberty. Occasion'd by his Royal Highness's Victory over the Rebels*, in the *London Magazine*, 15 (June 1746), 309–10; John Lockman's *Ode on the Crushing of the Rebellion* (London, 1746); the satiric *New Ballad on the Battle of Drummossie-Muir, near Inverness* (Edinburgh, 1746); *On the Duke of Cumberland's Late Defeat of the Rebels. By a West-Country Gentleman; An Ode on the Birth-day of His Royal Highness William Duke of Cumberland* (n.p., 1746); *An Epilogue on the Birth-Day of His Royal Highness the Duke of Cumberland* (n.p., 1746, BL shelfmark 1850 C10).

[20] Poems include "An Ode sacred to the Victorious Return of His Royal Highness the Duke of Cumberland from Scotland" (Foxon 056); "Britain's Ode of Victory, on the Happy Triumphant return of the Illustrious Duke of Cumberland, and his Suppression of the Horrible Rebellion"; "The Progress of Glory, an irregular ode on the Happy Suppression of the Rebellion," all

The poems, odes, epistles, and ballads celebrate William as champion of "Liberty," the "Patriot's Blessing" (*Epilogue on the Birth-Day*), and military "Hero" (the word appears in most of the poems). The battlefield, as readers of contemporary newspaper reports well knew, was clouded with smoke and confused with the clash of infantry, but somehow (so the poets claimed) William's "conduct shone / Conspicuous thro' the cloud of war" (*An Epistle on Liberty*). Combining the ideas of commanding general of a modern European army and Achillean warrior, the poets imagine that William defeated the villainous "rebels" virtually singlehandedly. One odist, John Lockman, probably remembers Addison's famous simile of the angel in *The Campaign* (1704), a poetic tribute to Marlborough's victory at Blenheim –

> Calm and serene he drives the furious blast;
> And, pleased the Almighty's orders to perform,
> Rides in the whirlwind and directs the storm.

– but still congratulates his royal hero for personal prowess:

> Calm, in the Storm, see WILLIAM ride!
> See him *Britannia*'s Fate decide,
> At one immortal Blow.
> (*Ode on the Crushing*, 11)

Poets probably knew they were competing with the "Authentick Accounts" of battles (at Culloden, Falkirk, Prestonpans, and Fontenoy), providing detailed reports on troop placements and movements, names and ranks of the participants, and tallies of those wounded and killed, which soon began appearing in London bookstalls and newspapers.[21] But the poets keep to epic heights – or fall into bathos:

> In closer Combat now the Heroes dare,
> Whilst Show'rs of Bullets whistle through the Air.
> Numbers on Numbers fall, whilst groans and cries
> And Shouts triumphant rend the vaulted Skies.

advertised in July and August 1746 editions of the *British Magazine*. See also Thomas Newcomb, "An Ode, presented to His Royal Highness the Duke of Cumberland, on his return from Scotland" (London, 1746).

21 See for example *An Authentick ACCOUNT of the BATTLE fought ... near Culloden* (1746); "A Succinct History of the REBELLION," in *The Museum*, beginning with first issue on 29 March 1746, and extending past Culloden; two accounts of *The Battle of Falkirk*, initially printed at Bannockburn and Edinburgh in January 1746, and reprinted in London. Even the "authentic accounts" make use of idealizing language: William is a "glorious young Hero," and the result a "glorious Victory" (*Authentick ACCOUNT*).

Th'undaunted *Britons* still renew the Fight,
Whilst the Oat-fed Heroes urge their shameful Flight.
(*On the . . . Late Defeat of the Rebels*)

Even before tripping over the oat-eating Highlanders, a contemporary reader might have found it difficult not to hear inadvertent echoes of the battle in *The Rape of the Lock*, where "Heroes' and Heroins' Shouts confus'dly rise, / And base, and treble Voices strike the Skies."[22]

Other Culloden poets took refuge in coarse humor and Scotticisms, as if to sharpen the ridicule of the ragged and "primitive" Highlanders. In *A New Ballad*, which apparently appeared in May 1746,[23] a "loyal Scot" exults in Culloden as revenge for the defeat at Prestonpans,

> When dev'lish Hacks and deadly Whacks
> Wi' their Claymores they gave, Man;
> But now their Swords are not worth Turds,
> Against a reg'lar Fae [Foe], Man.

Even a "glorious victory," as Culloden seemed to loyal Britons, had within weeks entered the low ballad tradition.

In restrospect, we might conclude that by the 1740s patriotic poetic accounts of battle had come to a kind of dead end, and that the last great English epic account of warfare was in Book VI of *Paradise Lost*. Poets in succeeding generations still had available the old epic conventions, but Homeric narrative was under pressure from several directions. Mock-epic had intervened to make straightforward epic on a contemporary subject less credible. The nature of warfare had changed so that the small scale (and sometimes single combat) of Homeric war had been displaced by the disciplined (and sometimes confused) movements of regiments and battalions, overseen by a commanding general safely removed from the action, and the best poets – like Addison – had understood that poems likewise needed to change. As Johnson observed, Addison took his images not from "books" (i.e., from classical epic) but from life. His Marlborough displays not "personal prowess" but "deliberate intrepidity, a calm command of his passions, and the power of consulting his own mind in the midst of danger. The rejection and contempt of fiction is rational

---

[22] *The Rape of the Lock*, v. 41–42. Cf. "*Restore the Lock!* the vaulted Roofs rebound" (v. 204). As Pope's Twickenham editors note, epic skies are often "vaulted" (as in Dryden's *Aeneid* IV. 962, and Pope's *Iliad*, I. 671, VI. 431).

[23] A copy of the poem is found in a volume of "Ballads and Broadsides" in the British Library, shelfmark 1850c10. It has been hand-dated "May 1746."

and manly."[24] Finally, eighteenth-century readers were the first generations to have relatively prompt and accurate reports, in newspapers and
magazines, of foreign military battles, and such reports probably made
it more difficult for them to accept the old epic forms. British battles in
the 1740s also presented a special problem: they rarely led to clear-cut
victories (Culloden is an exception), typically involved great losses on
both sides, and more than once led to cowardice and "shameful flight"
on the part of British soldiers, as at Prestonpans and Falkirk.[25]

Ignoring such pressures,[26] most Culloden poets – along with Jacobite
poets celebrating the military exploits of Charles Edward[27] – persisted
in conventional idealized description, following the classical example of
John Philips' *Bleinheim* (1705) rather than Addison's modern *Campaign*.[28]
Perhaps the silence of other poets, Collins for example, may be explained
by the realization that it would be difficult for the patriotic poet to succeed
in traditional battle narrative. Other Culloden poets perhaps sensed that
the patriotic poet needed to focus not on the martial hero but on the
"dear native Land" that his efforts helped preserve. Lockman's *Ode on the
Crushing of the Rebellion* ends with an apostrophe to Britain:

> Hail ISLE renown'd! dear, native Land!
> Far banish Tyrants from thy Strand,
> And awe the boundless Sea.

[24] *Lives*, II, 129. As Walter Scott was later to remark, Addison was "the first poet who ventured to
celebrate a victorious general for skill and conduct, instead of such feats as are appropriated to
Guy of Warwick, or Bevis of Hampton" (cited in Johnson, *Lives*, II, 129n).

[25] A military inquiry into the defeat at Prestonpans, published in London in September 1746 as
Report of the Proceedings and Opinion of the Board of General Officers on their Examination, &C (London,
1746), concluded that British troops panicked, "turned their Backs," and ran, "notwithstanding
all the Endeavours used by their Officers to prevent it" (42), and blamed the defeat on the
"shameful Behaviour of the Private Men" (103) rather than the commanding general and his
officers.

[26] In the summer of 1746 the author of *The Fourth Ode of the Fourth Book of Horace Imitated and Applied
to HRH the Duke of Cumberland*, urging that George now send Cumberland back to the Continent,
imagines that he will conquer like a Homeric warrior ("Resume the Sword, like great *Achilles*,
fear'd" [8]) Cf. also *The Progress of Glory: An Irregular Ode, Address'd to His Majesty, on the Happy
Suppression of the REBELLION* (London, 1746).

[27] See, for example, *To His Royal Highness Charles, Prince of Wales, Regent of the Kingdoms of Scotland,
England, France, and Ireland* (n.p., 1745), where the language of compliment is readily transferred
from Prince William to Prince Charles: "Hail Glorious Youth! the wonder of the Age, / The
future Subject of th'Historian's Page; / Oh best of PRINCES! best of PATRIOTS, deign / A loyal
Muse to hail thy happy Reign" (3).

[28] Johnson remarks that Philips "formed his ideas of the field of *Blenheim* from the battles of the
heroick ages or the tales of chivalry with very little comprehension of the qualities necessary to
the composition of a modern hero, which Addison has displayed with so much propriety" (*Lives*,
I, 317).

> Thee, from the Nations, *Neptune* rent;
> Bid thee shine, a new Continent;
> A WORLD, rever'd and free.
>
> (18, stanza 39)

Collins was in effect to follow Lockman's lead.[29]

Of the hundreds if not thousands of "victory odes" and other patriotic songs produced in the eighteenth century perhaps only two have achieved enduring fame. Two famous songs of the 1740s had by the nineteenth century come to be regarded as Britain's "national anthems." "Rule, Britannia" (1740), though it began life as the final ode in a masque about an English king (*Alfred*), is in fact centered not on the King but on the "blest isle" of "Britannia," its "happy coast," its "rural reign," and commercial "cities," and symbolized by the sturdily rooted "native oak." At the close of the masque a Hermit, before sending Alfred forth to lead the country into a future now revealed to him in a vision, bids him first listen to a "venerable Bard."

> Behold, my Lord, our venerable Bard,
> Aged and blind, him whom the Muses favour.
> Yet ere you go, in our lov'd country's praise,
> That noblest theme, hear what his rapture breathes.

There follows the "Ode." If Britain has any ruler, the bard sings, it is God himself, for it was "at Heaven's command" that Britain first "Arose from out the azure main." It was Heaven rather than King John who provided "the charter of the land." It is no mortal king (like Xerxes or Canute, who notably failed in their attempts[30]) but the country herself who "rules the waves." That she now wields the power implies that Britannia acts as the agent of a divine creator and redeemer, who first wielded it.[31] Reflecting the ongoing naval struggle with Spain, the song takes a militant stance

---

[29] Other poets continued to pour forth patriotic verse urging Britain to declare war in 1757 or celebrating British victories in 1763. See *The Patriot Muse, or Poems on Some of the Principal Events of the Late War; Together with a Poem on the Peace* (London, 1764), "by an American Gentleman" [Benjamin Young Price], and *The Patriot, or A Call to Glory; A poem. In Two Books* (Edinburgh, 1757), tediously seeking in blank verse "to rouse Britannia from her golden dreams, / In which, alas! she thinks herself secure," and "to show the Patriot what he ought to do" (3).

[30] Thomson might have expected the audience to remember the old story of King Canute, who attempted to rule the waves only a century after Alfred. Johnson's line in "The Vanity of Human Wishes" (1749) – "The waves he lashes, and enchains the wind" (232) – suggests that Thomson's audience might also have remembered that Xerxes had sought to impose his rule over the Hellespont.

[31] God the Father, by creating the world ("Let the waters under the heaven be gathered together unto one place," Gen. 1.9) and God the Son, by walking on the sea (Matt. 14. 25). Thomson may recall Milton, where Christ "walked the waves" ("Lycidas," line 173).

against Britain's enemies. First sung four months after news of Vernon's victory at Porto Bello reached London, it serves notice on the Spanish, who had notoriously "enslaved" British sailors in the War of Jenkins' Ear,[32] as well as on any other potential enemy, that "Britons never will be slaves" and furthermore that henceforth Britain intends to play the dominant role in global trade. It will be "the dread and envy" of all the nations. Even when it is attacked,

> Still more majestic shalt thou rise,
> More dreadful from each foreign stroke . . .
> Thee haughty tyrants ne'er shall tame;
> All their attempts to bend thee down
> Will but arouse thy generous flame,
> But work their woe and thy renown.

Britain will both control the sea lanes and, as its maritime power is exerted, control distant shores:

> All thine shall be the subject main,
> And every shore it circles thine.[33]

God Save the King, an old song which quickly attained nationwide popularity during the Jacobite rebellion of 1745,[34] declares the nation's attachment to its King, and invokes divine protection.

> God save our noble King,
> God save great George our King,
> God save the King.
> Send him victorious
> Happy and glorious,
> Long to reign over us,
> God save the King.

---

[32] As Rogers (*Whigs and Cities*, 58) notes, resentment that British sailors had been treated as "Spanish Galley Slaves" was roused by press discussion of Richard Copithorne's *The English Cotejo, or The Cruelties, Depredations and Illicit Trade Charg'd upon the English in a Spanish Libel Lately Published* (London, 1739).The frontispiece to Akenside's *The Voice of Liberty* [also published as the *British Philippic*] (1738) shows a Spanish dungeon with chained British captives. The caption, drawn from the ensuing poem, reads: "And dare they, dare the vanquish'd sons of *Spain* / Enslave a *Briton*?" Another 1738 print, entitled "Slavery" (see figure 6), with a text from *Richard II*, shows enslaved British sailors, forced to survive on roots, pulling a plow driven by a Spanish overseer. In the background a British ship is attacked by a Spanish man-o'-war, and Captain Jenkins loses his ear. In the right foreground the British lion, prepared to gain revenge, is threatened by Walpole, who chooses not to go to war with Spain.

[33] *Alfred. A Masque* (London, 1740), 42–43. For a reading of "Rule, Britannia" as an instance of "aggressive nationalism," see Suvir Kaul, *Poems of Nation, Anthems of Empire*, 1–8.

[34] See Percy Scholes, *God Save the King* (1942).

Figure 6. "Slavery" (1738). BM Cat 2355

Notably, the hymn is addressed not to the King but to God. By thrice imploring divine rescue the first stanza implies the King's grave danger. "Save" has a powerful Old Testament resonance.[35] And "God save the king" is a common choral cry in the books of Samuel and Kings, when the Jews were ruled by a king,[36] with a particular English resonance since Handel's *Zadok the Priest* (1727), a coronation anthem for George II.[37] To be "victorious"[38] over as yet unnamed enemies rhymes with and is syntactically parallel to (and perhaps equivalent to) reigning "over us" (i.e., his subjects) – apt enough at a time when his very right to the throne had been challenged both at home and abroad. Perhaps because in the minds of some subjects Charles Edward was the rightful king, the song takes the trouble to declare that it is "great George" who is in fact "our King." It is salutary to remember that the song was first sung on the night of 28 September 1745, just four days after Prestonpans.

The second stanza focuses not on God's "saving" the King but on his defeating the King's enemies:

> O Lord our God arise,
> Scatter his enemies
> And make them fall:
> Confound their politicks,
> Frustrate their knavish tricks.
> On him our hopes are fix'd.
> O save us all.

With further Biblical resonance,[39] the song contrasts the "scattered"[40] enemies with the united Britons – the repeated pronouns "our .. our .. us .. our .. our ... us all" emphasize that the chorus of British voices sings as one person. The enemies are not only the Jacobites but also the Catholic powers in Paris and Rome allegedly manipulating Charles Edward in their own interest – hence the "knavish [unprincipled, dishonest] tricks" and mere "politicks" (as opposed to the principled assertion

---

35 God "saves" Israel "out of the hand of the Egyptians" (Exodus 14.30)

36 1 Samuel 10.24, 2 Samuel 16.16 (where the context is the rebellion against the king), 1 Kings 1. 25, 34–40 (where Zadok the priest anoints Solomon king), 2 Kings 11.12 (where the context is a previously usurped throne). Cf. 2 Chronicles 23.11.

37 Handel's text, including the ringing words "God save the King, / Long live the King, / May the King live forever," is adapted from 1 Kings 1. 38–40.

38 On the aptness of *great, victorious, glorious,* and *happy,* see Donald Davie, "The Language of the Eighteenth-Century Hymn," in Donald Davie and Robert Stevenson, eds., *English Hymnology in the Eighteenth Century* (Los Angeles, 1980), 5–7.

39 "Arise, O Lord; / save me, O my God; / for thou hast smitten all mine enemies upon the cheek bone" (Psalm 3.7).

40 In the Old Testament God "scatters" the enemies of the Jews (Num. 10, 35, Psalm 68.1), or those (including the Jews) whom he curses (Gen. 11.8, 49.7; Lev 26.33).

of dynastic right).[41] After condemning the "enemies," the song returns to the King as the embodiment of the nation: just as "his enemies" are the country's enemies, so saving the King is the same as saving "us all."

Of the two anthems "Rule, Britannia," with its focus on the nation rather than the monarch and on Britain's control of the seas, is more characteristic of the patriotic poems of the major poets of the period.

LAUREATE ODES

Taught by Pope to laugh at Cibber's laureate verse, we usually assume that no serious poet after 1725, if inclined to write as a "patriot," would think of addressing a panegyrical ode to the sovereign, or even of agreeing to serve as Poet Laureate. (Gray refused the post in 1757.) But it is worth remembering that some of the laureate odes were in fact regarded as quite respectable, even by Gray. William Whitehead, who accepted the laureateship after Gray turned it down,[42] published birthday and New Year's odes annually from 1758 to 1785. Gray admired the November 1758 birthday ode tracing George's Hanoverian ancestry back to Ottoberto of Este, who "passed from Italy into Germany" in the tenth century. And he spoke well of the New Year's ode less than two months later, as the tide of battle in the Seven Years' War had begun to turn in Britain's favor:

> Already Albion's lifted spear,
>   And rolling Thunder of the main,
> Which justice [sic] sacred laws maintain,
>   Have taught the haughty Gaul to fear . . .
> Again Britannia's cross triumphant flies . . . [43]

In January 1759 Gray wrote to his friend and fellow poet William Mason that "I like both Whithed's Odes in great measure" (*Correspondence*, II, 604). Mason himself thought that "no court poet ever had fewer *courtly*

---

[41] A third verse, added later, prays that "Marshal Wade"(George Wade, who assumed field command of the British forces after Prestonpans) will "hush" Jacobite "sedition" and "crush" the "Rebellious Scots."

[42] In April 1758 Whitehead, newly named laureate, published "Verses to the People of England," praised by a reviewer as an attempt "to excite in us a patriotic zeal for the glory and safety of our country" and compared to the exhortations of Tyrtaeus (*Monthly Review*, 18 [April 1758], 334).

[43] Robert Anderson, ed., *The Poets of Great Britain*, 14 vols. (London, 1795), XI, 956–74. Whitehead probably remembers Pope's "And high in Air *Britannia's* Standard flies" (*Windsor Forest*, line 110).

stains."[44] When it came time to write an ode for 1760, Whitehead had a string of British victories to celebrate. His ode, set to music and performed before the King on New Year's Day, and simultaneously printed in the *Public Advertiser*, addressed the "Genius of *Albion*":

> Beneath thy tutelary care
>   The brave, the virtuous, and the wise
> Shall mark each moment's winged Speed
>   With something that disdains to die,
> The hero's, patriot's, poet's meed,
> And passport to eternity.[45]

Whitehead perhaps combines verbal echoes of Pope's *Epilogue to the Satires*, where virtue's "Priestless Muse forbids the Good to dye, / And ope's the Temple of Eternity," Milton's famous ambition to "leave something so written to aftertimes, as they should not willingly let it die," and Henry V's famous speech at Agincourt, where the "passport" back home of those who have "no stomach to this fight" is implicitly compared with the greater "passport" to fame of those who stay, their names remembered "to the ending of the world."[46] The poet both grants and receives a "meed" (compensating reward, such as Milton's uncouth swain offered Lycidas), and stands in the company of hero and patriot.

Writing after the poet's death, Mason observed that although Whitehead's laureate odes "have undergone all the usual obloquy of such compositions, there is certainly in them more delicacy of panegyric, if not more genius, than in any compositions of that kind that can be found from Chaucer to Cibber. If they are not equal to the odes of Pindar, they are not ridiculous." Still, "their annual production rendered the laureate contemptible."[47] Mason objected not to the panegyric ode itself, but to the command performance. He advised Whitehead to hire a "deputy" to write the official odes, and to "reserve his own pen for certain great occasions that might occur" (XI, 896). That was what Mason himself did, writing an *Ode to the Naval Officers of Great Britain* in 1779, to mark the vindication of Admiral Keppel after a court martial, and an

---

44 An allusion to Pope's "Epistle to Augustus," in which the "white page" of Addison's poetry has some excusable "Courtly stains" (lines 215–16), perhaps Addison's flattering address "To Her Royal Highness the Princess of Wales" (1714), accompanying a gift of *Cato*.

45 *Gentleman's Magazine*, 30 (January 1760), 38.

46 *Epilogue to the Satires*, lines 234–35; *The Reason of Church Government*, Bk. II; *Henry V*, IV. 3. 36.

47 "Life of Whitehead," in Anderson's *Poets of Great Britain*, XI, 900.

Ode to the Hon. William Pitt (the younger) in 1782, when he was named
Chancellor of the Exchequer at the age of twenty-three.[48] But Mason
clearly sensed that the occasional ode was ripe for parody, and himself
wrote satirical odes – mock-panegyrics – "To Mr. Jolliffe" (a taker of
profiles) in 1758 and to "Estimate" Brown and the newly ennobled Earl
of Chatham in 1766.[49] Plainly the panegyrical ode had by 1750 become
a genre to be used cautiously. Of the major poets, only Gray and Smart
attempt it.

THOMAS TICKELL AND DODSLEY'S *COLLECTION* (1748)

One of the most important barometers of public taste in poetry is Robert
Dodsley's famous and widely read *Collection of Poems, By several Hands. In
Three Volumes*, which began appearing in 1748, and went through three
more editions and numerous reprintings over the next twenty years.[50]
It is striking to rediscover that more than half of Dodsley's first *Collection*
is devoted to patriotic poems, and that "On the Prospect of Peace,"
a poem by Thomas Tickell first published in 1712, has pride of place.
More than thirty-five years after Tickell's poem first appeared, it was
still regarded – along with Johnson's "London," Dyer's "Grongar Hill,"
Shenstone's "The School-Mistress," and Collins' "Ode to Evening," all
of which appeared in Dodsley's first volume – as one of the best specimens
of contemporary English poetry. Indeed, Tickell in effect served as the
model of the patriotic poet well past mid-century.

Tickell's poem on the imminent signing of the Treaty of Utrecht,
"On the Prospect of Peace," preceded Pope's *Windsor Forest* (on the same
subject) by four months, and (perhaps because it was puffed by Addison
in the *Spectator*) had much greater initial popular success.[51] Unlike Pope's

---

[48] *Works*, 4 vols. (London, 1811), I, 59–62, and 68–72. Whitehead dated the *Ode to the Naval Officers*
11 February 1779, and added a note that it was "written immediately after the trial of Admiral
Keppel, and then printed." The *Ode to Pitt* is written at "ALBION's anxious hour" (I, 70), some
six months after news of the disastrous defeat at Yorktown reached London ("Scarce is the fatal
moment past / That trembling ALBION deem'd her last" [I, 71]).

[49] See Gray's *Correspondence*, ed. Paget Toynbee and Leonard Whibley, 3 vols. (Oxford: Clarendon,
1935), II, 547–50, III, 933–35, 1247–52.

[50] A second edition appeared in 1748; a fourth volume was added in 1755, and two more in 1758.
The *Collection* was revised and continued by George Pearch in 1775. It has been recently argued
that Dodsley's *Collection*, a commercial success, rather aimed to set taste than to reflect it. See
Michael Suarez, "Trafficking in the Muse: Dodsley's *Collection* and the Question of Canon," in
Alvaro Ribeiro and James Basker, eds., *Tradition in Transition* (Oxford: Clarendon, 1996), 297–313.

[51] Addison praised it in the *Spectator* as a "noble...performance" (no. 523, 30 October 1712).
Pope admired the poem's versification (*Correspondence*, ed. George Sherburn, 5 vols. [Oxford:
Clarendon, 1955], I, 157). The poem quickly went through six editions. Gray, who read it in

poem, it focuses on the battles of the war just concluding, on the soldiers now returning home to peace, on Blenheim Palace, gift of a grateful nation to Marlborough, and on the diplomats then negotiating the treaty. Britain is praised for binding up the wounds of Europe and maintaining a balance of power between "rival kings." Her role is not to conquer but to "civilize":

> Amidst the world of waves so stands serene
> Britannia's isle, the Ocean's stately queen;
> In vain the nations have conspir'd her fall,
> Her trench the sea, and fleets her floating wall;
> Who conquers, wins by brutal strength the prize;
> But 'tis a godlike work to civilize.[52]

Here Britain is the happy isle, a "queen" whose posture is defensive. Later Tickell addresses Queen Anne, with whom Britain is implicitly identified:

> Great Queen! whose name strikes haughty monarchs pale,
> On whose just sceptre hangs Europa's scale;
> Whose arm like mercy wounds, decides like fate,
> On whose decree the nations anxious wait;
> From Albion's cliffs thy wide-extended hand
> Shall o'er the main to far Peru command,
> So vast a tract whose wide domain shall run,
> It's circling skies shall see no setting sun.
> Thee, thee an hundred languages shall claim,
> And savage Indians swear by ANNA's name;
> The line and poles shall own thy rightful sway,
> And thy commands the sever'd globe obey.   (I, 18–19)

Although Anne is here presented not as global ruler but as judge among the great European nations, maintaining the balance of power ("Europa's scale"), this is a far more imperial vision than Pope's, a vision that Thomson and Dyer would later adopt.

Nine poems by Tickell are included in Dodsley's first volume, eight of them occasional pieces. Even when the occasion is the death of a famous man, it commemorates a public figure, the Earl of Sunderland (Secretary of State, and later First Lord of the Treasury), Earl Cadogan (one of Marlborough's generals), or Joseph Addison. The poem "On the Death of Mr. Addison" includes a survey of English "worthies" whom

Dodsley's *Collection*, deplored it as a "state-poem" displaying "a great poverty of sense, and a string of transitions that hardly become a school-boy" (*Correspondence*, II, 295).

52 Cited from a facsimile of the sixth edition (1782) of *Dodsley's Collection*, intro., notes, and indices by Michael F. Suarez, SJ (London, 1997), I, 12.

Addison will now join; it set a standard, followed by many poets at mid-century, for elegiac reflections on patriots and public men:

> Oft let me range the gloomy isles alone,
> (Sad luxury! to vulgar minds unknown)
> Along the walls where speaking marbles show
> What worthies form the hallow'd mould below:
> Proud names, who once the reins of empire held;
> In arms who triumph'd; or in arts excell'd;
> Chiefs, grac'd with scars, and prodigal of blood;
> Stern patriots, who for sacred freedom stood;
> Just men, by whom impartial laws were given;
> And saints, who taught, and led, the way to heav'n.
>
> (I, 27)

Goldsmith thought the elegy "one of the finest in our language" (*Collected Works*, V, 327). "Hallowed mould" reappears in Collins' "Ode, Written in the Beginning of the Year 1746" (line 4), "reins of empire" in the Eton MS of Gray's "Elegy." Johnson, who especially commended this passage, thought there was no "more sublime or more elegant funeral poem to be found in the whole compass of English literature."[53]

Much better known in his own day than in ours, Tickell in effect served as a model for public poetry of a patriotic cast for more than sixty years. His poem on the accession of George I, "The Royal Progress" (1714), was initially published in the *Spectator*,[54] and as a consequence remained, as Johnson noted in Tickell's *Life*, "well-known" as late as 1780. It celebrates the "royal progress" of "Brunswick" (George, Elector of Hanover and Duke of Brunswick), Tickell's "hero," from his German dominions to London, via Belgium and The Hague. Promising to do without classical furniture and (disingenuously) to be content with whatever "charms" are supplied by "the truth," Tickell, who had not yet fully committed himself to Whig patrons, greets the new king candidly, even daringly, as a "Great Stranger" – he is in fact a foreigner (the first meaning of the word in Tickell's day[55]), and his blood relation to James I is apparently thought by the poet so remote as not to bear mentioning. George is also "The World's Great Patriot," whose "extensive mind / Takes in the blended int'rests of mankind." This is not gross flattery but a tactful solution to a politically delicate matter, since George, continuing as Elector of Hanover, cannot be expected to be a wholly *British* "patriot." He will

---

[53] Goldsmith, *Collected Works*, V, 327; Johnson, *Lives*, II, 310. Gray later changed "reins of empire" to "rod of empire" (47).

[54] No. 620, for 15 November 1714.

[55] As the first meaning of "stranger" *OED* gives "One who belongs to another country, a foreigner; chiefly . . . one who resides in or comes to a country to which he is a foreigner."

presumably *blend* the interests not only of Hanover and Britain, but – with Europe at peace, Tickell excusably overstates – of all "mankind." In the spirit of celebration, factions (Whigs and Tories) forget they were foes, and the King "Rewards the faithful and restores the brave."[56] Among the faithful, Tickell focuses on Halifax, who years earlier had served as First Lord of the Treasury (guardian of England's "coin") under William III and was now restored to that post, and who had acted as a Maecenas to the nation's poets. If Halifax will look with favor, so Tickell concludes, perhaps his muse

> shall aim at more exalted themes,
> Record our monarch in a nobler strain,
> And sing the op'ning wonders of his reign.

That is, Tickell will assume the role of royal panegyrist, a traditional public and patriotic function of the poet since the Roman Silver Age, and a role played by English poets who greeted every monarch up to and including George's predecessor in this manner. It is clear that Pope, even after he broke with Tickell over their Homer translations, bore in mind his rival's patriotic verse as he considered his own political response to "great Brunswick" and his son. Pope may have found it politically distasteful, but the poem is not demonstrably inferior to Dryden's panegyric verse.

Tickell was followed in Dodsley's first volume by another poem on the Peace of Utrecht, Samuel Cobb's *The Female Reign*, a Pindaric ode celebrating "the wonders" of the pious and triumphant reign of Queen Anne. Cobb, who had earlier elegized Queen Mary, makes Anne his "heroine" and "the British Pallas." The poem looks back to Marlborough's victories and looks forward to the signing of the peace, and to the eventual succession of the Elector of Hanover, already designated by the Act of Settlement as the next monarch. Along with Tickell's poems, it serves to remind us that poetic celebrations of the monarch as the country's hero issued from both Whig and Tory pens in the early decades of the century, and that no amount of scorn at such patriotic panegyric from Pope and other Opposition writers during Walpole's twenty-year reign discredited this kind of poem in the eyes of as shrewd a judge of the literary market as Dodsley.

Other volumes in Dodsley's *Collection* confirm that political poetry of a patriotic cast remained popular through the 1750s and 1760s. In Dodsley's second volume (1748) appears Lyttelton's poem on *Blenheim*.

---

[56] Cf. "On the Prospect of Peace," which brings patriots and monarch together in a single line: "Such are the honours grateful Britain pays, / So patriots merit, and so monarchs praise" (I, 15).

Originally published in 1727, it celebrates Marlborough's princely Blenheim Palace and its gardens, and the efforts of the Duchess to honor her dead husband.[57] Blenheim is a grateful nation's "reward" for the Duke's "successful toils / For Europe's freedom, and Britannia's fame." Marlborough stands, Lyttelton declares, as inspiration to "British youth":

> So shall thy name,
> Dear to thy country, still inspire her sons
> With martial virtue; and to high attempts
> Excite their arms, 'till other battles won,
> And nations sav'd, new monuments require,
> And other BLENHEIMS shall adorn the land.
>
> (II, 27)

Other poems by Lyttelton include two "Epistles" from abroad, a genre that since Addison's "Letter from Italy" (1704) had served as a means to declare the superiority of one's native land. Addison had found "Oppression" and "Tyranny" in Italy's "golden groves," and assured his addressee, Lord Halifax, that Britons "envy not the warmer clime that lies / In ten degrees of more indulgent skies":

> 'Tis Liberty that crowns Britannia's isle,
> And makes her barren rocks and her bleak mountains smile.[58]

Lyttelton's "Epistle to Dr. Ayscough at Oxford. Written from Paris in the Year 1728" likewise celebrated his "native isle! Happiest seat!" (II, 34), and his "Epistle to Mr. Pope. From Rome," surveying the decline of "unhappy Italy," may have helped inspire his addressee to turn his attention to "the land, which yet alone can boast / That Liberty corrupted Rome has lost" (II, 42).[59]

Later in volume II comes Gilbert West's *Institution of the Garter*, a dramatic poem first published in 1742, when it served to advance the "Patriot" program of Frederick, Prince of Wales. Edward III, founder of the Order of the Garter, is hailed as "the great miracle of earth, a PATRIOT-King" (II, 173).[60] Also in volume II are three political poems by Robert Nugent,

---

57 Work on the Duchess's "column to thy praise" (the great Column of Victory in the palace grounds) was begun in 1727 – in effect the occasion of the poem.

58 *Poetical Miscellanies*, vol. 5 (1704), cited from *The New Oxford Book of Eighteenth-Century Verse*, ed. Roger Lonsdale (Oxford, 1984), 42, 44. Johnson reported that Addison's "Letter" was "justly considered as the most elegant . . . of his poetical productions" (*Lives*, II, 86). Addison's poem also celebrates England's role in maintaining the "balance" of power in Europe, thanks to "Nassau's sword."

59 See below, 62.

60 West echoes Bolingbroke's *Patriot King* (published in 1749, but circulated earlier), in which the "Patriot King" is hailed as "a sort of standing miracle, so rarely seen and so little understood" (*Political Writings*, 369). On West's *Institution of the Garter*, see Gerrard, *Patriot Opposition*, 224–29.

another "Patriot" writer.[61] Subsequent volumes included tributes to the Duke of Marlborough as national hero, and Akenside's political ode to Lord Huntingdon, affirming that the bard's task was to address "public themes" and "public arguments" if he wishes to win "the hero's and the patriot's love."[62]

POPE

Culloden poems, laureate odes, and most of the patriotic poems in Dodsley's *Collection* center on the King or on a military hero. The figure of the poet tends to be elided. Other models, centering on the patriot-poet himself, were also available, and may have proved especially suggestive to poets at mid-century who self-consciously sought to explore the possibilities of public and patriotic verse. Milton was consciously a literary patriot, resolving to devote his energy "to the adorning of my native tongue" and to be "an interpreter and relater of the best and sagest things among mine own citizens throughout this island in the mother dialect."[63] But Milton's poetic practice did not fulfill that ambition to write an English epic, and in any case his republican politics made some eighteenth-century poets wary of adopting him as a model patriot. Dryden too declared himself "ever studious to promote the honour of my native country," but, like Milton, he did not pursue his planned epic on an "*English* Hero."[64] Pope, though like his predecessors he failed to produce his English epic, wrote a series of poems on his native country, consciously bringing into those poems the figure of the patriotic poet.

---

[61] "Epistle to Lord Cornbury," "An Ode to William Pultney, Esq.," and "An Ode to Mankind. Address'd to the Prince," in which Frederick is hailed as the patriot-king who will "fix thy empire in a people's hearts" (*Collection*, II, 230), echoing Bolingbroke's conception of the patriot-king: "Nothing less than the hearts of his people will content such a prince, nor will he think his throne established till it is established there" (*Patriot King*, in *Political Writings*, 385). Joseph Warton later included Nugent in a group of "Patriot" writers. See below, 211 and n.

[62] See below, 108–11. Another early patriot-poet, not included in Dodsley's *Collection*, is John Hughes (1677–1720), whose *Poems on Several Occasions* (2 vols., London, 1735) includes odes on "The Triumph of Peace" (celebrating the 1697 Peace of Ryswick), "The House of Nassau" (marking the 1702 death of William III), and "The Patriot" (in praise of his patron, William Cowper, Lord Chancellor).

[63] From *The Reason of Church Government*, "The Second Book" (1642). In the *History of Britain* (1671) Milton commended the old stories from Geoffrey of Monmouth's *Historia Regum Britanniae* to "our English Poets, and Rhetoricians, who by their Art will know, how to use them judiciously" (*Complete Prose Works*, gen. ed. Don Wolfe, 8 vols. in 10 [New Haven, 1953–82], V, pt. 1, 37).

[64] From the "Preface" to *Fables*. In his "Discourse on the Original and Progress of Satire" Dryden reports his one-time plans to write an epic – on Arthur or the Black Prince – "for the Honour of my Native Country, to which a Poet is particularly oblig'd" (*Works*, gen. eds. E. N. Hooker and H. T. Swedenberg, Jr., 18 vols. [Berkeley and Los Angeles, 1961–], IV, 22–23).

Despite revisionist work in recent years by Gerrard and others,[65] non-specialists still tend to regard Pope primarily as a "Tory satirist," or to think of him as a poet who in youth foresaw a golden age under "great ANNA" and in maturity surveyed an age of lead under the "great Anarch." It is likewise conventional to note that, late in his career, Pope sought, in Johnson's words, "to join the patriot with the poet" (*Lives*, III, 181),[66] that is, to write in support of the political Opposition then cohering around the Prince of Wales. However, it might be more accurate to regard Pope as a writer who, throughout his career, aspired to serve the state as "My Country's Poet," but who – even from the beginning – looked with some ambivalence at the prospect of joining the patriot with the poet.

Windsor Forest opens promisingly for the patriot-poet: the "Forest" and its "green Retreats" are "At once the Monarch's and the Muse's Seats." Long associated with both poets and kings, Windsor serves as a symbol of the idea that the poet might stand beside the monarch and help him to do the work of the nation. Indeed, because endowed with a "Seat," the muse is in herself a kind of monarch. The poet goes on to salute the beneficent rule of Queen Anne, and closes by hailing the imminent Peace of Utrecht, negotiated by the Queen's ministers, and foreseeing a glorious future for a country restored to the status it enjoyed under Elizabeth:

> There mighty Nations shall inquire their Doom,
> The World's great Oracle in Times to come;
> There Kings shall sue, and suppliant States be seen
> Once more to bend before a *British* QUEEN.
>
> (lines 381–84)

One might argue that in this poem Pope confirms Tickell's model of the patriot-poet exulting in the triumph of the new imperial "*British*" nation – the very name sounds a nationalist note.

> Thy Trees, fair *Windsor*! now shall leave their Woods,
> And half thy Forests rush into my Floods,
> Bear *Britain*'s Thunder, and her Cross display,
> To the bright Regions of the rising Day.
>
> (lines 385–88)[67]

By describing the Thames as a river that flows from the heart of the country out into the mighty oceans, and linking its ancient oak forests

---

[65] Gerrard, *Patriot Opposition*, esp. 68–95; Bertrand Goldgar, *Walpole and the Wits: The Relation of Politics to Literature, 1722–1742* (Lincoln, 1976).

[66] Johnson was in fact silently alluding to Lyttelton's *Epistle to Mr. Pope* (London, 1730), urging Pope to "join the PATRIOT's to the POET's praise" (82).

[67] In the first edition, the fleets hoisted a "bloody cross," suggesting that Pope was at some level subverting the patriotic rhetoric.

(such as Windsor) with Britain's oak-built navy,[68] Pope amplifies the eighteenth-century British georgic tradition, visible already in Denham's *Coopers Hill*, of regarding "Britain" not as a small agricultural island protected by the sea but as a global power in which the sylvan rural heart is seamlessly connected to the maritime commercial empire. It is a tradition in which Thomson and Dyer will go on to work.

But in fact from the beginning of Pope's poem, the would-be patriot-poet is reluctant to commit himself fully to a role as Britain's voice. The opening line speaks of both Windsor's "Forests" – future navies – and "Retreats." And the poet of *Windsor Forest* shows a marked attraction to the "Retreats," to which he repeatedly withdraws. The panegyric on "sacred Peace" and the vision of Britain's future is in fact not given in the poet's own voice, but is quite specifically put into the mouth of Father Thames, a new character recruited to signal that the poet himself is only a "humble Muse" (line 427), hesitant to speak out as a public patriot.[69] Such a task should be reserved for others, like Granville (a minor poet, but recently named Anne's Secretary at War) – "The Thoughts of Gods let *Granville*'s Verse recite" (line 425) – who had literally found a way to join the patriot with the poet. (A poetic survey of English kings from Edward III to Anne had been assigned to Granville – "Oh wou'dst thou sing what Heroes *Windsor* bore, / What Kings first breath'd upon her winding Shore" – lines 299–300.) Pope's deference to the superior merit of his noble addressee, if conventional, is not merely so. Unlike Addison, who at the close of his "Letter from Italy" (1704) defers perfunctorily if graciously to Halifax,[70] Pope dwells on the idea that he is unfitted for the role of public celebrant. In a crucial passage the poem hints that perhaps the poet and the patriot are opposites, rarely if ever to be joined:

> Happy the Man whom this bright Court approves,
> His Sov'reign favours, and his Country loves;
> Happy next him who to these Shades retires,
> Whom Nature charms, and whom the Muse inspires.
>
> (lines 235–38)

---

[68] Cf. "Let *India* boast her Plants, nor envy we / The weeping Amber or the balmy Tree, / While by our Oaks the precious Loads are born, / And Realms commanded which those Trees adorn" (lines 29–32); "Where tow'ring Oaks their growing Honours rear, / And future Navies on thy Shores appear" (lines 221–22).

[69] Pope follows Horace, self-styled "parvus [small poet]" who leaves it to "concines maiore poeta" to sing of Caesar (*Odes*, IV. 1. 31–34). By contrast Tickell, though similarly professing humility, is "Fir'd with the views this glitt'ring scene displays," and attempts "the lofty theme" in his own voice.

[70] "My humble muse demands a softer theme, / . . . / Unfit for heroes, whom immortal lays, / And lines like Virgil's, or like yours, should praise."

Granville is the former figure, linked with the court and the monarch, loved by the whole country (and in turn one who loves his country). Pope himself is the latter, retiring from court and Queen to rural "Shades," and choosing rather to be inspired by the Muse than loved by his country. His surrogate is Lodona, whose prayer, "Let me, O let me, to the shades repair, / My native shades" (lines 200–1), implicitly serves as his own.[71] Even at a time when Pope delights in the state of the British nation, there is something that holds him back from embracing the role of national poet, something that makes him fear that a poet must ultimately choose between serving the muse and serving the state.[72]

In another poem, begun about the same time *Windsor Forest* was published, Pope reflected on the relationship between patriot and poet. The epistle "To Mr. Addison, Occasioned by his Dialogues on Medals" (first published 1720) looks ahead to a series of British medals, emulating "Greek and Roman fame" (54):

> Here, rising bold,[73] the Patriot's honest face;
> There Warriors frowning in historic brass.
>
> (lines 57–58)

Then follow Bacon and Newton, emulating Plato, "Or in fair series laurell'd Bards be shown, / A Virgil there, and here an Addison" (lines 61–62). Next come statesmen: proximity hints that, as in Whitehead's New Year's ode, the poet's rightful place is in the company of statesmen, warriors, patriots.

Twenty years later, in the *Essay on Man*, Pope continued to think of the affinity between poet and patriot. Surveying the "Restoration of *True Religion* and *Government* on their first Principle," he notes the role of the "Poet or Patriot" who "rose but to restore / The Faith and Moral, Nature gave before" (III, lines 285–86). But when in the late 1730s Pope throws in his lot with the "Patriots" around the Prince of Wales, he again holds back from full commitment. Even in the *Epilogue to the Satires* (1738), Pope drops hints that those standing in opposition to Walpole were not simply motivated by virtue and political idealism. In a note added to the first dialogue in 1751, glossing the word *Patriots* (I, line 24), Warburton remarks

---

[71] "Native shades" suggests that Lodona's "country" is found in the shades. Pope may allude to the derivation of *repair* from the late Latin *repatriare*, "to return to one's country" (*OED*).

[72] Pope's reluctance may be linked with his sense that the "thunder" of the British navy leads to "conquest" and "slavery." The recurrent figure of blood and gore (lines 310, 322, 348, 367, 372, 393, 417, 422) suggests an awareness that the patriotic story of British triumph is a dark story of the spilling of blood.

[73] A pun: 1) etched in relief, 2) standing up for their country.

that "This appellation was generally given to those in opposition to the Court. Though some of them (which our author hints at) had views too mean and interested to deserve that name." Another note (to I, line 51), glossing *Fleury* (i.e., French Cardinal Fleury), suggests that "patriotism" was little more than a slogan: "It was a Patriot-fashion, at that time, to cry up [Fleury's] wisdom and honesty." In the dialogue's concluding vision of the spread of corruption through the land, Pope does not find the "Patriot" exempt from its lure: "In Soldier, Churchman, Patriot, Man in Pow'r, / 'Tis Avarice all, Ambition is no more!" (lines 161–62). But in the final lines the poet himself succeeds in standing apart: "Yet may this Verse (if such a Verse remain) / Show there was one who held it in disdain" (lines 171–72). Again the poet and the patriot are posed as opposites.

Pope's suspicions about the Patriots emerge unmistakably in the fragmentary "One Thousand Seven Hundred and Forty," a poem he drafted in 1740 but left unfinished at his death. Here the "Patriot Race" are no more likely to save Britain than the "wicked men in place" (lines 3–4). Although Pope saves them with a dash, he makes plain that "C[arteret]" and "P[ulteney]" are frauds, and that even Gower, Cobham, Bathurst, Chesterfield – whom Pope had previously complimented in print – are content to sit on their hands rather than to take vigorous action to save their country from Walpole. The most damning words are reserved for Pulteney, who (so went the sneer), like everyone else, surely had his price – in his case a peerage: "Thro' Clouds of Passion P – 's views are clear, / He foams a Patriot to subside a Peer" (lines 9–10). Pope's brilliant and prophetic lines reduce Pulteney's political oratory to mere airy foam on a tankard of beer in the hand of a tavern statesman – the unspoken rhyme on beer /"peer" completes the haughty put-down.[74]

But it would be a mistake to conclude that by the 1730s Pope had abandoned altogether the idea that the poet could be a patriot. In the second dialogue of the *Epilogue to the Satires* he declares ironically that he is "So odd" that "my Country's Ruin makes me grave" (line 207) – the very pronouns unite the country's interest and the poet's. A few lines later he imagines a public role for the poet, the patriotic task of serving as the nation's moral watchdog, wielding the "sacred Weapon" of his satiric pen, ready not only to bark but (so his verbs suggest) to bite:

> To rowze the Watchmen of the Publick Weal,
> To Virtue's Work provoke the Tardy Hall,
> And goad the Prelate slumb'ring in his Stall.
> (lines 217–19)

---

[74] On the politics of Pope's "1740," see Gerrard, *Patriot Opposition*, 91–93.

The idea that the patriot-poet might somehow serve the nation even emerges in the "Epistle to Augustus" (1737), in which Pope declines to take up the traditional patriotic role of serving as panegyrist of the King. The poem's complex ironies are famous, whether we regard the epistle as exposing the shameful differences or the shameful similarities between George II and the Emperor Augustus. What has not been enough noticed is that lurking beneath the surface of the poem is the idea that, as Pope's "Advertisement" puts it, "Poets, under due Regulations, were in many respects useful to the State." In a properly regulated state, the "Muse" might indeed confer with the "Monarch" and advance – not "defraud" – "the Publick Weal" (lines 5–6).

The idea – a very traditional one, to be sure – that the poet can serve the state emerges in the middle of the poem, where it is apparently veiled in grave irony. Pope's Horatian voice offers to his monarch a mock-defense of the poets:

> Of little use the Man you may suppose,
> Who says in verse what others say in prose;
> Yet let me show, a Poet's of some weight,
> And (tho' no Soldier) useful to the State.
>
> (lines 201–4)

Pope's footnote acknowledges the "intermixture of irony," but points also to Horace's words on "the nobler office of a Poet."

> torquet ab obscenis iam nunc sermonibus aurem,
> mox etiam pectus praeceptis format amicis,
> asperitas et invidiae corrector et irae,
> recte facta refert, orientia tempora notis
> instruit exemplis, inopem solatur et aegrum.
>
> (lines 127–31)

("even then [the poet] turns the ear from unseemly words; presently, too, he moulds the heart by kindly precepts, correcting roughness and envy and anger. He tells of noble deeds, equips the rising age with famous examples, and to the helpless and sick at heart brings comfort.")[75]

Pope follows Horace's first three lines fair closely, offering Addison as an example of a poet who "pours each human Virtue in the heart" (line 220). For "noble deeds" (*recte facta*) and "brings comfort" (*solatur*), he

---

[75] From the Loeb translation, in *Horace: Satires, Epistles, and Ars Poetica*, tr. H. R. Fairclough (London, 1970), 407. Pope's footnote assumes that the reader knows the original passage. He only gives the opening words of three of the five lines: "*Torquet ab obscoenis – Mox etiam pectus – Recte facta refert, &c.*"

praises Swift's public services on behalf of the Irish "Nation," expanding Horace's two lines into an eight-line passage that offers, in miniature, a heroic image of the patriot-poet:

> Let Ireland tell, how Wit upheld her cause,
> Her Trade supported, and supply'd her Laws;
> And leave on SWIFT this grateful verse ingrav'd,
> The Rights a Court attack'd, a Poet sav'd.
> Behold the hand that wrought a Nation's cure,
> Stretch'd to relieve the Idiot and the Poor,
> Proud Vice to brand, or injur'd Worth adorn,
> And stretch the Ray to Ages yet unborn.
>
> (lines 221–28)

Even in laughingly declining to take on the role of fixing in verse an enduring image of kingly virtue, Pope manages to imply that the poet might serve the state – if not the King – in other ways.

Yet the fact remains that in the Britain of the late 1730s Pope finds no unimpeded way to join the patriot and the poet. In the voice of Martinus Scriblerus, Pope beginning in 1729 claimed, if only facetiously, that the satirist performs a public service.

Now our author living in those times, did conceive it an endeavour well worthy an honest satyrist, to dissuade the dull and punish the malicious, *the only way that was left*. In that public-spirited view he laid the plan of this Poem, as the greatest service of which he was capable (without much hurt or being slain) to render his dear country.

Here Pope may remember Dryden's conception of the satiric "Poet's Office,"[76] but at the same time he undermines his own bravery – suggesting that unlike the soldier the satirist can take his potshots "without much hurt." Pope may hesitate to proclaim himself the public servant of his own "dear country" since Dennis had deployed such rhetoric to justify a withering attack on Pope in his *Remarks on Homer*.[77] Furthermore, Gulliver's recent claims to patriotism had perhaps made it almost impossible for a satiric poet to speak of his "dear country" without a smile.

But the aspiration did not die, as is clear from a major literary project left unfinished at Pope's death. It is difficult to say much about the

---

[76] Cf. Dryden's defense of lampoon, in cases when we can "make ourselves no other Reparation," and it is an "Action of Virtue" to make an example of a "Publick Nuisance" (*Works*, III, 59, 60).

[77] Pope quotes Dennis's words – "I look on it as my duty to *King George*, whose faithful subject I am, to my *Country*, of which I have appeared a constant lover; . . . and to the *Liberty* of my *Country*, more dear than life to me, . . . to pull the Lion's skin from this little Ass." – in the *Dunciad* (1729), I, 106.

projected epic on *Brutus*, if only because he completed no more than its first eight lines. But together with the prose notes indicating that he had worked out the structure of the four-book poem in great detail, and in the context of both *Windsor Forest* and the *Epilogue to the Satires*, the lines from *Brutus* show that Pope still nurtured the idea that he might serve as "My Countrys Poet." Pope's "Patriot" friends had for some years been encouraging him to write a poem in praise of his native "Land." Lyttelton, as early as 1730, had in his "Epistle to Mr. Pope" urged him to abandon satire and to "raise / A lasting column to thy Country's Praise," and thereby to "join the Patriot's to the Poet's praise" (Dodsley's *Collection*, II, 42). In 1740 he was still seeking to inspire Pope to action: "Some sparks of Publick Virtue are yet Alive, which such a Spirit as Your's might blow into a flame" (*Correspondence*, IV, 369).

Both Spence and Warburton report that Pope gave the project serious consideration, and had sketched a poem based on the mythical founding of Britain by Brutus, "greatgrandson of Aeneas," and of his establishment there of "a Just Form of Governmt."[78] Most critics of Pope today pay little attention to *Brutus*, but if they did it might put Pope in a new light. As James Sambrook (who takes Pope's project seriously) has noted, it is clear that Pope "intended to crown his life's work by becoming the poet of Britannia."[79]

Had the poem been written, it would not have celebrated Britain's green and pleasant land – Pope had in effect done that in *Windsor Forest* – nor would it have given poetic form to English history, as Lyttelton perhaps hoped,[80] but it would have provided the country with a foundational myth. The poets of mid-century could have read, had they looked into Warburton's commentary or Ruffhead's *Life* (1769), that Pope had intended that the poem's hero, "in the office of legislation," would establish the "perfect form of Civil Government," which Pope planned to identify with "the old original plan" of pre-Norman England.[81] Brutus

---

78 Warburton's commentary, in his 1751 edition (III–2, xix–xx). Pope's manuscript notes on *Brutus* are transcribed in Paul Hammond's *Selected Prose of Alexander Pope* (Cambridge, 1987), 292–96.

79 *James Thomson 1700–1748: A Life* (Oxford: Clarendon, 1991), 205. Other good critics have been summarily dismissive. See Maynard Mack, *Alexander Pope: A Life* (New York, 1985), 774, and Lawrence Lipking, "The Gods of Poetry: Mythology and the Eighteenth-Century Tradition," in Albert Rivero, ed., *Augustan Subjects* (Newark, DE, 1997), 69. But Gerrard (*Patriot Opposition*, 143–44) and Miriam Leranbaum (*Alexander Pope's "Opus Magnum" 1729–1744* [Oxford: Clarendon, 1977], 155–74) treat the project respectfully.

80 In a letter in 1741 he had urged Pope to base a poem on the old English chronicles (*Correspondence*, IV, 348–49).

81 See Joseph Spence, *Observations, Anecdotes, and Characters of Books and Men*, ed. James Osborn, 2 vols. (Oxford: Clarendon, 1966), I, 153.

is said to be motivated by "benevolence" and by a desire to "redeem the remains of his countrymen." *Redeem* echoes "One Thousand Seven Hundred and Forty," in which Pope concludes with the fervent imagining that an "unministered" "Patriot King" might gain the throne, "And one man's honesty redeem the land." About the role of the poet in this great work Pope's notes for *Brutus* remain silent, although Brutus meets with several wise kings, oracles, and druids. But the patriot-poet was very much on Pope's mind, as the opening lines to the poem, the only ones Pope wrote, make clear:

> The Patient Chief, who lab'ring long, arriv'd
> On Britains Shore and brought with fav'ring Gods
> Arts Arms and Honour to her Ancient Sons:
> Daughter of Memory! from elder Time
> Recall; and me, with Britains Glory fir'd,
> Me, far from meaner care or meaner Song,
> Snatch to thy Holy Hill of Spotless Bay,
> My Countrys Poet, to record her Fame.[82]

The invocation of the muse and the introduction of the theme balance equally – four lines each for the country's founding "Chief" and "My Countrys Poet," assigning each a heroic task, the one to establish arts, arms, and honor in Britain, the other (given emphasis with the repeated "me ... me ... my") to record Britain's "Fame."[83]

It is as if Pope, at the end of his career, returned to the celebrative mode of *Windsor Forest*, this time not with a voice constrained by misgivings about Britain's imperial future and his own inadequacy to the poetic task of celebrating it. Instead, he would implicitly follow the path once chosen by Tickell, who in *The Prospect of Peace*, "Fir'd with the views" of Britain's global influence, declared himself "smit with passion for my country's praise" (Dodsley, *Collection*, I, 232).

PINDAR AND THE PATRIOT-POET

Pope's poetic practice directed attention to the role of the patriotic poet himself. So too, though in a different way, did the victory odes of Pindar, the eighteenth century's most respected classical lyric poet, not because

---

[82] Pope's lines were not published until 1954. Gerrard (*Patriot Opposition*, 93–94) notes that Pope's lines "carry echoes" of Lyttelton's "Epistle."

[83] In 1741 and 1743 copper medals were struck with a bust of Pope on one side and "Poeta Anglus," with the date, on the other. They are listed as portraits 62.1 and 62.2 in W. K. Wimsatt, *The Portraits of Alexander Pope* (New Haven, 1965), 270–72.

he self-consciously appears in his odes as celebrant – he does not – but because he stimulated an interest at mid-century in the idea that the poet in ancient Greece played a public and political role.

In affirming the poet's role as recorder of fame, Pope's final poem curiously echoes (and adapts) one of his earliest poems. *The Temple of Fame* (1715) places on the northern wall of the temple Gothic heroes including Odin, alongside "*Druids* and *Bards*," and the bold "Youths that dy'd to be by Poets sung" (line 128). The early Pope's druidic "Bards" immortalize the deeds and deaths of heroes; the late Pope's "Poet" records the fame not of a hero but the country. A few lines later in *The Temple of Fame* "the greatest Names in Learning in all Antiquity" – Homer, Virgil, Pindar, Horace, Aristotle, and Cicero – stand "In the midst of the Temple, nearest the Throne of *Fame*." Next to them stand "Heroes," Alexander and Caesar and (yet more virtuous since they fought "not for Empire" but for "their People's Safety") Epaminondas, Timoleon, Scipio, Marcus Aurelius, Socrates, Aristides, Phocion, Agis, Cato, and Brutus. Pope's choice of heroes was conventional in his day, but reminds us that the English "Augustans" were as familiar with Greek exemplars as they were with Romans. Through Plutarch and other sources the knowledge of Greek statesmen and poets was still part of the cultural inheritance of English readers. Plutarch's *Lives*, in the "Dryden" translation, made Lycurgus, Solon, Cimon, Aristides, Timoleon, and other statesmen familiar even to schoolboys.[84] Greek history and politics were often cited by political writers such as Harrington, who drew his picture of independent arms-bearing landowners from Rome, Sparta, and Timoleon's Syracuse.[85]

Pope himself projected an epic poem on Timoleon. His contemporaries were prepared to see the ancient Greek patriot, who placed the public good over the private, as a model for their own leaders. Benjamin Martyn's *Timoleon*, performed in 1730, closes with a tribute to its hero:

> May we like him all Self-Affection scorn,
> Think we are only for our Country born!
> When Freedom falls, forget the Ties of Blood,
> And fix our Interest in the publick Good.[86]

---

[84] Editions of Dryden's Plutarch appeared in 1685–88, 1693, 1700, 1727, and 1749. Thomson provides a survey of Greek worthies, including Socrates, Solon, Lycurgus, Leonidas, Aristides, Cimon, Timoleon, Themistocles, Pelopidas, Epaminondas, and Philopoemen, in *The Seasons* (*Winter*, 439–97).

[85] Timoleon appears prominently in the closing paragraphs of *Oceana*.

[86] *Timoleon* (2nd. edn., London, 1730), 66. The two prologues printed with the play repeat the sentiments: "Attentive then the *Grecian* Patriot view, / . . . Nor Love, nor Friendship, nor the Ties

Martyn dedicates the play to the King, claiming that he copies "from Your MAJESTY the Virtues of a King, who is a Blessing to his People." Timoleon is like George II "in a very early Appearance against Oppression, in being the Glory and Delight of his Country, and in (the greatest distinction of Heroes) a love for mankind" (A4v).

The Greek lyric poets were no less familiar to eighteenth-century readers than the Greek heroes. Basil Kennett's *Lives and Characters of the Ancient Grecian Poets* (1697, repr. 1735) was designed not for scholars but for a general audience presumed to be interested in, and familiar with, not only Pindar, but also such lesser poets as Tyrtaeus and Alcaeus. What modern readers have largely forgotten is that these Greek lyric poets were regarded by eighteenth-century critics as patriots. Critics today too often assume that Pindar's importance to his eighteenth-century imitators was purely stylistic, that he served primarily as a model of metrical complexity and sublimity of utterance, as Young put it in 1728, "rapturous, somewhat abrupt, and immethodical to a vulgar eye."[87] More recently, it has been suggested that in the minds of eighteenth-century critics, Pindar was regarded as the hired panegyrist of athletes and jockeys, and was no longer a suitable model for the modern ode-poet.[88] But this was not the view of Thomas Warton, who in an "Ode occasion'd by Reading Mr. West's Translation of Pindar" (1765), wrote that Pindar "our inmost bosom piercing, warms / With glory's love, and eager thirst of arms: / When Freedom speaks in his majestic strain, / The patriot-passions beat in every vein."[89] West's translation of selected *Odes of Pindar*, first published in 1749, proved remarkably popular.[90] In his translator's preface, West defends Pindar against current "prejudices," including the idea that his odes were inscribed "only" to "so many prize-fighters and jockeys" (xxix). He explains that the Olympic games were not simply athletic contests but a "great political institution" which tended to unite [the Greek city states] all in one great body, under one common name."[91]

---

of Blood / Abate his Ardor for the public Good"; "At once *Timoleon* open to our View, / The Man, the Hero, and the Patriot too."

[87] Young's Preface to "Ocean: An Ode." Anne Williams' *Prophetic Strain: The Greater Lyric in the Eighteenth Century* (Chicago, 1984) is typical in treating Pindar purely as a model for largeness and boldness of expression.

[88] Weinbrot, *Britannia's Issue*, 334–58.

[89] "On Reading Mr. West's Translation of Pindar" (1749), reprinted in Dodsley's *Collection* (1763), IV, 207 [(1765), IV, 228].

[90] The first edition (in one volume) was reissued in 1751. A second edition (in two volumes) appeared in 1753, a third edition (in three volumes) in 1766.

[91] "Dissertation on the Olympic Games," repr. in Francis Lee's edition of the *Odes of Pindar* (London, 1810), 149.

British readers saw Pindar's victors as more than just athletes. According to Robert Lowth, the bosom of every reader of Pindar glowed "with the desire of fame, with the most fervid emulation of virtue, with a patriotism, immodest perhaps, but honourable and useful in the highest degree."[92] For Basil Kennett, Pindar was to be praised for not limiting himself to the praise of athletic victories: "the Old Relations of the Acts of Heaven and Heaven-born Heroes, were what every Body long'd for and admir'd."[93] Pindar in Kennett's mind deserves "a much Nobler Praise" for his "*Morality*" and "Piety" than for his "Manners" and "Style."[94] As we will see, Akenside says nothing of Pindar's athletes; what he focuses on is Pindar's patriotic regard for his country:

Pindar was cotemporary with *Aristides* and *Cimon*, in whom the glory of ancient *Greece* was at its height. When *Xerxes* invaded *Greece*, *Pindar* was true to the common interest of his country; though his fellow citizens, the *Thebans*, had sold themselves to the Persian king. In one of his odes he expresses the great distress and anxiety of his mind, occasioned by the vast preparations of *Xerxes* against *Greece*. (*Isthm.* 8). In another he celebrates the victories of *Salamis*, *Plataea*, and *Himera* (*Pyth.* 1).[95]

Pindar himself exemplified the same dedication to "liberty" that he celebrated in his countrymen. He expressed "veneration . . . for that heroic spirit, shewn by the people of *Athens* in defence of the common liberty, which his own fellow citizens had shamefully betrayed." Pindar himself is "perhaps the most exemplary proof" of the "connection [between poetry and liberty], which occurs in history" (*Poetical Works*, 354–55).

In the common eighteenth-century view, Pindar was the greatest of Greek lyric poets, superior to Anacreon and Sappho, and worthy successor to Alcaeus of Mitylene. According to Kennett, Alcaeus was both poet and patriot: he "headed the People when engag'd by Arms to assert their Liberties against the Tyrant *Pittacus*." He "drove out the Tyrant, and restor'd the Ancient Privileges of his City." In a symbolic display of the poet's power, he even defeated Pittacus in a "Contention . . . in Verse."[96]

---

[92] *Lectures on the Sacred Poetry of the Hebrews* (1744), tr. G. Gregory (London, 1787), I, 21.

[93] Cf. Ogilvie, who remarks on Pindar's 7th Olympian ode, with its "noble panegyric upon the whole people of Rhodes, and the account of their Founder Tlepolemus." These are, he says, "happy and beautiful embellishments, whose introduction enlivens the whole piece with a proper variety of objects." *An Essay on the Lyric Poetry of the Ancients*, in Ogilvie's *Poems on Several Subjects* (London, 1762, repr. Augustan Reprint Society, 1970), lix.

[94] *The Lives and Characters of the Ancient Grecian Poets* (London, 1697), 84, 85.

[95] *Poetical Works*, ed. Robin Dix (Madison, NJ, 1996), 354.

[96] *Lives and Characters of the Ancient Grecian Poets* (London, 1697), Pt. 2, p. 35. Kennett also refers to reports that question Alcaeus' courage and patriotism. According to some stories, he ran away in battle, and had "some Designs on the State" (36).

For Akenside, Alcaeus was the exiled "Lesbian patriot," "Devoting shame and vengeance to her lords, / With louder impulse and a threatened land" ("On Lyric Poetry," lines 21–24).[97] In the eighteenth century, Alcaeus was often credited with writing the famous "Ode" of Callistratus, celebrating the patriotic daring of Harmodius and Aristogeiton of Athens, who succeeded in killing the tyrant Hipparchus in 514 BC, and although put to death were remembered by the Greeks as champions of liberty. His poems were republished in 1751.[98]

Contemporary with Alcaeus was Tyrtaeus, who for Kennett stands among "the Rank of the greatest Heroes as well as of the Noblest Poets." He was best known for his "exhortations" to the soldiers of Sparta. Horace in the *Ars Poetica* (401–2) notes that Tyrtaeus "with his verses fired manly hearts for battles of Mars." As Kennett explains, "by his continual Lectures of Honour and Courage, deliver'd in moving Verse to the Army; he ravish'd them to such a Degree with the thoughts of dying for their Country; that being all bent on another Attack," they rallied and won the battle (Pt. 2, p. 11). Stories known to Collins reported that Spartan warriors recited the poems of Tyrtaeus as they marched to battle. In his well-known essay "On Poetry," Sir William Temple noted that "the disheartened Spartans were new animated, and recovered their lost Courage, by the Songs of Tyrtaeus."[99] In 1701, on the occasion of "The King of France's Breaking the Peace of Ryswick," John Hughes translated Tyrtaeus' stirring call to "Spartan youths" as "The Praises of Heroic Virtue."[100]

The example of the Greek patriot-poets, exhorting troops to victory, or even leading the resistance to tyrants, probably stands behind some of the "Patriot" rhetoric of the 1730s and 1740s. In the *Debates in the Senate of Lilliput*, published in the *Gentleman's Magazine* in 1740, Johnson invokes the era when "*Poetry* and *Publick Spirit* were the same; . . . when the People caught the generous Flame from the Poet, when it spread from the People to the Prince, and united the Efforts of all against the common Enemy."[101] And as we will see, it prompted such poets as Akenside and Collins to invoke the patriotic Pindar and to call for a new Alcaeus.

---

[97] In a footnote, Akenside identifies Alcaeus as "ALCAEUS of Mitylene, the capital of Lesbos, who fled from his native city to escape the oppression of those who had inslav'd it, and wrote against them in his exile those noble invectives which are so much applauded by the ancient Critics" (in *Poetical Works*, 352).

[98] Together with poems of Anacreon and Sappho (Glasgow, 1751). A "fragment" of Alcaeus (the "Callistratus ode") was translated in the *Monthly Review*, 27 (1762), 248–49.

[99] *Critical Essays of the Seventeenth Century*, ed. Joel Spingarn, 3 vols. (New York, 1908–9), III, 77.

[100] Chalmers' *Works of the English Poets*, 21 vols. (London, 1810), X, 32–33.

[101] *Gentleman's Magazine*, 10 (1740), 230.

THE POET AS LEGISLATOR

In such a climate it was a short step further to think of the poet as leader in peace as well as war, in short, as legislator, and to invoke the example of Solon. As Benjamin Lowth notes, Solon was renowned as the "most venerable character of antiquity, the wisest of legislators, and withal a poet of no mean reputation."[102] Plutarch (as translated by Creech) notes that Solon was both lawgiver and poet: "his Numbers contain'd moral Sentences, and many transactions of the Commonwealth . . . sometimes to correct, chastise, and stir up the *Athenians* to noble performances." When Pisistratus threatened to take over the government, Solon engaged in "passionately exhorting them, not thus tamely to lose their Liberty." It would have been, he said, "an easier task to have stop'd the rising Tyranny, but now a greater and more glorious action to destroy it, when it was already begun, and had gathered strength."[103] In Horace's *Ars Poetica* Solonic poetry serves "to check vagrant union, to give rules for wedded life, to build towns, and grave laws on tables of wood" (398–99).

The idea of poet-lawgiver probably has its roots in the oldest Greek myths about poetry, the stories of Orpheus, who charmed even the savage beasts, and Amphion, at the sound of whose lyre the stones assembled themselves into the walls of Thebes. These myths continued to resonate in the eighteenth century: Orpheus and Amphion appear side by side in Pope's *Temple of Fame* (lines 83–86). Both are allegorical figures, Horace had said in the *Ars Poetica*, for the civilizing power of the poet.[104] The idea that the poet in some sense established and preserved the social order still had the power to move eighteenth-century critics and theorists of poetry. Bishop Lowth recalls the days when the poet had the power to "form the manners and maintain civil life."[105] As Thomas Blackwell remarked, "it was said of HOMER . . . 'that as a Poet, he had in a manner *formed* and *disciplined* barbarous *Greece*,'" that he "taught Men as much to Obey as to Command":

For both he, and so many other Bards, whose Works are equally grave and agreeable, aim at nothing so much as to celebrate the *useful Arts of Life*: They

---

[102] *Lectures on the Sacred Poetry of the Hebrews*, I, 27.
[103] *Lives*, 5 vols. (London, 1685–88), I, 279, 320.
[104] As Horace notes in the *Ars Poetica*, "While men still roamed the woods, Orpheus . . . made them shrink from bloodshed and brutal living; hence the fable that he tamed tigers and ravening lions; hence too the fable that Amphion, builder of Thebes's citadel, moved stones by the sound of his lyre" (391–95, Fairclough tr.).
[105] Lowth, *Lectures on the Sacred Poetry of the Hebrews*, I, 26.

breathe nothing but the public Good, Love of their Country, Social Virtue, and that wonderful Civility of Manners we admire among the *Grecians*.[106]

Blackwell went on to repeat the old idea, found in Aristotle, that "*Poetry, Philosophy* and *Legislation*" were "originally conjoined in one and the same Person" (294) – originally because "before the Invention of the Art of Writing, *Laws* were *sung*, lest they should be *forgotten*."[107] The idea of poet as legislator – most famous to us now in Imlac's "legislator of mankind" (in Johnson's *Rasselas*) and Shelley's formulation about the "unacknowledged legislators" – circulated widely in eighteenth-century Britain and France, and received its fullest exposition in the *Dissertation on the Rise, Union, & c. of Poetry and Music* (1763) by the cranky moralist, John Brown.[108]

Brown begins by observing that early Greek "Legislators were often Bards" as an aid to the memory, but quickly turns the phrase around as a means of dignifying his subject: "their Bards were Legislators" (40). Initially the character of the bard and legislator were united, but "after a certain Period of Civilization, the complex Character of *Legislator* and *Bard* would separate, or be seldom united" (30). But even then "the Profession of *Bard* would be held as very honourable and of high Esteem" (35).[109] In this "second period" the bard was "vested with a kind of *public Character*: and if not an original Legislator, yet still he would be regarded as a *subordinate* and *useful Servant* to the State" (35–36). Homer, says Brown, was "of a Genius truly *legislative*" (65), and after Homer Pindar was "the next great *legislative Bard*" (70):

we find, in his sublime *Songs*, the fullest and most perfect Union of salutary Principles, thrown out in Maxims religious, political, and moral . . . The intent of these *Songs*, sung by their Author at their most general and renowned Festivals, was to inspire his Countrymen with the Love of Glory and of Virtue . . . The Heroe of the Day was but the *occasional* and *incidental* Subject of his Ode. The main Interest was the Praise of his Country's gods and Heroes. (70–72)

Brown's Pindar is both legislator and patriot.

---

[106] *Letters Concerning Mythology* (London, 1748), 223, 291.

[107] This is John Brown quoting Aristotle. See below, n. 108.

[108] Blackwell cites Bishop Bossuet's *Discours sur l'Histoire Universelle*; Brown cites Aristotle, Voltaire's "Preface" to *Oedipus*, Shaftesbury's *Characteristics*, and Antoine-Yves Goguet's *De L'Origine Des Loix, des Arts, et des Sciences*, 2 vols. (Paris, 1759). Brown's *Dissertation* was republished in 1764 as *The History of the Rise and Progress of Poetry*.

[109] "When the Bard's profession had separated from that of the Legislator, [it] yet still retain'd it's Power and Dignity in full Union" (205).

Given's Brown's dark *Estimate* of his own countrymen's contemporary "manners," we are not surprised to discover that in his view the legislator-bard is now virtually "extinct" (207). Modern European poetry is but "the casual offspring of the corrupted *Roman* Arts, which were themselves no more than partial Imitation of the *Greek*, in their State of Separation and Weakness" (266). Even so, Brown discerns a few glimmerings of his hero in medieval Icelandic poetry, in Ossian and early Irish bards, and in the remnant of *"British Bards"* driven into Wales by Edward I, who was "so highly exasperated by the Influence of their Songs, which breathed the spirit of Liberty and War, and retarded his Conquest over a hardy People, that he basely ordered them to be slain" (202). Brown goes on to cite Gray's famous "The Bard," published only six years earlier, not only for the story about Edward I, on which Gray's poem is based, but also (one suspects) because "The Bard" seemed to offer a glimpse of the kind of poet that Brown celebrated.

The myth of Orpheus and the idea of poet as legislator had currency for the poets of mid-century as well as the theorists. In 1756 Joseph Warton reported having seen a manuscript ode "On the Use and Abuse of Poetry," in which Orpheus is "considered . . . as the first legislator and civilizer of mankind."[110] Once attributed to Collins, the lost ode may have been a poem by Warton himself, elsewhere entitled "Of the Usefulness of Poetry."[111] Warton's title suggests that in an effort to prove that – contemporary doubts to the contrary – poetry *was* indeed useful, he felt the need to go back to poetry's mythical origins. Other poets dropped the allusion to Orpheus but retained the idea of legislator. Three years after Warton wrote, Goldsmith remarked that, by acting as a "monitor" of the fashions, follies, and vices of the age, an author "may be considered as a merciful substitute to the legislature; he acts not by punishing crimes, but by preventing them."[112] But the context of Goldsmith's remark suggests that he regarded the idea of the author's national usefulness with some irony. It is even clearer in James Ralph's almost contemporary *The Case of Authors* (1758) that talk of the poet-as-civilizer was much in the air. Ralph observes skeptically that he is "neither an *Amphion* or an *Orpheus* – Nor

---

[110] He quotes nineteen lines, including an account of the effect of Orpheus' music: "Then sudden, while his melting music stole / With powerful magic o'er each softening soul, / Society, and law, and sacred order rose." As in Brown and other theorists, Orpheus is "Father of peace and arts." *Essay on the Genius and Writings of Pope*, 2 vols. (1756, 1757), I, 60–61.

[111] See *The Works of Collins*, ed. Richard Wendorf and Charles Ryskamp (Oxford, 1979), 224–25. Dodsley's *Collection* (1765) includes a poem on "The Power of Poetry," exemplified in Orpheus, Homer, Virgil, and Pope (III, 266–68).

[112] *An Enquiry into the Present State of Polite Learning in Europe* (1759), in *Collected Works*, I, 314–15.

are the Stocks, Stones, and Brutes of the present Time to be humanized by any Species of Incantation in my Power to practice upon them."[113]

THE EIGHTEENTH-CENTURY FANTASY
OF POET-AS-LEGISLATOR

In the closing sentence of his *Letters Concerning Mythology*, Blackwell locates the poet, even after he has been separated off from the legislator and philosopher, "above" the "Patriarch, Priest, or Lawgiver, that modelled the infant-State" (411). Why should the lofty, self-aggrandizing, and (to us) utterly fantastical idea of poet as legislator of the world – or as higher than legislator – have appealed so strongly to eighteenth-century poets and critics? Even if they did not harbor ambitions of serving their nation in parliament, why did they continue to imagine a prominent public role as metaphorical lawgiver? Even their irony suggests some effort to protect a pet idea. Before turning to the particular ways in which poets from Thomson to the end of the century tried on – with some ambivalence – the role of poet as legislator-patriot, I recall some of the features of the literary landscape being made familiar to us by recent studies of the changing circumstances of poetry in the age of print, and conjecture that it was precisely *because* poets feared that they were losing a public function that they dared to imagine that a poet might serve his nation as a patriot.

In the old order a poet might hope with Milton to be "doctrinal and exemplary to a nation" or to defend it in the court of world opinion. For Dryden, perhaps the last English poet of the old order, the poet in theory still stood beside the throne, as one of the virtuous monarch's trusted allies. If the monarch's function was to act on behalf of the people, the poet's function was to act as recording muse: "One to perform, another to record," as Dryden put it in the epistle to his honored kinsman. Or in a more exalted conception of the role, the poet not only records but actually confers fame. Pope may have still imagined such a role for the poet, but for many others the old rationale was breaking down.

In a world of print increasingly dominated by the theatre managers, the political factions, and the booksellers, the only choices available to the poet, James Ralph said at mid-century, were to write for the stage, to serve as political hireling, or as bookseller's drudge to be paid by the

---

[113] *The Case of Authors by Profession or Trade* (London, 1758), 59.

page.[114] Some writers, like Fielding, perhaps imagined that to write for the "Patriot" group of political leaders – Lyttelton, Dodington, Chesterfield – might mean to escape such narrow choices.[115] But the "Patriots" were themselves a faction, and held out the carrot of patronage. Even Fielding's *True Patriot* was designed, as Coley notes, to serve the political interests of a particular group. To aspire to be a "patriot" – small *p* – is to aspire to be free even of Patriot ideology, and to serve the state directly.

It is to imagine that the poet can still be a central figure in culture, and perhaps to ward off the suspicion that poetry during the course of the eighteenth century is becoming increasingly marginalized, as "literature" is both elevated in status and compartmentalized as the domain of the "aesthetic." Once considered as a source of knowledge as well as pleasure, "literature" shrinks from humane letters of all kinds (including history, political and economic theory, and philosophy) to a more modern notion of "imaginative" literature, what Joseph Warton called "pure poetry."[116] The poet who proclaims himself a patriot holds on to an older vision.

In subsequent chapters I focus on the efforts of a series of poets to imagine themselves as patriots. Some are the canonical figures of the mid and later eighteenth century – James Thomson, William Collins, Thomas Gray, Christopher Smart, Oliver Goldsmith, William Cowper. Others inhabit the margins of our current canon – Mark Akenside, John Dyer, and Ann Yearsley. For most of these poets, Britain is embodied not in its popular symbols (John Bull, or the Union Jack), not (Renaissance-style) in its monarch, or even in particular political heroes, but in its liberty, or its national church, its navy, its rural landscape. Characteristic too of these patriotic poets is their relatively infrequent use of national stereotypes designed to disparage a national adversary.[117] They do not seem to depend imaginatively on an Other: they typically focus on their

---

[114] *The Case of Authors*, 19.

[115] "The patriot utopia," W. B. Coley has noted (with reference to the Patriots of the 1730s and 1740s), "envisages a world without ministers, without factions, and without the selfish manipulations of political infighting. King and country would be more congenial themes for literature than the 'iniquitous Measures' of scheming ministers. And implicit in the 'pure' visions of the patriot ideology was the promise that if the patriots got in, they would reward the writers they had been cultivating." See his edition of Fielding's *The True Patriot and Related Writings*, lxxiv.

[116] See Steven Shankman, "The Pindaric Tradition and the Quest for Pure Poetry," *Comparative Literature*, 34 (1988), 219–44. Shankman argues that even the Pindaric ode was turned into "pure poetry" by poets and critics as early as the 1740s. Emphasizing Pindar as a narrowly focused encomiast, he overlooks the political/patriotic readings of Pindar in the eighteenth century.

[117] See Charles Knight, "The Images of Nations in Eighteenth-Century Satire," *ECS*, 22:4 (1989), 489–511, and the survey of eighteenth-century satirical prints in Michael Duffy, *The Englishman and the Foreigner* (Cambridge, 1986).

own nation, on its benevolent domination of world trade, on an idea of the public good, and in turn on the public good of the world. Cowper and Smart, writing in the heat of war with France, are exceptions. By the same token they typically avoid adopting a narrowly *English* (as opposed to a broader *British*) patriotism. Thomson, himself a Scot, explicitly praises Scots worthies, but praises "Britannia." Collins pleads for mercy for the largely Scottish Jacobite prisoners, and Gray's conception of "Britain" clearly includes Wales. Goldsmith, born an Irishman, avoids narrowly Irish political views. Churchill, vehement in his anti-Scots xenophobia, is the exception. And despite the strong current in the eighteenth century of what would later be called internationalism, British patriotic poets regard themselves as citizens of their native country. Here Goldsmith is the exception: attached to Britain but not fully at home there, and drawn at the same time to be a "citizen of the world." The patriot loves his (or her) country, and aspires to provide some service. But what distinctive service can the poet provide? Can the poet still record or confer fame? Can the poet create a sustaining vision that binds past, present, and future, what we would now call a *myth*? Can the poet, by redirecting attention to the still sylvan heart of the country, help save the nation from the dangers of commerce and of overseas expansion? Can the poet temper or soften the rough-edged British spirit? These are questions that the poets implicitly ask themselves as they watch their country complete its transformation into an increasingly urbanized nation of shopkeepers and a global empire.

CHAPTER 3

James Thomson: "to mix the Patriot's with the Poet's Flame"

Unlike Gray, Collins, or the Wartons, his fellow poets of the 1740s, James Thomson has long been viewed as a writer of patriotic verse. Few readers have believed that such work was Thomson's *best* work, and from the beginning of his career he was primarily recognized as a descriptive poet. But even in *The Seasons* Thomson himself announced his aspiration "To mix the Patriot's with the Poet's Flame" (*Autumn*, line 22), and to celebrate the glories of his country. His aspiration has not gone unnoted. In the 1920s, when literary historians were discovering the "Pre-Romantic" poets of the mid-eighteenth century, Cecil Moore firmly associated Thomson not with the visionary world of Collins and Gray but with "Whig panegyric."[1] And when the end of the Second World War prompted a skeptical reconsideration of nationalist sentiment, Dobrée noted the centrality of "the theme of patriotism" in Thomson's work, and A. D. McKillop refined Moore's term by characterizing Thomson's politics as "dissident [i.e., Opposition] Whig panegyric."[2] But literary historians have always been somewhat apologetic about what they regarded as the ebullient puffery of Thomson's patriotic verse (and of "Whig panegyric" in general), persuaded perhaps that poets who seemed to dissent from Tory "gloom" about the state of England must have been at best naive and at worst mere hacks in the pay of Walpole and his ministers. Thomson's defenders have usually gone on to deplore that he ever tried to write about politics, preferring that he had stuck to painting the works of nature, for which his genius was allegedly better suited. In recent years Thomson's patriotism has again drawn attention, this time from literary and political historians who have pointed to his close association with the "Patriot" group of politicians (Bolingbroke,

---

[1] "Whig Panegyric Verse," reprinted in *Backgrounds of English Literature*.
[2] Dobrée, "Theme of Patriotism," followed shortly by McKillop's influential "The Background of Thomson's *Liberty*," *Rice Institute Pamphlets*, 38, no. 2 (1951).

Lyttelton, Chesterfield, and Frederick, Prince of Wales) and his role in the opposition to Walpole in the 1730s.[3] It has been suggested too that Thomson's national allegiance is itself in question, that although he ostensibly writes as a loyal son of Hanoverian Britain he is more deeply an "Anglo-Scot" with anxious ambivalence about his Scottish origins.[4]

Such study as Thomson's patriotic poetry has received tends to view it in a narrow context – the decade of the 1730s, the opposition to Walpole, Anglo-Scot tension, or early-eighteenth-century fascination with Britain's maritime commerce. But Thomson needs to be read against a wider horizon. Though his origins are in the "Augustan" period – his career largely overlaps that of Walpole and Pope – he was a significant presence in English poetry well past the fall of Walpole in 1742 and the death of Pope in 1744. *The Seasons*, begun as early as 1726, continued to be revised as late as 1744 (with further minor revisions in 1746). Thomson himself died soon thereafter – in 1748 – but his poems had great impact on the poets for the remainder of the century. Following the example of Tickell and Pope, he is the first among the poets of the mid and late century who endeavored to join the patriot with the poet. His major poems, not only *Liberty* but also *The Seasons*, offered prototypes of the "panegyric of Great Britain" that was to become commonplace in later poets, and gave memorable form to a series of patriotic topoi – Britain as blest island, as temperate landscape, as the home of liberty, as naval power – that were to reappear throughout the century. At the same time, Thomson offered a critique of the very patriotic fervor he proclaimed by implicitly asking a series of unsettling questions: was commerce a danger to civic virtue? Was British "thunder" consistent with British "liberty"? Was "liberty" consistent with "public good"? – questions that gave Thomson and his successors considerable pause. Furthermore, he in effect asked a more fundamental question: are poetry and patriotism compatible? Is it possible for the poet to provide patriotic service to his country?[5]

Thomson's ambivalent response to the world of high politics dates from the beginning of his career, when the literary lowland Scotsman,

---

3 See especially Gerrard, *Patriot Opposition*, and William Levine, "Collins, Thomson, and the Whig Progress of Liberty," *SEL*, 34 (1994), 553–78.
4 Mary Jane W. Scott, *James Thomson, Anglo-Scot* (Athens, GA, 1988).
5 I leave out of consideration Thomson's verse dramas (except for *The Masque of Alfred*), though as Sambrook notes (*James Thomson*, 203), their protagonists – Gustavus Vasa, Edward I, Arminius, and Alfred himself – are clearly identified with the "royal patriot," Frederick Prince of Wales.

firm supporter of the 1707 Union of Scotland and England, arrived in London in hopes of making his way as a British poet. Walpole's Whig administration was then in control of the levers of patronage, and Thomson dedicated his first major poem, *Winter* (1726), to Sir Spencer Compton (later Earl of Wilmington), then Speaker of the House of Commons and a resolute ally of government. Thomson was soon introduced to other prominent Whigs, and the next year dedicated *Summer* to another Walpolean Whig and one of the Lords of the Treasury, George Bubb Dodington, and his *Poem Sacred to the Memory of Sir Isaac Newton* to Walpole himself. Thomson addressed Walpole as his country's "most illustrious *Patriot*," and would appear to have placed himself as solidly in Walpole's camp as had his fellow Scotsman, the minor poet Joseph Mitchell, who made a career of flattering Sir Robert. But within two years, Thomson's was one of the loudest voices in the Opposition, decrying Walpole's pacific policy toward Spain in the saber-rattling *Britannia* (1729), written to rouse the nation to revenge for Spanish "depredations" against British traders. For the rest of his career Thomson was to champion Britain's foreign trade and the naval "thunder" that underpinned it, thereby aligning himself with the nascent "Patriot" group in parliament that was beginning to coalesce around Bolingbroke and Pulteney. But Thomson, like his contemporary and friend Richard Savage (who also wrote both for and against Walpole), did not abandon hope that he might retain the patronage of the ministry and court, and a year later, in 1730, Queen Caroline accepted the dedication of his play, *Sophonisba*. Thomson, like Fielding after him, was willing to seek and accept financial support where he could find it. Whether this suggests a pragmatic flexibility or political principle is unclear. Unlike many poets later in the century, Thomson's "patriotism" can be aligned with that of the patrons from whom he received support.

In the early 1730s Thomson found another ministerial patron in Charles Talbot, Solicitor-General and in 1733 Lord Chancellor and member of the Privy Council, though not a highly partisan politician. But as the decade passed, Thomson, like his former patron Dodington and a number of leading Whig politicos including Chesterfield and Lyttelton, was increasingly aligned with the "Patriot" opposition to Walpole. *Liberty* (1735, 1736), Thomson's most obtrusively political poem, was dedicated to Frederick, Prince of Wales, the titular leader of the group opposed to the ministry and the court. Thomson was perhaps adjusting his opinions to suit those of his patrons, but there is good reason to believe that he, like many contemporaries, thought Frederick more likely than his father to support the arts. In 1737, when the Lord Chancellor died, Thomson lost a post that Talbot had given him, and received a pension from Frederick. In 1740 the masque of *Alfred*, written by Thomson and David Mallet, performed at the Prince's country estate at Cliveden, concluded with a patriotic "Ode in Honour of Great Britain," quickly to become famous as "Rule, Britannia."[6]

Thomson remained a pensioner of the Prince, and during the 1740s attached himself more closely to the Opposition Whig leaders Lyttelton (secretary to the Prince) and Chesterfield. When they went into government in 1744, Thomson in effect followed them. In the 1744 edition of *The Seasons* he inserted panegyrical paragraphs on both Lyttelton and Chesterfield, and a brief commendation of Claremont, the country estate of the prime minister, Thomas Pelham (later Duke of Newcastle). At a time when other patriotic poets, including Akenside and Collins, were still in Opposition, Thomson (following Lyttelton) became an adherent of the "Broad-Bottom" ministry. It was apparently his support of the government which led to the loss of his pension from Frederick in the last year of his life. The "Patriot" themes of the 1730s – especially the dangers of "Corruption" and the importance of "Independent Life" – are somewhat muted in Thomson's poems of the 1740s, not surprisingly since his patrons had gone into government. Though a supporter of government, Thomson, perhaps retaining his "Patriot" suspicions, is silent on the subject of the court of George II. It was to the Prince of Wales, dedicatee of the 1737 *Liberty*, that Thomson dedicated the revised and expanded *Seasons* of 1744.[7]

Thomson's patriotism revealed itself not in response to particular political occasions – the early *Britannia* is an exception – but in the 1730s as standard "Patriot" rhetoric and in the 1740s as "panegyric" of his country. Even such political events as the fall of Walpole and the alleged "apostasy" of Pulteney in 1742 pass unremarked in his poems. The heroic victory of Admiral Vernon at Porto Bello in 1739, the British success at Dettingen, and Anson's circumnavigation of 1740–44 provoke no patriotic outburst. Indeed, they go unmentioned.[8] During the years when the country was deeply divided about Britain's part in the continental War of the Austrian Succession (1740–48) and about the appropriate

---

[6] The "ode" was so described in the *Daily Advertiser* for 6 August 1740. It was first published separately in a 1752 collection.

[7] In 1745 Thomson dedicated to Frederick his *Tancred and Sigismunda*.

[8] Vernon appears in Thomson's poems only (in a passage added in 1744) as the unsuccessful besieger of Cartagena (*Summer*, lines 1040–51).

punishment for the defeated Jacobite rebels, Thomson was silent on these two great public topics. Although a Scotsman by birth, Thomson seems to have taken no public position on the merits of the Jacobite cause or on the honor of those fellow Scots who either opposed or supported Charles Edward. Mary Jane Scott's claim that Thomson wrote as a deeply conflicted Anglo-Scot, suffering from an "inferiority complex about being a Scot in London," "ambivalent about his national allegiance," "cautious" about expressing Scottish nationalism openly, and harboring "sentimental Jacobitism," is unsubstantiated by Thomson's writings. Sambrook more soundly identifies Thomson as a "true lowland Whig" who "regarded the Highland clans as barbarous."[9] Thomson rarely appears in his works as a Scottish patriot. The exception is a long panegyric on Scots worthies, and an implicit appeal for the development of Scottish industry, a passage that first appeared in *Summer* and was expanded and transferred to *Autumn* in 1744.[10] Thomson's nationalist allegiance is not to Scotland or to England but to a more inclusive "Britannia."[11]

It may be the relative absence of topicality, narrow Scottish sympathies, and partisanship (apart from his "Patriot" days in the 1730s) that helped make Thomson's literary patriotism a model for poets later in the century.[12] "Liberty" in his hands remains a loosely defined term rather than a polemical slogan, suggesting primarily freedom from an arbitrary monarch and from the religious bigotry of priestcraft, sometimes nothing more specific than "*Liberty* of *Mind*" (*Liberty*, II, line 247). As Linda Colley has recently emphasized, British patriots of all stripes boasted of the "liberty" that Britons enjoyed by comparison with continental autocracies such as France and Spain. McKillop notes that much of the political sentiment in *Liberty* (and, one could add, *The Seasons*) takes the form of "universally acceptable political, moral, and social generalizations."[13]

Thomson cannot be said to have initiated the stream of eighteenth-century patriotic verse. His celebrations of British liberty, British

[9] Scott, *James Thomson*, 174, 239, 248; Sambrook, *James Thomson*, 252. Sambrook cites Thomson's footnote to *Liberty*, IV, line 94, where the "*Rage of Slaves*" is identified as "Vassalage, whence the Attachment of Clans to their Chief."

[10] See Sambrook's notes.   [11] See his 1726 letter to Mallet, cited above, 11 n.

[12] *Liberty* did not fall quite so stillborn from the press as Johnson suggests, but Goldgar notes that "the poem in its vague loftiness seems to have passed above the grubby world of practical politics" (*Walpole and the Wits*, 144). For contemporary praise of the poem, see A. D. McKillop, "The Reception of Thomson's 'Liberty'," *Notes & Queries*, 198 (1953), 112–13.

[13] James Thomson, *The Castle of Indolence and Other Poems*, ed. A. D. McKillop (Lawrence, KS, 1961), 164.

worthies, British naval power, and the worldwide reach of British trade were all anticipated by poets earlier in the century – Tickell's "Prospect of Peace," Pope's *Windsor Forest*, Young's *Ocean* – and by the enthusiastic proponents (Defoe and others) of foreign trade.[14] But Thomson helped establish what were to become familiar elements in the celebrations of British greatness by later poets. It was Thomson above all who set the fashion for tracing Liberty's origins in classical Greece and Republican Rome and her peregrinations northward and westward to the Renaissance Italian city-states, Switzerland, Holland, and finally (at the time of Elizabeth) to Britain, where she revived ancient cults in her honor that predated the Romans. It is Thomson's version of the progress of Liberty, for example, that Collins uses as the basis for his "Ode on Liberty," published with his collection of *Odes* in 1746. But it was probably the vivid and sensuous descriptions of "Happy Britannia" in Thomson's *Seasons* rather than the windy abstractions of *Liberty* that moved later poets of patriotism.[15] Patriotism for Thomson is at bottom a love of the green and pleasant homeland, to which the poet returns after every distant excursion.

Britain in *The Seasons*, as in Thomson's *Liberty* and his patriotic anthem, "Rule, Britannia!," is a "Blest isle" (*Liberty*, V, line 633, "Rule, Britannia!" line 29), protected by God and Nature from the rest of the world by rocky cliffs and the same oceans that provide sea lanes for her merchant fleet.

> Island of Bliss! amid the subject Seas
> That thunder round thy rocky Coasts, set up,
> At once the Wonder, Terror, and Delight,
> Of distant Nations . . .
> Not to be shook thy self, but all Assaults
> Baffling, like thy hoar Cliffs the loud Sea-Wave.
> (*Summer*, lines 1595–1601)[16]

Both securely "bounded" (by the surrounding waves) and – one of Thomson's recurrent words – "unbounded" (because the seas both unite and divide), Thomson's Britain has it both ways.[17] Its climate is mercifully temperate, exempt from the extremes of heat and cold, drought

---

14 See also Lyttelton's *Blenheim* (1727).
15 But see the address to "the Goddess of Liberty, marking the Happiness and Grandeur of Great-Britain," in *Liberty*, V, lines 2–85.
16 Thomson makes plainer in "Rule, Britannia!" that Britain enjoys the special protection of heaven: "When Britain first, at Heaven's command, / Arose from out the azure main" (lines 1–2).
17 "Unbounded" may have been taken from Pope, whose "Unbounded Thames shall flow for all mankind" (*Windsor Forest*, line 398).

and deluge. Even on the hottest summer day, grateful shade is near, and compared to the heat in "Climes unrelenting," the sun's blaze is "feeble, and yon Skies are cool" (*Summer*, lines 633–34).

Thomson was among the first of poets to *invent* an enduring image of what we now think of as the "typically English" rural scene as viewed from a convenient hilltop, affording a prospect over

> Hill and Dale, and Wood and Lawn,
> And verdant Field, and darkening Heath between,
> And Villages Embosom'd soft in Trees,
> And spiry Towns by surging Columns mark'd
> Of houshold smoak   (*Spring*, lines 952–56)[18]

> Rich is thy Soil, and merciful thy Clime;
> Thy Streams unfailing in the Summer's Drought
> Unmatch'd thy Guardian-Oaks; thy Valleys float
> With golden Waves: and on thy Mountain Flocks
> Bleat numberless; while, roving round their Sides,
> Bellow the blackening Herds in lusty Droves.
> Beneath, thy Meadows glow, and rise unquell'd
> Against the Mower's scythe. On every hand,
> Thy Villas shine. Thy Country teems with Wealth;
> And Property assures it to the Swain,
> Pleas'd and unwearied in his guarded Toil.

> (*Summer*, lines 1446–56)

The description translates abstract "love of country" into deep and abiding affection for the *countryside* as its concrete embodiment. That the description is generic rather than particularized – it could fit hundreds of "prospects" throughout England and Scotland – only makes it more available to the self-consciously "British" reader as patriotic sentiment.[19]

Thomson was also among the first to associate the "happy rural seat" in Milton's Eden (*Paradise Lost*, IV. 247) with the "villa"[20] or "rural Seat" (*Spring*, line 766; *Autumn*, line 1038) of England's landed peers, Lyttelton's Hagley Park ("Thy British Tempe!" *Spring*, line 909), "The fair Majestic

---

[18] Cf. the "goodly Prospect... / Of Hills, and Dales, and Woods, and Lawns, and Spires, / And glittering Towns, and gilded Streams, till all / The stretching Landskip into Smoke decays!" (*Summer*, lines 1438–41).

[19] The passage at *Spring*, lines 950–62, describes the view of "Cambrian [Welsh] Mountains" from Hagley Park in north Worcestershire, *Summer*, lines 1406–41, the view of the Thames Valley from Richmond Hill.

[20] Not as Italianate as it sounds. *OED* notes that the word was naturalized by Shaftesbury in 1711. Thomson probably borrowed it from Pope, *Windsor Forest*: "Behold! th'ascending villas on my side" (line 375).

Paradise of STOWE" (*Autumn*, line 1042), Pelham's Claremont, with its "terrass'd Height, and Esher's Groves" (*Summer*, line 1429), and the "embowering Walks" (*Summer*, line 1420) of Queensberry's Ham House. The "stately homes of England," still in post-imperial Britain a powerful image of quintessential Englishness, were both literally and figuratively constructed – erected by architects and builders and endowed by poets with their symbolic power – in Thomson's generation. That the proprietors of the great country houses are also Britain's political leaders links the landscaped parks (many of them in the Thames Valley) with the political center in Westminster. The sylvan scene provides restoration ("By the soft Windings of the silent Mole, / From Courts and Senates PELHAM finds Repose" [*Summer*, lines 1431–32]) as well as inspiration: at Hagley, Lyttelton plans "with warm Benevolence of Mind / And honest Zeal / unwarp'd by Party-Rage, / BRITANNIA's Weal" (*Spring*, lines 928–30). The country house is made to seem not a site of private privilege but an integral part of the public good.[21] Marxicizing critics have noted that Thomson implicitly corroborates the "authority" of landed gentlemen "over the national landscape which they owned."[22] But just as the delighted spectator was taught by Addison to think he had a kind of "property" in what he could take pleasure in seeing, the reader of Thomson, situated on a prospect overlooking a gentleman's park, is induced to feel that the landscape somehow belongs not only to "the nation" but to its patriotic readers.

Indeed, the strength of the worldwide British empire itself is shown to rest on a solidly rural foundation. This theme is as old as Virgil's *Georgics*, but Thomson's is the classic English version:

> A simple Scene! yet hence BRITANNIA sees
> Her solid Grandeur rise: hence she commands
> Th'exalted Stores of every brighter Clime,
> The Treasures of the Sun without his Rage:
> Hence, fervent all, with Culture, Toil, and Arts,
> Wide glows her Land.   (*Summer*, lines 423–28)

> Such themes as these the rural MARO sung
> To wide-imperial Rome in the full Height
> Of Elegance and Taste, by Greece refin'd.

---

21 *Blenheim* (1727) by Thomson's patron, Lyttelton, is an earlier example. See above, 53–54.
22 Tim Fulford, *Landscape, Liberty, and Authority: Poetry, Criticism, and Politics from Thomson to Wordsworth* (Cambridge, 1996), 3, following the lead of John Barrell, in *English Literature in History, 1730–1780: An Equal, Wide Survey* (London, 1983).

In antient Times the sacred Plow employ'd
The Kings and awful Fathers of Mankind . . .

Ye generous BRITONS, venerate the Plow!
And o'er your Hills and long withdrawing Vales
Let Autumn spread his Treasures to the Sun,
Luxuriant, unbounded! (*Spring*, lines 55–59, 67–70)

Commerce, Thomson says, is "generous" (*Summer*, lines 138–39), binding the nations in a "golden Chain," and "social" (*Summer*, line 754,
Autumn, line 834). Like the ideologues of trade before him, Thomson
thinks of foreign commerce not simply as a source of riches and exotic
luxuries for his country but as a means whereby Britannia can benevo-
lently provide for the entire world.[23]

As the Sea
Far thro' his azure turbulent Domain
Your empire owns, and from a thousand shores
Wafts all the Pomp of Life into your Ports;
So with superior Boon may your rich Soil,
Exuberant, Nature's better Blessings pour
O'er every Land, the naked Nations cloath,
And be th'exhaustless Granary of a World!
(*Spring*, lines 70–77)

Trade (with its benefits) flows both ways: it "wafts" into British ports
and "pours" forth over the world. Indeed, Thomson goes so far as to
claim that Britain enjoys the special consideration of a god-like Nature
("superior Boon" and "better Blessings"), enacts a magnanimous role (the
"Blessings" it sends forth are "better" than the "Pomp of Life" it receives),
and even plays the role of divinity (clothing the "naked Nations" as Christ
clothes Adam and Eve in the garden).

Thomson's celebration of Britain's trading empire is calculated to
assuage the concerns of moralists who worried about the corrupting
effect of "luxury," and of those in the "landed interest" who worried
that an increasingly commercial England was deserting its traditional
economy (and political structure). His moralized vision of trade as a
means to worldwide benevolence helps to obscure the inflows of luxury
goods. His integration of rural land and overseas trade – for it is British
agricultural products (wool and grain) that are sent abroad – helps to
redefine "Britain" for new generations of patriotic "Britons" as a country

[23] Cf. *Windsor Forest*: "Unbounded Thames shall flow for all mankind" (line 398), and Dyer, *The Fleece* (see below, ch. 7).

that has safely preserved its rural soul even as "little England" was being transformed into a world empire.

That Britain now had a world empire was at the same time cause for patriotic pride, as was the naval power that opened the sea lanes and maintained British control of them. Thomson makes plain that Britain "commands / Th'exalted Stores of every brighter Clime" largely because of the "dreadful Thunder" of her navy that "Rides o'er the Waves sublime ... / Hence rules the circling Deep, and awes the World" (*Summer*, lines 423–24, 428–31). "Thunder," again appropriated from *Windsor Forest*,[24] is Thomson's recurrent metaphor (and metonymy) for British sea power, hinting at Zeus-like authority and boldly pointing to the ominously wide-mouthed cannon on a British man-o'-war. Britain can project its naval power to every corner of the world, "whose remotest Shore / Can soon be shaken by thy Naval Arm" (*Summer*, lines 1598–99).

But Thomson portrays no sea battles in *The Seasons* – having apparently sated his bloodthirst in the early *Britannia*. The British navy holds its power in reserve; even Britain's enemies are little in evidence. Though Britain was at war with Spain in the late 1730s and with France at the time of the 1744 and 1746 revisions to *The Seasons*, when fears of a French invasion were widespread, Thomson provides very little of the standard denunciations of French tyranny, absolutism, and territorial or commercial ambition. British thunder, he notes confidently in lines added in 1744, "now, even now, / Impending hangs o'er Gallia's humbled Coast" (*Summer*, lines 429–30), referring perhaps to British naval blockade of French ports. Other lines added that year glower at "the proud Foe / The faithless vain Disturber of Mankind, / Insulting Gaul," which has now "rous'd the World to War" (*Autumn*, lines 1075–77). Thomson may hint that Britain should punish the aggressor – British youth are said to be "keen, once more, within their Bounds to press / Those polish'd Robbers, those ambitious Slaves" (lines 1078–79). But compared to other patriotic poets of the day, Thomson is remarkably pacific, and little given to demonizing European adversaries or calling for blood. His harshest words are reserved for the "purple Tyranny" of seventeenth-century Jesuit missionaries (*Summer*, line 758) and for greedy Vasco da Gama, dead more than two hundred years (*Summer*, lines 1001–5).[25]

---

[24] "Thy trees, fair Windsor! now shall ... / Bear Britain's thunder ... / To the bright regions of the rising day" (*Windsor Forest*, lines 385–88). Cf. *Autumn*, lines 131–33: "ribb'd with Oak / To bear the BRITISH Thunder, black, and bold, / The roaring Vessel rush'd into the Main"; *Summer*, lines 1476–77: "like the mustering Thunder when provok'd, / The Dread of Tyrants."

[25] In this respect "Rule, Britannia" is more belligerent and invokes a world of threatening enemies ("Thee haughty tyrants ne'er shall tame / ... Britons never will be slaves").

The patriotic British reader is encouraged to think of his country as powerful but benevolent, an unbounded world empire but a safely and contentedly bounded island, a nation of merchants and traders but at heart a nation of sturdy farmers. In one sense Thomson takes a leading role in redefining national identity for a people who were still discovering what it meant to be "Great Britain" rather than just "England" and "Scotland," and were realizing that since the days of William III they had moved more firmly into the center of the European stage as the great adversary of France. His strategy of embracing a wider role for Britain while confirming its traditional agricultural and land-based economy was well suited for the times. And it provided a comprehensive patriotic vision that was available to later poets – Collins, Dyer, and Cowper – for their adaptive use.

MISGIVINGS

But Thomson's rapturous patriotic rhetoric and his insistent "both-and" strategy – Britain is *both* island *and* empire, *both* rich *and* virtuous, both "bounded" and "unbounded"[26] – suggests that, like many contemporaries, he sometimes doubted the truth of what he proclaimed. If Thomson's poems served as a kind of compendium of patriotic topoi, they also served as a catalog of cultural worries: perhaps the nation could not be both island and empire, both rich and virtuous. Editors have long noted that as *The Seasons* grew longer and longer from 1730 to 1746, its emphases shifted (more political, less devotional), and its contradictions widened. Progressivism sits next to primitivism, praise of rural simplicity next to praise of urban elegance, the delights of retirement next to the glories of active public virtue. The loose structure of the poem made it easy for Thomson simply to add whole new paragraphs without altering adjacent passages or worrying about consistency. And eighteenth-century editorial practices of reprinting the "beauties" of long poems encouraged readers to sample Thomson's set pieces rather than to try to discern the relation of part to part, and parts to whole. A reader dipping into Thomson's long poems might easily come away not with confidence in Britain's glorious future but with anxious doubts and fears.

This is even the case with *Liberty*, a poem in which Thomson is caught in a fundamental contradiction: he wants to celebrate Britain as the land of liberty, but he writes at a time when in his view and that of

---

[26] A particular obsession for Thomson: see *Spring*, line 110, *Summer*, lines 803, 1012, 1804, *Winter*, lines 799, 915, 1069.

other "Patriots" Britain, under Walpole, is enslaved to corruption. (The contradiction is found as early as *Britannia* [1729] – in which Britons are both "sons of freedom" [line 291] and "degenerate sons" [line 2]). Thomson's basic strategy is to contrast the corrupt present with the virtuous past and the idealized future, in order to define Walpolean corruption as a distortion of true Britishness. But he is uncomfortable with the strategy, and his rhetoric betrays his discomfort. After commending the three virtues that sustain British freedom, "Independent Life," "Integrity in Office," and "A Passion for the Common-Weal," the Goddess Liberty urges her Britons to "be firm! – nor let *Corruption* sly / Twine round your Heart indissoluble Chains" (v, lines 200–1), and then instantly regrets it: "Forbid it Heaven! that ever I need urge / Integrity in Office on my Sons" (lines 209–10). But her fear persists: "Should then the Times arrive (which Heaven avert!) / That Britons bend unnerv'd . . . / by *Corruption*'s Soul-dejecting Arts" (lines 304–7). And again she catches herself, and suggests such worries are needless: "But why to Britons this superfluous Strain?" (line 367). Why indeed? Perhaps because the worry is deep-seated in Thomson and his contemporaries that "true Britons" have indeed given way to the "*corrupting Flood*" (line 384), and that a nation "gorg'd with Wealth" from "Trade enormous" will surely sink into luxury: "*That Nation* must *another Carthage* lie" (lines 381–82, 388). Dyer and Goldsmith would later share Thomson's worry.

It is perhaps not surprising that Lyttelton, in his posthumous edition of Thomson's poems, omitted these lines from *Liberty*. The usual explanation is that Lyttelton thought the poem too long; but it seems equally likely that as a "Patriot" politician and supporter of the ministry – he was eventually made Chancellor of the Exchequer – Lyttelton preferred that Thomson's poem provide an unambiguously congratulatory picture of British liberty. Thus it is noteworthy to consider some of the other passages which Lyttelton deleted. Among them are lines in Part III which deplore the "deep Divisions" and "fierce Contentions" (lines 338, 341) that eventually destroyed the Roman republic: in Patriot ideology, the Roman republic stood as an unsullied model of classical liberty, and any suggestion (such as Thomson seems to make) that liberty might degenerate into "contentions" was to be dismissed. Lyttelton also deleted Thomson's suggestion that there may have been something inevitable in the republic's decline – "Rome / Began to feel the swift Approach of Fate" (lines 335–36) – though he left alone a line in Part II – "So States must die and Liberty go round" (line 420) – perhaps because the notion that every state must eventually degenerate was a commonplace in eighteenth-century political thinking, and seemed sufficiently abstract as not to reflect on British liberty. Thomson, though an adherent of the "Patriots," was not unaware that the term was claimed on all sides and probably not unaware that some of his "Patriot" friends had been accused of self-interest and of the kind of party-spirit they claimed to transcend. Liberty herself asks "Who can, unshock'd, behold . . . / Delirious Faction bellowing loud MY Name? / The false fair-seeming Patriot's hollow boast?" (*Liberty*, v, lines 279, 286–87). Lyttelton, who considered himself a "Patriot" whether in or out of office, omitted Thomson's querying lines.

Lyttelton also omitted a politically awkward passage in Part IV in which Thomson explains, as his original account of the "Contents" put it, "That sometimes Arts may flourish for a while under despotic Governments, tho' never the natural and genuine Production of them." Thomson's lines in fact trace the revival of sculpture, painting, and architecture, based on "antient Models from imperial Rome." That the arts should have flourished under the Roman emperors posed a problem for defenders of "Liberty," since they preferred to claim that the arts prosper best in free states. In Thomson's day the greater problem was France: what could explain the flourishing of the arts under the absolutist French kings? Thomson allows the question into his poem, devoting more than seventy-five lines (v, lines 441–518) to Boileau, Racine, Corneille, Molière, French painting, engraving, sculpture, and tapestry. Thomson then returns to his central theme, claiming rather lamely that had the same bounty been showered on the arts in Britain, they would have "branch'd luxuriant to the Skies" (line 527), and warning that courtly largesse is an "uncertain Spring" that gives a "transitory Gleam" (line 531), and can just as easily be withheld as given. Lyttelton omits the lines about art under imperial Rome, and the flourishing of the arts in France, leaving only the brief concession that arts, "by casual beams of *Favour* rais'd / May sometimes in a tyrant's garden bloom," and the insistence that arts under Liberty enjoy "perpetual spring." Lyttelton, who had himself acted as patron and as the conduit of the patronage of the Prince of Wales, might well be expected to take a benign view of the supportive climate for the arts in a free state. Thomson, who throughout his career but especially until about 1738 depended for a significant part of his livelihood on the uncertain favors of patronage,[27] not surprisingly took the view, shared

---

[27] For an account of Thomson's dependence on both patrons and booksellers, see James Sambrook, " 'A Just Balance between Patronage and the Press': The Case of James Thomson," in John A. Dussinger, ed., *Questions of Literary Property in Eighteenth-Century England* (*Studies in the Literary Imagination*, 34:1 [2001], 135–53).

by many writers of his day, that Britain ought to be more like France in this matter.

In another respect, Thomson asks whether England and France might be more alike than the champions of liberty would prefer to think. The French under Louis XIV were long thought to have ambitions of "*universal Sway*," ambitions which England stoutly resisted in a series of wars beginning in the 1690s, at the cost of "Seas of Blood and Treasure" (IV, lines 1080–81). By the 1730s Britain had successfully challenged French aspirations:

> Despairing *Gaul* her boiling Youth restrains,
> Dissolv'd her Dream of *Universal Sway*:
> The Winds and Seas are Britain's wide Domain;
> And not a sail, but by Permission, spreads.
>
> (*Liberty*, V, lines 634–37)

Thomson invites a reader to ask whether there is a real difference between French and British imperial ambitions, between France's "Universal Sway" and Britain's "wide Domain." Again, Lyttelton omitted the entire passage.

Liberty concludes with "The Prospect" of "the Happiness and Grandeur of Great-Britain." Thomson seems intent on restoring the celebratory mood of the poem, and his vision of an idealized future for his country probably warmed the heart of his patrons, from Lyttelton to the Prince of Wales (who himself hoped to lead the nation into its glorious future). But Thomson's final lines do not leave the reader dazzled by British glories. Instead, restoring the frame of the dreaming visionary, they return to the poet's starting point amidst the ruins of Rome:

> As thick to View THESE VARIED WONDERS rose,
> Shook all my Soul with Transport, unassur'd,
> The VISION broke; And, on my waking Eye,
> Rush'd the still RUINS of dejected ROME.
>
> (V, lines 717–20)

The "VISION" of the glorious future is only a vision. Perhaps, the poem implies, Britain will not survive the flood of wealth and the "felon undermining Hand / Of dark CORRUPTION" (IV, lines 1189–90) so vividly described in Part IV. Perhaps Britain will go the way of imperial Rome, and end in ruins. The curious insertion of "unassur'd" (V, line 718) suggests that Thomson wanted to underline the uncertainty with which he faced the future. Lyttelton deleted the line.

That Thomson's fears about his country sometimes overwhelmed his hopes is clear from his letters, even those written at the time he was working on *Liberty*. In August 1735 he complained in Popean terms of the "new Gothic night" that covered the land. (He had lamented "this general night" as early as 1730.[28]) Two weeks later, in a letter to Aaron Hill, he lamented the "vast Temple of *Corruption*, under which this Generation, more than any other that ever boasted Freedom, worships the dirty, low-minded, insatiable Idol of Self-interest." He expects to see "all Learning absorb'd into the Sink of hireling scurrilous News-Papers," but hopes that Hill will seek to "stem the Torrent of Barbarism. I wish you could find an Assistant, tho' never so weak a one, in Dear Sir, Your most affectionate humble Servant, James Thomson" (98). In another letter to Hill the following May, while Thomson is engaged in the printing of *Liberty*, he laments that "the continual Tides of Riches, pour'd in upon this Nation in Commerce, have been lost again in a Gulph of ungraceful, inelegant, inglorious Luxury." He can only hope that "the better Genius of this Nation," which has "often nobly exerted itself," will once again "struggle hard before it expire" (105–6).

Those fears and hopes find their way not only into *Liberty* but also into the *Seasons* of 1730 and 1744. In a passage added to *Winter* in 1730 Thomson commends the work of "The Jail Committee, in the year 1729," a parliamentary committee investigating charges that Britons, "That for their country would have toiled or bled," were being tortured in their country's jails. Thomson dwells on the shameful contradiction: even "in the Land of Liberty – the Land / Whose every Street and public Meeting glow / With open Freedom – little Tyrants rag'd" (*Winter*, lines 365–67). And trade, which Thomson could see as a kind of benevolent exchange, or as pure generosity, has a dark side. He wrote when British ships were fully engaged in the "triangular trade" that carried manufactured goods to Africa in exchange for slaves, then transported in the middle passage to the New World. Like many of his contemporaries, Thomson seems to have acknowledged the cruelty of slavery but implicitly to have recognized it as an essential part of Britain's system of world trade. In his mental excursion to the "torrid zone" Thomson's muse reviews "many a happy Isle; / The Seat of blameless Pan, yet undisturb'd / By Christian Crimes and Europe's cruel Sons" (*Summer*, lines 853–55). The "happy Isle" is a reminder of Britain's own island state, but its happy pagan natives are soon to be converted by Christian Europeans – Thomson does not go so

---

[28] To Valentine Munbee, 27 October 1730, quoting the closing lines of Pope's 1728 *Dunciad*, to William Cranstoun, 7 August 1735, again citing Pope's Dulness, in *Letters and Documents*, 76, 96.

far as to call them Britons, though the Society for the Propagation of the Gospel was already at work – whose "Crimes" presumably include enslavement. In a later passage in *Summer* Thomson is unambiguous, and enacts a kind of rough poetic justice by portraying a slave ship caught in a tropical storm. A shark circles,

> And from the Partners of that cruel Trade
> Which spoils unhappy Guinea of her Sons
> Demands his share of Prey, demands themselves.
> The stormy Fates descend: one Death involves
> Tyrants and Slaves; when strait, their mangled Limbs
> Crashing at once, he dyes the purple Seas
> With Gore, and riots in the vengeful Meal.
>
> (*Summer*, lines 1019–25)

The gory scene, which inspired Turner's famous *Slave Ship*, implicitly condemns the "cruel Trade" by imposing a greater cruelty. But it holds back from calling for an end to the trade, or even for banning British participation. Thomson's lines go so far as to make the slaves themselves (perhaps through their African captors) jointly responsible for their fate – who else are the "Partners of that cruel Trade" but the "Tyrants" and "Slaves"?

Even if the slave trade can be safely cordoned off as one of the horrors of the "torrid Zone," far from the green hills and dales of Britain, Thomson at two key points seeks to distinguish the mental traveling of his imperial muse from the voyages of avaricious merchants, bent on exploitation and gain. "Come, my Muse" he says, "the Desart-Barrier burst, / . . . Shoot o'er the Vale of Sennar . . . / Thou art no Ruffian, who beneath the Mask / Of social Commerce, com'st to rob their Wealth" (*Summer*, lines 747–54). Commerce is here only a "Mask," and its "social" aspect a cruel deceit – a sharp rebuke to the ideologues of trade, Thomson among them, who praise its beneficent effects. Why, one may ask, does Thomson bother to *deny* what few readers would have suspected, that the poet is like a merchant, in effect an agent of British imperial expansion, unless the poet suspects it himself? Later, in *Autumn*, Thomson distances himself more completely from the venturing foreign merchant:

> Let others brave the Flood in Quest of Gain,
> And Beat, for joyless Months the gloomy Wave.
> Let such as deem it Glory to destroy
> Rush into Blood, the Sack of Cities seek –
> Unpierc'd, exulting in the Widow's Wail,
> The Virgin's Shriek, and infant's trembling cry.
> Let some, far distant from their native Soil,

Urg'd or by Want or harden'd Avarice,
Find other Lands beneath another Sun.

(Autumn, lines 1278–86)

Foreign trade of the kind that enriches Britain now seems conducted by men whose human sensibilities have been deadened by the avaricious "Quest of Gain." The poet, by contrast, will wrap himself in "conscious Peace," and escape from the world into "still Retreats, and flowery Solitudes" (lines 1302–5).

What drives this kind of merchant is apparently pure self-interest, which throws into relief Thomson's recurrent praise of "social" feeling. "Social" is indeed one of the most common of Thomson's honorific terms in *The Seasons*, a virtual synonym for love – "The Sympathies of Love and Friendship dear, / With all the social Offspring of the Heart" (*Autumn*, lines 1028–29).[29] It is the key element in Benevolence:

> The social Tear would rise, the social Sigh;
> And into clear Perfection, gradual Bliss,
> Refining still, the social Passions work.
>
> *(Winter*, lines 356–58)

As Sambrook notes, "social Love" (*Summer*, lines 939, 1605) is Thomson's "constant theme."[30] It receives such emphasis in his poems, I suggest, in part because Thomson thinks of "self-love" and "social love" not in Popean terms as cooperating principles, the first leading inevitably to the second, but as separate impulses, the latter not only morally superior but often called upon to oppose the dictates of the former. "Heroes, Patriots, and Martyrs," he notes, are "so strongly actuated by Social Love, as frequently to act in direct Contradiction to that of Self."[31] But Thomson is acutely aware that without social love "Liberty" becomes an expression of pure, unlimited self-interest and "self-love," freedom *from* all restraint and all ties. Like Goldsmith later in the century, Thomson seems to have sensed that unrestrained liberty led not to social harmony but to the kind of independence that cuts man off from man. In the paradisal close of *Spring*, married lovers retire from the world and, both at the end of the day and the end of their lives, together "sink in social Sleep" (*Spring*, line 1174). But when love sinks to "sordid Interest" (line 290),

---

[29] Cf. also *Liberty*, IV, line 437 ("social Earth") and *Castle of Indolence*, II, line 20 ("social Commerce").
[30] *James Thomson*, 72.
[31] See his 1726 letter to Aaron Hill, which distinguishes self-love from social love as opposed to those who are "ill-natur'd enough" to find the "Original" of social love in self-love (*Letters and Documents*, 26). Pope derives social love from self-love in *Essay on Man*, III.

> deeply rankling, grows
> The partial Thought, a listless Unconcern
> Cold, and averting from our Neighbour's Good;
> Then dark Disgust and Hatred, winding Wiles,
> Coward Deceit, and ruffian Violence.
> At last, extinct each social Feeling, fell
> And joyless Inhumanity pervades,
> And petrifies the Heart.
> (*Spring*, lines 300–7)[32]

In his darker moments Thomson seems to have thought of such loss of "social Feeling" as man's fallen condition.

THE PATRIOT AND THE POET'S FLAME

Thomson was by no means alone, even among zealous patriots, in worrying that unrestrained commerce and imperial expansion might lead to luxury, moral decline, and ultimately to the general decay of civilization in Britain.[33] Such warnings were commonplace, and do not in themselves form a distinctive feature of Thomson's patriotic poetry. But underlying his doubts and fears about Britain's transformation into a trading empire is a more basic anxiety that would have especially attracted the attention of poets. Thomson seeks to join "the Patriot's with the Poet's Flame," but is this just a poet's foolish dream? Returning to the line in context, we note that his muse "*pants* for public Virtue" (emphasis added) but may not have the "Power" to become herself a "Patriot":

> she,
> Tho' weak of Power, yet strong in ardent Will,
> Whene'er his Country rushes on her Heart,
> Assumes a bolder Note, and fondly tries
> To mix the Patriot's with the Poet's Flame.
> (*Autumn*, lines 18–22)

Perhaps the "bolder Note" is only *assumed* or put on; there may be something "fond" or foolish in the attempt to join poet with patriot, private with public, retired with active life. In a 1730 letter Thomson had claimed that it was "no less my ambition to be capable of serving my country

---

[32] Cf. "Let this thro' Cities work his eager Way, / By legal Outrage and establish'd Guile, / The social sense extinct" (*Autumn*, lines 1287–89).

[33] Suvir Kaul repeatedly emphasizes both Thomson's celebration of British foreign trade and imperial reach as well as the poet's worries about the costs and consequences of empire (*Poems of Nation, Anthems of Empire*, 85, 134, 145, 157, 176).

in an active than in a contemplative way,"[34] though what that active service might be is not made clear: the letter hints only at his ambitions to write an epic poem. But elsewhere in *The Seasons* Thomson suggests that aspirations to public virtue may have to be repressed by those, unlike "Patriots" and "Heroes" (line 597), who can never attain it:

> if doom'd
> In powerless humble Fortune to repress
> These ardent Risings of the kindling Soul,
> Then, even superior to Ambition, we
> Would learn the private Virtues; how to glide
> Thro' Shades and Plains along the smoothest Stream
> Of rural Life.
>
> (*Winter*, lines 597–603)

This is a note of poetic modesty that Thomson could have learned from the ending of *Windsor Forest*, where Pope, whose "humble Muse, in unambitious strains, / Paints the green forests and the flowery plains," defers to Lord Lansdowne, a man "whom this bright court approves, / His sovereign favours, and his country loves" (lines 234–35, 427–28). But unlike Pope, who emphasizes contented retirement, Thomson focuses on repressed ardor and on the poet's "weakness." The poet James Hammond is a figure for the poet who would serve his country – he was both a member of parliament and a member of "Cobham's Cubs," a group of young "Patriots" who gathered around Richard Temple, Viscount Cobham, at Stowe – but is prevented from doing so, in his case by early death:

> Ah why, dear Youth, in all the blooming Prime
> Of vernal Genius, where disclosing fast
> Each active Worth each manly Virtue lay,
> Why wert thou ravish'd from our Hope so soon?
> What now avails that noble Thirst of Fame,
> Which stung thy fervent Breast? That treasured Store
> Of knowledge, early gain'd? That eager Zeal
> To serve thy Country, glowing in the Band
> Of YOUTHFUL PATRIOTS who sustain her Name?
>
> (*Winter*, lines 557–65)

Hammond serves only to "check our fond Pursuits, / And teach our humbled Hopes that Life is vain!" (lines 570–71). Thomson ostensibly draws a broad and conventional moral – that "life is vain" – but his language

---

[34] *Letters and Documents*, 74. Thomson promises, perhaps facetiously, that in a projected tour of Italy he will not travel "like a Poet" (i.e., with an eye for beauties of landscape).

(*fond, humbled*), recalling his own "humble Fortune" and "fond Hopes," suggests that he is thinking specifically of the vain ambitions of would-be patriotic poets to "serve [their] Country."

Why, one might ask, should Thomson put such emphasis on the poet's weakness, at a time when "Patriot" poets like him were being eagerly encouraged and rewarded by leading political figures such as Lyttelton and Chesterfield? By sending his muse or his excursive eye forth on a mental tour of "the torrid Zone" (*Summer*, line 632), Thomson would seem to offer himself as an agent of imperial expansion, implicitly laying Britain's claim to the undeveloped tropics.[35] His views from a "Prospect" (*Summer*, line 690) seek to organize the visual field and (symbolically) possess it. But his "wandering Eye" (line 693) fails to contain the scene: it becomes "lost" (line 693), beholding unframeable "Wastes" of sand (line 963) and natural wealth (line 860). And when he imagines adopting a Roman civilizing role, carrying "the softening Arts of Peace, / Whate'er the humanizing Muses teach" (*Summer*, lines 875–76) as a means of justifying imperial command, he pulls back: wisdom, truth, "Investigation calm" (line 879), and "the Government of Laws" (line 881) cannot be instilled in the "Ill-fated Race" (line 875) that dwells in the torrid zone: "These are not theirs" (line 884). In the remainder of his excursion Thomson beholds "Terrors" and "gloomy Horrors" (lines 1013, 1033).

What led Thomson to hint that, despite his georgic assumptions, there was no public role for the poet to play? The poems, with their apparently sanguine rhetoric, offer no obvious answer, but they do offer a few clues. One clue lies in the pose adopted by the poet in *The Seasons*. If anything apart from the cycle of the four seasons provides Thomson's poem with continuity, it is perhaps the device of the wandering poet, walking through the natural settings he describes, or taking a mental excursion beyond the seas: "I pursue my Walk . . . Long let us walk . . . Should I my Steps turn . . . Hence let me haste . . . Pensive I stray . . . ," and so on.[36] The device is itself conventional – Thomson perhaps borrowed it from Milton's *L'Allegro* and *Il Penseroso*. It suggests that the poet is a man of leisure, a gentleman free from the demands of daily labor and thus at liberty to walk reflectively through the rural scene. Thomson was of course no landed gentleman, but very much a poet largely dependent on the bounty of various patrons. And at times he seems uncomfortable with his pose, as when

---

[35] Shaun Irlam's view in "Gerrymandered Geographies: Exoticism in Thomson and Chateaubriand," *Modern Language Notes*, 108 (Dec. 1993), 891–912.

[36] *Spring*, lines 106, 498, 766; *Summer*, lines 9, 197. Cf. also *Summer*, lines 516, 585, 622, 1379.

he refers to his "vagrant Muse" (*Summer*, line 1101), a word that links the poet not with leisured gentlemen but with the "new-shorn Vagrant," sheep who must be marked with a "Master's Cipher" (*Summer*, lines 407–8) and "vagrant" birds (*Summer*, line 864) rather than industrious insects. The poet, so "vagrant Muse" hints, is himself a kind of vagrant, a landless man (like Thomson himself) who wanders the countryside without settled home or regular work, and maintains himself by begging charity.[37] Such a vagrant in fact appears a little later in *Summer* in the story of Damon and Musidora, when Damon (who, poet-like, writes some penciled "lines") protects Musidora against "each vagrant Foot / And each licentious Eye" (lines 1343–44). Perhaps, so the lines worry, the poet's "Eye" – an organ to which Thomson obsessively returns[38] – is not "sage-instructed" and "pure" (*Spring*, lines 210, 859), but "licentious."

The poet's "wandering Song" sometimes needs to be "recalled" (*Autumn*, line 150) to its main business. His "roving" eye (*Spring*, line 508, cf. "the hurried Eye / Distracted wanders", line 518) is implicitly contrasted to the more productively busy bees at their "delicious Task" (line 508). Furthermore, in a georgic poem that places a high value on labor and "Industry" (*Autumn*, line 43) it is not clear that the poet has any particular *work* to do. To paint the "breathing Prospect" may be a "pleasing Task," but Thomson feels unequal even to that: "Ah, what shall Language do? Ah, where find Words . . . " (*Spring*, lines 474–75). But even if it is "successless," the "Toil" will nonetheless "delight" him (*Spring*, line 480). Elsewhere the task is assigned to someone other than the poet. It is loving parents who enjoy the "Delightful Task" of rearing the "tender Thought" and teaching "the young Idea how to shoot, / To pour the fresh Instruction o'er the Mind" (*Spring*, lines 1152–54).

Perhaps, after all, the poet's work is to provide georgic instruction and advice, but Thomson is consciously neither "Master" nor "Husbandman." In a poem that celebrates the security of British "Property" – "Thy Country teems with Wealth; / And Property assures it to the Swain" (*Summer*, lines 1454–55) – the poet himself is a propertyless man, unless one is to count literary property – which he typically sells to the bookseller.[39] It is only by his patron's invitation he has the right to walk

---

37 Vagrancy – a problem exacerbated by the demobilization of veterans and by enclosures – worried the political projectors of the day. See for example *Proposals for Maintaining of the Poor, and Discouraging of Vagabonds, and Vagrants and Sturdy Beggars* (Edinburgh, 1726) and *Observations upon the Vagrant Laws* (London, 1742).

38 *Spring*, line 956, *Summer*, lines 477, 1386, 1409, 1417, *Winter*, lines 582, 1049.

39 A 1736 letter to Hill suggests that selling copyright, even when it produces a good income, left Thomson troubled: he wishes for "one good Act of Parliament for securing to Authors the Property of their own Works"; he fantasizes about buying back his "Property" in *Liberty* from

in the grounds of Lyttelton's Hagley.[40] When Thomson applies the georgic metaphor to prison reform, urging the need for "the Patriot's weeding Hand" (*Winter*, line 383) to remove tyrannical jailers, he acts as cheerleader from the sidelines.

Thomson seems to have some sense of the poet's traditional role of distributing praise and inspiring emulation, but little or no sense of the poet as "recording muse." Even in *Liberty* he had worried that in an age of corruption the "*recording Arts*" – "monumental Brass," "sculptur'd Marble," and the "deathless Page" – are neglected.[41] He finds Patriots (and patrons) to commend in *The Seasons* – Lyttelton, Chesterfield, Pitt, Peter the Great – but in a curious sense he is displaced by them. Lyttelton is a statesman, but he also discharges the role of poet, "Courting the Muse" as he strays through Hagley Park and wandering "thro' the Philosophic World," climbing the hills to view the "bursting Prospect" (*Spring*, lines 904–62). If Lyttelton the man of public virtue can perform all the functions of the wandering philosopher-poet, what need is there for Thomson? Chesterfield too is both patriot and polished writer, graced by "Apollo's animating Fire." His wit, sense, "Attic Point," and "kind welltemper'd Satire" make him the paragon of "elegant Politeness," and the "vary'd Maze" and "gracious Power" of his eloquence make him a persuasive orator before the "listening Senate." Here is the man who combines the patriot's and the poet's flame. Thomson can only beg that Chesterfield will "Indulge" his muse's "fond Ambition" to have a place "in thy Train," there "to Grace Thee with her Song! / Ere to the Shades again she humbly flies" (*Winter*, lines 656–90).[42] Here again is the *humble* poet with an ambition he knows to be *fond*. Even Peter the Great is a figure who combines, as Thomson implicitly cannot, the active and the contemplative lives: "what his Wisdom plann'd, and Power enforc'd, / More potent still, his great Example showed" (*Winter*, lines 986–87). With such men to shape a nation,[43] what need for poets to instruct them? The

---

Millar; he is shocked that writers who "impress Paper" with "the best and everlasting Riches of all civiliz'd Nations" should have "less Property in the Paper . . . than those who deal in the Rags, which make that Paper" (*Letters and Documents*, 105–6).

[40] Cf. the walk up Richmond Hill for its famous view, from which the poet imagines that he and his "Amanda" can see the surrounding hills, silver Thames, and landscaped estates (*Summer*, lines 1401–37).

[41] As a consequence, the work of the sage, the legislator, the hero, and the patriot are all "in vain" (*Liberty*, v, lines 386–97).

[42] William Pitt is another young political leader with poetic abilities against whom Thomson implicitly compares himself unfavorably. See *Autumn*, lines 1048–57.

[43] In praising Arthur Onslow, Speaker of the House, Thomson emphasizes his eloquence ("while listening Senates hang upon thy Tongue" – *Autumn*, line 15). Cf. the Duke of Argyll, a noted orator in the Lords: "from thy rich Tongue / Persuasion flows, and wins the high Debate" (*Autumn*, lines 940–41).

emphasis lies on Peter's (as on Chesterfield's) "Power" – and by implication on the poet's weakness.

The hints here gathered – suggesting that the poet can no longer hope
to serve his nation in the way he hoped – remain just that, only hints.
But they lie in *The Seasons* for later poets to notice. And they may help
explain the curious tension in Thomson's last great poem, *The Castle of
Indolence*, apparently planned as early as the 1730s but not published until 1748. As commentators have suggested, the *Castle* seems ambivalent
about the attractions of Industry and Indolence. John Sitter observes
that while the "official" meaning of the poem is the triumph of Industry,
Thomson's own "unoffical sympathies" seem to lie rather with Indolence,
and with "the world of reverie and retreat." The Knight of Industry is
accompanied in the poem by a "little Druid wight," perhaps based on
Pope, or on Thomson himself, in either case a figure of diminished potency. Sitter sees in the poem only a "wistful allegiance to the notion of
poetry as a political force."[44] Although critics have recently offered political readings of *The Castle of Indolence*, finding an allegory of indolent Scots
or English gentlemen who need to be roused to civic virtue and Hanoverian industry,[45] Thomson's best biographer has wisely suggested that
evidence for any political allegory – Thomson's contemporaries noticed
none – remains very thin.[46] The poem more clearly seems to meditate
on the poet's own ambivalent engagement with patriotically inflected
poetry. While dwelling in the Castle of Indolence the poet rouses himself
to "sing of War, and Actions fair, / Which the bold Sons of BRITAIN will
inspire" and to paint "the Heroe's Ire, / The Sage's Calm, the Patriot's
noble Rage, / Dashing Corruption down through every worthless Age"
(I, xxxii, lines 3–4, 8–10). These are odd lines from a poet who had already devoted much of his career as a poet to painting the patriot's noble
rage dashing corruption. Did he wonder whether it was all for nought?
Odd too, since in the following stanzas the poet sings not of the hero and
the patriot but of the delicious pleasures of the pavilions of Indolence.
In the second canto the call to action must be delivered again, this time
by the Knight of Industry, whose "chosen Isle" is Britain (II, xviii, line 3).
Having retired, Cincinnatus-like, from his role as lawgiver to the country,
where he successfully "Commixed the Chief, the Patriot, and the Swain"

---

[44] *Literary Loneliness*, 95, 94.
[45] See Scott, *James Thomson, Anglo-Scot*, 278–79; Barrell, *English Literature in History*, 89; and Christine
Gerrard, "*The Castle of Indolence* and the Opposition to Walpole," *Review of English Studies*, 41
(1990), 45–64.
[46] Sambrook, *James Thomson*, 269–70.

(II, xxv, line 4), the Knight, summoned back to save the state, warns that
if mortals only indulged the pleasures of indolence

> Great Homer's Song had never fir'd the Breast
> To Thirst of Glory and heroic Deeds;
> ...
> Dumb too, had been the sage Historic Muse,
> And perish'd all the Sons of antient Fame;
> Those starry Lights of Virtue, that diffuse
> Through the dark Depth of Time their vivid Flame,
> Had all been lost with Such as have no Name.
> Who then had scorn'd his Ease for others' Good?
> Who then had toil'd rapacious Men to tame?
> Who in the Public Breach devoted stood,
> And for his Country's Cause been prodigal of Blood?
>   (II, lii, lines 1–2, liii, lines 1–9)

If the Knight is convinced of his own plea that the poet perform his traditional role of inspiring "heroic Deeds" and then conferring "Fame,"
his rhetoric does not show it: his negatives ("Great Homer's song had
never fired the Breast") and his series of questions ("Who . . . ? Who . . . ?
Who . . . ?") fall short of confident assertion that the poet's patriotic
words can prompt his countrymen to patriotic action. The "Swain" and
"Patriot" may be "commixed," but perhaps it will not prove possible, as
Thomson had hoped, to "mix the Patriot's with the Poet's Flame."

Thomson then seems to have left a double legacy for the poets who
read and appropriated his work: on the one hand, a politically engaged
writer who openly enlisted under the banner of the "Patriot" Opposition
and frankly embraced public themes, setting forth an idealized vision
of a British present (or future); on the other, a poet who allowed into
his poems doubts about the very land of freedom he celebrated, and
underlying doubts about what public role the poet, as poet, might hope
to play in his country's future.[47]

---

47 Johnson, always skeptical about the political enthusiasm of poet-patriots, regarded Thomson not
as a patriot but a "poet": "he looks round on Nature and on Life with the eye which Nature
bestows only on a *poet* [emphasis added], the eye that distinguishes in every thing presented to it
whatever there is on which the imagination can delight to be detained" (*Lives*, III, 298–99).

CHAPTER 4

Mark Akenside: "great citizen of Albion"

For most readers of eighteenth-century poetry, Akenside remains a lesser "poet of sensibility," author of *The Pleasures of Imagination*, a precursor of Wordsworth, and a minor practitioner of the ode, overshadowed in that fashionable poetic form of the 1740s and 1750s by his contemporaries Collins and Gray. But a fresh look at Akenside's two books of odes, published in 1745 and 1760, prompts the rediscovery of what was once a commonplace – that he is a vigorously political poet.[1] When Akenside's politics have attracted the attention of biographers and literary historians, they have been persistently and melodramatically mischaracterized as radical Whiggism – even republicanism – ending in apostasy. It would be more accurate to describe Akenside as a "Patriot" Whig who came to political maturity in the last years of Walpole's administration, and who preserved his principles for the remainder of his public life. Furthermore, the full implications of his "politics" – obscured by what Johnson dismissively called his "rage for liberty" – show that he ambitiously conceived of a significant public role for the poet as small-*p* patriot.

Before focusing on the literary dimension of his patriotism, however, it is best to clarify the nature of Akenside's political commitments. That avowed republicanism is an unlikely political stance in mid-eighteenth-century England has not deterred the repetition of claims that Akenside in his youth held "radical" and "republican" views.[2] Even

---

[1] Sitter (*Literary Loneliness*, 114–20) recognizes the patriotic–political side of Akenside, but emphasizes his indulgence of fancy and pensive retreat. The strongest case for Akenside as politically informed poet is made in Harriet Jump's 1987 Oxford D. Phil. thesis, "Mark Akenside and the Poetry of Current Events, 1738–1770."

[2] See, for example, George Saintsbury: "windy, theoretical republicanism" (*Peace of the Augustans* [London, 1916], 83); Charles T. Houpt: "republican tendencies" (*Mark Akenside: A Biographical and Critical Study* [Philadelphia, 1944], 96, cf. 118); George Rousseau: "radical, republican views" (*The Perilous Enlightenment: Pre- and Post-Modern Discourses* [Manchester, 1991], 137; cf. 127); John

recent Akenside scholars have accepted this idea.[3] The idea of Akenside as republican is in fact an old one: it probably derives less from his poems than from the satirical portrait of a "republican" physician in Smollett's *Peregrine Pickle* (1751).[4] But literary historians have incautiously concluded that Smollett, fellow physician and London litterateur, was speaking about Akenside on the basis of first-hand knowledge as well as common reputation. They forget that Smollett was primarily writing as a satirist, with license to invent and exaggerate. Furthermore, the future Tory propagandist was ready, like many of his party, to paint a noted "Whig" as a political extremist.

The evidence for republican principles or sympathies is in fact very thin. Those who claim to find republicanism quote the same handful of examples from Akenside's poems and letters, but when those examples are looked at carefully, the republicanism disappears.[5] The earliest example occurs in a youthful letter in which Akenside expresses admiration for James Harrington and Algernon Sidney, but Harrington's principles – the fount of "Country Party" ideology – were fully consistent with loyalty to a constitutional monarch, and Sidney was commonly honored in the eighteenth century for his principled resistance to the tyranny of the largely discredited Stuarts. When, in the same letter Akenside says that the word *king* "has naturally a bad or sordid idea," the context is not the political world but the "intellectual World," in which, as in the republic of letters, no man is subject to the sovereign authority of a "king."[6] When, in the early ode "On Leaving Holland," Freedom "tells a monarch on his throne, / Tells him he reigns, he lives but by her voice,"[7] the sentiment is perfectly consistent with conventional mid-century ideas about England's limited (not absolute) monarchy, in which the King is

Mahoney: "nearly republican politics" (*Dictionary of Literary Biography*, vol. 109, *Eighteenth-Century British Poets: Second Series*, ed. John Sitter [Detroit, 1991], 8).

3 Harriet Jump: "enduring reputation for republican principles" ("High Sentiments of Liberty: Coleridge's Unacknowledged Debt to Akenside," *Studies in Romanticism*, 28 [1989], 212); Robin Dix: "republican undertones"(*The Poetical Works of Mark Akenside*, 481, 492, and "The Literary Relationship of Mark Akenside and David Fordyce," *Scottish Literary Journal*, 23 [1996], 17).

4 The episode in question appears in chapter 47. See Howard S. Buck, "Smollett and Dr. Akenside," *JEGP*, 31 (1932), 10–26.

5 For detailed discussion, see Dustin Griffin, "Akenside's Political Muse," in Robin Dix, ed., *Mark Akenside: A Reassessment* (London, 2000), 20–24.

6 The letter is quoted from the transcription by Robin Dix in "The Literary Relationship of Mark Akenside and David Fordyce," 14.

7 Akenside's poems are generally quoted from *The Poetical Works of Mark Akenside*, ed. Robin Dix, hereafter cited as *Poetical Works*. In this instance, I cite lines 26–28 from the 1745 edition of the poem (regarded by some critics as more "republican" than the 1760 edition).

not above the law, and in which monarchy (within a mixed government) and liberty are wholly compatible.[8]

In the later ode "To Francis Earl of Huntingdon" his country is again the land of "freedom," where

> empire's wide-establish'd throne
> No private master fills:
> Where, long foretold, the People reigns:
> Where each a vassal's humble heart disdains;
> And judgeth what he sees; and, as he judgeth, wills.
>
> (*Poetical Works*, 304)

An anachronistic reading might find incipient republican – even democratic – sentiment here: the reign of "the People." But in eighteenth-century political language "the People" usually refers not to the entire citizenry but to "the political nation" – the traditional political class who elect the members of the Commons and who participate in government. "The swelling democratic tide" (*Poetical Works*, 304) is not welcomed as a sign of liberation; it is watched closely as a sign of imbalance in England's carefully mixed and balanced government, in which neither King, nor nobles, nor commons should become too powerful, in which faction and partisan politics threaten to divide and weaken the country. The tenth Earl of Huntingdon, Akenside's addressee, would hardly have welcomed or even countenanced the expression of "republican" sentiments.

Akenside's context, furthermore, contrasts the "wide-establish'd [i.e., solidly settled and broadly accepted] throne" of Huntingdon's day with the dark days of feudalism, in which Huntingdon's ancestors quarreled with other powerful barons, leading their tenants (who owed military service to their lord) into battle for a merely "private strife" while the weak kings of the day stood by in impotence or fear. Huntingdon's king, by contrast, is "No private master." He rules in the name of the people and the public good. His independent-minded subjects disdain to consider themselves humble "vassals" of an overlord. Freeborn Englishmen, they judge things for themselves. All the "valiant sons" of freedom enjoy her "equal throne" (lines 131–32) – "equal," a Latinism, here means fair, equitable, impartial[9] – since their liberties under the law are guaranteed to them, and all are equal before the law.[10] They are also "conscious of

---

[8] Cf. "An Epistle to Curio," where the British people are a "Race Erect!" with "native Strength of Soul, / Which Kings, nor Priests, nor sordid Laws controul" (lines 189–90).

[9] *OED*, 5, from the Latin *aequus*. Cf. "equal law" ("To Drake," line 28).

[10] Cf. James Thomson, on Britain as "The Land where, *King* and *People* equal bound / By guardian Laws" (*Liberty*, I, lines 318–19).

her cares" – i.e., careful to preserve their freedoms, and in that sense they "share" the "power, that rules [them]" (lines 133–34). In mid-eighteenth-century England "the People" may be said to "reign" since the monarch, as even a Tory like Johnson believed, ruled by the consent of the people.

When these few repeatedly cited examples of alleged republicanism are reconsidered in full context, Akenside's politics become recognizable as those of a mid-century Whig "Patriot," eager to preserve and champion English "liberties," alert to the dangers of an entrenched ministry that ruled, as did Walpole's, by corruption, and impatient to defend British interests abroad by aggressive action against Spain and France.[11] Like many a "Patriot," Akenside called for war against Spain in his *British Philippic* (1738). In a 1742 letter to Fordyce he reported himself "quite sick of politics – our present politics, I mean," as well he might in the disappointing aftermath of the fall of Walpole. In the *Epistle to Curio* (1744), he denounced the apostasy of the Patriot leader William Pulteney. Also in 1744, he enthusiastically supported England's decision to join the War of the Austrian Succession against France as the efforts of "a mighty and free people proclaiming war against the most formidable people in the world, in defence of justice and drawn to it by the disinterested succour of an oppress'd and insulted ally."[12] His letter to Fordyce takes a similarly high-minded "Patriot" view of how English politics ought to be conducted at home, praising that "independence" and "manly and rational spirit of thinking and acting which ought to be the very end of society."[13] When in a 1754 ode he praised "generous William" and condemned the "ignoble reign" of James II ("To Drake," lines 38, 40), he was uttering standard Hanoverian Whig doctrine. And in 1758, after the early setbacks in the Seven Years' War, his *Ode to the Country Gentlemen of England* was read by the *Monthly Review* as a "patriot performance" and a "call to arms."[14] Johnson, who did not (after the mid 1740s) think English liberties were threatened, and who harbored grave doubts about the advisability of England's war for empire, judged Akenside's politics severely: "He certainly retained an unnecessary and outrageous zeal for what he called and thought liberty."[15] But he pointedly does not call Akenside a "republican." What Johnson thought Akenside's "envious desire of plundering wealth or degrading greatness"

---

[11] Neither Gerrard, *Patriot Opposition*, nor Harris, *A Patriot Press*, has much to say about Akenside.
[12] A letter to his patron, Jeremiah Dyson, 21 April 1744, quoted in Alexander Dyce, ed., *The Poetical Works of Mark Akenside* (London, 1857), xxii.
[13] Dyce, ed., *Poetical Works of Akenside*, lxxxiii.   [14] *Monthly Review*, 18 (April 1758), 335–36.
[15] *Lives*, III, 411.

and "impetuous eagerness to subvert and confound, with very little care what shall be established" (412) links him in Johnson's thinking with Milton,[16] but also with mid-eighteenth-century Whigs and Patriots who clamored to limit the power of the throne, and were, so Johnson thought, "not willing to be governed."[17]

After 1760 Akenside's politics, in the traditional account, changed "entirely and radically," when both the poet and his patron Jeremiah Dyson accepted places under the new king George III and the new administration of Lord Bute. According to one eighteenth-century observer who knew them both, Dyson and Akenside became "bigoted adherents to Lord Bute and the Tories, having at every earlier period been, as it were, the High Priests of the opposite Creed."[18] The claim of apostasy was taken up by Akenside's foremost nineteenth-century editor, Alexander Dyce, and by twentieth-century critics who pointed to revisions in Akenside's poems that allegedly display a tempering of the political radicalism of his youth.[19] But it is important to note that the source of the idea of Akenside's apostasy was George Hardinge, a Whig who confessed that he took his political principles from his uncle, the great Whig Lord Chancellor, Lord Camden. No admirer of Lord Bute, Hardinge, writing more than fifty years after the alleged apostasy, was not an unbiased observer.[20]

Furthermore, to accept office or favor from Lord Bute should not mark a man of Whig principles as a turncoat. After all, many Whigs held office under George III, including the Great Commoner, Pitt himself (an ally of Lord Camden). It was Bute's stated policy not to govern through the Tories but simply to admit them – along with the long-established Whig oligarchy – to a share of government. Dyson, who succeeded Hardinge's father Nicholas as Clerk of the House of Commons in 1748, accepted a place as Cofferer to the Royal Household,[21] and he was

---

[16] Cf. the similar phrasing in Johnson's account of Milton's politics: "Milton's republicanism was . . . founded in an envious hatred of greatness, and a sullen desire of independence; in petulance impatient of control, and pride disdainful of superiority . . . His predominant desire was to destroy rather than establish" (*Lives*, I, 157).

[17] From an uncorrected proof page of *Taxation no Tyranny*, in *Political Writings*, 455n.

[18] George Hardinge, in John Nichols, *Literary Anecdotes of the Eighteenth Century*, 9 vols. (London, 1812–15), VIII, 523.

[19] See Jeffrey Hart, "Akenside's Revision of *The Pleasures of Imagination*," *PMLA*, 74 (1959), 68; Michael Meehan, *Liberty and Poetics in Eighteenth-Century England* (London, 1986), 52.

[20] Writing in 1813, Hardinge acknowledged that he was "the victim" of Akenside's and Dyson's "politics," and that after 1761 there was a "coolness between us" (Nichols, *Literary Anecdotes*, VIII, 523).

[21] Houpt, *Mark Akenside*, 156.

no doubt instrumental in securing for Akenside in September 1761 one of the places as Physician-in-Ordinary to the Queen. (Perhaps his friend Francis Hastings, Earl of Huntingdon, who became Groom of the Stole in 1761, also put in a good word.)[22] It is likely that what attracted ministerial attention were not Akenside's political principles (any more than did Johnson's politics when he received a pension from Bute in 1762), but his standing as a well-established London physician. He was the author of several medical works, had obtained medical degrees from Leiden and Cambridge, had served as a medical lecturer at the College of Physicians, was Physician at St. Thomas's Hospital and Assistant Physician at the school of Christ's Hospital, and in October 1759 had delivered the prestigious Herveian lecture to the College of Physicians. The lecture was published the next year. If Bute wanted to secure the services of the best physicians for the Queen, and wanted to be seen to be rewarding merit wherever he found it, he could hardly have done better than to have offered a place to Akenside. By accepting the place, Akenside was not obliged to become a "bigoted" Tory. And there is little or no evidence that he revised the political Whiggery of his poems of the 1740s.

One often-cited instance of such political revision is the line in *The Pleasures of Imagination* (1744) about "Harmony" attended by "Truth" and "Her sister Liberty" (I, lines 20, 23–24). In the revised *Pleasures of the Imagination* (1772) the line refers to Harmony attended by "Wise Order" and "Her sister, Liberty" (I, lines 40–41). Several critics have suspected political significance in the substitution of "Order" for "Truth," suggesting that Akenside, having signed on as a placeman, now assigns a higher value to "Order" than he once did.[23] But there is nothing distinctively "Tory" about "Order,"[24] and in any case Akenside had in the earlier version of the poem already invoked "Order."[25] If the lines are simply examined for their sense, it might be argued that Order more properly serves as "guardian" than Truth, and that the pairing of Order and Liberty, a combination of potential opposites, is superior to the pairing of Truth and Liberty, which are only linked by convention.

---

[22] Akenside's friend Dr. Caleb Hardinge was Physician Extraordinary to the King (Charles Bucke, *On the Life, Writings, and Genius of Akenside* [London, 1832], 78).

[23] George Hardinge was the first of them (Nichols, *Literary Anecdotes*, VIII, 525).

[24] Bucke finds "no derogation of principle" (*Life, Writings, and Genius*, 140) and Dyce nothing "indicative of violent Tory zeal in the alteration" (Dyce, ed., *Poetical Works of Akenside*, 81).

[25] A point made by Robin Dix, *Poetical Works*, 464. The revision in question may have been made as early as 1757, the date Dyson assigns to Book I of the revised poem (*Poetical Works*, 46), and thus well before Akenside accepted his place.

Another instance of alleged political revision concerns the lines in the ode "On Leaving Holland" that in 1760 say that Liberty "tells a monarch on his throne, / He reigns not but by her preserving voice." In the 1745 version Liberty "tells a monarch on his throne, / Tells him he reigns, he lives but by her voice" (*Poetical Works*, 263). Some have suspected a softening of the "republican" sentiment.[26] But the political sense of the 1745 lines – that the King "reigns" with the support or "voice" of Liberty – remains the same in 1760.[27] The change might be justified on grounds of sense: the 1745 version contains two limp redundancies ("tells a monarch...tells" and "he reigns, he lives") that Akenside removed in the tighter 1760 version.

In short, the evidence for a moderation of Akenside's earlier ideas about liberty and monarchy seems very weak. He probably remained what he always was – a Patriot Whig who with his like-minded contemporaries put his emphasis where Whigs always put it, on the liberty of the people rather than the authority of the crown. In this respect Akenside perhaps deserves to be remembered not as a republican but as a political poet, and "the greatest poetic spokesman, after Milton, for the cause of liberty."[28] But there were many spokesmen for the cause of liberty in the eighteenth century. What makes Akenside distinctive and a significant figure at mid-century are not his political opinions but his claims for the political function of poetry and his poetic implementation of those claims.

POLITICAL ODES

Poets after 1740 are said to have turned away from the verse *epistle* – a social form (commonly in couplets) addressed to a friend and implicitly to the reader and the larger world – in favor of the *ode* – an oracular form (commonly stanzaic) addressed not to anyone in particular or to an abstraction. Such poems as Collins' "Ode on the Poetical Character" or "Ode to Evening" and Gray's ode on "The Progress of Poesy," it is suggested, indicate that mid-century poets were typically preoccupied with their own sensibilities and with the possibilities for (or the impossibility

---

[26] The first was Andrew Kippis, in *Biographia Britannica*, 2nd. edn., 5 vols. (London, 1778–93), I, 105.
[27] Here I disagree with Dix, who finds the 1745 lines contain a "more explicitly republican" sentiment (*Poetical Works*, 481). Bucke (*Life, Writings and Genius*, 141) found "no difference...that can be twisted into any...variation of sentiment."
[28] Meehan, *Liberty and Poetics*, 53, on Akenside's eighteenth-century reputation.

of) poetry in their day. Akenside himself devoted several odes to the uses of poetry ("On Lyric Poetry," "On the Use of Poetry") and to his own poetic aspirations ("To the Muse," "On a Sermon Against Glory," "To Sleep," "At Study"). A number of other odes are of the smaller Horatian kind, dealing with intimate experience (love, suspicion, cheerfulness). But Akenside also wrote a number of more ambitious "greater" odes on political topics, particularly for about a decade from the late 1740s through the late 1750s. A review of these half-dozen poems underscores the idea that for him the ode is by no means always a meditative-rhapsodical exercise in solipsism. It is often a social form – an ode addressed, commonly upon a particular occasion, to a named friend or public figure. Many of Akenside's "odes" are in fact verse epistles in all but name and verse form.[29] He addressed a number of his odes to contemporary political leaders: to "Curio" (a transparent disguise for William Pulteney); to Sir Francis Henry Drake, a baronet and Whig MP from Devon; to the Hon. Charles Townshend, MP, nephew of a prime minister, member of the Board of Trade, and future Chancellor of the Exchequer; to the young Francis Hastings, tenth Earl of Huntingdon; to Benjamin Hoadly, the well-connected Whiggish Bishop of Winchester; and to "the Country Gentlemen of England."

In one of those odes to a young political leader, Akenside declared explicitly that the task of the poet in a land of freedom is to take up "public themes" and "public arguments." In absolutist Florence and France poets may be forgiven for retiring from "public themes," for what could they write but flattery of priests and tyrants? To write on such themes can bring nothing except "venal honors to an hateful lord." But England is different.

> Here let the bard, whose dastard tongue
> Leaves public arguments unsung,
>   Bid public praise farewell:
> Let him to fitter climes remove,
> Far from the hero's and the patriot's love,
> And lull mysterious monks to slumber in their cell.
>   ("To Huntingdon," lines 135–40)

It is only by writing on "public arguments" that a poet may hope to win "public praise." And indeed, it can be said that Akenside devoted his

---

[29] Of the thirty-three odes in Akenside's two books, fourteen are addressed to a "friend" or a named addressee.

attention for twenty years – though not exclusively – to matters of great public moment: the agitation for war against Spain in 1738, the disgrace of Pulteney in 1742, the Jacobite rising in 1745,[30] the continuing military and cultural threat from France, the "near and loud alarms" occasioned by French victories in the first years of the Seven Years' War, and the controversy over the Militia Bill of 1757. In its account of the ode "To the Country Gentlemen of England," the *Monthly Review* declared that its verses "glow with the sacred fire of liberty," and that "our publick-spirited Doctor well deserves to be stiled, *The Poet of the Community.*"[31]

The greatest "public argument" of course, from Akenside's point of view, is British "liberty," and Akenside addressed that theme throughout his work, from the *British Philippic* of 1738 – a poem also published under the title *The Voice of Liberty* – to the revised *Pleasures of the Imagination*, published posthumously. To Johnson, Akenside's "outrageous zeal" for liberty may have seemed "unnecessary" in a country where liberty was secured. But to other readers such zeal was commendable. The *Monthly Review* in 1772 observed that instead of limiting himself to lighter topics Akenside throughout his career had applied his genius "to the interests of truth, of morals, or civil and religious liberty."[32]

Akenside himself took the view that liberty should always be on a poet's mind. Thus the early ode "On Leaving Holland" closes with a panegyrical apostrophe to his "native land," in which "freedom" itself is hailed as the "Great citizen of Albion" (line 66). In a later ode entitled "The Remonstrance of Shakespeare" appears another apostrophe to England, chosen by heaven "To check the inroads of barbaric power" – so much for the vaunted "civilization" of France! – and "The rights of trampled nations to reclaim" (lines 91–93). And in *The Pleasures of Imagination* (1744) the arts thrive in England because "freedom's ample fabric" has long been "fix'd . . . / on Albion's happy shore," where it serves as a "common mansion, a parental roof" for the Virtues, the Muses, and the

---

[30] See the sneering reference to "that servile band [of Jacobite supporters who hesitated to take up arms on behalf of Charles Edward, but remain a threat to political stability] who kneel / To freedom's banish'd foes; / That monster, which is daily found / Expert and bold thy country's peace to wound; / Yet dreads to handle arms, nor manly counsel knows" ("To Huntingdon," lines 176–80).

[31] *Monthly Review*, 18 (April 1758), 336. "Our Poet," the reviewer goes on, "after exposing the extreme folly, as well as danger, of trusting entirely to either our fleets or standing armies, for the defence of Britain, which, (in proportion to its wealth, will only prove the more tempting to invaders)," urges the country gentlemen to become master of "the only art by which these invaluable blessings can be preserved to themselves, and transmitted to posterity."

[32] In a review of the revised *Pleasures of the Imagination*, *Monthly Review*, 48 (Dec. 1772), 436.

Graces.[33] In a note to the ode to Huntingdon, Akenside declares that *"great poetical talents, and high sentiments of liberty, do reciprocally produce and assist each other"* (*Poetical Works*, 355). (To David Hume, who asked why poetry had flourished in absolutist France, Akenside would have complained, as he did in "The Remonstrance of Shakespeare," that French dramatic art was a kind of "fettered" eloquence, "gentle prattle" on love, "nought but what the king may hear.")

Akenside even claims that English freedom has stimulated the rejoining of philosophy and poetry in such philosophical poems as his own: "the general spirit of liberty," growing ever since the Revolution, "naturally invited our men of wit and genius to improve that influence which the arts of persuasion gave them with the people, by applying them to subjects of importance to society" (Akenside's own note to *The Pleasures of Imagination*, II, line 30, *Poetical Works*, 162). It may have been words such as these which led Johnson to complain that Akenside's zeal for liberty was "unnecessary" in a philosophical poem about the pleasures of imagination. Akenside's implicit response is that the implications of his poem go beyond the workings of imagination. His purpose, he noted in "The Design," was no less than to "dispose the minds of men to a similar taste and habit of thinking in religion, morals, and civil life" (*Poetical Works*, 88).

In Akenside's view the poet's role was not simply to address "public themes" and to assert British liberty. Remembering the example of Pindar, whose odes serve as a model for his own, Akenside called for the English poet once again to play a vital role in the public life of his nation, as Pindar had done, recording great deeds, conferring honor on those who perform them, and inspiring readers to emulate their example. For an epigraph for his 1745 *Odes*, Akenside chose Greek lines from Pindar's eighth Nemean Ode: "... until I am buried I will continue to praise the praiseworthy and cast blame on the guilty."[34] The Pindar he praises is not the mythical poet who was fed by Apollo, and on whose lips bees once settled and gave him sweetness,[35] but the bold Theban whose song was bitter rather than sweet, and provoked his readers not

---

33 Akenside's prose argument states that the poem deals with the reunion of the works of imagination and the works of philosophy "under the influence of public liberty." Cf. also Akenside's note on "the general spirit of liberty." On the old (and still vigorously renewed in the eighteenth century) theme that the arts thrive under conditions of freedom, see Meehan, *Liberty and Poetics*, passim.

34 Robin Dix's translation (*Poetical Works*, 475).

35 In a note (*Poetical Works*, 354), Akenside contrasts such mere "tradition" with the "real historical facts" of Pindar's political stance.

to praise but to vengeance:

> proud to unfold
> What thy base rulers trembled to behold;
> Amid corrupted Thebes was proud to tell
> The deeds of Athens and the Persian shame.
> Hence on thy head their impious vengeance fell.
>
> (lines 71–75)

Despite the dangers, Pindar remained "faithful" to his own reputation as liberty's champion.[36] The ultimate end of Pindar's account of the great deeds is not simply to confer honor upon heroes but to inspire emulation in his listeners, "and other minds to virtue raise" (line 79).

In Akenside's own high conception of poetry, the task of the bard in mid-eighteenth-century England is to celebrate heroic achievement and nourish the spirit of freedom. God himself keeps "the faithful records" of human actions, but (as it were) bids the poets to act as his agents on earth, to

> Dispose of honor and of scorn;
> Discern the patriot from the slave;
> And write the good, the wise, the brave,
> For lessons to the multitude unborn.
>
> ("To Huntingdon," lines 237–40)

Mindful of his public function, the poet serves as recording historian, discerning judge, and the one who disposes of or bestows honor. Although he disapproved of Akenside's politics, Johnson shared this traditional conception of the poet's moral responsibilities. "To encourage merit with praise," Johnson wrote in *Rambler*, 136, "is the great business of literature," and to preserve the "distinction" between good and evil essential to that end. It is the "sons of learning," says Johnson, who have the "power of bestowing" the "honours of a lasting name."

When moved by the example of Alcaeus and Pindar, Akenside writes not only to instruct –

> How life its noblest use may find,
> How well for freedom be resign'd;
> And how, by glory, virtue shall be crown'd.
>
> ("To Huntingdon," lines 38–40)

---

[36] In Akenside's pantheon, Pindar is akin to Alcaeus, praised earlier in the same poem as the exiled "Lesbian patriot," "Devoting shame and vengeance to her lords, / With louder impulse and a threatening land" ("On Lyric Poetry," 22–24). Akenside's 1745 note identifies Alcaeus as "ALCAEUS of Mitylene, the capital of Lesbos, who fled from his native city to escape the oppression of those who had inslav'd it, and wrote against them in his exile those noble invectives which are so much applauded by the ancient Critics" (in *Poetical Works*, 352).

– but also to inspire political courage:

> They best the soul with glory fire;
> They noblest counsels, boldest deeds inspire;
> And high o'er Fortune's rage inthrone the fixed heart.
>
> ("To Huntingdon," lines 8–10)

His words will "move" the soul of the listener "with noblest passions" (line 152), will "throw incense on the vestal flame / Of liberty" ("On Lyric Poetry," lines 113–14). "Letters and the Muses powerful art" serve to "Exalt the ingenuous heart, / And brighten every form of just and true. / . . . lend a nobler sway / To civil wisdom, than corruption's lure / Could ever yet produce" ("To Townshend in the Country," lines 162–67).[37]

To inspire champions of liberty, Akenside chose to address his political odes not to the widely known "Patriot" heroes of the 1740s and 1750s but to several little-known patrician MPs at the beginning of their careers – Charles Townshend, Francis Hastings, Francis Henry Drake – of whom only Townshend ever attained eminence. Perhaps because he is exhorting unproven young men by means of precept and remote (typically classical or seventeenth-century) rather than recent example, there remains in the minds of many readers something abstract or merely theoretical about Akenside's call to action. Does it reveal a rhetorical weakness, or a deeper anxiety beneath the confident declamation about English liberties?[38] Why Akenside should not have been able to find any English political leader worth emulating since the days of Somers and "Nassau, great deliverer, wise and bold,"[39] remains unclear. Pulteney had once seemed to be the hero he looked for, but had bitterly disappointed all Patriot hopes in 1742, and this perhaps made Akenside wary of great men, including such Patriot heroes as Frederick, Prince of Wales, and William Pitt the "Patriot Minister."[40] His 1744 *Epistle to Curio* may be his farewell to all that. Nor does Akenside celebrate mid-century military heroes such as Admiral Vernon or the Duke of Cumberland, even though he voiced strong support for naval war with Spain in 1738 and land war

---

37 When Akenside declares in the ode "On Lyric Poetry" that in order to celebrate British heroes and liberty he needs "Nor Theban voice nor Lesbian lyre," he is not repudiating the Theban Pindar or Lesbian Alcaeus as models. Rather, he concludes his poem about Greek lyric poetry with an assertion that he is not simply an imitator: he finds inspiration in his own "genius" and "presaging mind."

38 Cf. the end of the ode "To Curio" where Akenside urges the champions of liberty to "protect her from yourselves," from "selfish fierceness" prompted by luxury and commerce, and from "fantastic demagogues."

39 See "To the Hon. Charles Townshend in the Country. 1750," lines 71–74, 131–40. Akenside also names Fairfax and Pym.

40 Akenside supported Pitt's policies (the 1757 Militia Act, for example), but he nowhere praises him – or even names him – in his poems.

on the Continent in the early 1740s. There is perhaps something unreal about his bold assertion in 1745 that "From envy and from death" he will "claim / A hero bleeding for his native land" ("On Lyric Poetry," lines 111–12).[41]

His 1748 ode "To Huntingdon" hints, too, that for him the experience of the 1745 Jacobite rising, though in the end a victory for English liberties and Protestantism, was ultimately a sign of British weakness rather than strength. In Akenside's account the rising was not a foreign invasion funded by French papists (as some contemporaries portrayed it) but a civil war – "Our fields in civil blood imbru'd" (line 212) – betraying some internal defect. It was no trivial challenge to Hanoverian supremacy: the "barbarous host" of Charles Edward's Highland soldiers seized fully "half the astonish'd isle" before they were turned back. At this point in the poem one expects a tribute to the defenders of the Hanoverian throne. But rather than singing the glory of loyal resistance to "papal snares and lawless arms" (line 199) – his tribute in the previous stanza to the those who made the Revolution of 1688[42] – Akenside turns instead to the cowardice of English Jacobites who did not rush to the support of their lord:

> Did one of all that vaunting train,
> Who dare affront a peaceful reign,
> Durst one in arms appear?
> Durst one in counsels pledge his life?
> Stake his luxurious fortunes in the strife?
> Or lend his boasted name his vagrant friend to chear?
>
> (lines 215–20)

One wonders whether the questions are implicitly directed not only at the enemies of the "peaceful reign" but also at its friends. Why, the poem implicitly asks, was there no greater patriotic defense? The ode identifies no heroes of the '45, and closes with an implicit challenge to its addressee. The English Jacobites, he says to Huntingdon, are the ones "Who challenge to themselves thy country's love" (line 222) – that is, they claim to be true patriots. Akenside's reply – "let their works declare them" (line 225) – while contrasting Huntingdon's "free" and

---

[41] Unless Akenside refers here not to a contemporary English hero but to a figure from Greek history. He was planning an epic poem on Timoleon.

[42] Akenside distinguished between good plots and bad ones: he commends "Ca[ve]ndish, Booth, and Osborne" (line 196) for having "privately concerted the plan of the Revolution" in what later became known as "*the plotting parlor*" [Akenside's note to line 192], but condemns the "confederate hours" and "lurking slander" of Jacobite plotters (lines 227–28).

"generous" powers with the enemy's "lurking slander," is in effect directed at all who claim to be patriots. Akenside's stirring political odes in fact may mask his doubts about England's political virtue, the same doubts that provided John Brown's gloomy *Estimate of the Manners and Principles of the Times* with such a receptive audience when it appeared in 1757.

Akenside's stern ode "To the Country Gentlemen of England" (1758), like Brown's *Estimate*, urges its audience to forsake the pursuit of "pleasure's lying tales" ("riot's orgies" and "the gamester's dark, destroying snare") and the lure of the "courtly shrine." The animus of the ode is focused sharply not only by the threat represented by France in the third year of the Seven Years' War – the great British victories were still a year away – but by the resistance to Pitt's Militia Act of 1757. Akenside's task is to convince the "country gentlemen," traditionally suspicious of the designs of the central administration in London, that instead of delegating the defense of the nation to foreign mercenaries, they ought to take up their traditional responsibilities of teaching "war's heroic arts" to the sons of their tenants:

> Ye chiefly, heirs of Albion's cultur'd plains,
> Ye leaders of her bold and faithful swains,
> Now not unequal to your birth be found:
> The public voice bids arm your rural state,
> Paternal hamlets for your ensigns wait,
> And grange and fold prepare to pour their youth around.
>
> (*Poetical Works*, 339)

Akenside appeals both to the sense of ancient honor ("Europe's ancient spirit," "the laurels which your fathers won," "the old simplicity") and to modern shame (that English warmaking should be left to mercenaries, "slavish ruffians, hir'd for their command"). The virtues he praises are those of the Harringtonian "Country gentleman." They are also the virtues of the "warrior," a word which Akenside does not hesitate to use.[43]

But this ode is not typical of Akenside's political poems, which more commonly treat the victories of peace than war, the force of eloquence than the force of arms. Benjamin Hoadly, Bishop of Winchester, is a more characteristic hero. He is a champion of liberty and even a "conqueror,"

---

43 By making the implementation of the unpopular Militia Act a test of patriotism, Akenside was implicitly taking part in a Pittite publicity campaign. For analysis of the debate, see Eliga Gould, "'What Is the Country?': Patriotism and the Language of Popularity During the English Militia Reform of 1757," in Gerald Maclean, Donna Landry, Joseph P. Ward, eds., *The Country and the City Revisited: England and the Politics of Culture, 1550–1850* (Cambridge, 1999), 123.

but not a warrior:

> For not a conqueror's sword,
> Nor the strong powers to civil founders known,
> Were his: but truth by faithful search explor'd,
> And social sense, like seed, in genial plenty sown.
> Wherever it took root, the soul (restor'd
> To freedom) freedom too for others sought.
>   (*Poetical Works*, 328)

Hoadly's great deed, Akenside reports in a note, was "to distinguish himself in the cause of civil and religious liberty," against doctrines of passive obedience and the divine right of kings preached by the "Jacobite faction" and the "nonjuring clergy." His "war" was with "sacred folly," and the clear light of his reason "Could a whole nation disengage / From the dread bonds of many an age, / And to new habits mould the public mind." It is to such intellectual liberators, "that heroic throng / Who rescu'd or preserv'd the rights of human kind," that Akenside is chiefly drawn. Like his admired Milton, Akenside looks more often to the heroism of the "achievements of the peaceful gown" than those of "the imbattled field" ("To Townshend in the Country," lines 101–2). Thus John Pym who stoutly challenged the "proud force" of the Earl of Strafford on the floor of parliament is preferred to the soldier Fairfax who won the contemporary battle of Naseby ("To Townshend in the Country," lines 105–10).

"NOT FAR BENEATH THE HERO'S FEET"

In this regard, it is significant that the "Huntingdon" ode, urging the political defense of English liberties, closes not with the young earl but with the bard whose "Honest praise / . . . nobly sways / Ingenuous youth" (lines 229–31). To end the poem in this way suggests that Akenside is as much interested in the power of the poet to "sway" the "ingenuous youth" as he is in the "prevailing mind" of the hero.[44] Indeed, it is characteristic of Akenside's political poems to set the bard alongside the military and the political leader: art and arms are allied with the ruler in the defense of the nation.

Akenside is not content to assign an ancillary role to the poet, or a merely supportive role to "the blest function of the poet's tongue" ("To

---

[44] The echo of the key term "prevailing" – the "prevailing . . . charm" of the Muse (line 11), the "prevailing mind" of Huntingdon (line 226) – suggests that Akenside is claiming that the poet, too, wields a kind of power.

Huntingdon," line 22). Through compressed allusion and syntactic linkage he implicitly puts the poet on a level with two other figures, the warrior "hero" and the political "patriot."[45] This symbolic trio recurs with some frequency in Akenside's poems, in the odes "On a Sermon Against Glory," where Timoleon, Cicero, and Milton share immortal glory (lines 17–18), "To Huntingdon," where Aristides, Cimon,[46] and both Homer and Pindar characterize Greece's "happiest age" (lines 61–64), and "On Leaving Holland" where "the honors of a poet's name" share space with "Somers' counsels" and "Hamden's arms" (lines 63–64). Elsewhere ("To Townshend in the Country"), Somers the "patriot" is joined in "the unfading groves" by both the warrior-king William (to whom he provided advice) and the poets Milton and Spenser, whom Somers served as "guardian of their fame below" (lines 135–36, 156–60) – apparently by encouraging editions of their works.[47]

In this poem Akenside is implicitly appealing to Townshend to be a Somers – i.e., a patron – to him. This appeal (if it is one) is unique in the poems of a man who throughout his career was in fact dependent on the beneficence of patrons.[48] Indeed, he strenuously and repeatedly repudiates – perhaps because he half-mistrusts his own motives – the corrupted relationship of venal "polluted bard" and flattered "tyrant" ("To Huntingdon," lines 81–90, 121–30).[49] This denunciation of lying bards is probably linked to Akenside's own wariness about addressing the Great Men of his day, and a sense that there was something inherently corrupting about the practice.[50] (It was perhaps because he had accepted

---

45 "To Huntingdon," lines 135–40, where the deficient "bard" who "leaves public arguments unsung" is banished "Far from the hero's and the patriot's love" to the cells of slumbering "monks." By implication, the *true* bard dwells with the hero and the patriot.

46 Athenian general who, as Akenside's note explains, won "two great victories . . . over the *Persians* by sea and land."

47 Tonson dedicated his 1705 edition of *Paradise Lost* to Somers, who was thought by some to have sponsored Tonson's elegant 1688 folio edition of the poem. John Hughes dedicated his 1715 edition of Spenser's *Works* to Somers.

48 Johnson remarks not only on Dyson's pension of £300 per year, but on the assistance the young Akenside received "from the fund which the Dissenters employ in educating young men of scanty fortune" – and on his insistence on repaying the "contribution" when he decided to study medicine rather than theology (*Lives*, III, 411, 414–15).

49 Cf. earlier lines in the same poem on "the blandishments of Tuscan strings" and the "servile notes to Celtic kings / By flattering minstrels paid in evil hour" (lines 25–28), "On Leaving Holland," where the poet dares "from impious thrones [of Latium and Gaul] reclaim / . . . The honors of a poet's name" (lines 59–63), and "To Curio," where the "vain wreaths" bestowed by "lying bards" are finally "despoiled" by "old Time" (lines 121–30).

50 Akenside may have written the anonymous *Epistle to the Right Honourable William Pultney, Esq; Upon his Late Conduct in Publick Affairs* (1742), effusively praising Pulteney's "most generous, I might almost venture to say supernatural Concern for the Welfare of his country" (from "To the Reader"). It is attributed to Akenside by Harriet Jump, in "Akenside's Other Epistle," *Notes and Queries*, n.s. 33 (1986), 508–12.

an annuity from the politically connected Dyson that Akenside was careful not to address to him any of his politically charged poems.[51])

But Akenside does more than link the king, the warrior, and the bard. He embodies the extraordinary fantasy that of the three figures it is really the bard who wields the most "power." In the ode "On the Use of Poetry" the familiar triad appears:

> Not far beneath the hero's feet,
> Nor from the legislator's seat
> Stands far remote the bard.
>
> (lines 19–21)

But the bard's "rule" is "wider," and his "award" more "lasting." The fame and imperial rule that Lycurgus and Pompey won for Sparta and Rome have disappeared – "Where are they?" (line 28) – but "Homer's reverend page / Holds empire to the thirtieth age" (lines 29–30), and "Shakespeare's powerful art" will rule men's hearts when England's political and military heroes – Sidney, Russell, even William the Deliverer – have long ceased to "move the patriot's breast" (line 35). In the ode "To Huntingdon" the Muse's "power" to compel obedience and prevail upon the heart ("the vengeful bosom to disarm; / To melt the proud with human woe, / And prompt unwilling tears to flow") exceeds that of the statesman and the general: "Can Cromwell's arts, or Marlborough's sword, / An equal empire claim? / No" (lines 11–18). In the ode "To Sleep" Akenside prefers the "honorable visions" and "prophetic dreams" of Milton even to "those awful forms ... / For chiefs and heroes only meant," such as the "choral songs" and "glad applause" that greeted Timoleon when he offered counsel to a "rescued people."[52]

Elsewhere, and particularly in the last decade of his career, Akenside curiously elides the differences between bard, patriot, and hero, so that the poet himself takes on the functions of the legislator. This theme appears most prominently in the revised *Pleasures of the Imagination*. But it is anticipated in the curious 1751 ode addressed to Frederick the Great of Prussia. Significantly, the poem is entitled "To the Author of Memoirs of the House of Brandenburgh," identifying Frederick not as "the hero and the king" (line 20) but as an "author." Like Caesar and

---

[51] Akenside refers to Dyson directly only twice in his published verse: in the dedication to him of the revised *Pleasures of the Imagination* (I, lines 48–97), and in the ode "On recovering from a Fit of Sickness, in the Country [i.e., at Dyson's estate in Highgate]," line 58.

[52] "After Timoleon had delivered Syracuse from the tyranny of Dionysius, the people on every important deliberation sent for him into the public assembly, asked his advice, and voted according to it. PLUTARCH" (Akenside's note).

Xenophon before him, Frederick, having achieved renown as one of the "chiefs of human race, / And born to lead in counsels or in arms," turns away "from glory's chace / To dwell with books [and] court the Muse's charms" (lines 1–4).[53] If a king can be a poet, a poet can also be a king. This is hinted at in Akenside's language – his repeated references to the muse's "reign," "power," "prevailing charm" and "prevailing lyre," her "command," "powerful art," and "powerful strain," her "awful art" and "awful throne."[54]

The theme is developed more fully in *The Pleasures of the Imagination* (1772), and particularly in the two new books which Akenside added to the earlier *Pleasures of Imagination*. The new "Book the Third," left apparently incomplete at Akenside's death, is devoted to a mini-epic narrative of the return of Solon, the lawgiver-poet, to Athens after an absence of ten years, a story designed to explain why God permitted "the viper Evil" to "pollute / The goodly scene" of man (III, lines 10–11). In Akenside's poem he is sage, "wise patriot" (line 100), and lawgiver "whose voice / Through Athens hush'd the storm of civil wrath; / Taught envious want and cruel wealth to join / In friendship; and, with sweet compulsion, tam'd / Minerva's eager people to his laws" (III, lines 33–37). But he is also a poet, who once "with strains / Of glowing harmony" taught Athens "to soften war's / Dire voice, or in fair colours ... / To clothe the form of civil counsel" (lines 350–54), and in old age pays vows "To the sweet Muses, teachers of my youth / And solace of my age" (lines 327–28). Most of the book is devoted to his epic-style speeches to the Athenians (lines 111–24, 134–37, 298–337, 344–540), seeking to arouse their resistance to the tyrant Pisistratus. Akenside-as-narrator quite consciously speaks through the lawgiver Solon, and "assumes" his speech:

> Could i the speech of lawgivers assume,
> One old and splendid tale i would record
> With which the Muse of Solon in sweet strains
> Adorn'd this theme profound.   (lines 25–28)

This is only the last and most explicit of Akenside's many attempts to find in the poet a figure who can give laws to the people.

---

53 As it happens, Frederick's book – because two "extraordinary passages" in it laugh at the principled emigration of the Huguenots after the revocation of the Edict of Nantes – prompts Akenside's scorn rather than his admiration. See stanza III, and Akenside's note (*Poetical Works*, 357).

54 "To Huntingdon," lines 3, 21, 29; "On Lyric Poetry," lines 114, 118; "On the Use of Poetry," lines 37, 39; "To Charles Townshend in the Country," line 162; "To the Muse," line 19. Cf. also "The Powers of Imagination" in *The Pleasures of Imagination* ("The Design").

Just what role Akenside planned for the poet-legislator, and how the story of Solon was intended to illustrate the "theme profound" of evil, cannot be known, for his narrative breaks off while Solon is still telling the Athenians how he made his way back to his homeland.[55] It seems likely that Akenside, following his sources, would have balanced Solon's despair on his return to Athens from Cyprus with the survival of his legal code well past the era of Pisistratus. But he wrote enough of the tale of Solon to prompt the reviewer in the *Monthly Review* to declare that Akenside's poem, and in particular Book III, was designed "to shew the great influence of poetry, in enforcing the cause of Liberty."[56]

Akenside's fragmentary tale of Solon may have been designed to enforce the cause of liberty. But it also raises for us the question of whether his conception of the political function of the poet, based as it was on classical Greek example, was wholly idealized, so visionary as to lose all touch with contemporary British reality, where national politics was a matter of shifting coalitions of parties and factions both in parliament and "without doors," and where poets no longer played the prominent role in their nation's affairs that Milton, Dryden, and even Pope had done. Before we dismiss Akenside as a utopian who did not realize, as we with the advantage of hindsight do, that a gap was opening in his day between the aesthetic and the political worlds, we should remember the flowering of a high Pindaric conception of poetry at mid-century. As I have suggested, this conception was a serious and considered attempt to reassert the traditional public role for the poet at the very time when that role was being called into question by political practice in Westminster, indeed, *because* it was being called into question. Perhaps it was to protest the reduction of the serious writer to a paid producer of pamphlets that Akenside and his contemporaries proposed a Pindaric alternative.

Another kind of evidence suggests that Akenside might have taken seriously the idea of poet as legislator. Because he maintained close relationships not only with the Clerk of the House of Commons but also with several gentleman MPs, Akenside, who followed contemporary political events closely, was not unacquainted with the workings of the country's legislature. While a medical student at Edinburgh, he was apparently an eloquent participant in a local debating society,[57] and was ambitious to

---

[55] Johnson thought the tale of Solon "too long" (*Lives*, III, 418).

[56] *Monthly Review*, 48 (Dec. 1772), 436.

[57] Bucke reports that Akenside was "distinguished by the eloquence which he displayed in the course of the debates [at the Edinburgh Medical Society]" (*Life, Writings, and Genius*, 17).

gain a seat in parliament, for which he felt himself highly qualified.[58] Several passages in his poems seem to hint at what Dugald Stewart (who knew of Akenside's Edinburgh days) called "a secret consciousness of powers adapted to a higher station in life than fell to his lot." Stewart cites lines from the ode "To Sleep" on the "rescued people's glad applause" that greeted the counsels provided by Timoleon – scenes now "too grand for fortune's private ways":

> And though they shine in youth's ingenuous view,
>   The sober gainful arts of modern days
> To such romantic thoughts have bid a long adieu.
>   (*Poetical Works*, 312)[59]

But the evidence of Akenside's later poems suggests that he may not have fully abandoned his aspiration of serving as a modern Timoleon.

In his last years, however, Akenside may have been rethinking his idea of poet-as-lawgiver. In the famous closing lines of the uncompleted "Book the Fifth," the "bard" is celebrated not as the recording muse or the source of fame or even as legislator, but as an "imperious" creator who rules his own imagined world with limitless power and authority. To the poets, he says,

> A field is open'd wide as nature's sphere;
> Nay, wider: various as the sudden acts
> Of human wit, and vast as the demands
> Of human will. The bard nor length, nor depth,
> Nor place, nor form controuls. To eyes, to ears,
> To every organ of the copious mind,
> He offereth all its treasures. Him the hours,
> The seasons him obey: and changeful Time
> Sees him at will keep measure with his flight,
> At will outstrip it.   (v, lines 105–14)

The "prevailing hand" of the poet, like that of God himself, gives life to "corporeal essence." Whatever he wills within his own "delightful world," he performs. At this outer limit of Akenside's exalted conception, the social and political world of Solon has been transcended, and poet-as-lawgiver has yielded to poet as absolute monarch. We have come some

---

[58] William Robertson reported to Dugald Stewart that "the great object of [Akenside's] ambition then [i.e., in Edinburgh] was a seat in Parliament" (*Elements of the Philosophy of the Human Mind*, 3 vols. [London, 1829], III, 501).

[59] Stewart also cites lines from the ode "To Townshend in the Country" in which the poet considers what remains if a life of heroic action is no longer possible: "Yet where the will divine / Hath shut those loftiest paths, it next remains / With reason clad in strains / Of harmony, selected minds to inspire, / And virtue's living fire / To feed and eternize in hearts like thine" (lines 45–50).

distance from the Akenside who celebrated not power but liberty, not an imperious monarch but freedom's "equal throne."[60] But it was only in his last years that Akenside seemed to want to transcend the world of politics, and we should not read back into his poems of the 1740s and 1750s the impulse to move beyond "history" into "the solitary imagination."[61]

[60] In the ode "To Curio," Akenside had warned that "dangerous power" is often the "mortal bane" to "freedom" (lines 31–32). One occasionally senses a strain of worship of the strong leader in Akenside's praise of heroic William, the "great deliverer" ("To Charles Townshend," line 74), who "This reign, these laws, this public care, / . . . gave us all to share" ("To Huntingdon," lines 201–2).

[61] This is William Dowling's description of Akenside's political poems as early as the "Ode to Curio" (*The Epistolary Moment: The Poetics of the Eighteenth-Century Verse Epistle* [Princeton, 1991], 124).

CHAPTER 5

William Collins: "Virtue's Patriot Theme"

It has been customary since the 1920s to think of Collins' *Odes on Several Descriptive and Allegorical Subjects* (1746) as consisting of two separate groups of poems, those concerned with poetry itself, and the so-called "patriotic odes." Ricardo Quintana, who in 1963 saw no reason to dissent from the distinction, concluded his essay by remarking that if Collins had two purposes in writing his odes, "exploring the resources of poetry" and "expressing the hopes and desires of a civilized community," those two purposes "must have seemed to him very close to each other."[1] But the implications of this suggestive remark have never been pursued. Perhaps we can see the twelve odes in Collins' book as forming a single group, united not just by a concern for "the possibilities for poetry" (including political or patriotic poetry) but by an overarching principle to which both "patriotism" and "poetry" are subordinate.

Collins himself left several hints that the patriot and the poet are, in his mind, near allied. In the early "Epistle to Sir Thomas Hanmer," it is the "Patriot's Hand" that "protects" the "Poet's Lays" (line 2): Hanmer, who initially made his name in parliament as a champion of the Protestant succession, is now, as editor, the protector of Shakespeare, and perhaps a potential protector, or patron, of Collins. In the "Ode to Fear," the relationship between poet and patriot is even closer: Aeschylus, who fought at Marathon, encompassed both roles: he "nurs'd the Poet's flame" but also "reach'd from Virtue's Hand the Patriot's Steel" (lines 32–33). Like Thomson, Collins is drawn toward figures who combine the contemplative and active lives.

A fresh glance at the biographical evidence confirms that Collins himself was not content to take up the quiet position in the church for

---

[1] "The Scheme of Collins' *Odes on Several...Subjects*," in Carroll Camden, ed., *Restoration and Eighteenth-Century Literature* (Chicago, 1963), 376, 380. H. W. Garrod was apparently the first to speak of the "patriotic odes" as a group or a "series." See his *Collins* (Oxford, 1928), 47, 70, 79.

which his university training qualified him.[2] Far from being a bookish Oxford scholar and dreamy, unstable literary genius, the "poor Collins" of literary legend was an energetic and ambitious young man in the London of the early 1740s, with a keen patriotic interest in the military crises facing his country. One of his uncles, Colonel Edmund Martin, was a professional soldier. (His two sisters would later marry army officers.)[3] In 1745 he appears to have traveled to Flanders to discuss with Colonel Martin his hopes of serving his country in some capacity. Carver even surmises that he wanted to "offer himself as a volunteer" in resisting the Jacobite invaders.[4] Colonel Martin seems to have proposed instead that he try to "get a chaplaincy in a Regiment."[5] Collins made a second trip to the Low Countries the following summer, where he visited army camps and reported encountering "many wounded & Sick Countrymen."[6] In London and later in Richmond he made the acquaintance of veterans of the battles of Fontenoy, Falkirk, and Culloden.[7] Collins may have been more drawn, as Alexander Hay thought, to "letters, and the improvement of his intellect" than to the army,[8] but he also felt the pull of a wider public world in which a poet might play a role.

As Collins considered the options open to a poet who sought to present himself as a patriot, he implicitly declined several of the literary models. He tends to avoid sabre-rattling rhetoric designed to rally the nation to resistance or reprisal – the "Ode on the Death of Colonel Ross" is an exception. He also ignores the Patriot political campaign against minis-terial corruption. Although British forces won some notable victories on land and sea, at home and abroad, in the 1740s, Collins gravitates not toward British victories but defeats – at Fontenoy and Falkirk. As for the patriotic role of recording muse who honors fallen heroes by preserving their names, Collins is curiously reticent.

The literary tradition of honoring the dead was very much alive in England in the 1740s. In the *British Magazine* for May 1746 there was advertised "A Poem on the Death of Col. Gardner, slain at the Battle

[2] He was offered a position by the Duke of Richmond as a country curate, but seems to have preferred a life in the larger world of London.

[3] P. L. Carver, *The Life of a Poet: A Biographical Sketch of William Collins* (London, 1967), 180.

[4] Carver, *Life*, 62–63.

[5] According to a September 1745 letter from John Mulso to Gilbert White (Rashleigh Holt-White, ed., *Letters to Gilbert White* [London, 1907], 9).

[6] Holt-White, ed., *Letters*, 15.

[7] Including John Home and Thomas Barrow, who fought at Falkirk. The Duke of Richmond, Collins' would-be patron, served with George II at Dettingen and with Cumberland at Culloden. His uncle, Colonel Martin, attracted royal comment for his service at Culloden.

[8] Carver, *Life*, 35.

of Prestonpans."⁹ This was Colonel James Gardiner, a regimental commander whose "glorious Death" was much reported in newspapers and remembered in pamphlets, including two by Fielding.¹⁰ The "Poem" on his death addresses him as "Great Spirit":

> speak, for who can better tell?
> O! speak the Ecstacy of dying well;
> Say, what choice Blessings are reserv'd as due
> To those, who for their Country fall, like You:
> That we, thus taught what Glories wait the Brave
> May love that Liberty, you dy'd to save.   (3)

The battle at Prestonpans resulted in defeat for the soldiers loyal to King George, in part because English regiments (including Gardiner's) turned tail and fled under fire.¹¹ The publication of the "Poem" in May 1746 was probably part of a campaign to preserve Gardiner's honor.¹² Collins almost certainly knew this poem, but in his own memorial poems on the death of soldiers he decided to take a different tack.

In his "Ode on the Death of Colonel Ross," which was first printed a month after the poem on the death of Colonel Gardiner, Collins remembers

> The warlike Dead of ev'ry Age,
> Who fill the fair recording Page,
> (lines 25–26)

and he summons those dead English war chiefs – the "Sons" of Edward III – who won fame at "*Cressy*'s laurell'd Field" to witness the honors paid to Ross.¹³ But it is noteworthy that Collins' odes on fallen soldiers are far more elegiac than celebrative, and that, since he rarely honors any soldier by name, he implicitly disavows the role of the poet as the muse who records fame. (The "recording *Sister*" in the "The Passions" is not Poetry but Clio, the Muse of History.) Rather than name the soldiers who

---

⁹ It was published on 6 May as *On the Death of the Hon. Colonel James Gardiner, And the Flight of the Rebels on the Approach of His Royal Highness the Duke.*

¹⁰ His death was noticed in the *Daily Advertiser*, 1 October 1745; the *London Magazine*, 14 (1745), 543–44; and the *Gentleman's Magazine*, 15 (1745), 530. Gardiner is celebrated in Fielding's *History of the Present Rebellion in Scotland* (1745) and in the introductory number of *The True Patriot* on 5 November 1745.

¹¹ A formal inquiry in September 1746 cleared the officers and blamed the private soldiers. See the *Report on the Proceedings and Opinion of the Board of General Officers . . .*, found among "Tracts on the Rebellions of 1715, 1745" in the British Library.

¹² He was still being remembered a year later in "An Ode, To the Memory of Colonel Gardiner, In Imitation of Milton," which appeared in the *British Magazine* in February 1747.

¹³ Cf. the "Ode to Liberty," in which "The Chiefs who fill our *Albion*'s Story" appear "In warlike Weeds, retir'd in Glory" (lines 109–10).

fell at Falkirk, Collins in his poem on that event, "Ode, Written in the beginning of the Year 1746," does not even name the battle, much less any of the men who died there.[14] (Indeed, when the "Ode" was reprinted two years later, Collins may have taken further steps to distance the poem from a particular time and place, and to obscure its reference to particular soldiers. It appeared simply as "Ode, Written in the same Year [as the former poem, i.e., the "Ode on the Death of Colonel Ross, Written May, 1745]," as if Collins wanted to delete the reference to Falkirk altogether.)

Even the "Ode on the Death of Colonel Ross" is in its printing in the December 1746 collection of *Odes* stripped of some of the features that a "recording Muse" would preserve. When first printed in Dodsley's *Museum* in June 1746 it was entitled "Ode to a Lady, On the Death of Col. Charles Ross, in the Action at Fontenoy, Written May, 1745." Perhaps Collins was thinking of the poem on the death of Colonel Gardiner advertised a month earlier. As editors have noted, the real Ross (whom Collins seems not to have known) was a captain rather than a colonel: Collins may have been thinking more about the literary recognition of *Colonel* Gardiner than the death of *Captain* Ross. But six months later Collins reconsidered. In his collected odes, as Roger Lonsdale notes, "the date of composition and Ross's Christian name were omitted from the title."[15] The details may seem trivial, but they probably indicate that Collins was rethinking the commemorative role of the poet, and was moving away from the idea that he could best serve as recording muse.[16] In his collection of twelve odes there appear only two proper names of his contemporaries.[17]

But if Collins implicitly declines the roles of recording muse, and declines as well to rouse English troops to war or to celebrate their victories, he does not turn away from the world of contemporary history, nor does he decline to think of the poet as a kind of patriot. Indeed, Collins seems to have focused his attention on the particular contribution that a

[14] Compare the "Ode, To the Memory of Colonel Gardiner" (*British Magazine*, February 1747), which borrows much from Collins' "1746" ode, and in which three soldiers who fought at Falkirk and Culloden are named among the mourners.

[15] *The Poems of Gray, Collins, and Goldsmith* (London, 1969), 455.

[16] Here I part company with Howard Weinbrot, who in an otherwise fine essay suggests that one of Collins' chief concerns in the odes was "the memorial function of poetry" ("William Collins and the Mid-Century Ode: Poetry, Patriotism, and the Influence of Context," in Howard Weinbrot and Martin Price, *Context, Influence, and Mid-Eighteenth-Century Poetry* (Los Angeles, 1990), 28.

[17] Ross and William, Duke of Cumberland ("Ode on the Death of Colonel Ross," line 46 – a line deleted in a later edition). In Collins' other odes only two contemporary names appear, Thomson (in the title of the "Ode Occasion'd by the Death of Mr. Thomson," but not in the poem itself), and "H- - -" [for John Home] in the opening line of the "Ode to a Friend on his Return &C" [i.e., the "Popular Superstitions" ode].

poet – as opposed to a historian or a political journalist – might make in a time of national crisis.

One such contribution was to remind readers of Britain's cultural heritage. In this Collins was by no means alone; he was one of many poets and critics who at mid-century were engaged in celebrating native British literary tradition and establishing Spenser, Shakespeare, and Milton as Britain's canonical writers. They are the three English poets most prominently named, praised, and borrowed from or alluded to in Collins' odes.[18] As we have become increasingly aware in recent years, canon-formation in the eighteenth century is not simply a matter of the inexplicable changing tides of taste; arguably, Spenser, Shakespeare, and Milton emerged at mid-century as Britain's classic writers for discernible reasons.[19] Among those reasons, I suggest, is what was increasingly perceived as their distinctive *Britishness*, at a time when Britain was more or less continuously at war with France, and when some critics like John Brown were anxiously worrying about the corrupting French influence on English culture.

As his editors point out, Collins is often indebted to Pope and to Dryden, to the former for his *Persian Eclogues*, the "Epistle to Hanmer," and the several elegiac odes, and to the latter for "The Passions." But it is significant that Collins never names them,[20] and does not draw attention to these debts to poets who were increasingly thought of at mid-century as belonging to what Thomas Warton called "The School of France." Instead, Collins names Thomson ("YOUR DRUID"), Otway (from Collins' own "native Plains" of Sussex), and "British Fairfax,"[21] emphasizing their native character. In the "Ode to Liberty" he draws attention, both in his poem and in explanatory notes, to native "Tradition" of which he now seeks to make "Poetical Use." And in the "Ode on the Popular Superstitions" he reviews the possibilities of distinctively *Scottish* legends and folk beliefs, which had once inspired Spenser and Shakespeare, as

[18] Shakespeare most prominently in the "Ode to Fear" and the "Ode on the Popular Superstitions of the Highlands of Scotland," Milton and Spenser in the "Ode on the Poetical Character." Collins also published two songs inspired by Shakespeare ("To fair Fidele's grassy Tomb," and "Young Damon of the vale is dead").

[19] See Jonathan Brody Kramnick, "The Making of the English Canon," *PMLA*, 112 (Oct. 1997), 1087–101, later incorporated into his *Making the English Canon: Print-Capitalism and the Cultural Past, 1700–1770* (Cambridge, 1998).

[20] Richard Wendorf suggests that Collins was engaged in a "continual attempt to escape the early influence of Pope" (*William Collins and Eighteenth-Century English Poetry* [Minneapolis, 1981], 72).

[21] In the "Ode occasion'd by the Death of Mr. Thomson" (line 44), the "Ode to Pity" (line 17), and the "Ode on the Popular Superstitions" (line 197).

materials for modern poetry. If Collins promotes a kind of "cultural patriotism," however, he stops short of the nationalistic claims for cultural superiority found, for example, in Akenside's contemporary "The Remonstrance of Shakespeare," in which British supremacy over French art and taste is loudly asserted. While the logic of the progress poem (which provides the structure for several of Collins' odes) calls for the migration of Poetry or Liberty from Greece and Rome to "*Britain*'s favor'd Isle" ("The Manners," line 52) and a "*British* Shell" ("Ode to Pity," line 42), Collins typically avoids mentioning France, or comparisons between British and French culture.[22]

Thoughts of a poet's patriotic function make Collins think less of contemporary France than of classical Greece, and of the lyric poets Pindar and especially Alcaeus who, as I have shown, retained a reputation in the eighteenth century as authors of patriotic odes inspiring and honoring their countrymen. Pindar is the model for perhaps four of the larger odes in the 1746 volume, and provides Collins' epigraph, but it is not the political poet so much as the enraptured singer of sublimity that Collins invokes. Alcaeus, on the other hand, is invoked in the "Ode to Liberty" as the model for the poet (a "New *Alcaeus*") who might arouse the champions of "*Freedom*" and "sing the Sword" until it "leap'd in Glory forth, and dealt her prompted Wound" (lines 1–12). Collins provides a note, explaining his allusion to a "beautiful Fragment of *Alcaeus*" – probably in fact, as editors point out, by Callistratus, but commonly attributed to Alcaeus in the eighteenth century – which he then quotes in Greek. But this is the only allusion to Alcaeus in Collins' poems, and this is the only moment when, like his contemporary Akenside, the poet issues a call to heroic action.[23] Indeed, Collins seems to betray some misgivings about an Alcaic role, for in lines immediately following, he refers to his "Shell's misguided Pow'r" (lines 15), and resolves *not* to "tell / How *Rome*... fell" (lines 17–19). The figure of *preteritio*, though it permits Collins to tell what he says should remain unspoken, again suggests some misgivings about the idea of addressing stirring words to his countrymen or to the Goddess of Liberty herself.

The misgivings may spring not from a sense of poetry's impotence but of poetry's power. "Power," in fact, is a recurrent term in Collins' odes, beginning with the epigraph from Pindar, in which the poet asks that

---

[22] In a rare reference to a French writer, Collins in a note to "The Manners" praises Alain-René Le Sage, "Author of the incomparable Adventures of *Gil Blas de Santillane*" (note to line 67).

[23] Unless we count the stanzas in the "Ode on the Death of Colonel Ross" implicitly urging Cumberland to avenge the defeat at Falkirk.

he might find the right "words," and might be attended by "boldness and ample power."[24] Fear, Simplicity, Music, and the Passions are possessed of "Power" to which the poet implicitly seeks to gain access.[25] It is to those few who possess the "Poetical Character" that the "Cest of amplest Pow'r is giv'n." The idea that a poet may have a kind of "power" is an ancient one, descending from the conception of poet as *vates*, possessed of prophetic power, and before that from mythical poets such as Orpheus, who were said to have power over the animals and the sun itself, or historical figures such as Archilochus, whose satiric poems allegedly had the power to kill. Such beliefs in the potency of poetry largely faded to metaphor by the eighteenth century, although Pope still attributes to his "Muse" great powers of prophecy and preservation. Collins, with Pindar on his mind, may simply be thinking in traditional ways about the power of poetry. Gray, about the same time, began conceiving an "Ode in the Greek Manner" which he intended to call "The Powers of Poetry" (later to be published as "The Progress of Poesy").[26] It is nonetheless somewhat surprising that the old language of poetry's "power" should resurface in the midst of the Enlightenment, when belief in occult influences had largely disappeared. Writing about poetry's "power" may be an indication that poets want to reaffirm poetry's ancient role as a civilizing influence; paradoxically, it may also be a sign that poets fear that poetry has largely lost its old power.[27]

For most readers in the 1740s "Power" was of course an implicitly political term, and is joined in the odes by recurrent appearances of "rule" and "reign." We might be tempted to dismiss Collins' language here as merely metaphorical, but should consider that he may be providing his odes with an additional political resonance. It is worth noting that in the 1740s the ideas of power and royal rule were very much on the minds of political observers. Wars in Europe had been fought since the 1690s over the "balance of power" – particularly to prevent France from establishing a "universal monarchy" – and how to maintain the "balance" was much

---

24 From Pindar's 9th Pythian Ode, lines 80–83 (tr. W. H. Race, Loeb Library, 1997). See S. Musgrove, "The Theme of Collins's Odes," *Notes and Queries*, 185 (1943), 214–17, 253–55.
25 "Ode to Fear," line 31, "Ode to Simplicity," line 6, "The Passions," line 16 (the "expressive Pow'r" of each Passion) and line 100 (Music's "all-commanding Pow'r").
26 Horace Walpole reported that Gray changed the title of the poem because Thomas Cooke preempted the title in his 1751 "Ode on the Powers of Poetry" (*Horace Walpole's Correspondence*, ed. Lewis, XL, 102).
27 Cf. Bishop Hurd's famous remark that poets of his own day had, as a result of the progress of "truth," gained "a great deal of good sense" but "lost" a "world of fine fabling" (*Letters on Chivalry and Romance*, ed. Edith Morley [London, 1911; repr. New York, 1976], 155).

debated in contemporary periodicals and in pamphlets.[28] The other key issue of the several "wars of succession" of the day was the determination of who would hold the thrones of Spain, Austria, and even Poland – that is, who should "rule" or "reign."[29] Closer to home was the dynastic conflict in Britain: was the country to be ruled by the Hanoverians or the Stuarts? When Collins ends the "Ode to Liberty" with the ringing declaration that "Thou, Lady, Thou shalt rule the West!" his readers were perhaps intended to recall that their country had just put down an invasion from the *north* which would have supplanted the "rule" of King George, and was at that moment fighting in Europe to determine whether another "Lady" (Maria Theresa) would "rule" in the *east*.[30] When he ends the "Ode to Mercy" by vowing that "Thou, Thou shalt rule our Queen, and share our Monarch's Throne!" the reader in 1746 would probably find it difficult to exclude the memory that months earlier much British blood had been spilt to settle the question of who would "rule [as] our Queen" and "share our Monarch's throne."

   What can one infer from Collins' use of the categories of mid-century international politics? Perhaps not very much, and certainly not much with any certainty. Some will conclude that Collins, in Sitter's terms, is in fact turning his back on contemporary history, and enacting a kind of retreat where he meditates on the power of *fancy* and the realm of the *imagination*. My own view is that his calculated use of these words – power, rule, reign[31] – indicates that he has not left the world of politics behind. Thinking like a *poet*, he suggests that the questions of who "rules" or holds "power" in a culture are deeper and more encompassing matters than who sits on the throne of Austria or holds the balance of power in Europe.

   If we look at the *Odes* from this angle, we can see more clearly that they do not fall into two separate subgroups, the "patriotic" and "poetic"

---

[28] *Britannia in Mourning, or a Review of the Politics and Conduct of Great Britain with Regard to France, the Balance of Power, and the True Interest of these Nations* (1742); *A Letter to the E- - of S- -, in which Are Examined the Conduct of the Several Ministries with Respect to the Ballance of Power in Europe, and the Necessity of Supporting the House of Austria, and Prescribing Bounds to the Power of France* (1743); *German Politics, or, the Modern System Examin'd and Refuted . . . and the Nature of the Ballance of Power Explained* (1744).

[29] The War of the Spanish Succession was set off in 1701 by the death of Charles II, and the issue was whether he would be succeeded by a French or an Austrian heir. The War of the Austrian Succession began in 1740, at the death of Charles VI, when the question was whether or not Maria Theresa, named by Charles as his heir, would in fact be allowed to succeed. Britain was deeply engaged in both wars. The War of the Polish Succession in 1738, in which Britain remained neutral, involved France and Spain against Russia and Austria.

[30] Only one year earlier her husband Francis was named Holy Roman Emperor.

[31] Even "supremely" in the "Ode to Liberty" ("O how supremely art thou blest," line 143) has a political resonance: for "supreme" *OED* gives "Highest in authority or rank; holding the highest place in authority, government, or power," A.2.

odes, but that they make up a single set. Collins seems to have taken some trouble to intermingle them, the explicitly "patriotic" poems occupying positions 5, 6, 7, 8, and 10 in the series of twelve, framed by "poetic" odes. Early commentators make no distinction between two subgroups. Twentieth-century critics have noticed that the collection seems to have a single "scheme" – Collins exploring various "kinds" of poetry, or experimenting with various metrical and strophic patterns. It has not been sufficiently noticed that numerous verbal links between the "patriotic" and "poetic odes" suggest that Collins wanted them to be considered together.[32]

In the "Ode to Simplicity," for example, Collins invokes "holy *Freedom*" (line 23) as well as "Virtue's Patriot Theme" (line 32), and in lines from the "Ode to Fear" cited earlier Aeschylus "reach'd from Virtue's Hands the Patriot's Steel" (line 33). In the ode on "The Passions," "*Anger*" ("his Eyes on fire," his hand rudely striking the lyre) and "*Revenge*" (who "threw his blood-stain'd Sword in Thunder down, / And with a with'ring Look, / The War-denouncing Trumpet took") are linked with Anger in the "Ode to Liberty" and "the Fiend of Nature" and other warlike figures in the odes to Mercy, Peace, and Colonel Ross. "Wan Despair," whose "Grief" is beguiled with "woful Measures" in "The Passions," likewise recalls not only "Impatient *Freedom*," "sunk in deep Despair" (from the ode on the death of Colonel Ross), but also the several grieving figures in the elegiac odes.

The "Ode to Evening," perhaps the quintessential "poetic" ode, occupying ninth position, is recurrently linked to the overtly "patriotic" poems. In its first printing, Evening was hymned not by "rose-lip'd *Health*" (line 50) but by "smiling *Peace*," said to be "regardful of thy quiet Rule"[33] – which links it to the "rule" of Mercy and Liberty ("Ode to Mercy," line 26; "Ode to Liberty," line 144) and the "holier Reign" of Peace ("Ode to Peace," line 18) and restored "Reign" of Freedom ("Colonel Ross," line 45). Evening's "genial lov'd Return" (line 20) echoes the "blest Return" of Peace ("Ode to Peace," line 12). And the hints of violent sexual assault at the hands of Winter ("rudely rends thy Robes," line 48) combine the "Garments torn" and "Bosom bare" of Freedom in the "Ode on the Death of Colonel Ross" (line 38), the "rude tyrannic Sway" of War and the "injur'd Robes" of Peace in the "Ode to Peace" (lines 7, 13), and

---

[32] Horace served implicitly as a model for the ode-poet who would mingle the public and the private: his "Roman odes" (addressed to Augustus and other political leaders) are mixed with smaller odes celebrating private pleasures.

[33] Rather than, as in later editions, "sure-found beneath the Sylvan Shed" (line 49).

the "rude repeated Stroke" and "barb'rous Yell" (cf. "*Winter* yelling thro' the troublous Air," "Ode to Evening," line 46) at the fall of Rome in the "Ode to Liberty" (lines 24–25). Such verbal echoes suggest that Evening herself is another embodiment of the calming and soothing presence that is elsewhere in the odes given the name of Mercy, Peace, Concord, Freedom, or the Muse.[34]

Another structural feature of the series suggests a deeper unifying principle. The collection of *Odes* begins with a pair of poems on Pity and Fear, and it has long been suspected that in writing these odes Collins had Aristotle in mind, especially since he is known to have begun a translation of and commentary on Aristotle's *Poetics* about 1745, when the odes were being planned and composed.[35] It is not often enough observed that these two poems at the beginning of the series are matched by two odes at the end of the series on topics drawn from the tragic drama, "The Manners" and "The Passions." In Aristotelian critical tradition, the two topics are related.[36] The ode on "The Passions" no longer strikes us as one of Collins' better poems, perhaps because for seventy years we have thought of the "Ode to Evening" as the defining center of his work.[37] But "The Passions" was once very highly regarded,[38] and we should consider that Collins may have carefully made it the final poem in the series, not simply because it was composed last but because it serves as a kind of summation.[39]

Like the tragic drama, poetry of the kind Collins wants to write is based both on the representation of passion and the arousal of passion in poet and reader. His first two odes deal explicitly with the arousal of the passions of pity and fear in the poet and reader, and his final ode with the broader topic, the various human passions (fear, anger, despair, hope, revenge, pity, jealousy, melancholy, cheerfulness, joy) and the ability of

---

[34] "Evening" is linked to other odes as well, through Milton's "Ev'ning Ear" in the "Ode on the Poetical Character," line 64, and the "Ev'ning Musings slow" in the "Ode to Simplicity," line 17.

[35] Johnson seems to have thought Collins still at work on Aristotle in 1748. See his "Preface" to *The Preceptor*, which seems to refer to a forthcoming edition of the *Poetics* (by Collins?).

[36] In *The Grounds of Criticism in Tragedy*, Dryden remarks that "Under this general head of manners, the passions are naturally included" (cited in Richard Wendorf and Charles Ryskamp, eds., *Works of William Collins* [Oxford, 1979], 155).

[37] Carver finds "The Passions," despite its apparently late date of composition, a retrograde poem, "not revealing a natural development of the powers which had produced the *Ode to Evening*" (*Life*, 133).

[38] See the notes in Lonsdale, ed., *Gray, Collins, and Goldsmith*, and Wendorf and Ryskamp, eds., *Works of Collins*. The poem was often recited publicly in the eighteenth century. The *Gentleman's Magazine* spoke of its "universally-acknowledged excellence" (52 [January 1782], 22).

[39] Garrod says that "The Passions" holds "the place of honour" (*Collins*, 101).

art to express them.[40] I would argue that Aristotle is more important to *Collins'* poetics than has been realized,[41] that an Aristotelian concern with the passions runs through the entire set of odes, and provides Collins with another way to think about the relation of poetry and patriotism.

In the tradition of odes on music, it is the power of the poet (or of the musician – a closely related figure in Collins' mind) to arouse and to modulate the passions – in Dryden's words, to "raise and quell" them. "The Passions" systematically surveys how the several passions "in early *Greece*" were "By turns... Disturb'd" by Music, and then "delighted, rais'd, refin'd" (lines 7–8). What Collins describes here sounds remarkably like a gloss on Aristotle's *catharsis*, that process whereby passion is first aroused in the listener/spectator and then purged, cleansed, purified, tempered, or otherwise transformed (depending on the translation of Aristotle's Greek term). Not surprisingly, in the "Ode to Pity" arousal ("frantic Woe" [line 3], "broke forth" [line 5], "raise a wild Enthusiast Heat" [line 29]) yields to a kind of release and easing of tension ("balmy Hands" [line 2], "charm" [line 3], "sooth'd" [line 18], "melt away" [line 38]). The "Ode to Fear" offers to the "disorder'd" and "throbbing Heart" (line 42) of the "madly wild" (line 25) devoté of Fear a vicarious shudder, especially through the tragic drama of Aeschylus, Sophocles, and Shakespeare – "Teach me but once like Him to feel" – that will provide a kind of protection or immunity from real harm. One might well expect Collins, in odes on Pity and Fear, to invoke ideas of catharsis. What is surprising, however, is that this same process of arousal followed by "soothing" takes place in a number of the other odes, both "poetic" and "patriotic."

The pattern is perhaps clearest in the "Ode to Liberty." The poem begins by arousing the defenders of "Freedom."[42] A "New *Alcaeus*" shall "sing the Sword" until it leaps into action and deals "her prompted Wound" (lines 1–12). But by the end of the poem passions are quelled: the poet calls on a "Laureate Band" to "sooth" Liberty so that she can be

[40] Dryden distinguishes between the passions "belonging to the characters" (e.g. "anger, hatred, love, ambition,..." which the dramatist must describe) and the passions of pity and terror ("which are to be moved in the audience by the plot").

[41] Carver thinks the "Ode to Simplicity" influenced by Aristotle's idea of unity (*Life*, 104–5), but generally believes that personal experience is more important than Aristotle in shaping Collins' poems. He conjectures (100) that by the publication of the 1746 collection Collins had bade farewell to Aristotle.

[42] Mrs. Barbauld heard a patriotic clarion call: "The opening of this spirited ode rouses the mind susceptible of patriotic feelings, as with the sound of a trumpet" ("On the Poetical Works of Mr. William Collins," in *Poetical Works of William Collins* [London, 1797], xxvii).

joined by "Blithe *Concord*'s social Form" (lines 129–32). Anger's "blood-shot Eyes" are closed in sleep, "*Rage* drops his Steel, and Storms grow calm" (lines 134–36). In the "Ode to Mercy" the warmongering "*Fiend of Nature*" is loosed but ultimately disarmed: Mercy is said to have "stop'd his Wheels, and look'd his Rage away" (line 19). In the "Ode to Peace," War has "bad his Storms arise" (line 6), and "injur'd" the robes of Peace; but by poem's end the "blest Return" of Peace restores her "holier Reign" (lines 12–18). The ode on the death of Colonel Ross moves from aroused passion – Fancy that "Awakes to Grief" (line 11) and "Impatient *Freedom*" (line 39)[43] – through attempts to "sooth" the heart (line 49), to final "Relief" (line 55). Britannia's mourning Genius, tearing laurels from his own hair as the poem opens, is replaced by the gentler "social Grief" of the Muse at the close. In other odes, where the pattern of arousal and tempering is not clearly discernible, Collins hints at the disturbing power of "the dang'rous Passions" (which keep aloof from the weaving of the "Cest of amplest Pow'r" in the "Ode on the Poetical Character"), "the Wizzard *Passions*" (which haunt the "Fairy Field" of Philosophy in "The Manners"), and the rude and intemperate "yelling" of Winter that frightens "chaste" and "modest" Evening.

It is rare for Collins to banish the passions altogether: in the "Ode on the Poetical Character" the "dang'rous Passions" are supplanted by a purified passion, the "Rapture blind" of the aspiring poet. What interests Collins is not the suppression of passion but its tempering or regulating. It is significant in this regard that Simplicity's vale is "temp'rate" (line 51). "The Passions" are not absent; they "own [Simplicity's] Pow'r" (line 38), that is, would submit to be inspired and regulated by her. This has some implicit bearing on the "patriotic odes." Collins seems to be experiment-ing with the idea that a poet might best be a "patriot" not by promoting patriotic sentiment but by subjecting patriotic sentiments to a searching reexamination, seeking to foster a kind of national tempering or catharsis of political passions. Rather than limiting his focus to particular events and controversies in 1745–46 – debates over British interests in Hanover, the war in Europe, negotiations for peace, the suppression of the Jacobite rebellion and the punishment of its leaders – Collins uses those occasions to raise larger questions about the meaning of such contemporary slogans as "British Honor" and "British Liberty," and about the kind of politi-cal culture Britain might hope to develop. Rather than simply arousing strong and simple patriotic feeling (by calling for revenge for past defeats

---

[43] As Wendorf and Ryskamp note, "impatient" in Johnson's *Dictionary* means "Vehemently agitated by some painful passion."

or victory over his country's foes, as in contemporary odes in praise of Cumberland), he seeks something more complicated and less definable in contemporary political terms: a means whereby powerful public passions can be acknowledged, aroused, contained, and ultimately soothed and softened. It is within such a frame that I want now to look more closely at Collins' five "patriotic odes."

THE PATRIOTIC ODES

Collins does not seem to have worked out a consistent way of understanding the role of the patriotic poet. Although it has seemed to some critics that a consistent politics – based on peace, mercy, restraint, and reconciliation – can be inferred from Collins' patriotic *Odes*, I would point rather to their complexities and inconsistencies, which make it difficult to align Collins with any identifiable political faction in his own day. At some points, furthermore, Collins seems to have his eye more on the literary context than the political one, concerned more about responding to the patriotic odes and elegies of his contemporaries than to the events that occasioned them. Most of the poems have a fairly well-defined political occasion – a battle, or the debates about peace and mercy in late 1747 – but in the most substantial of the five poems, the "Ode to Liberty" (longer than the other four put together), the occasion, if there is one, is much obscured and the poem's politics very difficult to define.

The first of Collins' patriotic poems to be published was the "Ode, to a Lady on the Death of Colonel Ross in the Action of Fontenoy," which first appeared in June 1746 in Dodsley's *Museum*. In some ways this would seem to be the most straightforward of the patriotic odes: a simple lament for the death of a brave and loyal Scotsman who died in the service of his country in a major battle in Flanders against France in May 1745. But the simplicity is deceptive. To begin with, although the poem was apparently written (as was claimed in its first edition) "in May 1745," it appeared not (as did many French poems on Fontenoy) in the immediate aftermath of the battle, but more than a year later. When it did appear, British readers were full of the news of a much more recent battle – fought at Culloden on 18 April, about six weeks earlier. In that context the poem served in part as an indirect tribute to the many loyal Scots who had fought (and continued to fight) not only in the Low Countries against the French but also in Scotland against the rebellious Jacobites.

One might infer from such an elegy that Collins was both honoring the dead and encouraging the living soldiers to continue the fight to preserve "Freedom" against French tyranny, that is, endorsing Britain's role in the continental land war. And the poem indeed summons "The warlike Dead of ev'ry Age" to honor Ross and to give voice to a desire for vengeance:

> Again for *Britain*'s Wrongs they feel,
> Again they snatch the gleamy Steel,
> And wish th'avenging Fight.

But Collins is quite vague about the *casus belli*, and does not define Britain's interest in the conflict. He never specifies what "Wrongs" Britain has suffered, and says nothing at all about French tyranny or overweening ambition. Indeed, the enemy army is never named. His readers of course knew that the enemy was France, and were no doubt aware that there was considerable debate in the newspapers and magazines of the day, and in parliament, about whether Britain ought to be engaged in a land war in Europe at all.[44] When the poem appeared in the collected *Odes* six months later, Collins (perhaps like many of his countrymen more supportive of the war now that Britain had won – in the summer of 1745 – an important victory at Cape Breton Island) added lines to suggest that Ross had "fall'n to save" an "injur'd Land." But whether it is Ross's own "Land" or the land of "Imperial *Honor*" (i.e., perhaps of the Holy Roman Empire, a British ally) is never made clear. In any event, by the time the poem next appeared (in the *British Magazine* in July 1747), Collins, having apparently reconsidered his implicit political endorsement of the war, had deleted the reference to "his injur'd Land." By December 1748, when the poem appeared in a fourth version in Dodsley's *Collection*, the Peace of Aix-la-Chapelle had been signed,[45] and Collins may have again decided that the war (despite the fact that Britain had gained very little) had been justified after all, and once again Ross is said to have fallen to save an "injur'd Land."

As it happens, whether or not Britain should have fought in Flanders was a question on which Ross himself had an opinion. Despite the fact that he had a commission in the Scots Guards, he seems to have sided with those in the Patriot Opposition who thought that Britain had no business

---

[44] See for example the *Westminster Journal* of 11 May 1745: "what are the Effects of our connexion with Han---r! Behold those Fields *crimson'd* o'er with the Blood of our *Countrymen*, who fell a sacrifice to the scheme of *France* for obstructing her views!", quoted in Harris, *A Patriot Press*, 188.

[45] The preliminaries to the peace were signed in April 1748 and the peace treaty itself was signed in October 1748.

fighting for Hanoverian interests in Europe.[46] It is not clear whether Collins, who apparently was not acquainted with Ross personally, knew this. If he did, the poem gains an added dimension of bitter irony: Ross died in a war of which he himself disapproved. Collins himself may have been ambivalent, or found himself changing his mind as the war progressed. In effect, he found a means of including – and personalizing – what the Opposition journals were saying about the terrible *waste* of British blood.

Collins' ambivalence (or changing opinion) is evidenced too by other revisions to the text. The poem when published in June 1746 imagines that the heroes of *"Cressy's* laurell'd Field" – the 1346 victory over the French at Crécy – will wish that the loss at Fontenoy might be avenged. Six months later Collins developed the desire for vengeance by adding two stanzas in which "Impatient *Freedom"* herself refuses to leave the battlefield at Fontenoy until she is avenged:

> But lo where, sunk in deep Despair,
> Her Garments torn, her Bosom bare,
>   Impatient *Freedom* lies!
> Her matted Tresses madly spread,
> To ev'ry Sod, which wraps the Dead,
>   She turns her joyless Eyes.

> Ne'er shall she leave that lowly Ground,
> Till Notes of Triumph bursting round
>   Proclaim her Reign restord:
> Till *William* seek the sad Retreat,
> And bleeding at her sacred Feet,
>   Present the sated Sword.

Editors suggest that Collins added the lines in December 1746 in compliment to William, Duke of Cumberland, victor at Culloden, and hailed as the hero who would then return to Flanders to defeat the French. But the lines on Cumberland would have been far more apt in June 1746 than in December. Within days of the victory in Scotland it was hoped that William would lead his troops back to Flanders to fight the French. By the end of July it was widely reported that Cumberland would in

---

[46] Carver notes that Ross, a member of parliament for Ross from 1741, was criticized in his Scottish constituency for his "constant way of voting with ye Opposition" (quoted from a collection of local documents, *Life*, 76). See also the evidence identifying Ross as a member of the opposition collected and assessed by Mary Margaret Stewart, in "William Collins' Ode on the Death of Charles Ross: The Search for Audience and Patronage," *Age of Johnson*, 8 (1997), esp. 212–17.

fact not be going to the continent "this Campaign."[47] Perhaps Collins, who apparently wrote the stanzas after June and before December 1746, decided to include them in the December *Odes* as an expression of a hope he seems at the time to have still shared that William would before long return to Flanders. By December 1748, when the poem appeared in Dodsley's *Collection*, the two stanzas on William's vengeance were withdrawn, perhaps as editors suggest because of the embarrassing fact that William in July 1747 had led a British army not to victory but to another defeat in Flanders. The more likely reason is that by December 1748 England and France were at peace. Perhaps too Collins came to think that the stanzas naming the Duke of Cumberland were too particular in a collection of odes that largely tended toward general statement.[48]

He may also have felt that fostering in his readers by means of luridly eroticized details a desire for bloody revenge – half-naked Freedom is presented as a victim of rape, crazed by grief[49] – was not consistent with the patriotic role he wanted to play. This cry for vengeance is unique in the patriotic odes; it is unusual for Collins to seek to arouse vehement passion rather than to allay it. Indeed, the lines themselves seem to reveal his misgivings. The "sated Sword" suggests that an avenging William will somehow satisfy a felt need, and thereby restore stasis, but it also hints at an excessive and even unnatural appetite for blood: for "sate" Johnson's *Dictionary* gives "To satiate; to glut; to pall; to feed beyond natural desires." Perhaps Collins was uneasy, as were many contemporaries, about reports of excesses by "Butcher" Cumberland and his zealous subordinates as they mopped up after Culloden.

What is more, Collins suggests that even revenge would ultimately fail to console those mourning for Ross's death. And it is the process of mourning that concerns Collins in this poem far more than the patriotic ceremony of honoring the war dead. The poem is addressed "to a Lady" who was said to have been Ross's "intimate acquaintance," perhaps his "intended bride." It is the grieving lady rather than the dead officer

---

[47] *General Evening Post* 29–31 July 1746, quoted in Lonsdale, ed., *Gray, Collins, and Goldsmith*, 460.

[48] The only other contemporary particular in the poem, apart from its title, is "rapid Scheldt's descending wave," which locates the poem at Fontenoy. "*Rapid* Scheldt" is, however, a puzzle, since the river, as Collins who had visited the area must have known, flows slowly through the flat Low Countries. Perhaps, thinking metaphorically, Collins wanted to echo the falling of the dying Ross.

[49] The image of a ravished female figure was not uncommon in contemporary satirical political prints. See, for example, "The Whipping Post: Britannia Stripped and Flogged" (no. 113 in Herbert Atherton, *Political Prints in the Age of Hogarth* [Oxford: Clarendon, 1974]) and "The Queen of Hungary Stript" (1742, in Paul Langford, *Walpole and the Robinocracy* [Cambridge, 1986], 229).

on whom this elegiac ode focuses. While elegy conventionally passes from initial grief via tribute to consolation, Collins declines to follow this path, and suppresses any strong sense of relief.[50] The poem offers the muted comfort of "fond Remembrance," the pagan "Delight" on the part of the "warlike Dead" who "hail" another hero, and the assurance that Peace itself will "protect" him in his grave. But Collins ends not with confidence that Ross has gone to a better place. He remains in his "lonely Bed," perhaps (in fearful fancy) still "bleeding." What is worse, the location of the grave is apparently unknown: Collins can only say that "his Country's Vows shall bless the Grave, / *Where'er* the Youth is laid" (emphasis added). Nor can Collins promise that Ross has not died in vain. Immediately following the desire for vengeance, both in the original and second versions, Collins explicitly questions whether "pictur'd Glories" (of Britain's dead heroes, or of future triumphs) will serve to assuage a mourner's grief:

> If, weak to sooth so soft an Heart,
> These pictur'd Glories nought impart,
>   To dry the constant Tear:
> If yet, in Sorrow's distant Eye,
> Expos'd and pale thou see'st him lie,
>   Wild War insulting near

What is "constant" is not love or memory, but the still-flowing tears. The body of the dead man seems to lie unburied on the battlefield – Ross, belly-shot, apparently died in a ditch – and war, far from being concluded, still seems to be "insulting near." The poem in effect ends where it began. All the poet can "Promise" is that the lady will not mourn alone: the muse offers "social Grief." All he can do is to "repeat" the same "sad . . . Tale,"[51] so that even those who never knew Ross will – in the poem's final word – also "weep."[52]

What more, the poem seems to ask, can the patriotic poet say about soldiers who die in the service of their country? The question seems to have continued to trouble Collins, for he included in his collection a

---

[50] Herein I again depart from Weinbrot, who finds Collins' patriotic odes "deeply but optimistically elegiac" ("William Collins," 28).

[51] Cf. the ode on the death of Thomson, which ends ("In yonder Grave YOUR DRUID lies!") virtually as it began ("In yonder Grave a DRUID lies").

[52] Collins' final lines – "Even humble Harting's cottaged vale / Shall . . . / . . . bid her shepherds weep" – reverses the elegiac perepeteia in Milton's "Lycidas": "Weep no more, woeful shepherds weep no more" (line 165).

second elegiac ode that editors have supposed to be a "reworking"[53] of the ode "To a Lady," and perhaps a further response to Fontenoy and the war in Flanders. Because it is better known, the "Ode Written in the beginning of the Year 1746" need not deter us long, but several features of the poem's patriotic feeling deserve comment. First, the poem was initially designed to make readers think primarily not of Fontenoy (a battle fought in May 1745) but of Falkirk, a battle in January 1746 (i.e., "in the beginning of the Year 1746") in which Jacobite rebels defeated English and Scots troops loyal to King George.[54] But by omitting to be specific about the location or date of the battle, Collins allowed readers to think generally about British battles in both Scotland and Flanders. (And when the poem was revised for Dodsley's *Collection* in December 1748 either Collins or Dodsley decided that for whatever reason it was better to steer readers away from Falkirk: the new title declares that the poem was "Written in the same year [as the "Ode, to a Lady"]," and thus seemed to refer to Fontenoy – or perhaps Prestonpans in September 1745.)[55] As patriotic poet Collins focused not on the memorial details – which he perhaps found merely accidental – but, as in the "Ode, to a Lady," on the response of mourners, here not a particular grieving friend but a grateful grieving nation.

Second, the poem probably had a more particular purpose. It has been suggested that the poem was designed to answer charges that British troops disgraced themselves at Falkirk. Taking note of the fact that soon after the battle British newspapers reported on the cowardice of the men and the "scandalous" behavior of some of the officers, Weinbrot argues that Collins "swims against the current of national rage by mourning the defamed."[56] This puts the case too strongly: the bravery of British officers both at Falkirk and Prestonpans was being publicly asserted. Falkirk may no longer have been a national controversy in December 1746, but it no doubt remained in the minds of the men who fought there. And since Collins knew several of the officers well, he may have wished to honor and please them.

[53] Lonsdale, ed., *Gray, Collins, and Goldsmith*, 436; Wendorf and Ryskamp, eds. *Works of Collins*, 136.
[54] There is no hard evidence to support Weinbrot's suspicion ("William Collins," 20) that the "1746" ode was "conceived after Fontenoy [but before September 1745]."
[55] Contemporary evidence about reception is inconclusive. That Langhorne in 1765 noted that the poem was written on the "occasion" of "the late rebellion, . . . in memory of those heroes who fell in defence of their country" indicates that he thought he knew Collins' intention, but also that he thought readers only twenty years after the event would not have understood without his assistance.
[56] Weinbrot, "William Collins," 16–17, 19, quoting *Gentleman's Magazine*, 16 (1746), 41–42, 244, 594.

But his deliberately generalized and delayed response to the event suggests that he saw the patriot-poet not as a gazetteer who salutes the dead by name and seizes the occasion to maintain patriotic fervor, or as a man of prudential wisdom who at a time of national crisis urges his countrymen to close ranks, honor their dead, and turn their hostility toward the French foe, but as a musing observer who takes a longer view and strikes a deeper chord. With the rebellion safely put down, Collins could afford to reflect soberly on the darker hours of 1745–46 and on the ceremonial language used for paying public honor to the war dead. The scene he paints has been emptied of particularity and of human substance, as if the event commemorated were long ago and far away. Some readers have been struck by the poem's impersonality, others by its coldness and insistence on the physicality of the grave – its "Mold," "Sod," "Turf," and "Clay" – still others by the "delicate elegiac mood" created by the "fairy hands" and "forms unseen."[57] In the context of elegiac tradition and of other contemporary elegies, what emerges is the ode's refusal to allow passion to well up, its cool, unblinking, even-handed envisaging of the grave site (cold but hallowed, a place of honor but also weeping), and its insistence that no patriotic elegy can wholly console. As in the "Ode, to a Lady," the final image is of a weeping mourner, here not a weeping shepherd but Freedom herself. But in contrast to the "Ode, to a Lady," Collins now suggests that the weeping will soon have to stop. Yet even the restoration to life's daily rhythms, toward which most elegy tends, is given a dark shadow. Collins makes clear that Freedom will only remain there "a-while," for, regardless of these devastating losses, there are other battles to be fought, and presumably other losses endured, in defense of British Freedom. But the weeping is measured and even, the feeling not permitted to overflow its narrow octosyllabic bounds, all passion spent.

The "Ode to Mercy" at first seems different from Collins' other patriotic poems. It may have had a more specific political purpose than Collins' two elegiac odes. Langhorne said that like the "1746" ode it was written on the "occasion . . . of the late rebellion, . . . to excite sentiments of compassion in favour of those unhappy and deluded wretches who became a sacrifice to public justice."[58] Recent editors have followed Langhorne by suggesting that the poem was composed during the national debate, waged in London's newspapers in July and August 1746, as to whether

---

[57] Lonsdale, ed., *Gray, Collins, and Goldsmith*, 437.
[58] *Poetical Works of Collins*, ed. John Langhorne (London, 1804), 133.

the defeated and imprisoned Jacobite lords deserved justice or mercy. Langhorne's language – "excite sentiments of compassion" – suggests another anomalous feature: that Collins in this poem sought not to calm the passions but to stir them up. But it is easy enough to see, from another angle, that Collins' poem seeks to defuse strong feelings of anger and revenge. One might also question whether the poem has a specific purpose – winning mercy for the leading Jacobite lords. Two of the three lords condemned on 29 July were hastily executed on 18 August, and a third was pardoned. A fourth, the Earl of Derwentwater, was executed on 8 December. And for at least one contemporary preacher, the mercy men should think about was God's "*Publick* and *National Mercy*" in freeing England from the Jacobite threat.[59] But it is probably true that Collins was urging mercy as a *general* policy at a time when hundreds of lesser Jacobite prisoners still in British prisons in December 1746 were being tried and sentenced.[60]

What is curious about Collins' plea for Mercy is that it takes rhetorical risks, not simply in arguing for mercy (a position that many contemporary writers adopted) but in making room in his ode for provocative images of the very horrors of war that prompted many other writers to call for nothing less than rigorous Justice – the "deathful Field" (on which loyal soldiers as well as rebels died) and the "Wound[s]" that the "Country's Genius" suffered, even "The *Fiend of Nature*" (probably War itself personified) whom Collins' syntax links with Charles Edward, who "rush'd in Wrath to make our Isle his Prey." It is as if Collins, by acknowledging the "Salvage Deeds" of the enemy, disarms his rhetorical opponent (the proponents of Justice), much as Mercy herself disarmed the "*Fiend of Nature*" when she "O'ertook Him on his blasted Road, / And stop'd his Wheels, and look'd his Rage away." The violent passions that swirl around the issue are thus admitted to the poem, but defused or tempered by the "tender melting Eyes" of the "Gentlest of Sky-born Forms" – a gentle tenderness being precisely the emotion Collins prompts in his reader.

[59] *National Gratitude Due For National Mercies* [a thanksgiving sermon preached at Peckham, Surrey, 9 October 1746] (London, 1746), 4.

[60] Collins may have known that his erstwhile patron, the Duke of Richmond, was strongly opposed to mercy for the lesser Jacobites. In letters to Newcastle during the months of November and December 1746, Richmond deplores the "very great lenity" and "ill timed mercy" shown "to so many notorious rebels." He highly approved of the execution of the Earl of Derwentwater. Richmond claims to be moved by "the spirit of '*true patriotism*'" (Timothy McCann, ed., *The Correspondence of the Dukes of Richmond and Newcastle, 1724–1750* [Lewes, 1984], 235–37). Collins implicitly disputes Richmond, and claims that a true patriotism is consistent with a policy of mercy.

But he is careful not to allow himself to be pigeonholed as a mere partisan, a spokesman for one side of the Mercy–Justice debate. Mercy is said to be the "smiling Bride" of "*Valour*" himself, that is, she meets and gratifies all the reasonable claims of martial courage.[61] With "Bosom bare," hanging over "the Youth who sinks to Ground," she is plainly akin to the half-naked figure of "Freedom" lying on the battlefield in the "Ode, to a Lady." This links the fallen youth for whom she pleads with fallen British soldiers: Mercy disregards battle lines. And the poet offers to build a "roseate Bow'r" for Peace "Where *Justice* bars her Iron Tow'r," that is, not *in place of* but *in the same place*, perhaps hinting that Mercy is not the adversary but the partner of Justice. The final line of the poem is equally reassuring: "Thou, thou shalt rule our Queen, and share our Monarch's Throne!" Queen Caroline having died in 1737 and left the King without a consort, Mercy cannot rule the Queen: she rules *as* the queen, and "share[s] our Monarch's [i.e., George II's] Throne." The important point is that Mercy is said not to be sole ruler (as Liberty is said to "rule the West"), but merely to "share" the throne. The pair of rulers in the final line ("Queen" and "Monarch") are linked with the opposing pair of divinities in the previous two lines (Justice and Mercy), suggesting that Mercy and Justice should share the throne. Collins thus ends with a safely moderating position, having appeared to acknowledge the claims of both Justice and Mercy, as well as the powerful feelings prompted by both figures.

The "Ode to Peace" deploys a similar rhetorical and political strategy. In praising peace, Collins carefully avoids alienating the proponents of war: his Peace is said to be the bride of "warlike *Honour*." Again, Collins' tendency is to repair the breach between two parties, to bind up the nation's wounds, just as Peace is said to "up-bind" her "injur'd Robes," to join rather than to separate, "and not leave one behind / Of all thy beamy Train." Some peace-lovers may be so "Tir'd of [War's] tyrannic Sway" that they will simply "burn" his "sullen Shrines" themselves (rather than burn sacrifices at the shrines), calling in effect for peace at any price. "But" – Collins carefully distinguishes their response from the one he promotes – Peace, who listens to the higher music of the "turning spheres," has a larger view.

[61] Collins adapts the conventional trope of valor as bride of victory. Cf. *A Joyful Ode* (1743), where "*Victory*," with "*Fame* and *Honour* at her Side / Descends like an Imperial Bride, / And perches on auspicious *William*'s Crest" (7).

This poem, like the "Ode to Mercy," may have a less specific political occasion than has been suggested. Editors note that domestic opposition to Britain's participation in the War of the Austrian Succession continued throughout the summer of 1746, and that peace talks were convened in Breda in August. But the talks did not go well, and were broken off by November of that year.[62] Still, so Lonsdale supposes, the poem (written at some point between June and December) expresses a longing for an end to the fighting in Europe, and a "peace with honour." Collins may well have privately hoped for peace in Europe, but his poem, as I read it, seems preoccupied with matters closer to home. More than six weeks before Collins' ode appeared, it was clear that there were no prospects for peace – and in fact the war continued for another two years. Some members of the ministry were eager to pursue Britain's successes of the previous summer. Others, like the Duke of Newcastle, wanted peace but felt themselves in a distinct minority. As Newcastle wrote with some exasperation on 23 December 1746, a week after Collins' poem appeared,

The nation is now universally for war. All parties in Parliament seem to agree to it, and that which has thus united everybody, I am convinced, is their hopes, and expectations, of keeping Cape Breton [captured from the French in July 1746], and distressing and making impression upon the French in North America.[63]

Collins' poem in fact seems to turn away from the prospects of peace in Europe and to focus on Britain. Indeed, this has been his real concern from the first stanza, which remembers when "*War*, by Vultures drawn from far, / To *Britain* bent his Iron Car, / And bad his Storms arise!" This must be the Jacobite landing of 1745, for the war in Europe never spread to the British Isles, though a French invasion was feared. From the moment that war and war fever gripped the nation, Peace has been absent, having withdrawn to seek her "native Skies." In contemplating the return and reign of Peace, Collins thinks not of the reconciliation of warring nations, but of the "*British Lion*" lying down to kiss the feet of Peace. That is, he looks forward to some pacification of Britain's martial spirit. "Let others," says Collins, "court thy transient Smile, / But come to grace thy western Isle." The contrast drawn is between those statesmen trying to negotiate what must surely remain only a temporary

---

[62] The letters of the Dukes of Richmond and Newcastle in the autumn of 1746 eagerly follow the progress of the war in Europe, and say nothing of any prospects for peace.

[63] Quoted in Harris, *A Patriot Press*, 223, from H. Richmond, *The Navy in the War of 1739–1748*, 3 vols. (Cambridge, 1920), III, 49.

or "transient" peace in Europe, and a more permanent peaceableness that, so Collins hopes, might pervade the separate and distinct "western Isle" of Britain. Collins has in mind not a particular peace conference, nor does he call for a general laying down of arms: his Peace is allied to "warlike *Honour*." (As I have noted, biographical evidence suggests that Collins was attracted to soldiers and to battlefields: while traveling through a war zone near Antwerp in July of 1746 he was "in Raptures" and "high spirits."[64]) Instead, he seems to look for a softening of the national spirit, a spirit that expresses itself too often by dividing men against each other in warring factions, not just Jacobite against Hanoverian.[65] It is that same spirit of faction in Britain that Goldsmith began to write about some ten years later in what became *The Traveller*.

> Here by the bonds of nature feebly held,
> Minds combat minds, repelling and repelled.
> Ferments arise, imprisoned factions roar,
> Repressed ambition struggles round her shore.
>
> (lines 343–46)

At the return of Peace, even Britain's "Ports" will rejoice, a hint perhaps (unusual for Collins) at the restoration of overseas trade interrupted by war,[66] or a return to Britain's traditional orientation toward a reliance on a blue-water navy rather than a land army. Implicitly avowing himself a lover of his country, Collins joins the "Sons" of Peace who "adore" her "Choice" of "Honour" as her spouse – "With Him for ever wed!" – and Britain as her new permanent home.

The "Ode to Liberty," placed prominently at the midpoint of Collins' 1746 volume, carries on the same critical examination of British national character, and implicitly urges the nation to temper its proud spirit of Liberty. Freeing himself even more than in the other patriotic odes from any particular political occasion, Collins in this poem retraces the conventional history of Liberty's northward and westward progress since its birth in Greece, invents a new history, gratifying to any patriot, which locates Liberty's origins in pre-Roman Britain, and foresees a day when Liberty, soothed and softened by "*Concord*'s social form," will "rule the West."

---

[64] So reported Mulso, in a letter to Gilbert White, dated 1 August 1746 (Holt-White, *Letters to Gilbert White*, 15).

[65] The sermon on *National Gratitude Due for National Mercies* calls for union among all Protestants.

[66] Cf. Venice, the "Port of Glory" in the "Ode to Liberty" (line 46).

The large historical sweep of the poem and the politically charged but politically vague final words suggest that Collins is not primarily reacting to particular political events in 1745–46. Modern editors suppose that "sad *Liguria*'s bleeding State" (line 49) is a reference to the capture of Genoa by the Austrians from the occupying French in October 1746, an event reported in the *Gentleman's Magazine*.[67] If this was designed as a topical allusion to the events in the War of the Austrian Succession, then it is the only such reference in a long sequence of places in which Liberty once resided – Rome, Florence, Pisa, San Marino, Venice, Genoa, Switzerland, and Holland. By the time Collins was writing, only San Marino among the Italian city-states preserved its independence. For that reason it seems unlikely that Collins thought it important for readers of his ode to think about what the *Gentleman's Magazine* called the "thorough humiliation" of the "proud city" of Genoa at the hands of Britain's allies.[68] His eighteenth-century editor Langhorne thought that "sad *Liguria*" alluded to "those ravages in the state of Genoa, occasioned by the unhappy divisions [in the twelfth century] of the Guelphs and Gibelines."[69] But it seems more likely that his source, as Lonsdale implies, is Thomas Salmon's survey of *Modern History* (1739).[70]

The only other phrases that even hint at a topical application are the mythical "blest Divorce" (line 87) that separated Britain from the continent and her "ravag'd Shore" (line 138). Weinbrot may be right in suspecting that the former is a "covert disagreement with Hanoverian attempts to wed British and German interests,"[71] but it seems more likely that this ancient event is a celebration of Britain's providential insularity (Thomson and other English writers had long thought of the encircling sea as a kind of protective barrier[72]), and an answer to the symbolic (and in the event ineffectual) espousal between Venice and the sea.[73] In any

[67] Lonsdale, ed., *Gray, Collins, and Goldsmith*, 446; Wendorf and Ryskamp, eds., *Works of Collins*, 140.
[68] At the same time, the recent capture of Genoa may have added a resonance to Collins' phrase.
[69] *Poetical Works*, 1765 edn., 165.
[70] Salmon notes that "no state has ever suffered greater or more frequent revolutions" than Genoa (*Modern History*, 3rd. edn., 3 vols. [London 1744–46], II, 291).
[71] "William Collins," 20. But why should an opponent of Britain's embrace of continental Hanoverian interests imagine the relation to Hanover as a marriage that needs to be broken up? Why dignify a thirty-year liaison between two states – the Hanoverians arrived in Britain in 1714 – by thinking of it as a wedding?
[72] Cf. Thomson's praise of the "Island of Bliss! Amid the subject Seas, / That thunder round thy rocky Coasts" (*Summer*, lines 1595–96), and the closing lines of Joseph Warton's "Ode to Liberty" (1746): "On deep foundations may thy freedom stand, / Long as the surge shall lash thy sea-encircled land."
[73] "Divorce" need not be an allusion to the married state. Topographical writers spoke of the "divorce" of British islands from the mainland (William Lambard, *A Perambulation of Kent* [London,

case, when Collins' contemporaries wanted to protest the wedding of British and German/Hanoverian interests, they felt free to speak out boldly, as did young Charles Ross on the floor of the House in 1743 and 1744, supporting Opposition attacks on the hiring of Hanoverian mercenaries.[74] "Ravag'd shore" may not have registered as a topical allusion in December 1746: action in the ongoing continental war was thus far limited to the continent, though fears of invasion were not uncommon.[75] If "ravag'd shore" refers to an invasion at all, it might more likely point to the landing of Charles Edward in northern Scotland over a year earlier. But by the spring of 1746 that invasion no longer offered a threat.[76] Again, it seems more likely that Collins' reference is generalized – to the spirit of rancor that continued to divide freedom-loving Britons against each other, and the vigorous campaign throughout the early 1740s by the Opposition press.[77]

Attempts to identify a precise political context distract attention from what is of equal importance, its literary context. William Levine has effectively shown that Collins' ode "borrows and transforms" the "stock of Whig poetical commonplaces" in Thomson's five-part poem *Liberty* (1736–38), which had confidently celebrated (in the words of its dedication) the "excellent establishment" of Liberty in Great Britain. As Levine argues, Collins ignores Thomson's "Patriot" praise of commerce and industry, as well as his emphasis on the need to guard against internal political corruption. More important, Thomson's "triumphant narrative" of the "progress" of Liberty from Greece and Rome to Britain becomes "problematized" in Collins' poem, where Liberty is "always accompanied by violence" (567) and where her true British home is found not in the heroic present but in the "idealized, precultural" (560) – and

1576], 78). For Johnson, the word can mean "to force asunder, to separate by violence." He cites Carew's *Survey of Cornwall* (1602, new edition 1723) on Cornwall and St. Michael's Mount, now "divorced by the downfallen cliffs." Cf. Cowper: "Till knees and hassocks are well nigh divorced" (*Task*, 1, line 748).

74 Stewart surveys the Opposition's efforts through motions in parliament and extraparliamentary pamphlets ("Collins' Ode on the Death of Charles Ross," 213–17).

75 William Levine thinks the phrase is a "metaphoric projection of a country's anguish over its military losses on the Continent" ("Collins, Thomson, and the Whig Progress of Liberty," 566).

76 Carver imagines that the poem was begun "during Collins' warlike mood, a little before or immediately after the Battle of Culloden" and finished "at a time [i.e., autumn 1746] when the country was sated with the fruits of victory of home and wearied by the prolongation of the war with France" (120). His unsubstantiated biographical speculation breaks up on historical rocks: much of "the country" was eager for war in late 1746.

77 See Harris, *A Patriot Press*, 95–177. Ironically, the spirit of opposition largely subsided at the time of the Jacobite rebellion, and, according to Harris, led to an upwelling of loyalist sentiment. Collins' poem more accurately reflects the temper of the years up to 1745 than thereafter.

thus inaccessible – past. But in the end Levine is more interested in what he sees as the poem's political context, "the later stages of an unpopular war" and a desire for an end to "militarism" (570, 571). As I have argued, this mistakes both the mood of the country in 1746 (when the war against France was much more widely supported than before) and Collins' own praise of "Warlike Honour"[78] in the "Ode to Peace" or Albion's "Chiefs... / In warlike Weeds" in this poem. And it puts the emphasis on the international arena, when the poem, beginning with the second epode, is almost completely concerned with Liberty *in Britain*.

Levine also overlooks what is probably a more immediate part of the poem's literary context, an "Ode to Liberty" published almost simultaneously in Joseph Warton's *Odes on Various Subjects* (December 1746), a poem Collins very likely knew, since he and Warton had been projecting a joint publication.[79] Like Thomson's *Liberty*, Warton's ode is patriotic in a largely self-congratulatory way. Britain has "for ages past" been Liberty's "choicest darling care." Warton comfortably assumes that Liberty is attended by Pleasure, Health, Joy, Wealth, Plenty, and Science. His poem is structured by easy oppositions, contrasts between liberty and conventional figures of the pining prisoner, the galley slave, the sultan's harem, and the captive African king, and such cartoon villains as Doubt, Murder, Tyranny, and Revenge. Britannia must remember the fate of Greece and Rome, and stand "watch" to prevent the loss of liberty to "some death-dispensing tyrant," but Warton himself doesn't seem to believe in this bogeyman, or in any real threat to British liberty.[80]

By contrast, Collins' patriotism is critical. He worries about Britain's "ravag'd Shore" and suggests that the high-water mark of British Liberty was the reign of Elizabeth if not the distant pre-Roman past. Collins is less confident than Warton, but he finds grounds for hope. Fortunately for

---

[78] Levine also goes astray in suggesting that Collins (or Thomson, for that matter) shows support for "republican forms of government," "republican rhetoric," or "benevolent autonomous republicanism" ("Collins, Thomson," 559, 566, 567). There is no evidence to support the idea that either poet was anything but a Whig who supported limited monarchy.

[79] Foxon lists yet another contemporary poem on the topic, *Liberty: An Ode* (July 1746).

[80] Incongruously, Warton acknowledges that Liberty requires violent acts in its defense, alluding to Lucius Junius Brutus who killed his own sons when he discovered their conspiracy to restore the Tarquins, Marcus Junius Brutus who killed his friend Caesar, Leonidas who died at Thermopylae, and Gustavus Vasa who freed the Swedes from Danish rule. It was perhaps Warton's poem that prompted Collins to acknowledge the "bloody cycle of liberation and violence" that Levine ("Collins, Thomson," 570) has noticed in his ode.

Britain, "The beauteous *Model* still remains" (line 106), and the poet may yet be able to offer a glimpse of its majesty and "mix'd Design" of Gothic and Grecian principles. But Collins remains troubled by something inherent in British Liberty that needs correction.[81] "Now sooth Her," he urges,

> to her blissful Train
> Blithe *Concord*'s social Form to gain:
> *Concord*, whose Myrtle Wand can steep
> Ev'n *Anger*'s blood-shot eyes in Sleep.

Liberty must be "soothed" so that Concord, who unlike Liberty has a "social Form," is willing to join her train. What Collins means is not made very clear, but "social" suggests that he means something like what Goldsmith worried about in *The Traveller*, where Englishmen are "Fierce in their native hardiness of soul, / True to imagined right, above control," and where an unalloyed Freedom carries its own price:

> foster'd even by Freedom, ills annoy:
> That independence Britons prize too high,
> Keeps man from man and breaks the social tie.
> (lines 331–32, 338–40)[82]

What Collins hopes for is another figurative marriage, a softening of the hard edge of Liberty (which, he implies, expresses itself in Anger and Rage).

But he took little care to articulate just what this means in political terms, and has left readers puzzling over his final lines:

> Her let our Sires and Matrons hoar
> Welcome to *Britain*'s ravag'd Shore,
> Our Youths, enamour'd of the Fair,
> Play with the Tangles of her Hair,
> Till in one loud applauding Sound,
> The Nations shout to Her around,
> O how supremely thou are blest,
> Thou, Lady, Thou shalt rule the West!

"Her" probably refers back not to Concord (three lines earlier) but to Liberty (called "Her" just six lines earlier), for it seems bizarre that an

---

[81] Collins' worries were lost on one reviewer in 1764 (when Britain was in a triumphant mood), who remarks that the "ancient tradition that there was formerly a temple of liberty in Britain, awakes, at once, the enthusiasm and the patriotism of our liberal Bard" (*Monthly Review*, 30 [1764], 25).

[82] Cf. the importance of "social" ties in Thomson. See above, 90–91.

ode "to Liberty" would end with the arrival and reign not of Liberty
herself but of Concord. The allusion to "Lycidas,"[83] which seems to
turn Liberty into a "fair" inamorata available for love-play, has been
thought equally bizarre. Perhaps Collins, in recommending that Liberty
acquire a "social" dimension, was trying to invoke Milton's context, in
which the "uncessant care" of single-minded and solitary poetic aspiration is contrasted with a more relaxed pursuit of pleasure and society. In
fact, the poem is studded with Miltonic allusions. The "Youths" in the
ode's opening lines, with Adamic "Locks . . . / Like vernal Hyacinths,"[84]
"Applauding *Freedom*," and hot for glorious deeds, now are diverted
into milder pastimes. Their applause is transferred to the "Nations"
all "around" Liberty. If we read this line in a political context, it oddly
suggests that Britain has an international role after all, not the nations
of continental Europe but the three "Nations" of England and Wales,
Scotland, and Ireland joined in the United Kingdom.[85] But Collins'
language – *hail, the nations, shout, supremely, blest, rule* – suggests that he
is probably thinking biblically rather than politically. Like Mary before
her, Liberty is "hailed" as "supremely blest"[86] (cf. "hail . . . blessed art
thou among women," Luke 1.28); and Britain is like favored Israel:
"All nations shall call you blessed" (Malachi 3. 12).[87] The ode does
not end with a contemporary Pax Britannica or a patriotic hymn to a
Britannia that "rules the waves." It ends rather with an apocalyptic vision, in which "the West" suggests the Fortunate Isles in the western
ocean – Collins had earlier compared the "little Isles" of Britain to the

[83] "Or with the tangles of Neaera's hair" (line 69).
[84] Cf. Adam's "Hyacinthine Locks" (*Paradise Lost*, IV. 301). Cf. also "Beyond the Measure vast
   of Thought" (line 64) and "what thought can measure thee" (*Paradise Lost*, VII. 602); "pillar'd
   Earth" (line 76) and "pillar'd firmament" (*Comus*, line 598); "like Gems . . . / The little Isles"
   (lines 80–81) and "Sea-girt Isles / . . . like . . . gems" (*Comus*, lines 21–22); "Navel . . . / . . . In some
   religious Wood" (lines 90–91) and "navel of this hideous Wood" (*Comus*, line 520).
[85] Cf. Pope's "three realms" of England and Wales, Scotland, and Ireland in *Rape of the Lock*, III. 7.
[86] The probably unconscious echo of Pope's *Essay on Man*, II. 270 ("Supremely blest, the poet in
   his muse") masks the allusion to the power of the "Supreme Being," whom Hooker calls "the
   Supreme Guide and Monarch of the whole world."
[87] "Nations" in biblical use denotes the gentiles or "heathen nations." With Collins' oddly *shout-
   ing* "Nations," cf. Ezra 3:11: "All the people shouted with a great shout, when they praised
   the Lord," and 1 Samuel 4. 5: "And when the ark of the covenant of the Lord came into
   the camp, all Israel shouted with a great shout." For "rule" in conjunction with "nations," cf.
   Revelation 12.5: "a man child who was to rule all nations." The Collins who in later years,
   according to Johnson, carried with him only one book – "but that is the best" (*Lives*, III, 339) –
   must have been a Bible-reader ten years earlier. Perhaps too Collins echoes the *Joyful Ode*
   (1743), where Victory "hears the Conq'ring Shout, / Once more, in her oft-wedded Nation
   blest" (7).

"Islands blest" (line 107)[88] – and figures as a mythical alternative to the world of actual domestic and international politics.[89]

The political vision at the end of the "Ode to Liberty" takes the reader far from the contemporary situation and proposes an idea of national harmony that is difficult to align with any faction. It may have been in part for those reasons that Collins' odes failed to get the kind of reception for which their author hoped. During a decade when readers of periodicals and pamphlets were being eagerly solicited to take sides on the political issues of the day, Collins declines to be a partisan poet or to satisfy a taste for occasional verse.[90] (His political reticence may have been a matter of calculation as well as temperament: when his *Odes* were published, the Habeas Corpus Act, suspended at the outbreak of the '45, had not yet been restored.) Like his contemporaries, the Warton brothers, Collins seems to have wanted to distinguish poetry from mere "moralizing in verse," and to have aimed at a denser, richer texture, highly figurative and allegorical, even when he was addressing contemporary patriotic subjects. At a time when readers of poetry were still accustomed to encounter what Joseph Warton called "didactic Poetry" and "Essays on moral Subjects," Collins' odes – even his patriotic odes – may have seemed insufficiently clear. It must be conceded too that several long-familiar features of Collins' poems probably made it difficult for readers to understand him: his dense syntax, his vagueness about agency, his habit of altering and revising epithets, stanzas, and titles.

Furthermore, Collins seems not to have worked out a consistent politics, a consistent idea about how patriotism and poetry might best be joined, or a consistent sense of what the patriotic poet might hope to accomplish. In the elegiac odes his ambitions seem modest, but the poet of the odes to Mercy and Peace, and especially the ode to Liberty and the summary ode on "The Passions," is a figure of great enthusiasm, energy, and ambition. Still clinging to an idea of Collins as poet of anxiety, Wendorf notices that, in the "Ode to Liberty" a "desire to

[88] In so doing, Collins is pursuing to its end the idea, found in Thomson's *Liberty* and elsewhere, that Britain is a "blest isle" (v, line 633).

[89] Cf. the visionary language at the end of Bolingbroke's *Idea of a Patriot King* (circulating in the 1740s): in "the whole glorious scene of a patriot reign . . . things so seldom allied as empire and liberty are intimately mixed," in the place of "civil fury . . . concord will appear, brooding peace and prosperity on the happy land," and the Patriot King will appear "at the head of a united people" (*Patriot King*, in *Political Writings*, 141).

[90] Harris argues that, as evidenced by the waning vigor of the press debate, "concern with issues of national politics" sharply declined after 1746 (*A Patriot Press*, 219).

fulfill his patriotic obligations" draws Collins into "celebration of his own poetic powers." If we expect a mid-century poet to be anxious and self-doubting, we may find such "celebration" both "uncharacteristic" and unconvincing, and the confidence unjustified, as Wendorf does.[91] But if we dispense with the idea of the solipsistic poet, still wandering (despite what he claims in "The Manners") in the "dim-discover'd Tracts of Mind" (line 2) and barred (in the "Ode on the Poetical Character") from the Miltonic bower, and if we read his odes in the context of the patriotic aspirations of his poetic contemporaries, we can find in the patriotic Collins a poet who eagerly explores "that ampler Range, / Where Life's wide Prospects round thee change" ("The Manners," lines 21–22). And we can find a patriot-poet who writes not to arouse the pride of his countrymen but to temper their rough devotion to liberty, independence, and revenge.

[91] *William Collins and Eighteenth-Century English Poetry*, 114.

CHAPTER 6

Thomas Gray: "some great and singular service to his country"

Matthew Arnold thought it strange and regrettable that Gray "never spoke out." Regarding him as the "poetical classic" of an unpoetic age, Arnold hoped for more "volume" and "power" from Gray, greater poetic production and poems of greater scope than the *Elegy* and a few odes.[1] For today's readers, less inclined to blame the age and more inclined to regard his major poems as bold utterances, it remains remarkable that a poet of Gray's gifts and convictions, who came to maturity about 1750, should apparently have had so little to say in his poems about the major public issues of his day – war with France, the Jacobite rebellion, empire, the protection of English liberties, the dangers and delights of commerce and luxury. And it remains paradoxical that the author of the *Elegy*, probably still today the best-known and best-loved poem in English, as well as "The Progress of Poesy" and "The Bard," which many of his contemporaries regarded as "the best odes in our language,"[2] should in his poems seem so little concerned with national politics. In some real sense he spoke (and speaks) for "the nation," but does one ever feel that, like Pope or Thomson, Goldsmith or Cowper, he speaks as a patriot, a self-conscious lover of his country?

Gray's reticence as a public spokesman is more remarkable when one considers both his own situation and the state of literature in his day. Though not born to great privilege, Gray was from his youth educated as a member of his country's elite – at Eton and then at Cambridge, at the Inns of Court and on the Grand Tour. Not only that, his closest school friend was son of the sitting Prime Minister, and his classmates included men who in their twenties could already be regarded as

[1] The famous words are in fact those of James Brown, Master of Pembroke College, Cambridge, in Gray's lifetime, adapted by Arnold to be a sort of critical key to Gray's life and work. Arnold's essay, entitled "Thomas Gray," first appeared in 1880.
[2] The words of John ("Estimate") Brown. See W. Powell Jones, "The Contemporary Readers of Gray's Odes," *Modern Philology*, 28 (1930–31), 61–82.

"Statesmen."[3] In his adult years Gray counted among his intimates several members of parliament, including Horace Walpole and Thomas Pitt (nephew of the Earl of Chatham), as well as Richard Stonhewer, who was eventually to hold high office in the Treasury and the Excise (and who was instrumental in securing for Gray the post of Regius Professor of Modern History at Cambridge).[4] Gray's own letters to and from his politically connected friends show that he had the keenest interest in the political maneuverings in parliament and at court, and that he avidly sought out and passed on news of the fortunes of Britain's armies and navies as they fought the French on the continent and in North America. To judge by his letters, no poet of the century – apart from Swift and perhaps Pope – had as lively and informed an interest in high politics. His extraordinarily wide reading kept him abreast of – and prompted his vigorous response to – not only current poetry and scholarship but also broad cultural controversy, such as that aroused by John Brown's *Estimate of the Manners of the Age* (1757). As the most important of the arts, poetry in his view required of its practitioners "a liberal education, a degree of literature, & various knowledge " (*Correspondence*, II, 811). Both Mason and Johnson reprinted a "character" written a year after Gray's death in which he is called

perhaps . . . the most learned man in Europe. He was equally acquainted with the elegant and profound parts of science, and that not superficially but thoroughly. He knew every branch of history, both natural and civil; had read all the original historians of England, France, and Italy; and was a great antiquarian. Criticism, metaphysicks, morals, politics made a principal part of his study; voyages and travels of all sorts were his favourite amusements.[5]

A poet with Gray's knowledge and interests, Johnson implies, might have written about anything.

The literary climate within which Gray worked also offered him implicit invitations – which he steadily declined – to write on the political issues of the day. As we have seen, Thomson, Akenside, and even Collins had in the 1740s published poems responding directly to the

---

3 See Gray's own May 1742 letter to Walpole about his Eton years, *Correspondence*, I, 210.

4 Other close friends included John Lord Cavendish, son of the Duke of Devonshire, member of parliament for more than forty years, and ultimately Chancellor of the Exchequer; William Mason, who served as chaplain to both George II and George III; and Richard West, whose father was Lord Chancellor of Ireland.

5 Johnson, *Lives*, III, 429–30. Cf. Johnson's own account of Gray's letter about his 1765 trip to Scotland: "as his comprehension was ample his curiosity extended to all the works of art, all the appearances of nature, and all the monuments of past events" (427). Gray's letter is found in *Correspondence*, II, 887–95.

Jacobite rebellion, the war in Europe, or the political infighting in parliament. Dodsley's famous *Collections* of poetry, which began appearing in 1748, gave prominence to political poems from the 1710s and 1720s by Thomas Tickell and Lord Lyttelton. The conventions of public elegy, freshly deployed in Tickell's elegy on the death of Addison (also included in Dodsley's *Collection*), invited reflections on the lives and deaths of great men. The Pindaric ode, a form in which Gray chose to work, was in eighteenth-century England intimately associated with the celebration of British "Liberty" or with military victories or important occasions in the lives of the country's political leaders. Although Gray turned down an invitation to become the country's Poet Laureate, he in fact admired the official Pindaric odes produced by the man who took up the post (and with it the responsibility for producing birthday and New Year's odes), William Whitehead.[6] By the time Gray wrote his "Ode on a Distant Prospect of Eton College," the "prospect" tradition (with its long view from a hilltop) was already well established as a means of surveying the symbolic landscape of the nation. And when Gray wrote on "The Progress of Poesy," the "progress" form had long been used to celebrate the triumphant cultural and political achievements of the poet's own day. Despite all of this, Gray in his poems seems to have turned his eyes from the state of the nation.

INTERPRETING GRAY

How are we to interpret Gray's aversion and his silence? There has been no lack of critical response. Gray's case, in fact, seems to prompt critics to large-scale theoretical claims about the literature of the age, or about literature generally. An Arnoldian answer is to argue that the times in which Gray wrote, what Arnold himself called the leaden "age of prose and reason," were (regardless of contemporary poetic conventions) simply not "favourable" to the production of a politically engaged poetry or to poetry on a heroic scale. An answer from Harold Bloom or Walter Jackson Bate would point to Gray's weakened position as a poet who followed in the shadow of literary greatness that, in the end, intimidated him or left him with the sense that there was nothing left to be done.[7]

---

[6] See below, 175.

[7] Bate in fact does not mention Gray in his *The Burden of the Past and the English Poet* (Cambridge, MA, 1970), or in his earlier *From Classic to Romantic: Premises of Taste in Eighteenth-Century England* (Cambridge, MA, 1946). Gray is also absent from Harold Bloom's *Anxiety of Influence* (New York, 1973).

Gray's best modern editor, Roger Lonsdale, writes of Gray's sense that the poet in his age no longer has any "social function."[8] John Sitter was later to write of Gray as an exemplar of the large-scale "flight from history" in mid-eighteenth-century English poetry, and of the consciousness his contemporary poets had of themselves not as acute observers and analysts of a social scene but "as solitary writers for solitary readers."[9] More recent historicist critics point to Gray's fastidious loathing of the developing literary marketplace, and to his reluctance to put himself forward in public as an "author" or a "man of letters."[10]

Given the tradition of viewing Gray as an essentially private and even solipsistic poet, it comes as a surprise to remember that there is another critical tradition which has always examined Gray's poems for their implicit politics. The tradition begins with those eighteenth-century readers of "The Bard" whom Johnson was concerned to refute: "I do *not* see that *The Bard* promotes any truth, moral or political" (III, 438, emphasis added). But Gray's nineteenth-century editor, John Mitford, found a central political truth: "The tendency of *The Bard* is to show the retributive justice that follows an act of tyranny and wickedness."[11] William Empson argued in a famous passage at the beginning of *Some Versions of Pastoral* that even the "universal" *Elegy Written in a Country Churchyard* contains "latent political ideas." After quoting the stanza about the flower that wastes its sweetness on the desert air, Empson observes that Gray makes a particular "social arrangement" (that few opportunities are open to the poor) seem an "inevitable" part of nature. There is something "pathetic" about the waste, "but the reader is put into a mood in which one would not try to alter it." In other words, the poem sustains and endorses a hierarchical social order, and deters any reader from thinking that social arrangements ought to be different.[12]

---

[8] *Gray, Collins, and Goldsmith*, 115. In a later essay tellingly subtitled "Versions of the Self," Lonsdale viewed Gray's poems as "a sustained struggle to find decorous ways of talking about the self and about the meaning of one's own life" ("The Poetry of Thomas Gray: Versions of the Self," *Proceedings of the British Academy* [1973], 112).

[9] *Literary Loneliness*, 9.

[10] See, for example, Linda Zionkowski, "Bridging the Gulf between the Poet and the Audience in the Work of Gray," *ELH*, 58 (1991), 331–50, and William Levine, "'Beyond the Limits of a Vulgar Fate': The Renegotiation of Public and Private Concerns in the Career of Gray and other Mid-Eighteenth-Century Poets," *Studies in Eighteenth-Century Culture*, 24 (1995), 223–42. By contrast with most critics, Wallace Jackson points not to any cultural pressures, but to Gray's "utterly and completely personal" failure as a poet ("Thomas Gray and the Dedicatory Muse," *ELH*, 54 [1987], 277).

[11] *Works of Gray*, 5 vols. (London, 1835–43), II, Preface.

[12] *Some Versions of Pastoral* (London, 1935, rev. edn., Harmondsworth, 1965), 11–12.

Empson himself, writing as a Marxist in the 1930s, and primarily interested in twentieth-century "proletarian literature," is unclear as to
whether he regards Gray's political point of view as "aristocratic" or
"bourgeois." But his hint that Gray should be read *politically* has been influential. Some later critics, taking the lead from Empson, have tried to locate Gray within a specific eighteenth-century political milieu. For James
Steele, Gray's "world vision" was "consistently that of a Whiggish, im-
perialistic bourgeois, latterly a Pittite."[13] Primarily citing evidence from
Gray's letters, Steele emphasizes Gray's family connections and financial
circumstances. But he gives little attention to Gray's poems and, when
he does, is remarkably inattentive to tone and nuance. His approach
to Gray is undergirded by a teleological Marxist theory of history, in
which Gray's benighted fellow bourgeois imperialists "had a bloody but
constructive contribution to make to the world" (235).

John Sitter takes up Empson's hint that Gray should be read *politically*.
In his 1982 book, Gray is an instance of the "politics of melancholy," a
widespread sentiment in the mid eighteenth century (and not merely a
psychological condition affecting neurotic poets) that success and ambition are suspect, and commerce and cities unattractive, that war and
poetry are incompatible, in short "a general protest against various capi-
talistic tendencies."[14] Without citing Empson explicitly, he too finds that
Gray, in the *Eton Ode*, "cannot or will not make a distinction between
necessary and unnecessary human suffering."[15] Responding to the influential idea from the 1970s that to claim to be above politics is itself
a political stance, Sitter finds in the middle decades of the eighteenth
century a new but "unconscious politicization of poetry."[16] Ten years
later Suvir Kaul, also citing Empson, proposed again (in opposition to
Steele) that the key political category in Gray is not party but social class.
Unlike Sitter, who saw a "Flight from History," Kaul sees "an insistent engagement with its contemporary discursive, cultural, and social

---

[13] "Thomas Gray and the Season for Triumph," in James Downey and Ben Jones, eds., *Fearful Joy: Papers from the Thomas Gray Bicentenary Conference at Carleton University* (Montreal, 1974), 198–240, here 235. Steele's paper was not in fact delivered at the conference.

[14] *Literary Loneliness*, 106, 107.

[15] *Literary Loneliness*, 89. Empson is also the unacknowledged source for John Lucas' sentences on the *Elegy* – it "underwrites an almost entirely complacent account of a 'settled' society ... Its recommendation of 'the cool sequestered vale of life' produces an 'innocent' reading of the actual labour and social relations of the vale" (*England and Englishness: Ideas of Nationhood in English Poetry, 1688–1900* [London, 1990], 45).

[16] *Literary Loneliness*, 89. Sitter acknowledges that while Gray "offers no political platform," what is "politically significant" is that "childhood and rural innocence are being used as new norms by which to measure the passionate tragedy of the world adults make" (89).

forms." Reflecting contemporary critical affinities for ideological contradictions, he also set himself apart from Steele by claiming that where
Steele saw "zeal and fervour" in Gray's commitment to the "ideology
of empire," Kaul sees "hesitations and dialogic uncertainties." He finds
Gray a "reluctant public prophet."[17] Prompted by Marxist social history ("the country aristocracy," he says, were in Gray's day "giving way
to the mercantile bourgeoisie" [148]), he uncovers ideological traces by
putting great pressure on isolated lines from Gray's poems. His readings
are bizarrely strained: even the "Ode on the Death of a Favourite Cat"
"serves both imperial and domestic ideological interests . . . Man's anxi-
eties about the progress of Britain as a trading empire are systematically
re-written as narratives of women's lust and depravity" (179).

Marxist and deconstructive readings of Gray have begun to recede,
but he continues to attract attention as a reflection of political tensions
in his day, particularly from critics interested in British "national myths."
Christine Gerrard wants to link his poems of the 1750s with the Patriot
Opposition to Walpole in the 1730s, and, observing that "The Bard" was
written "on the eve of the Seven Years War and Pitt's imperial victories,"
finds in the poem "an implicit identification with the oppressed victims of
English victories."[18] Quite apart from the fact that in 1757 British fortunes
of war were distinctly bleak – the tide did not turn until 1759 – and thus
Gray's "ruthless king" (Edward I) seems remote from George II, even a
casual reading of Gray's letters will show, as Steele notes, that Gray on
the whole had great admiration for Pitt.

Sharing Gerrard's interest in "national myth," but approaching the
topic from literary rather than political history, Howard Weinbrot's
Britannia's Issue has intriguingly regarded Gray as a kind of cultural patriot, a champion of a distinctly native (rather than classical) culture.
Taking for the title of his book a phrase from "The Bard," Weinbrot goes
so far as to see the poem as a "national ode," and Gray as expressing the
"public voice of the nation." Gray is deployed to support the governing
thesis of Weinbrot's book, that a self-consciously "British" culture arose
in the eighteenth century, and that poets such as Gray both reflected
and created that culture.[19] Whether we can demonstrate that Gray's

---

[17] *Thomas Gray and Literary Authority: A Study in Ideology and Poetics* (Stanford, 1992), 149, 212, 221.
[18] *Patriot Opposition*, 148. Gerrard seems to take her view of Gray from Lucas, who finds in Gray
   an "oppositional" voice. *The Bard* looks to him to be "a statement against xenophobic, anti-
   libertarian nationalism," but he sensibly concedes that Gray, "no radical," wouldn't want the
   poem to say that (*England and Englishness*, 44–45).
[19] *Britannia's Issue*, 333, 397.

eighteenth-century readers read him as a patriotic or "national" poet, or can legitimately link Weinbrot's "native values and models" with other aspects of a developing British national identity, remains to be seen.[20]

In the light of such large and contradictory claims about the nature of eighteenth-century culture both from those who see Gray as essentially apolitical and those who find him politically engaged, it may be well to launch a more modest inquiry into Gray's politics and his poetry, seeking – by means of more patient attention to what Gray wrote – to arrive at a defensible account. That will require a broader survey of Gray's writings, from the letters to his early Latin poems, from the *Alliance on Education and Government* to his late "Ode for Music." It will also involve careful attention to Gray's indirections and disguises, the bias for facetiousness and irony in his letters, the bias for decorous generalized utterance in the odes, and for habitual self-deprecation whenever he comments on his own poems, which he affected to call mere trifles, and things with or without endings to them.

GRAY'S POLITICS

The best evidence for Gray's politics is found in his extensive correspondence. By extracting from Gray's letters many of his incidental remarks about contemporary political events, James Steele (whose essay constitutes the most thorough account of Gray's political principles and affiliations) confidently concludes that he was a lifelong Whig, a champion of English "liberty," unwilling to support Britain's military adventures in the 1740s, but by the mid-1750s an ardent Pittite, eager for the expansion of British commercial and military interests. It is easy for the reader of Gray's letters to confirm that he avidly followed the progress of Pitt's war for empire, anxiously awaiting the latest news reports and promptly passing them on to his correspondents:

What are we to believe about Silesia? am I to make bonfires, or keep a general fast? pray, rid me of this suspense, for it is very uneasy to me. (December 1757, *Correspondence*, II, 542–43)

News is hourly expected of a Battle in Westphalia. (July 1759, II, 628)

The season for triumph is at last come [Gray's response to the victory at Minden, August 1759]. (II, 632)

[20] Gray's obvious admiration for Pindar (in "The Progress of Poesy") has to present a problem for Weinbrot, who argues that British poets tend to depreciate Pindar as a mere celebrant of jockeys.

This is a very critical time, an action being hourly expected between the two great Fleets, but no news as yet. (November 1759, II, 652)

You will have heard of Hawke's Victory [at Quiberon Bay] before this can reach you. (II, 654)

We are in great alarms about Quebec. (June 1760, II, 679)

It is also easy to find Gray declaring that his "Principles in Government" are those of "every true and rational Whig" (II, 469), and avowing his admiration for Pitt, as he does in 1765 when it was said that Pitt, "dangerously ill" with the gout, might not survive: "I hope & rather believe, it is not true. when he is gone, all is gone, & England will be old England again, such as (before his administration) it always was eversince we were born" (II, 873).[21] And like many Whigs, Gray was disappointed that Pitt accepted a pension and a peerage in 1761.[22] It seems clear too that, like many a Whig, Gray, though uninclined to republicanism, had no special reverence for monarchy. George II – seventy-three years old when the Seven Years' War broke out – appears in the letters of the late 1750s with some irony as "old *Priam*" (II, 511) and "the old Gentleman" (II, 659). "It is an odd contemplation," Gray wrote in 1759 in England's great year of military triumph, "that *somebody* [i.e., George II] should have lived long enough to grow a great & glorious Monarch" (II, 655). When the King died, Gray reported the news in an utterly matter-of-fact tone: "This event happens at an unlucky time, but (I should think) will make little alteration in publick measures" (II, 708). It was the ministry rather than the King who, in Gray's view, really controlled "publick measures."

But it is unsafe (*pace* Steele's confidence) to infer much more about Gray's politics than that. Even his intimate friend Walpole said that he never understood Gray's political opinions: "sometimes he seemed to incline to the side of authority; and sometimes to that of the people."[23] The persistently facetious tone of Gray's letters also makes it difficult to tell how much irony we should hear in any particular phrase, e.g., "We are all very sorry for poor Queen Hungary" (I, 207), or "I give you joy of Porto-Bello" (I, 147) and "Admiral Vernon will shine in our medallic history"

---

[21] On their surface Gray's words fear the loss of an extraordinary leader, who made England into a greater nation. But they hint at an opposite meaning: with the imperialist Pitt gone we can recover the timeless "old England" that we had nearly lost.

[22] See especially *Correspondence*, II, 761, 763, 771.

[23] *Walpoliana* (Dublin, 1800), I, 21. Reflecting further, Walpole thought this "natural" enough: "When a portion of the people shews gross vices, or idle sedition arising from mere ignorance or prejudice; one wishes it checked by authority. When the governors pursue wicked plans, or weak measures, one wishes a spirited opposition by the people at large."

(I, 171) – which Steele takes to be the ironic remarks of a Whig opposed to war with Spain in 1740. Furthermore, Gray's ostensible political loyalties did not prevent him from laughing at the foibles of the great, as when he reports on Pitt's 1759 speech on the death of Wolfe with mingled derision and deadpan irony: "a studied & puerile declamation on funereal honours . . . in the course of it he wiped his eye with one handkerchief, & Beckford (who seconded him) cried too, & wiped with two handkershiefs at once, wch was very moving" (II, 651). It is as if some dry skepticism in Gray prevents him from full-hearted admiration or patriotism. After Hawke's victory at Quiberon Bay, Gray urbanely imagines the popular celebrations: "as to the Nation, I fear, it will not know how to behave itself, being just in the circumstances of a Chambermaid, that has got the 20,000£ Prize in the Lottery" (II, 655). Even William III figures in the letters as a sort of sacred cow whom no Whig dares to criticize.[24]

In some respects Gray's politics can be plausibly coordinated with his family background and his political connections. In his early years he was in effect a ministerial Whig, a supporter of the pacific policies of Sir Robert Walpole at a time when Patriot poets such as Thomson and Akenside were denouncing him for corruption. Gray appears to be no friend of the Patriot group either in the early 1740s or the 1750s, when he refers to Charles Townshend (whom Akenside addressed with admiration) as "a most unprincipled Patriot" (I, 450). But some other elements are difficult to square. In 1757 Gray reported that he admired in John Brown's *Estimate* "the dissertation against Trade, for I have always said, it was the ruin of the Nation" (II, 499). If he genuinely believed that trade was "the ruin of the Nation," Gray was rejecting the principles on which his own family's wealth had been built – as Steele notes, his grandfather was a rich East India merchant and his father both a scrivener and draper – as well as the commercial interests who were the most prominent supporters of Pitt and the war for empire. Perhaps his animus against trade was the disdain of the scholar-gentleman who sought to distance himself from his family background. Gray withheld assent from the remainder of Brown's famous diatribe, perhaps because he could not agree with its central thesis that aristocratic English culture had become "effeminate," infected by an uncritical admiration for all things French. Neither Gray's letters nor his poems suggest that he shared the anti-Gallicanism that prompted much of the pro-war sentiment

[24] *Correspondence*, III, 1007, 1021.

and, as Colley and others have argued, helped define what it meant to be a "Briton." He was an avid reader of – though not always an admirer of – Rousseau, Voltaire, D'Alembert, Buffon, Crébillon père and fils, Montesquieu, and other French writers. Gray's political sensibility was not built on xenophobia or nationalism.

Nor was it built on a sharply partisan view of domestic politics. Gray was no less fascinated with the shifting political scene in the court and parliament than with the fortunes of foreign wars, but he beholds politics as a kind of spectacle about which he is very curious but in which he has no real concern. Acting as a kind of conduit between well-placed sources at Westminster – especially Stonhewer and Walpole (whom he calls his "Gazette") – and friends in Cambridge or Durham, Gray reports on the ministerial changes at the end of the Newcastle administration. His letters constitute a kind of political gossip:

> my Gazette says, that Mr. P: will be Sec: of State, & has accepted it (tho' ill of Gout in the Country) that the D: of Devonshire has consented (wch was one of the conditions of acceptance) to be at the head of the Treasury. (Oct. 1756, II, 485)

Gray confesses that "the present revolution of affairs" is "some spur to my curiosity," but that he himself has no real stake in the matter: "my own interests have no more concern in it, than those of any Cottager in the nation." Even when his own hero is involved, Gray is dispassionate:

> The Ministry are much out of joint. Mr. P: much out of humour, his popularity tottering, chiefly occasion'd by a Pamphlet against the German War, written by that *squeaking* acquaintance of ours, Mr. Mauduit: it has had a vast run. the Irish are very intractable, even the Lds J:s them-selves; great difficulties about who shall be sent over to tame them: my Ld H:ss again named, but (I am told) has refused it. every body waits for a new Parliament to settle their ideas. (Jan. 1761, II, 728)

High parliamentary politics are for Gray not an art or a mystery, but a matter of opposing interests and of politicians actuated by ordinary human motives and feelings – Pitt is "much out of humour." Gray, a privileged observer with access to private discussions, beholds the scene with affected equanimity, in which avid curiosity is checked by haughty detachment.

Furthermore, political intrigue at the center of the British state is no different, Gray implies, from the jockeying for position, office, and glory that goes on everywhere – even at Cambridge, where the resolution of the dispute between the Master and the Fellows of Pembroke College is parodically described in the terms of high politics: "Shall I be expeditious enough to bring you the News of the Peace, before you shall meet with it in the Papers? not the Peace of Aix la Chapelle, . . . , no, nor the Peace between Adil-Shah & the Great Mogol; but the Peace of Pembroke" (II, 314).

A major question of course remains: in what ways, if at all, did Gray's political temperament – Whig principle and a fascination with political power, both held at ironic distance – shape the poems he wrote from his early years in Cambridge in the late 1730s to his last years as Regius Professor of Modern History? Was Gray able, as has been suggested, to compartmentalize his mental life, leaving his greedy appetite for political intrigue and for imperial geopolitics behind him when he turned to write ode, elegy, and sonnet? Or did his political imagination, his readiness to see the world in terms of interest, gain, loss, and glory, who's in and who's out, insensibly color the poems he wrote? Was he a kind of British "patriot" in ways that neither he nor his readers – because they so shared his political assumptions – were aware?

THE EARLY POEMS

Even Gray's early poems show signs of a poet who conceived of a public and even a political role for poetry, and at the same time of a poet who held back from embracing such a role. Given his reputation as retired scholar-poet, it is striking to rediscover that Gray's first published poem was a set of Latin verses celebrating the marriage of the Prince of Wales. It appeared as part of a Cambridge University collection, *Gratulatio Academiae Cantabrigiensis* in 1736. Written, as one of Gray's Cambridge friends noted, in "the Manner of Claudian" (i.e. in high encomiastic style), it salutes Frederick as *Angliacis spes optima regnis* ("best hope of the English realms"). The occasion of a royal marriage conventionally called forth congratulatory verses from aspiring poets hoping for royal patronage. The young Gray responded to the occasion as the older poet refused to do. When Mason felt obliged to apologize in 1775 for Gray's youthful poem – "Every person, who feels himself a poet, ought to be above prostituting his powers on such occasions, and extreme youth . . . is the only thing that can apologize for his having done it"[25] – he was probably echoing Gray's decision in 1757 to decline the laureateship and the literary prostitution that both he and Gray thought it entailed.

[25] William Mason, ed., *Poems of Mr. Gray. To which are prefixed Memoirs of his Life and Writings* (London, 1775), 10n.

Gray's poem reflects institutional loyalty rather than any strong royalism on the poet's part, or any nascent Patriot sentiment for the Prince, whose open opposition to his father did not take place until September 1737, a year and a half after Gray's poem appeared. Nor do Gray's Latin verses "In D: 29am Maii" and "In 5tam Novembris," though they celebrate two royalist holidays (the Restoration of Charles II and the discovery of the Gunpowder Plot), signify any youthful attachment to the Stuart family. As Lonsdale notes, the poems are probably conventional undergraduate exercises.[26] There are signs of routine patriotism – England is *patria cara* ("dear country"), *innumeris belli clara triumphis* ("famous for innumerable triumphs in war"), illustrious both *artibus et bellis, et orbis decus* ("for arts and wars, and the adornment of the world")[27] – of the sort that reappear in Gray's Pindaric odes of the later 1750s.

In a more ambitious Latin work dating from the early 1740s, *De Principiis Cogitandi* ("The Principles of Thinking"), Gray addresses Locke as *Angliacae lux altera gentis* ("second light of the English people"), and declares his hope to have done for England what Lucretius did for Rome: *primus Britanna per arva / Romano liquidum deduxi flumine rivum* ("I first led a lucid stream from the Roman river through British fields"). His aspiration recalls both the literary ambition and nationalism of Milton and of Pope. But where his predecessors vowed to adorn their native language – Milton to write "in the mother dialect" and Pope to be "My Countrys Poet" – Gray deflected their linguistic patriotism by choosing to write not in English but in Latin.[28] It is a characteristic step for a poet who in one way or another held back from adopting the role of "My Countrys Poet." A letter to West, written just as Gray was beginning work on *De Principiis Cogitandi*, hints at the reasons he held back. Gray is weighing the advantages of a "public life and a private one."

To me there hardly appears to be any medium between [them]; he who prefers the first, must put himself in a way of being serviceable to the rest of mankind, if he has a mind to be of any consequence among them: Nay, he must not refuse being in a certain degree even dependent upon some men who already are so. If he has the good fortune to light on such as will make no ill use of his humility, there is no shame in this: If not, his ambition ought to give place to a reasonable

---

[26] *Poems of Gray, Collins, and Goldsmith*, 296. When Gray met the Old Pretender in Rome in 1740, he regarded him as something of a curiosity. In letters home he refers (with dry irony) to "his majesty of Great-Britain," "Il Serenissimo Pretendente (as the Mantova gazette calls him)," and plain "Mr. Stuard" (*Correspondence*, I, 146, 154, 158).

[27] "In D: 29am Maii," line 8, "In 5tam Novembris," lines 13, 16.

[28] Johnson notes that according to Mason, Gray's "first ambition was to have excelled in Latin poetry" (*Lives*, III, 424).

pride, and he should apply to the cultivation of his own mind those abilities which he has not been permitted to use for others' service. (*Correspondence*, I, 169)

Unlike Johnson, for whom the use of one's "talent" was a sacred obligation, Gray weighs the gains – being "of consequence" – and the costs – being dependent, and ill-used – of using his "abilities" so as to be "serviceable to the rest of mankind." He seems unprepared to embrace the idea that the poet may be serviceable to his country.

But he was still attracted to the idea. One other early – and uncompleted – project suggests that in Gray's view poetry (and, more generally, learning) might, indeed must, as he put it in a letter to Wharton, "concur [with government] to produce great & useful Men" (*Correspondence*, I, 310). In 1748 Gray's letters show that he was at work on another long didactic poem on the subject of "The Alliance of Education and Government." This time the poem was in English, and took the form of a Popean ethical essay in couplets. As editors have noted, Gray had been reading and taking notes in his commonplace book on several classical works bearing on his topic, including Book VI of Plato's *Republic* (dealing with the fitness of the philosopher-king to rule) and an oration by Isocrates *On the Peace*, urging Athens to make a general peace with her neighbors, and to return its government to virtue and justice.[29] What may have especially interested Gray was Isocrates' concluding sentence: "when the affairs of Hellas are in a happy and prosperous condition, it follows that the state of learning and letters also is greatly improved."[30] The fragment of some hundred lines that Gray completed before he abandoned the poem indicate that he had been reading or remembering recent English poems dealing with the ends of political society, including Pope's *Essay on Man* (1733–34), Thomson's *Liberty* (1735–36) and *The Seasons* (1730–44), as well as Sir Richard Blackmore's *The Nature of Man* (1711), a poem arguing for the "Advantages" that Englishmen receive from having been born "in a mild Air and temperate Climate." In early 1748 he was also reading Dodsley's new *Collection*, in which the lead poem, Tickell's "On the Prospect of Peace" (written in 1712, at the end of the War of the Spanish Succession), may have prompted Gray to consider the proper

---

[29] In a 1770 letter Gray says that he read Isocrates "20 years ago" (*Correspondence*, III, 1121). W. Powell Jones gives the date with more precision, noting entries on Isocrates' oration in Gray's commonplace book between 26 December 1747 and 1 March 1748 – while Gray was at work on *Alliance* (*Thomas Gray, Scholar* [New York, 1937], 58–61). The signing of the general Peace of Aix la Chapelle on 18 October 1748, ending the War of the Austrian Succession, may have prompted Gray to read Isocrates again.

[30] Quoted from *Isocrates*, vol. II, tr. George Norlin, Loeb Classical Library (Cambridge, MA, 1929), 97.

role of government as the War of the Austrian Succession was coming to a close. He did not care for Tickell's poem – "This is not only a state-poem (my ancient aversion), but a state-poem on the peace of Utrecht" (*Correspondence*, I, 295) – and his own poem may have been designed as a response to Tickell.

It is the influence of climate on the political character of a nation – a topic that much interested his contemporaries – that Gray explores in the fragmentary "Essay I" of what was apparently intended to be a long poem consisting of several such "Essays." Why was it that some nations were disposed to despotism and others to freedom, some to "Industry and Gain" and others to war ("force and hardy deeds of blood")? His initial reflections do not extend beyond an introduction to his topic, but Mason, working from Gray's notes for the poem ("scattered papers in prose"), suggests the directions in which Gray would have proceeded. He was broadly concerned with the difference between the "effeminate Southern nations" and the "warlike Northern people," whose "invasions" are necessary "in order to revive the spirit of mankind" and "to restore them to their native liberty and equality." Gray apparently had in mind not only the enervated Roman empire, invaded and reinvigorated by "Northern" barbarian invaders, but modern exemplars, especially since he associated with "effeminacy" the "arts of commerce."[31] As modern European economies turned increasingly from agriculture to commerce, moralists worried about the enervating effects of "luxury." Gray shared those worries, as evidenced by one of the "maxims" Mason found among his papers:

Commerce changes intirely the fate and genius of nations, by communicating arts and opinions, circulating money, and introducing the materials of luxury; she first opens and polishes the mind, then corrupts and enervates both that and the body.

It appears that Gray's poem would have examined both the effects of luxury and the devotion to "philosophic ease" (line 40) and to pleasure that John Brown was to declaim against ten years later in his *Estimate*.

The doctrine of Epicurus is ever ruinous to society: It had its rise when Greece was declining, and perhaps hastened its dissolution, as also that of Rome; it is now propagated in France and in England, and seems like to produce the same effects in both.[32]

---

[31] If Gray came to think that modern commercial England was acting like an enervated "Southern" country, he may have had another reason to pursue his interest in early "Northern" (Norse and Welsh) poetry.

[32] The "maxims," printer in Mason's *Memoirs*, are reprinted in Lonsdale, ed. *Poems of Gray, Collins, and Goldsmith*, 91.

To counteract the pursuit of pleasure Gray seems to have intended to recommend "education" and "government," working together: "It is the proper work of education and government united to redress the faults that arise from the soil and air" – and presumably the faults that arise from commerce and pleasure. What Gray apparently wanted particularly to promote was the "desire for fame," which "continues and propagates virtue" and "prevents the prevalence of vice in a generation more corrupt than our own." Promoting the desire for fame is the business of government: "Any nation that wants public spirit, neglects education, ridicules the desire of fame, and even of virtue and reason, must be ill-governed." But it seems likely that Gray would also have invoked the traditional role of poetry in conferring fame, and of extending the example of good men "into future ages."

Patriotic love of country was, in Gray's outline, a sign of a well-governed state which promoted the love of fame: "To a native of free and happy governments his country is always dear." By the same token, where tyranny was found, there was "no country" to love, pure selfishness, and thus "no desire of fame." England was of course in Gray's Whiggish view a "free and happy government," but it perhaps gave him pause that in such a state the "contempt of fame" was "one principal characteristic of vice in the present age." Perhaps the country was in fact "ill-governed."

Why Gray did not complete his poem cannot be known with certainty.[33] Mason proposed that it was reading Montesquieu's *L'Esprit des lois* soon after it appeared in November 1748 – while Gray was at work on *The Alliance of Education and Government* – that "made him drop his design." Montesquieu had, so Mason thought, "forestalled some of [Gray's] best thoughts." One may also speculate that Gray could not convince himself that the "contempt" and "ridicule" of fame could be overcome, or that poetry's still small voice would gain listeners or would be able to help produce "great & useful Men." Readers of Mason's *Memoirs*, including Johnson and Gibbon, regretted that Gray never completed the poem.[34] Had he done so, it seems unlikely that we would still think of him as a retiring and essentially inward poet.

But the extent to which Gray can be considered a political or a public poet, engaged with matters of national or patriotic concern, must be determined on the basis not of fragments and uncompleted projects but

---

33 For several speculations, see Lonsdale, ed., *Gray, Collins, and Goldsmith*, 86–87.
34 *The History of the Decline and Fall of the Roman Empire*, ed. David Womersley, 3 vols. (London, 1994), II, 211 n. Johnson thought the fragmentary poem contained "many excellent lines" (*Lives*, III, 424).

of the poems he completed and printed, and in particular on the *Elegy* (1750), the Pindaric odes of 1757, and the "Ode for Music" (1769).

THE *ELEGY*

In what ways, if at all, does Gray's *Elegy* – praised since Johnson's day for its universality – engage the historical circumstances in which it was written and first read, or identify itself as a poem produced at a particular point in England's history? Gray's generalizing rhetoric offers few invitations to contextualization, but this has not deterred critics from making (broadly speaking) two attempts to situate the poem in the political world of mid-century England, neither of which has proved satisfactory.

One set of biographically minded critics have attempted to situate the poem within Gray's own life, and to identify the poem's immediate occasion. Thus the Reverend Duncan Tovey was the first of many commentators to argue that the country churchyard in question must have been that at Stoke Poges, in Buckinghamshire, where Gray spent many summers (including the summer of 1750, when the poem was completed), and that Buckinghamshire – where Milton spent several years, and where Hampden lived – was in turn a setting that recalled the turbulence of the Civil War. Tovey also argued that it was the triumphant return to London of the Duke of Cumberland in July 1746 that prompted Gray to think of the contrast between men remembered by history and those who lived and died unknown.[35] F. W. Newman developed Tovey's hint, and argued that it was the shocking spectacle of the trial of the Jacobite lords in London in August 1746 – a trial at which Gray was present – that provoked a poem about the paths of glory leading but to the grave. But as Roger Lonsdale and his many predecessors have argued, Gray's reflections on glory, fame, and death are so generalized, so commonplace, and so demonstrably similar to (if not derived from) phrases found in the writings of classical and contemporary authors, that they require no particular occasion. Evidence for any inspiring event comes largely not from the poem but from Gray's letters and our knowledge of what he did or might have done in the summer of 1746. Nor does the poem's generalizing rhetoric seem to seek to arouse in the reader the memory of any particular event. One possible exception – "wade through slaughter to a throne" (line 67) – would seem to allude, in a way that a contemporary reader might be expected to recognize, to the attempt by Charles

---

[35] *Gray's English Poems*, ed. D. C. Tovey (Cambridge, 1898).

Edward Stuart to "cut his passage to the British Throne," as Edward Young put it in a poem published in 1745.[36]

Another set of critics, their argument derived from Empson's throw-away remark about "latent political ideas," have claimed not that Gray responds to a particular occasion, but that his poem confirms in a rather deliberate way the views of Gray's comfortable readers about the economic inequities of the social order. This idea has been most thoroughly developed by Richard Sha, who argued in 1990 that Gray reflects contemporary debates about how to deal with the problem of "the poor," and in effect offers the reassurance that the only poor people of whom one had to take notice were sturdy hard-working peasants who kept themselves busy and out of trouble, returned responsibly to their families at night, and, because they seemed to have adequate food and shelter, did not need either charity or the workhouse.[37] One can grant the main point, that (not surprisingly) Gray (along with many of his contemporaries) broadly supported the existing social order and regarded the working poor as decent deserving people and the unemployed poor as idle, shiftless, undeserving, and dangerous.[38] But it is going too far to claim, as Sha does, that Gray "actively suppresses the rebellious history of the poor" and is "actively silencing the peasants." Gray's poem seems *actively* engaged in other quarters. It is only if we interrogate Gray's poem from the perspective of Crabbe or Cobbett – or of a twentieth-century parlor radical – that we would even notice Gray's implicit social attitudes. It ought to be possible, without setting out grimly to *expose* Gray's adherence to an outworn ideology, to say that his rural poem seems calculated for the liberal sentiments of urban readers ready to recognize and even honor the humble working peasants in a spirit of Christian fellowship but not inclined to take any steps to alter their material condition. But this is a long way from saying that such a confirmation of the social order is Gray's primary purpose or interest.

It is quite possible that the nearly universal popularity of Gray's poem among English-speaking readers is due not to its "universality" but to its accommodating social attitudes. For the poem *accommodates* a wide

---

36 "Reflections on the Publick Situation of the Kingdom," added to the nine-night edition of *Night Thoughts* in 1745. It is also possible (as Newman suggested) that Gray had in mind *another* throne – that of Maria Theresa, Queen of Hungary, for example, besieged in the 1740s by both Frederick the Great and Louis XV.

37 Richard C. Sha, "Gray's Political *Elegy*: Poetry as the Burial of History," *Philological Quarterly*, 69 (1990), 349, 351.

38 The note of social protest is not absent from the poetry of mid century, as witness the poems of Goldsmith: "But a bold peasantry, their country's pride, / When once destroyed, can never be supplied" ("The Deserted Village," lines 55–56).

range of readers, from Whiggish admirers of the John Hampden who resisted "Ship Money"[39] and French revolutionaries (who, as Ellis notes, delighted in translating the poem), to the deeply conservative who are not asked to change the social order, from the devout Christian to the secular reader ready to acknowledge "the voice of nature."[40] Even the details – "Some Cromwell guiltless of his country's blood," for example – are calculated for wide appeal. Since the line occurs in a stanza about villagers whose "growing virtues" were "circumscribed" by their narrow "lot," it ostensibly suggests that the original Cromwell, like his village analogue, was "guiltless."[41] But the line also makes room for readers who still maintained that the historical Cromwell was guilty of bloodshed, and regard the village-"Cromwell" as a man whose "crimes" were luckily "confined."

But the poem's popularity among English readers may also be due to some central and often overlooked features of the poem – perhaps overlooked because they are so central: its "Englishness," its "country" setting, and the sense of perdurability (rather than timelessness) that it conveys. First published at a time when England was being rapidly transformed from island nation to world empire, from an economy based on agriculture to one based on commerce and world trade, Gray's *Elegy* offered a reassuring image of an enduring "England," an image that would be developed in English rural writing for the next two centuries.[42]

A comparison of the "Eton manuscript" (the poem's first version) and the published text reveals that Gray deliberately "Englished" the poem, most prominently by substituting for classical names – Cato, Tully, and Caesar – solidly English ones – Hampden, Milton, Cromwell. For the poem's stanza form Gray chose the old ABAB quatrain, in use in English poetry since the sixteenth century, that he regarded as distinctively and

---

[39] Cf. Gilbert Wakefield on Gray's "honourable testimony and the noble detestation of arbitrary power": "What son of freedom is not in raptures with this tribute of praise to such an exalted character... ?" (*Poems of Mr. Gray* [1786]). Hampden's "talents and virtues" were honored in Catharine Macaulay's *History of England* (1772), III, 449; he was commonly toasted at Whig political dinners.

[40] Raymond Williams observes that Gray's "structure of feeling" temporarily holds together "the luck of the 'cool sequester'd vale' and the acknowledged repression of 'chill Penury'" (*The Country and the City* [Oxford, 1973], 74).

[41] Cowper remarks that prior to Catharine Macaulay's *History of England*, Cromwell was regarded by many "sensible and learned men" as "the greatest Hero of the world" and "the Dignity of the British Empire during the Interregnum" (*Letters and Prose Writings*, ed. King and Ryskamp, II, 31).

[42] Goldsmith may have had its "Englishness" in mind when in a review of Gray's Pindaric odes he hinted a regret that an "English Poet," "one whom the Muse had mark'd for her own," had chosen to "force the exotics of another climate" instead of "cultivating such as are natives of the soil" (*Collected Works*, I, 113).

traditionally English.[43] Gray's language is an artful combination of the native and the Latinate that manages to sound "English" even when Gray is translating sentiments from classical or Italian writers. Some passages are markedly native in sound. Consider the diction of the first stanza, adapted (as Gray acknowledged) from Dante: *toll, knell, day, lowing, herd, lea, ploughman, plods, darkness* are all words of Saxon derivation.[44] Even *curfew*, though derived from the Norman French couvre-feu,[45] carries impeccably English associations because of its use by Shakespeare and Milton, and because, as Tom Paine was to confirm, it preserved native English resentment of Norman tyranny: "Though not a courtier will talk of the curfew-bell, not a village in England has forgotten it."[46] Gray's ear was acute – he thought Joseph Warton had "a good Ear" and Collins had a "bad" one[47] – and he effectively created, through a selection of simple English monosyllables, a rural scene that generations of readers found to be characteristically "English."[48] When Gray's diction is Latinate, it is often borrowed from Spenser, Milton, or Pope, from whom it acquires an "English" feeling.

Although Gray was by no means the first to send a poet into the countryside, his poem established in the minds of readers of poetry powerful associations between a twilit rural scene, a calm country churchyard, and the very idea of "England." Indeed, it is unlikely that Goldsmith and Cowper, in the 1770s and 1780s, would have made of the rural village, with its humble parish church, an emblem of what is most fundamental and valuable in English culture without the example of Gray's poem and its extraordinary popularity – twelve separate editions in its first dozen years, along with numerous reprintings in literary periodicals.

43 See Gray's "Observations on English Metre," in *Works*, ed. Edmund Gosse, 4 vols. (London, 1884), I, 344.

44 Despite Gray's admiration for Milton, relatively few of the words in the poem are "Miltonic" or even Latinate (e.g., provoke, sequestered, tenor), and with rare exceptions they are well naturalized: solitary, cell, clarion, sire, jocund, destiny, annals, pomp, inevitable, Memory, urn, animated, empire, penury, genial, serene, tyrant, inglorious, senates, despise, circumscribed, confined, ingenuous, ignoble, memorial, erected, precincts, pious, contemplation, fortune, science, melancholy, recompence.

45 In the *Dictionary* Johnson, citing Cowel, preserves the tradition that the word refers to the "evening-peal, by which the conqueror willed, that every man should rake up his fire, and put out his light." *OED* notes that the tradition is unsupported by early historical evidence.

46 *The Rights of Man*, Part 2 (1792), ch. 2. Cf. Shenstone's "Elegy 15" (1742), on the "dull curfew" that spoke to Britons of "their freedom fled," and Wordsworth's *Excursion* on "the curfew-knoll / That spake the Norman Conqueror's stern behest" (VIII, 172).

47 *Correspondence*, I, 261.

48 See the amusing footnote in Lonsdale (ed., *Gray, Collins, and Goldsmith*, 117), surveying the reaction to Thomas Warton's claim that Gray's first stanza was "classical" and did not reflect the "natural circumstance of an English evening."

Gray's villagers, unlike Goldsmith's, are not an image of something precious in English culture that is being lost, but of a sturdy yeoman strain that readers could imagine connected the present with the remote past and assured the survival of the race. The choice of famous seventeenth-century names – Hampden, Milton, and Cromwell – both extended the village's history back for at least a century and suggested that even the violent disruptions of the Civil War are peacefully absorbed into the soil of the nation.

The village is not timeless; rather it has endured through time. Those in the graves are not the peasants of the passing generation but the "rude forefathers of the hamlet" – where "forefathers" suggests generations of "fathers" extending backward in time, even (so "rude" hints) into pre-history. Numerous details of the scene contribute to the sense of endurance through time: the "ivy-mantled tower," the owl's "ancient solitary reign," the "old fantastic roots" of the "nodding beech" tree. That the "annals" of the poor are "short and simple" suggests not that the poor live brief lives but that they will always be there, year in and year out, part of the landscape, their records short and simple as in the oldest English historical chronicles. Though Gray's poem is sometimes thought to exemplify a morbid "graveyard" sensibility, it devotes most of its energy not to creating an atmosphere of gloom and religious horror at the thought of *death*, but to setting the drowsy, fading scene and to imagining the *life* of the unknown villagers as they "kept the noiseless tenor of their way." Even in their ashes "*live* their wonted fires." Their "memorial" grave markers are "frail" but they are "still" to be found in the churchyard, and, though nameless, they are remembered by the "mindful" poet. By keeping their memory alive, he preserves the nation's sense of itself.

It is not clear how soon Gray's poem came to be thought of as a kind of metonymy for the nation. On the night before the battle of Quebec in 1759, according to a hoary legend, General James Wolfe recited the *Elegy* and declared that "he would prefer being the author of that poem to the glory of beating the French to-morrow." This famous anecdote dates from 1822, and reflects growing sentiment in the nineteenth century that Gray's *Elegy* was a kind of national poem. But the sentiment may well have arisen earlier: the source of the anecdote was a man who had been present at the time.[49] However, it is by no means certain that

---

[49] The anecdote first appears in the *Works* of John Playfair, 4 vols. (Edinburgh, 1822), IV, 126, and is attributed to a "Professor Robison" who "was on the boat in which Wolfe went to visit some of his posts." Cf. also McNairn, *Behold the Hero*, 235–37.

Gray fully shared the idea that the poem somehow spoke for the nation. Indeed, there is much in the *Elegy* to suggest that it represents for him the recognition that a poet can no longer expect to serve the nation.

To begin with, there are the stanzas about the desire of the simple peasants to be remembered ("Yet even these bones ... "), the passage Johnson found most striking and most original.[50] There is reason to think that they were also central to Gray's purposes in the poem. For it was with these lines that Gray recommenced (and redirected) a poem he had apparently left unfinished. As Lonsdale has suggested, they embody a thought that Gray had been meditating during the composition of the *Alliance of Education and Government*: "It is impossible to conquer that natural desire we have of being remembered."[51] Just as Gray's abandonment of the *Alliance* may have something to do with his doubts about the poet's role in turning that "desire" to the service of the nation, so too the *Elegy* may reflect his conclusion that the poet as dispenser of "fame" no longer had a public role to play.

That role was still being played by some poets in the 1740s. Thomson in *The Seasons* had recited a roll call of English heroes, including both Hampden and Milton from an earlier era and a number of Scots and Patriot statesmen from his own,[52] with the intention of perpetuating their names and inciting others to follow their example. Akenside's ode "To Sleep" had celebrated the heroic oratory of Timoleon before the "applause" of a "listening senate," and offered him as a model of the patriot-hero. Gray not only knew the poem, but alluded to it – or at least remembered it – in the *Elegy*.[53] In the 1748 edition of Dodsley's *Collection* were found Richard West's *Monody on the Death of Queen Caroline*, a poem discharging the poet's traditional role of commemorating the death of the Great, along with Tickell's "On the Death of Mr. Addison," an elegy seizing the occasion of the death of a famous man to urge him on readers as an exemplary figure. Gray knew these poems well, and alluded to them both in the *Elegy*.[54]

---

[50] "I have never seen the notions in any other place; yet he that reads them persuades himself that he has always felt them" (*Lives*, III, 442). Johnson had in fact seen them in Swift's *Thoughts on Various Subjects*: "There is in most people a reluctance and unwillingness to be forgotten. We observe even among the vulgar, how fond they are to have an inscription over their grave." Johnson cited the sentences in the *Dictionary* as an illustration of the word *unwillingness*.

[51] *Poems of Gray, Collins, and Goldsmith*, 91.

[52] See especially *Summer*, lines 1488–1571, *Autumn*, lines 929–49, *Winter*, lines 656–90 [1746 edition line numbers]. Milton first appeared in the 1727 edition, Hampden in 1738.

[53] "The applause of listening senates to command ... " (line 61).

[54] Lonsdale notes that Gray's lines 33–36 were apparently "inspired" by West's poem, and that Gray echoes Tickell's poem at lines 47 and 84. Mitford also noted that line 63 ("To scatter plenty

By encompassing the poems of Thomson, Akenside, Tickell, and West, Gray implicitly acknowledges their readiness to distribute fame for moral purposes, and to use the funeral elegy for the same end, but at the same time he signals his own tacit revision of that role. Like Collins in the exactly contemporary "Ode, written in the Beginning of the Year 1746," Gray is moved by the unnamed and "unhonoured" dead. (A canceled stanza from the *Elegy* suggests that Collins' poem was very much in Gray's mind.[55]) His *Elegy* honors the "celestial fire" that animates the poet and enables the orator to command the "applause of listening senates," the "dauntless breast" that enables a man to resist tyranny or to sway "the rod of empire", and even the "useful toil" of the sturdy ploughman. And it recognizes that the "desire of fame" lies within every breast. But by declining to provide names either of great men or of humble Men of Ross, or even to provide as much identification as did Collins by tying his soldiers to a battle in early 1746, Gray in effect breaks the link between fame and virtuous deeds and implicitly resigns from the role as the nation's distributor of fame. Although he writes his own epitaph, he himself remains, like the villagers he honors, "A youth to fortune and to fame unknown," declining to identify himself or to lay claim to any "merits." His function is to honor the "unhonoured dead," and in effect to teach the rustic moralist (and the reader) how to die. But he does not presume to call this service "useful toil." Just as circumstances prevented the "village Hampden" from deploying his talents on a national stage, so they prevent Gray, despite unquenched aspiration, from playing any more than a private role.

THE PINDARIC ODES

It is customary to note that, after the embarrassing popularity of the *Elegy*, Gray took refuge in the formal difficulty and substantive obscurity of the Pindaric odes of 1757. But if we focus on Gray's ambivalence about a public role for poetry, the odes are less a departure than a further step in the same direction. In the context of public poetry, what is most striking about Gray's Pindaric odes is that in the second year of Britain's Seven Years' War with France, they decline to celebrate contemporary British power and greatness – even though we know from Gray's letters that he followed the progress of the war with avid interest and patriotic

o'er a smiling land") comes from "To scatter blessings on the British land" in Tickell's poem on Addison.
55 See Lonsdale, ed., *Gray, Collins, and Goldsmith*, 138.

concern[56] – or British "liberty," even though it had itself been the topic of Pindaric celebrations by Collins and Thomson. What has particularly attracted critical attention are the endings of Gray's odes, each of which seems to suggest that the voice of the daring poet can be "heard no more" ("Progress of Poesy," line 111). This has led some to conclude that the poems express Gray's doubts and fears about the ability of mid-eighteenth-century poets to reach the heights of their great predecessors. But other critics, by focusing on the Bard's heroic defiance of Edward I, have teased out political meanings.

Steele regards the odes as "stern poems of war," sensing a "militant mood" at the end of "The Progress of Poesy" and a "triumphant note" at the end of "The Bard." Both poems, he claims, "celebrate the beauties of empire." When the Bard confronts Edward I, the reader reflects on Britons then confronting French tyranny across the globe: "The Bard dies . . . not just so that liberty might prevail within Britain, but also in order that a Britain where liberty had been achieved might prevail in the world."[57] The difficulty with this reading, of course, is that nothing in the poem associates Edward I, a mighty *English* king, with the French Bourbons. Indeed, Gray took steps to efface suggestions that the Bard's defiance was a figure for the contemporary defense of British "liberty."[58] By having a Welsh bard stand in mighty opposition to an English king, Gray seems, in the minds of other recent critics, to take a stand "against xenophobic, anti-libertarian nationalism" and even to express "implicit identification with the oppressed victims of English victories."[59] But the idea of Gray as a crypto-oppositional voice founders on the plain patriotic evidence from the letters, and on the absurd discrepancy between old George II (then seventy-four years old) and the "ruthless king," mounted at the head of an invading army, in the opening line of "The Bard." It comes as no surprise to learn that none of Gray's contemporary reviewers thought that either ode offered reflections on Britain's ongoing war for

---

[56] Gray seems to have known, and perhaps in a sense to have been "rewriting," the Pindaric odes of Samuel Cobb, including *Pax Redux* (1697), on the Peace of Ryswick, *The Female Reign* (1709), on Queen Anne, and *The Progress of Poetry*.

[57] "Thomas Gray and the Season for Triumph," 215, 224.

[58] In an earlier draft the Bard's final line is "Lo! to be free, to die, are mine." Gray also considered "Lo! Liberty & Death are mine" (*Correspondence*, II, 504). But the printed version obscures any link between the Bard and eighteenth-century liberty. By the same token Gray admired the "priestly pride & obstinacy" of the druids in Mason's *Caractacus*, who, "after all is lost . . . resolve to confront the Roman General, & spit in his face" but advised Mason to omit the words "*Liberty & Freedom*" (*Correspondence*, II, 551).

[59] Lucas, *England and Englishness*, 44; Gerrard, *Patriot Opposition*, 148.

empire.[60] If Gray's poems hold back from an affirmation of Hanoverian Britain, it is not for Gray's lack of political confidence.

The two poems, it is worth reemphasizing, address themselves to "the power of poetry" (Gray's initial title for "The Progress of Poesy") and not to political power. If Gray is reflecting on contemporary affairs, he presumably has in mind the state of English poetry. But one can still take a political view of that subject, as does Howard Weinbrot, who argues that Gray's poems are "national odes," ultimately asserting the cultural superiority of Britain over Greece and Rome, and British literature over the classical odes of Pindar, devoted as they were to celebrating the winners of athletic contests and horse races. There are several difficulties with this reading. Gray's own notes, printed with the poems in 1768, make clear that he is following Pindar's model closely;[61] his epigraph to "The Progress of Poesy" is from second Olympian ode; Pindar is lavishly praised as "the Theban eagle . . . sailing with supreme dominion / Through the azure deep of air" ("The Progress of Poesy," lines 115–17); and Gray's own contemporaries, from Walpole to the reviewers, regarded his poems not as implicit critiques of Pindar's odes but as imitations of them.[62]

A more promising angle of approach is to reconsider Gray's suggestion that English poetry in his own day is somehow inadequate to its political occasion. Near the end of "The Progress of Poesy," Gray considers the lyric manner of Dryden's Pindaric odes – "Thoughts that breathe and words that burn" – but concludes that it is "heard no more" (line 111). It was at this point, apparently, that Gray broke off his own progress on the poem, uncertain how to continue and to complete a "progress poem" which was expected to conclude with the triumph of English poetry at mid century. When he returned to complete it, he offered himself as the "daring spirit" who might succeed Dryden and awaken the lyric lyre, but ranked himself well below Pindar (inheriting "Nor the pride nor ample pinion" of his predecessor). In a note to line 111 added in 1768, Gray explained that "We have had in our language no other odes of the

---

[60] The reviewers for the *Critical Review*, the *Literary Magazine*, and the *Monthly Review* in August and October 1757 find nothing topical in either of Gray's odes.

[61] See, for example, the note to "The Progress of Poesy," line 3: "The subject and simile, as usual with Pindar, are united," and line 13, "The thoughts are borrowed from the first Pythian of Pindar."

[62] Walpole, *Correspondence*, XXI, 120; *Critical Review*, 4 (August 1757), 167 ("Perhaps he has imitated him too closely"), and *Monthly Review*, 17 (August 1757), 239–43. Of "The Progress of Poesy," Mason told Gray that it "breathed the very spirit of Pindar" (*Memoirs*, 145n).

sublime kind, than that of Dryden on St. Cecilia's Day," dismissing the odes of Cowley and Pope by name. More to the present point, he implicitly dismisses (since he says nothing of them) the odes of Akenside and Collins from the decades of the 1740s and 1750s on patriotic and poetic subjects.[63] Akenside had written repeatedly about the "power" of lyric poetry to inspire devotion to liberty and resistance to tyranny, but Gray implicitly refuses to follow this path.[64] (In this regard it is significant that he abandoned the provisional title of "The Power of Poetry" and settled instead on "Progress"). And his ambiguous concluding line – "Beneath the Good how far – but far above the Great" – perhaps suggests that Gray's Pindaric poet will sever any connection with politics (the world of "the Great") and turn instead to the pursuit of virtue.[65]

Gray held off publishing "The Progress of Poesy" until he had completed "The Bard," perhaps in part because he wished to offer the latter poem as the fulfillment of the ambition to "mount" and soar in Pindaric style that he had announced at the end of the former. But "The Bard" is in its own way undercut by poetic doubt. Its ending, like that of the "Progress," suggests that English poetry of Gray's own day had failed to match the vigor of Spenser, Shakespeare, and Milton. It is perhaps not coincidental that Gray also had difficulty providing this poem with a satisfactory conclusion. By the summer of 1755 he had carried his vision of English history as far as the conclusion of the War of the Roses and the founding of the House of Tudor, the first kings who, because they came from Wales, might be regarded as "Britannia's issue." When he finally completed the poem in 1757, he began with Queen Elizabeth ("her lion-port, her awe-commanding face") and the poets who celebrated "Fierce war and faithful love, / And truth severe." But he celebrated no later monarch, and no later poet except for two lines on Milton (whose "voice" is heard "from blooming Eden"). At that point the Bard refers only to the "distant warblings" that "lessen" on his ear and that "lost in long futurity expire." Gray anticipated that these somewhat obscure lines might make some reader think that "Poetry in Britain was some time or other really to

---

[63] The only contemporary poet who receives Gray's approval in the 1768 note is Mason, who "of late days [in *Caractacus*, published in 1759] has touched the true chords, and with a masterly hand."

[64] In 1768 Gray added a note at line 54 remarking on the "poetic Genius" and its "connection with liberty, and the virtues that naturally attend on it." But in the poem, Gray does not celebrate modern English "liberty."

[65] Gray perhaps adapts Horace's "Extremi primorum, extremis usque prioris" (I stand behind the first, but still before the last) from *Epodes*, II. 2. 204.

expire," and insisted to Mason that he meant to suggest that it "was lost to [the Bard's] ear from the immense distance" (*Correspondence*, II, 504).

Mason was dubious, and provides the basis for seeing in the odes Gray's ambivalence toward poetry's traditionally public role. In Gray's commonplace book Mason found what he called the "original argument" of "The Bard," an argument that Gray was unable to complete. In this plan the Bard, after foretelling "the misfortunes of the Norman race,"

with prophetic spirit declares, that all [Edward's] cruelty shall never extinguish the noble ardour of poetic genius in this island; and that men shall never be wanting to celebrate true virtue and valour in immortal strains, to expose vice and infamous pleasure, and boldly censure tyranny and oppression. (*Poems of Gray*, 91)

The plan embodies the same lofty Pindaric conception of the poet's role that can be found in the work of many poets and critics at mid century. But Gray was unable to execute this plan, according to Mason, "because instances of English Poets were wanting." True virtue and valor were celebrated by Spenser, but only in allegory. No great poet, not even Shakespeare, exposed vice and infamous pleasure. (Apparently Ben Jonson was not in his view a great poet.) Milton "of all our great Poets, was the only one *who boldly censured Tyranny and Oppression*," and that was in prose rather than poetry. Dryden, though a great lyric poet, was in politics "a mere court parasite." Pope expressed "detestation of corruption and bribery," but he was "a Tory" – apparently this put him beyond the Whig pale – and Addison, though a Whig, "was not enough of a Poet." The same criticism apparently applies to the patriotic Whigs, Thomson and Akenside. Because Gray could find no poets who had performed the high role of public moralist, he was, according to Mason, "necessitated to change his plan towards the conclusion," and to refer vaguely to the "distant warblings" (133) of "The succession of Poets after Milton's time" (Gray's 1768 note). It is noteworthy that although Gray could find no monarch after Elizabeth whom he wished to praise (not even William III), he put his emphasis not on any decline of British liberties – he presumably thought that they were well preserved – but on the failure of the poets (and Gray presumably includes himself here) to perform their traditional Pindaric role of inciting the people to valor.[66] Weinbrot suggests, rightly I think, that the bard speaks "with a public voice

---

[66] Thomas Carte's *General History of England* (1750), usually regarded as Gray's source for the tradition about Welsh bards, remarks that they "used to put those remains of the antient *Britains* in mind of the valiant deeds of their ancestors" (II, 196).

of the nation."[67] But he does not recognize Gray's doubts about the possibility of speaking with such a voice.

"SOME GREAT AND SINGULAR SERVICE"

To judge by the published form of "The Progress of Poesy" and "The Bard," Gray seems to have abandoned that role and to have turned the Pindaric ode inward – toward a consideration of poetry rather than politics. But to arrive at this conclusion is to overlook one prominent feature of "The Bard": in Gray's poem the Bard, from a position of great symbolic power, speaks directly to the King.[68] At some level Gray had not abandoned the dream that the poet might indeed play some great public role. But what service might he perform? In his last years, though he wrote little, Gray apparently continued to ponder this question.

Late in 1757 Gray was offered the opportunity to serve as Poet Laureate to King George, but in his well-known letter to Mason he explained his reason for refusing: "the office itself has always humbled the Possessor hitherto (even in an age, when Kings were somebody) if he were a poor Writer, by making him more conspicuous, and if he were a good one, by setting him at war with the little fry of his own profession" (*Correspondence*, II, 545). It is worth noting that Gray does not object to the service he would be expected to perform – the birthday and New Year's odes that he facetiously refers to as catching "a mouse or two (for form's sake) in publick once a year" (II, 544). It is rather that he would have to expose himself to envious attacks. But he wishes that the office might be held in more respect, and hopes "somebody may accept it, that will retrieve the credit of the thing, if it be retrievable or ever had any credit" (II, 544). After William Whitehead was named laureate in his place, Gray commended his first efforts, the birthday ode in November 1758 and the New Year's ode in January 1759: "I like Whithed's [*sic*] Odes in great measure ... they are far better than any thing he ever wrote" (*Correspondence*, II, 604, 618).

Even though he turned down the laureate, Gray through the 1760s kept a poet's eye on the state of the nation and on its great men, primarily (but not only) as a satirist. The best known of these poems today is "On

---

[67] *Britannia's Issue*, 397. Paul Odney argues that the Pindaric odes try to "establish the legitimacy and authority of ... a national poet" but in the end propose an "alternative nationalism" ("Thomas Gray's 'Daring Spirit': Forging the Poetics of an Alternative Nationalism," *Clio*, 28:3 [1999], 247, 260).

[68] Sitter refers in passing (*Literary Loneliness*, 97n) to this and other "similar fantasies" in the poems of Thomas Warton of "the poet's access to the king and power over him."

176 *Patriotism and poetry in eighteenth-century Britain*

Lord Holland's Seat" (written 1768). Henry Fox, Lord Holland, was by 1768 in disgrace (accused of bribery and corruption) and in bitter retirement. Although Gray himself never acknowledged it as his, the poem, first published in 1769, was attributed to him in its frequent reprintings. One contributor to the *Gentleman's Magazine* claimed that the poem demonstrated Gray's credentials as a patriot, declaring that it showed him to be not only a great lyric poet but "a lover of his country, and an abhorrer of its intestine foes, . . . possessing a constitutional spirit of liberty congenial to Churchill's."[69] The comparison with Churchill obscures the fact that while Churchill recklessly attacked great men in power when he thought their policies endangered the country, Gray could not have imagined that he performed a patriotic service by striking at Holland after his fall from office. It also obscures some suggestive links between "On Lord Holland's Seat" and "The Bard." The latter poem begins by wishing "Ruin" on a "ruthless king," the former by setting Holland amidst "ruins" that he himself designed. Holland is "abandoned by each venal friend," and in a note Gray added to "The Bard" in 1768 (the year he wrote "On Lord Holland's Seat"), Edward III is "abandoned by his Children, and even robbed in his last moments by his Courtiers and his Mistress." It is as if the curse visited by the bard on his English oppressors falls even on Lord Holland. But in the end Gray turns the poem – and the curse – over to Holland, who dreams of the vengeance he would have wreaked if he had not lost power and place:

> Purged by the sword and beautified by fire,
> Then had we seen proud London's hated walls:
> Owls might have hooted in St. Peter's choir,
> And foxes stunk and littered in St. Paul's.

This is no simple satire. Something in Gray seems stirred by the imagined ruin of Britain's capital city.

In "The Candidate" (1764), described later by a contributor to the *Gentleman's Magazine* as "a very proper *companion*" for the poem on Lord Holland,[70] Gray beheld the sordid spectacle of two political factions in Westminster angling to strengthen their influence by lobbying for the election of their man as High Steward of Cambridge University. Again Gray focuses on a discredited politician, this time John Montagu, Earl of Sandwich and First Lord of the Admiralty, who held on to his offices despite his reputation for gross immorality in his private life. But Gray's coarse satire does not exempt the several faculties of the university, represented in the poem as vying for Sandwich's favors.

[69] *Gentleman's Magazine*, 47 (1777), 624. [70] *Gentleman's Magazine*, 52 (1782), 39.

Had his final poems been "The Candidate" and "On Lord Holland's Seat" we might have inferred that Gray in his last years saw no public role for the poet except to laugh at the vices and follies of the great. But his last poem, the "Ode for Music," shows that Gray had one more opportunity to serve his nation as a poet, and this time he took it, even though with some reluctance. When the Duke of Grafton was elected Chancellor of the University of Cambridge in 1769, Gray offered to write the text of an ode to be performed at his formal installation in the office. He acted largely out of gratitude to a patron – Grafton as Prime Minister had arranged for him to be named Regius Professor only a year earlier – and Gray may have felt that Grafton, then under attack by Junius and others, deserved public praise. But he probably also acted from his sense that it was necessary that university tradition be observed: "as somebody was necessarily to do this, I did not see why Gratitude should sit silent and leave it to Expectation to sing" (*Correspondence*, II, 1062). Gray was concerned to make the point that he was not *asked* to write, as if his volunteering "unasked" (II, 1070) somehow preserved more of his dignity.

He had a sense of the dignity of the occasion, admiring the installation ode his friend Mason had written for Newcastle, the previous Chancellor, in 1749.[71] And the beginning of his own ode invokes the memory of Milton's *Comus*, first presented in 1634 before the Earl of Bridgewater, recently installed as Lord President of the Council of Wales. Gray goes on to borrow repeatedly from Milton's poems, and to introduce Milton himself who offers a kind of blessing on the holy place. But for the structure of his ode Gray again goes back to his own "Bard," as if to find a way in which a poem about the confrontation between a thirteenth-century bard and king could be adapted to a modern alliance of poetry, "education," and "government." Like the earlier Pindaric, Gray's "Ode for Music" begins with a bold and "indignant lay" in defense of the "holy ground" of the Muse: "Hence, avaunt, ('tis holy ground)." This time, however, instead of calling down ruin on the "ruthless king," the bard ritually banishes Ignorance and his Comus-crew, in preparation for the arrival of a "noble son" with "inborn royalty of mind" (lines 67, 81). Again, as in "The Bard," there is a chorus of fellow spirits ("the sainted sage, the bard divine, / The few whom genius gave to shine / Through every unborn age"). In place of the vision of Edward's bloody descendants and successors, the "Ode for Music" presents a procession of the university's benefactors, some

---

[71] "Mason's Ode was the only Entertainment, that had any tolerable Elegance; & for my own Part I think it (with some little abatements) uncommonly well on such an Occasion" (*Correspondence*, I, 323).

of them the same kings who appeared in the bard's prophecy (Edward III, Henry VI), all of them royal. Just as "The Bard" looks ahead to the rise of the House of Tudor under Henry VII, so the "Ode for Music" concludes its historical review with Margaret, Countess of Richmond, mother of Henry VII, founder of both St. John's and Christ's Colleges, and ancestor of the Duke of Grafton.

Gray's ode thus manages to interweave the history of England with the history of the university, and (for the first time in his poetic career) to connect England's historic past with its present. The poem closes with high encomium of the new Chancellor, and a brief bow to the reigning King, George III, "the Star of Brunswick" – the first poem since his early hymeneal on the Prince of Wales in which Gray offered praise to a contemporary "great man." Anxious that his poem not seem venal flattery – Gray ritually banishes "Servitude," "Flattery," "creeping Gain" (lines 6, 8, 9) and declares that he offers "no vulgar praise, no venal incense" (line 79) – he is careful to praise Grafton only for his distinguished ancestry, his "liberal heart" and "judging eye" (line 71). And by another act of self-quotation, Gray makes Grafton a kind of figure for the poet who in the *Elegy* had lamented the neglect of buried talent, the "gem" in the caves of ocean, and the "flower . . . born to blush unseen." In the "Ode" it is Grafton whose "judging eye"

> The flower unheeded shall descry,
> And bid it round heaven's altars shed
> The fragrance of its blushing head:
> Shall raise from earth the latent gem
> To glitter on the diadem.
>
> (lines 72–76)

James Beattie told Gray in November 1769 he thought the ode "the finest panegyrical poem in the world." And he implicitly recognized that Gray had taken on a role he had first dreamed of in the *Alliance of Education and Government*, the conferring of fame: "it will make the name of the Duke of Grafton known as long as the English language is understood; which is an honour, no other great man of this age has any chance of obtaining at the hands of the muses" (III, 1082).[72]

What Gray thought of Beattie's praise is not known. But in the next letter Gray wrote to him – in July 1770 – it is striking to find that he takes up the idea that the muses have a public role to play. Asked for his

---

[72] Coleridge found "something very majestic" in the ode (*Table Talk*, in *Collected Works*, XIV, Pt. I, ed. C. Woodring [Princeton, 1990], 447).

opinion of Beattie's *Minstrel*, which he had read in draft, Gray thought there was something "imperfect" at the end of the first book: "Why may not young Edwin, when necessity has driven him to take up the harp, and assume the profession of a Minstrel, do some great and singular service to his country? (what service I must leave to your invention) such as no General, no Statesman, no Moralist could do without the aid of music, inspiration, and poetry" (*Correspondence*, III, 1140). Even at the end of his career Gray was still imagining that the poet might do "some great and singular service to his country."

CHAPTER 7

John Dyer: "sedulous for the public weal"

John Dyer's *The Fleece* (1757), says Bonamy Dobrée, in the lecturer's throwaway manner, is "in many ways the greatest patriotic poem in the language."[1] What he has in mind is Dyer's celebration of Britain's overseas trade, and his confidence that a "great commercial nation" can bring about a *pax Britannica*. Dobrée suspects that, given what we know now about the motives and the consequences of commerce, Dyer's vision of Britain is rather naive and innocent, "if not deliberate self-deception, at least what we should call wishful thinking."[2] This idea has largely colored what critical attention Dyer has received in the last twenty-five years, and has tended to shift attention from his patriotism to his understanding of the world of labor and trade. One critic thinks Dyer's poem "evasive of bedrock realities,"[3] another that Dyer was simply unaware that "the forces he was celebrating were inevitably part of a new order, very different from that sense of things which sustains the pastoral vision."[4] A recent discussion of *The Fleece* focuses primarily on Dyer's demonstrably accurate knowledge of sheep-farming.[5] The best critic of the poem, John Barrell, is primarily concerned to show that Dyer aims to harmonize the worlds of pastoral and georgic, "holding together rural and industrial, industrial and mercantile, domestic and imperial."[6] This is an idea that needs to be explored more intensively and extensively.

---

[1] *English Literature in the Early Eighteenth Century*, 518. His comments on Dyer are based on his 1948 British Academy lecture, published in 1949 as "The Theme of Patriotism in Early-Eighteenth-Century Poetry."

[2] "The Theme of Patriotism," 63.

[3] Laurence Goldstein, *Ruins and Empire: The Evolution of a Theme in Augustan and Romantic Literature* (Pittsburg, 1977), 57.

[4] Richard Feingold, *Nature and Society: Later Eighteenth-Century Uses of the Pastoral and the Georgic* (New Brunswick, 1977), 116–17.

[5] John Goodridge, *Rural Life in Eighteenth-Century English Poetry* (Cambridge, 1995), 91–187.

[6] Barrell, *English Literature in History*, 104.

In defending Dyer against charges of naiveté, and in arguing that the vision of the poem extends beyond the world of sheep-farming and even of the wool trade, I propose to return to the idea that *The Fleece* can be usefully regarded as a "patriotic" poem. In the words of one of Dyer's first reviewers, "The subject of his poem is peculiarly interesting to an English reader, by being *national*, and conveying to us the most pleasing ideas of our own wealth and happiness . . . Mr. Dyer seems ambitious of uniting the character of patriot and poet, he takes every opportunity of paying his tribute of praise to his native country."[7] Implicitly locating Dyer in the tradition of Thomson, who had in *The Seasons* sought to "mix the Patriot's with the Poet's Flame," the reviewer implies that it is the double task of the patriot-poet to honor his native country and to serve it. The poet's special service is to invent a vision of the nation, and by means of this imagined community to convey to readers "the most pleasing ideas of our own wealth and happiness." Dyer, I will argue, invented a powerful vision of Britain as a community of labor – sheep-farmers, carders, spinners, weavers, and traders – united by their participation in one stage or other of the wool trade. It is a single comprehensive vision of the nation sustained over a long four-book poem, extending from the rural paradise of Book I by way of England's many navigable rivers to its small country towns, its thriving cities, and its seaborne merchant fleet.[8] Dyer writes as a man inspired by the "public weal" and the "universal good of the nation." But, more in Thomson's manner than in Pope's, he hesitates to step forward as "My country's poet," or define a public role for himself. And his vision of commercial Britain is shadowed, like Thomson's, with doubts and misgivings about the fate of a trading nation, especially one that exchanges the solid good of woolen cloth for the dubious delights of consumer luxuries.[9]

It seems likely that Thomson was for Dyer the most formative model of the patriot-poet. They were exact contemporaries, both born in 1700 in rural surroundings on the Celtic fringe, Thomson in Lowland Scotland, Dyer in Wales. Both made their way to London and in 1726 came to public notice for *Winter* and *Grongar Hill*. Thomson pursued a literary

---

7 An anonymous reviewer in the *Critical Review*, 3 (May 1757), 402, 406.
8 Barrell asserts that "*The Fleece* offers us . . . the most whole vision of 18th-century English society that is offered anywhere in its poetry" (*English Literature in History*, 104).
9 Kaul's discussion of *The Fleece* (in *Poems of Nation, Anthems of Empire*, 219–29), while taking note of the "familiar fear of the corrupting effects of wealth" (224), emphasizes Dyer's celebration of Britain as commercial empire.

career in the metropolis for the next twenty years, courting the attention of great men, and of the "Patriot" group, steadily expanding his first "Season" into a poem of over 10,000 lines. Dyer hovered on the edges, studying law and painting, and supervising the daily operation of a family farm. He eventually took holy orders, and won some small ecclesiastical patronage from the family of the Earl of Hardwicke and others, and devoted himself – intermittently – to the labors of composing *The Fleece*, a poem of some 2700 lines.

Both *The Seasons* and *The Fleece* are written in blank verse occasionally colored by Miltonisms; both are centered in an idealization of rural, agricultural England, but are at the same time poetically stimulated by Britain's expanding commercial empire, and argue – in Virgilian fashion – that British imperial grandeur is established on the sturdy foundation of agricultural labor. If Thomson called on Britons to "venerate the plough" (*Spring*, line 67), Dyer asked them to honor the herdsman. Even that subject is implicit in Thomson, where he imagines that the products of Britain's "rich soil" will "pour / O'er every land" and "the naked nations clothe" (*Spring*, line 76), and in a related passage in *Liberty*, that Britannia,

> whitening o'er her Downs, diffusive, pours
> Unnumber'd Flocks: She weaves the fleecy Robe,
> That wraps the Nations.   (v, lines 36–38)[10]

These lines in effect constitute a program for Dyer's poem, which in its final vision brings out the god-like role played by a benevolent and paternalistic commercial empire:

>   'Tis her delight
> To fold the world with harmony, and spread
> Among the habitations of mankind,
> The various wealth of toil, and what her fleece,
> To clothe the naked, and her skilful looms,
> Peculiar give.   (iv, lines 664–69)[11]

"Fold" quietly and wittily combines the actions of the shepherd folding his sheep and the clothier enfolding the naked nations in good British

---

[10] Thomson is remembering Pope's "Spring," in which two herdsmen "Pour'd o'er the whitening Vale their fleecy Care" (line 19). Cf. Thomson's *Liberty*, where Britannia is addressed as "Great Nurse of Fruits, of Flocks, of Commerce" (v, lines 81).

[11] For convenience of reference, *The Fleece* is quoted from the Everyman's Library *Minor Poets of the Eighteenth Century* [Parnell, Green, Dyer, Collins, Winchelsea] (London, 1930), which provides line numbers in the text.

woolens. Because God (or his Son) is also the Good *Shepherd, clothed* the naked Adam and Eve, and brings his people to dwell "in a peaceful *habitation*" (Isa. 32. 18), Dyer's Britannia, who "folds the world with harmony," in effect serves as a divine agent.

Thomson may have provided Dyer the seed of a program, but it took a more disciplined poet than Thomson to produce a four-book poem focused on "The care of sheep, the labours of the loom, /And arts of trade" (I, lines 1–2). Thomson's *Seasons* might be said to be georgic in spirit though not in form. Dyer goes back to Virgil for formal discipline. Even the proposition of the tripartite subject recalls the Virgilian original.[12] As in Virgil's *Georgics*, a vision of empire is given the shape of instruction in a rural art. But Dyer adapts his model for the world of eighteenth-century Britain. By selecting "The care of sheep" for the first part of his subject, Dyer finds an agricultural topic that Virgil (who wrote of cows but not of sheep) left open and honors a distinctively English industry. By writing a "georgic" about *sheep* (the traditional "pastoral" topic), he engages in a kind of witty revisionism. By adding "the labours of the loom, /And arts of trade," Dyer extends the georgic sphere to include agriculture, manufacturing, and commerce.

Thomson had seemed to sense that it was Britannia herself, rather than her king or its political and military leaders, who should serve as the center of a patriotic poem. But he nonetheless found himself writing panegyrics to the politicians of the Patriot group, Lyttelton, Chesterfield, and others, and calling out an honor roll of British heroes. Dyer wants to avoid partisan politics.[13] When he salutes a "patriot" by name, it is John Russell, the fourth Duke of Bedford, honored not for his service as Secretary of State under Pelham, but for draining the fens on his Cambridgeshire estate:

> Bedford Level, erst
> A dreary pathless waste, the coughing flock
> Was wont with hairy fleeces to deform;
> And, smiling with her lure of summer flowers,
> The heavy ox, vain-struggling, to ingulph;
> Till one, of that high-honoured patriot name,

---

12 Cf. Virgil's "qaue *cura* boum, qui *cultus* habendo / sit pecori, apibus quanta *experientia* parcis" (I. 3–4, my emphasis) – "what care the kine need, what care the herd in breeding, what skill the thrifty bees" (Loeb tr.).

13 On the eve of the publication of *The Fleece*, Dyer worried in a 31 January 1757 letter to William Duncombe "whether this is a proper time for publishing it," since "people are so taken up with politics" (John Duncombe, *Letters by Several Eminent Persons Deceased*, 3 vols. [London, 1773], III, 65).

Russel, arose, who drained the rushy fen,
Confined the waves, bid groves and gardens bloom,
And through his new creation led the Ouze,
And gentle Camus, silver-winding streams:
Godlike beneficence; from chaos drear
To raise the garden and the shady grove.

(II, lines 165–76)

This is a new kind of patriot-hero, whose greatest service to his nation was not in governing or in leading troops but in improving his landed estate, not by enclosing a pleasure park but by turning waste land into agriculturally productive acres. Like Britannia herself, he is "godlike," this time for an act of "new creation." His highest service to his native land is in effect to create more of it.[14]

Most of Dyer's few compliments to British heroes and to great men seem perfunctory, mere vestiges of Thomson's practice.[15] His patrons are lesser lights, "Heathcote" (III, line 16, Sir John Heathcote, who provided Dyer a church living), and "Wray" (II, line 4, Daniel Wray, the conduit for church patronage from the Lord Chancellor, Philip Yorke.) Dyer follows Thomson in complimenting the country seats of his patrons, but while Thomson lingers at Lyttelton's Hagley Park for more than fifty lines, Dyer does little more than name a single feature of each house.[16] He has nothing to say about the role of their owners – only one of whom is named in the poem – in the political and cultural life of the nation.[17] Other

---

[14] Elsewhere Dyer salutes as a "patriot" the statesman who is able to devise means to control the illegal export of the distinctively English "comber's lock" – England's "golden fleece" – while leaving other importing and exporting open: "Happy the patriot, who can teach the means / To check [the smuggler's] frauds, and yet untroubled leave / Trade's open channels" (II, lines 456–58).

[15] At IV, lines 116–17, he merely names the "patriot sages, Walsinghams, and Yorkes, / And Cecils," the first and third of them Elizabethan worthies, and only the Yorkes (Philip Yorke, first Earl of Hardwicke, Lord Chancellor; and his son Philip, Viscount Royston) Dyer's contemporaries. Royston is also named at II, line 10. Dyer briefly notices Peter the Great ("Illustrious Peter," IV, line 17), Sir Walter Raleigh ("active Raleigh" the admiral, IV, line 500), and a conventional set of Whiggish worthies ("our Edwards, Henrys, Churchills, Blakes, / Our Lockes, our Newtons, and our Miltons" – I, lines 161–62). He devotes more lines to the Duke of Marlborough (III, lines 501–12), and George Lord Anson, the circumnavigator of 1744 (IV, lines 599ff).

[16] See the brief compliments to Heathcote's country seat at Normanton (I, line 44), and to three lesser houses in Herefordshire, Sir Archer Croft's at Croft (Croft was Dyer's kinsman), the third Earl of Oxford's at Eyewood (Oxford was a political ally of the Yorkes), and John Viscount Bateman's at Shobden (I, line 52–55). For details, see Goodridge, *Rural Life*, 110–11.

[17] *Pace* Barrell, who refers to "a number of aristocrats [two of Dyer's four landed gentlemen are in fact only gentry]" whose "upland estates ... permit them an extensive view of England" (*English Literature in History*, 105). Later Barrell concedes that Dyer seems to make no room for those leisured gentlemen "who merely observe" (106).

figures who appear in *The Fleece* – "benevolent Mackenzie" (I, line 314), "Nuceus" (I, line 444), and "Blasius" (II, line 525) – play humbler but more useful roles in the nation. "Mackenzie" is Dr. James Mackenzie, a country physician; "Nuceus" is Mr. Joseph Nutt, an apothecary at Hinckley; "Blasius" is Bishop Blaise, the alleged "inventor of wool-combing." Lewis Paul, the inventor of an "engine for cotton and fine wool" and of another "to spin cotton" (II, line 281n, III, line 392n), is named only in a footnote.

But Dyer is fully aware of the political significance of his topic, and does not completely ignore the great men of the day. In his "dedicatory verse," asking that good people of "all degrees, all sects, be present to my song," he specifically includes "princely merchants" and members of both houses of parliament:

> And ye, high-trusted guardians of our isle,
> Whom public voice approves, or lot of birth
> To the great charge assigns.   (I, lines 4–6)

And he even addresses the King, but in terms derived from his subject:

> But chiefly thou,
> The people's Shepherd, eminently placed
> Over the numerous swains of every vale,
> With well-permitted power and watchful eye,
> On each gay field to shed beneficence,
> Celestial office! thou protect the song.
>   (I, lines 12–17)

Dyer perhaps concluded that his first readers might think he was addressing God, in his capacity as "chief Shepherd" (1 Peter 5.4)[18] or beneficent Providence, especially since his "office" is "Celestial" and Dyer's opening is suggestively Miltonic,[19] for he felt obliged to add a footnote to explain that by "The people's Shepherd" he meant "The king, namely."[20] It is significant that he does not in fact *name* the King, and that he assigns him an office that makes him *primus inter pares* – "eminently placed / Over the numerous swains of every vale" – and makes all of his people both sheep and shepherds ("swains"). The care of sheep is in effect the business of every man and woman, from the King down to the "rural nymphs" and

---

[18] Cf. "Shepherd of Israel" (Psalm 80.1).

[19] "But chiefly thou" plainly recalls "And chiefly thou O Spirit," from the opening of *Paradise Lost* (I. 17).

[20] James Grainger, in his review of *The Fleece* in the *Monthly Review*, recognized that "the People's shepherd" was "the emphatic language of Homer" (16 [1757], 329).

"swains" (I, lines 2–3). By the end of the poem, the King having as it were disappeared, it is an office that is subsumed by "Britannia" herself.[21]

In both *The Seasons* and *The Fleece* "Britannia" is the recipient of the poet's most rapturous address. Thomson's extended "Panegyric to Great Britain" (*Summer*, lines 1442–1619) is probably the model for Dyer's, more compressed and more focused on the rural landscape, a distinctively English scene (and climate):

> Hail noble Albion! where no golden mines,
> No soft perfumes, nor oils, nor myrtle bowers,
> The vigorous frame and lofty heart of man
> Enervate: round whose stern cerulean brows
> White-winged snow, and cloud, and pearly rain,
> Frequent attend, with solemn majesty:
> Rich queen of mists and vapours! These thy sons
> With their cool arms compress; and twist their nerves
> For deeds of excellence and high renown.
>
> (I, lines 152–60)

Britain's hardy "sons" plainly derive from Thomson's "Bold, firm, and graceful" youth, "By hardship sinewed" (*Summer*, lines 1467–68), but Dyer finds a witty way to attribute their sinewy strength to the English climate. Thomson had called the climate "merciful" (line 1446) – i.e., neither too hot nor too cold (the conventional compliment) – but Dyer doesn't hesitate to name mists, vapors, rain, and snow. (His transformation of the "clouded majesty" of Pope's Queen of Dulness is deservedly praised.)

Thomson was a model familiar to Dyer's readers. His other English poetical model for patriotic verse would have been less familiar in the 1750s: Michael Drayton, the only poet to whom Dyer refers in the course of *The Fleece*. In Book II he is the one "whose rustic Muse / O'er heath and craggy holt her wing displayed, / And sung the bosky bourns of Alfred's shrines," and who in his geographical survey "Has favoured Cotswold with luxuriant praise" (II, lines 381–84). Dyer was referring to Drayton's *Poly-Olbion* (1616, 1622), an encyclopaedic poem made up of thirty "Songs" (typically extending to 350 lines), subtitled "a Chorographical Description of Tracts, Rivers, Mountains, Forests, and other Parts of this Renowned Isle of Great Britain, with Intermixture of the most Remarkable Stories, Antiquities, Wonders, Rarities, Pleasures, and Commodities of the same." Dyer probably had particularly in mind Drayton's "Fourteenth Song," which celebrates "Cotswold" as "that

---

[21] Biblical and epic convention allowed Dyer to call the King "the people's Shepherd" but not "the prince of merchants."

great King of shepheards" (line 219), describes in considerable detail "the sheepe our wold doth breed" (line 251), and a sheepshearing festival, in which "each lustie jocund swaine" sings "roundelayes" to "their country-girles, whose nosegayes they doe weare" (lines 275–78).

Because *Poly-Olbion* is not much read today, we have largely forgotten that the "chorographical" tradition was a means by which Renaissance poets could celebrate their native land, not by embodying the nation in the person of the monarch, but by surveying the body of the land, its "Tracts, Rivers, Mountains, Forests," along with the "Antiquities" of each region and the products of the soil.[22] "Chorographical" works, especially Camden's *Britannia* (1586, and frequently reprinted, sometimes in abridged form), were still being widely consulted a century later. Defoe's *Tour of the Whole Island of Great Britain* draws heavily on Camden.[23] In Drayton, Dyer found a poet who "industriously pursu'd / This noble countries praise" (XIV, lines 172–73), its "sundry varying soyles" (I, line 2), and especially its rivers.

Drayton is perhaps the most prolific of the Renaissance river-poets: his poetical tour of English counties typically traces rivers upward to their springs and downward to the Severn, Wye, Trent, or Thames. "River-painting," as the *Monthly Review* noted in 1757, is one of the most prominent features of Dyer's poem: "Scarce any Poet, antient or modern, has surpassed the Author of *The Fleece* in river-painting" (16: 340). Dyer names thirty-two English and Welsh rivers, and several of them more than once. Rivers have an appropriate place in an account of the wool trade, for sheep must be washed in rivers before they are shorn (I, lines 566–78), and the fulling-mills are driven by flowing streams (III, lines 161–65). They are especially prominent in Book III, and interest Dyer chiefly as the means by which wool is transported to the spinners and weavers (II, lines 65–69), and the "labours of the loom" are taken to market (III, lines 558–79). The poetry in such passages sometimes sinks to the pedestrian, but the underlying feeling of the nation on the move – "all is here in motion, all is life" (III, line 321), reflects the excitement that trade could inspire in the country's mid-century poets. This is no vision of a nation of shopkeepers, but of the pulsing flow of British products from field to village to town to metropolis, developed from a Renaissance topos to an extent that Drayton could not have foreseen.

---

[22] For a recent study, see Richard Helgerson, *Forms of Nationhood: The Elizabethan Writing of England* (Chicago, 1992), esp. 107–47.

[23] It was republished in 1695 and 1722. Defoe's editor, Pat Rogers, regards Camden as Defoe's principal source.

The circulation of goods had long been of interest to Dyer. About 1737, before he began thinking about *The Fleece*, he drafted plans for a "Commercial Map of England," which would show the products of each region as well as the roads and the navigable rivers.²⁴ The project was set aside, so he wrote later, for lack of "proper encouragement."²⁵ It seems likely too that Drayton helped Dyer see that the country's rivers might be represented best not on a map but in a poem. The *Critical Review* was to praise him as a "poetical geographer" (3 [1757], 411).

THE DISCOURSE OF WOOL

The seeds of Dyer's patriotic poem are present in Drayton and Thomson. And the idea that Virgilian georgic might be adapted for specifically British agricultural topics had been demonstrated by John Philips and other early-eighteenth-century poets.²⁶ But for the idea that the country was ready for a long poem devoted exclusively to sheep, Dyer was implicitly counting on the fact that since at least the 1720s the wool trade had been heatedly debated in print by projectors and politicians. *The Fleece* in effect responds to and participates in a national discussion about the wool trade. Two key themes emerge from that cumulative discussion: the wool trade was essential to British prosperity; and the wool trade was in decay.

Defoe, who wrote avidly about most aspects of British manufacturing and commerce, also wrote about the wool trade. In 1727 appeared his *Brief Deduction of the Original, Progress, and Immense Greatness of the British Woollen Manufacture*. To his readers, who are assumed to think that the wool trade is thriving as it always has, Defoe brings the news that production is up but the markets have declined. Wool had long been the basis for English commerce, accounting (by one estimate) for 90 percent of her exports in 1621. But by 1700 woolens made up only 50 percent of exports. In retrospect, it was possible for Defoe to report that the "full glory and perfection" of English woolen manufacturing was the century from 1580 to 1680. The remedy to the problems, Defoe thought, included limiting production, concentrating on high-quality broadcloth

---

²⁴ The MS plans are found in the Longstaffe Collection at Durham Cathedral. See also Ralph Williams, *Poet, Painter, and Parson : The Life of John Dyer* (New York, 1956), 97–98, and the recent discussion of the "Commercial Map" by John Barrell in his "Afterword" to Maclean, Landry, and Ward, eds., *The Country and the City Revisited*, 238–44.
²⁵ W. H. D. Wagstaffe, "Notes Respecting the Life and Family of John Dyer, the Poet," *The Patrician*, 5 (1848), 81.
²⁶ It is very likely that Dyer, with his interest in "Siluria," knew Philips' *Cyder* (1708). He may have known William Somerville's *The Chace* (1735). Dyer lived in Nuneaton, Warwickshire, from about 1738 to 1742, near Somerville's Warwickshire estate.

rather than cheaper goods, buying British ("The only way to restore our manufactures is to wear them" [208]), and expanding overseas markets. It is not clear how many readers Defoe reached. His title signaled that his tract might only be of interest to economists and the Board of Trade. A different kind of strategy – calculated to appeal to a wider audience – was adopted in 1736 by the author of a short tract given a catchier title: *The Golden Fleece*. The title promises to set the topic within a context of heroic effort and national pride. The subtitle laments the "Decay" of the wool trade, lays out the argument, specifies a new problem (illegal exports), and establishes the importance of the topic:

Or the Trade, Interest, and Well-Being of Great Britain Considered. With Remarks on the Rise, Progress, and Present Decay of our Woolen Manufactures. Also An Estimate of this Valuable Trade, fairly and clearly stated, and the great Proportion given up yearly to Foreigners. By Suffering (or Conniving at) the illegal Exportation of *British* and *Irish* Wool, and Woolen Goods thoroughly manufactured in *Ireland*, to Foreign Parts. Likewise Heads for a BILL, to put an effectual STOP to this matchless Evil, so injurious to both KING and COUNTRY.

Wool, says the author, is our "peculiar National Blessing" (28). It is for that reason that English judges are seated on "Wool-Packs" in the House of Lords, "that they might always remember themselves to be Guardians of the Blessing Providence hath so peculiarly bestowed on this Land" (14).[27] *The Golden Fleece* is addressed not only to economists or to traders, but to all public-spirited men, "such as are truly inclined to the Service of their Country" (11). The language of the tract is clearly designed to show that the issue is genuinely *national*: exportation of raw wool is "manifestly destructive of the Honour, Interest, and Wealth of the whole Nation" (13).

The Golden Fleece attracted readers; it went into a second edition the following year, and it was regularly referred to by other pamphleteers.[28] Its central political theme – that the wool trade was essential to the health of the nation – was quickly picked up in William Webber's *The Consequences of Trade* (1740), where "The Consequences of the Woollen Trade" are said to be "more beneficial than any other, even than all our other Branches of Trade."[29] In *The Grasiers Advocate: or, Free Thoughts of Wool, and the Wool*

27 *OED* notes that the chief judge, the Lord Chancellor of England, sits on a special "Woolsack." His office is itself sometimes called "the Woolsack."
28 It is cited in William Ellis's *The Modern Husbandman*, 3 vols. (London, 1744) and John Smith's *Memoirs of Wool*, 2 vols. (London, 1747).
29 *The Consequences of Trade* was reprinted in the *Gentleman's Magazine*, 10 (1740), 500. Ellis's *The Modern Husbandman* agrees with the several "Authors of Pamphlets on the Woolen Manufacture" whom he cites – *The Golden Fleece*, *Remarks upon Mr. Webber's Scheme* (1741), and *The Draper's Pamphlet* (1741) – that the wool trade is "the most beneficial and extensive of all the Manufactures of this Kingdom" (143).

Trade (1742), occasioned by a reading of Webber's pamphlet, the price of wool "may well deserve to be looked upon as a NATIONAL CONCERN" (31).[30] Dyer, who began planning *The Fleece* about 1741,[31] probably owes his rhetorical strategy, whereby he declares that his topic is a *national* one, of concern to "high-trusted guardians of our isle," to the cumulative pamphlet discussion.[32] It is significant that he had originally intended to entitle his poem "The Golden Fleece."[33]

The national discussion of the wool trade continued through the 1740s, and probably shaped the final form of Dyer's poem. From 1741 to 1744 William Ellis, a Hertfordshire farmer, published monthly installments of what he would collect in three volumes as *The Modern Husbandman*, offering practical advice to farmers, organized by the tasks that need to be performed each month. Each month has at least one chapter on the care of sheep: the treatment of sheep rot in May, shearing in June, and so on. The instructions probably interested Dyer, who supervised sheep farms himself in the 1730s, and may have encouraged him to think of a didactic poem about the care of sheep as well as the wool trade itself. In 1747 John Smith, author of *The Grasiers Advocate*, addressed not the sheep-farmer but the gentleman, in publishing a two-volume compendium of lore about the wool trade entitled *Chronicon Rusticum-Commerciale, or Memoirs of Wool, Woollen Manufactures, and Trade, (Particularly in England) From the Earliest to the Present Times*. Complete with a distinguished subscriber list, including six earls and the Duke of Newcastle himself (who ordered three sets), the *Memoirs of Wool* attempted to make the wool trade a branch of English history. It includes reprinted extracts from scripture and the classics, concise summaries of statutes and exchequer records, abstracts of pamphlets on the wool trade, a discourse on the "mixed and mutual Interest" of land and trade, and Smith's own "Scheme" for imposing a duty on exported wool. Building on earlier writers, Smith claims that his subject "is very peculiarly the Gentlemens Care and Study; not only by Reason THEY are of all others most interested in WOOL; but because it is of POLITICAL Consideration likewise; and

---

30 Published anonymously, but attributed to John Smith, author of the later *Memoirs of Wool*. The author also remarks that he is responding to Joseph Gee's *Impartial Inquiry into the Importance and Present State of the Woollen Manufactories of Great Britain* (Gainsborough, 1742).

31 In verses "Written on Recovery from a Dangerous Illness" (1741), Dyer looks ahead to poetic plans: "Shall I attune the old Arcadian reed, / And sing the Fleece and loom?" (see Williams, *Poet, Painter, and Parson*, 106).

32 Dyer's readers got the message. Johnson, in his *Life of Dyer* more than twenty years later, called wool "our native commodity" (*Lives*, III, 346). Cf. the *Critical Review* on Dyer's subject as "peculiarly interesting to an English reader, by being *national*" (3 [1757], 402).

33 Wagstaffe, "Notes," 221.

THEY have, besides a considerable Stake in their Country, Leisure for Speculation" (xiii–iv). Smith's work, if Dyer knew it, and one assumes he did,[34] would probably have suggested to Dyer that a poem on the wool trade would appeal to patriotic gentlemen with leisure for speculation.[35] *The Fleece*, with its opening book on "The care of sheep," its middle books on "the labours of the loom," and its fourth book on the "arts of trade," in effect combines Ellis's practical instruction for sheep-farmers with Smith's synoptic view of the wool trade and its "POLITICAL" implications.

But Dyer's poem does not offer any new solution to the problems of wool exports, the declining price of wool, the imbalance of power between farmers and wool buyers, or the increased competition from printed cotton, problems that continued to be debated in print.[36] He recognizes the export problem, and hopes that some British "patriot" will discover a way to control illegal exports (II, line 456). Rather than entering into the current debate about whether the price of wool was being held down, Dyer simply advises that sellers of raw wool not "Reject" the "artists" who come to buy, and accept the price established by the market: "let the season's price / Win thy soft treasures" (II, lines 63–64). On the competition from cotton and other materials, Dyer doesn't see a problem. At one point he reviews the various materials for clothing, and concludes that wool is simply the best (II, lines 393–413). Elsewhere he dismisses the linen, silk, and cotton fabrics produced abroad as "gauds and dresses, of fantastic web," mere "feminine toys" for the luxury trade (III, lines 374, 381). But he recommends the blend of wool with flax, cotton, or silk woven by British mills in Manchester (III, lines 486–92, cf. IV, line 526).

What is more surprising, given the ongoing discussion about the "decay" of the wool trade,[37] Dyer nowhere acknowledges that the British wool trade has decayed. For him it is still a thriving national industry

---

[34] A second edition of Smith's *Memoirs of Wool* appeared in 1756 and 1757. The reappearance of this major treatise (it was advertised in the *Gentleman's Magazine* in January 1757) may have prompted Dyer to bring his own prolonged labors on *The Fleece* to an end.

[35] Twenty years later Henry Lord Kames assumed that "Every gentleman farmer must of course be a patriot" (*The Gentleman Farmer* [1779], xvii).

[36] In the *Gentleman's Magazine* for February 1757, one month before Dyer's *Fleece* appeared, is "An Appeal to the Public Occasioned by the Low Price of Wool" (59). For a modern discussion of the eighteenth-century politics of wool vs. cotton, see Beverly Lemire, *Fashion's Favourite: The Cotton Trade and the Consumer in Britain, 1660–1800* (Oxford, 1991).

[37] Other contemporary tracts on the topic include *The Sinking State of the Woolen Exportation Trade, humbly represented by the British Woolen Manufacturers, to the Members of Parliament* (1737); *A Method to Prevent, Without a Registry, the Running of Wool from Ireland to France . . . [and] to Re-Establish the Woolen Manufacture of England* (1745); James Bradshaw, *A Scheme to Prevent the Running of Irish Wools to France* (1744, 1754). Adam Smith discussed the imbalance of power between buyers and sellers of wool in *The Wealth of Nations*, Book, IV, ch. 8.

with a yet more glorious future. It hardly seems possible that Dyer could be unaware of the widespread assumption that the wool trade had been in trouble for decades.[38] On the other hand, as a free-trader Dyer would perhaps have discounted many of the gloomy reports about decay – most of the pamphleteers were seeking relief from parliament in the form of protective legislation. His assumption seems to be that even if the British wool trade is past its peak, it is still fundamentally healthy, and responsible for a good deal of Britain's economic power. This is not to retract my claim that *The Fleece* responds to and participates in a continuing national debate. Dyer was not alone in his optimism. Blackstone maintained that the "universal good of the nation" depends "in great measure" on the production and trade of wool, and Adam Smith that the country's woolen manufacture was in a "flourishing state."[39] Furthermore, Dyer writes not as a projector but as a poet.[40] Although he makes various "recommendations" about the wool trade,[41] his real interest does not lie with improving the economy. He is primarily interested in conveying to his readers, at a time of strenuous debates about Britain's increasing reliance on trade, and of publicly expressed doubts about the nation's moral fiber, a comprehensive and an inspiring vision of Great Britain. At the same time, like Thomson before him, Dyer lets a reader see that he has some misgivings of his own about Britain's future as a trading nation.

DYER'S VISION

Dyer's most significant accomplishment in *The Fleece* is to devise a simple poetic means – tracing the path whereby the sheep on English hillsides produce the woolens that clothe the world – which enables him to produce a comprehensive picture of the country, seen whole and all at once, as a nation working together for a common and generous end.

---

[38] But it is quite plausible that Dyer was unaware of the threat to the wool trade represented by cotton, which by 1800 was to account for almost as much of Britain's trade as did wool.

[39] *Commentaries on the Laws of England*, 7th. edn., 4 vols. (London, 1775), I, 126; *The Wealth of Nations*, Book I, xi.

[40] With nothing to say of Dyer's literary models (Virgil, Drayton, Thomson), Cecil Moore regards *The Fleece* as "mere versification of ideas" also found in contemporary tracts on the wool trade ("Whig Panegyric Verse," *Backgrounds of English Literature*, 127).

[41] One should distinguish between the up-to-date advice to sheep-farmers (see Goodridge, *Rural Life*, 137 for evidence that Dyer knows his sheep) and the points where Dyer enters into contemporary debates. His prose "arguments" include several "recommendations," "proposals," and "censures." One reviewer, probably only reading the "arguments" and skimming the poem, took specific note of Dyer's "exhortations to benevolence to the brute creation" (Book II), his recommendation of country work-houses, his "censure of those who refuse an asylum to persecuted foreigners" (Book III), and his "censure of the dispute between the English and French East-India companies" (Book IV). See *Monthly Review*, 16 (April 1757), 336–37; *Critical Review*, 3 (May 1757), 410.

Dyer adopts the basic assumptions of georgic poetry since Virgil that the greatness of a nation or an empire is founded on a firm agricultural base, and that there is no discontinuity between the sturdy simplicities of the farmer's life and the glories of the metropolis, and implements them systematically. A vision of an integrated and harmoniously united nation can be seen in the smallest and largest features of the poem. Take, for example, the way Dyer's river-painting is tied into the distribution of British goods:

> From little tenements by wood or croft
> Through many a slender path, how sedulous,
> As rills to rivers broad, they speed their way
> · · · and thence explore
> Through every navigable wave, the sea
> That laps the green earth round: through Tyne, and Tees,
> Through Weare, and Lune, and merchandising Hull,
> And Swale, and Aire whose crystal waves reflect
> The various colours of the tinctured web;
> Through Ken, swift rolling down his rocky dale,
> Like giddy youth impetuous, then at Wick
> Curbing his train, and, with the sober pace
> Of cautious eld, meandering to the deep;
> Through Dart, and sullen Exe, whose murmuring wave
> Envies the Dune and Rother, who have won
> The serge and kersie to their blanching streams;
> Through Towy, winding under Merlin's towers,
> And Usk, that frequent, among hoary rocks,
> On her deep waters paints the impending scene,
> Wild torrents, crags, and woods, and mountain snows.
>
> (III, lines 559–79)

As in Renaissance tradition, each river carries its epithet, or more commonly an identifying clause. Dyer's eye jumps all over the map of Britain, from the Tyne in Northumberland to the Dart and Exe in the West Country. He is less concerned to trace a particular watery trade route than to suggest that the country is one vast system of navigable waves. Interlinked with the rivers is a network of paths and roads,[42] teeming with British goods being carried home or to market:

> trade and business guide the living scene,
> Roll the full cars, adown the winding Aire

---

[42] Barrell notes that Dyer's "Commercial Map," by emphasizing the national "structure of communications" by road and river, de-emphasizes the difference between agriculture and manufacturing ("Afterword," 239–40).

> Load the slow-sailing barges, pile the pack
> On the long tinkling train of slow-paced steeds.
> As when a sunny day invites abroad
> The sedulous ants, they issue from their cells
> In bands unnumbered, eager for their work;
> O'er high, o'er low, they lift, they draw, they haste
> With warm affection to each other's aid.
>
> (III, lines 311–19)

Like the most social of animals – Dyer elsewhere compares men to bees – each laborer helps another; the transfer of goods, in this idealized vision of trade, is for "mutual benefit" (line 347).

> The creaking wain brings copious stores of corn:
> The grazier's sleeky kine obstruct the roads;
> The neat-dressed housewives, for the festal board
> Crowned with full baskets, in the field-way paths
> Come tripping on.   (III, lines 322–26)

In the busy, crowded roads women mingle easily with men,[43] human beings with animals. And Dyer takes some trouble with consonance and assonance – *loa*d the *slo*w-*sai*ling barge, slee*k*y *k*ine, *dressed / fest*al, *fest*al *b*oard / *f*ull *b*askets – to suggest that the harmony of the scene can even be heard. By the same token, when Dyer visits the busy weavers in their workshops, he hears "the sounding loom / Mix with the melody of every vale" (III, lines 398–99).[44] Men at their mechanical work are part of the harmony of the natural scene. Even the new spinning or carding machine is itself a "harmonious frame" (III, line 296), and poses no threat to the operators – it is "easy-tended work" (III, line 84). In this idealized world, no laborers are displaced: "Fear not surcharge; your hands will ever find / Ample employment" (III, lines 89–90); all that is replaced is "the tedious toil of needless hands" (III, line 294).

Wherever Dyer looks he sees the possibility of harmony and "union." Individual men may themselves be "feeble," but "man / With man united, is a nation strong" (II lines, 488–89). Canals, Dyer suggests, might easily be dug "and through the centre of the isle conduct / To naval union" (III, lines 602–3). If the right economic policy is followed – promoting the

---

43 The poem begins by addressing both "nymphs" and "swains" (I, lines 2–3). As opposed to Duck's *Thresher's Labour* (1736) and Mary Collier's *Woman's Labour* (1739), it represents men and women working happily together.

44 Cf. the "notes" of the "swiftly-circling engines," which "Warble together, as a choir of larks" (III, lines 283–84), and the "echoing hills" which "repeat / The stroke of axe and hammer" (lines 326–27).

Ierne breed of sheep in Wales, Lancashire, and Cumberland; and letting
"Caledonia" (Scotland) concentrate on "fisheries and flaxen webs" –
the three nations of England, Wales, and Scotland would enjoy mutual
prosperity:

> Then would the sister realms amid their seas,
> Like the three Graces in harmonious fold,
> By mutual aid enhance their various charms,
> And bless remotest climes.   (II, lines 459–70)

Dyer's unifying vision extends beyond Britain's borders to the ends of
the empire. Indeed, he urges that the traditional border surrounding the
British Isles be effaced. Britain's "gates" and "arms" should stand "open"
(III, lines 470) to welcome virtuous refugees like the Huguenot weavers,
whose presence will only strengthen the home economy. Indeed, Britain
should stop thinking of itself as an island, cut off from the world:

> Why to the narrow circle of our coast
> Should we submit our limits, while each wind
> Assists the stream and sail, and the wide main
> Wooes us in every port?

Nature itself invites Britons to go to sea, as does the example of other
nations (such as the Belgian fishery):

> Thus our isle,
> Thus only may Britannia be enlarged.
> (III, lines 545–52)

In this mood Dyer rejects the idea of little England and embraces the
future of a *Greater* Britain.

As a trading nation, Britain need not expect to engage in deadly
rivalry. (Here Dyer, ignoring decades of competition with the French,
invokes the universal benefits of trade, a theme more common at the
beginning of the century.) Disputes between trading nations are unnecessary: "Peace, peace, ye blinded Britons, and ye Gauls; / Nation to
nation is a light, a fire, / Enkindling virtue, science, and arts" (IV, lines
328–30).[45] Even Britain's imperial ambitions are consistent with internal strength. Rather than draining the nation (Goldsmith's fear), new

---

45 By the time the poem was published in 1757, Dyer knew that his vision was remote, for by then
France and Britain were again at war. One wonders whether it was at the last minute that Dyer
added the lines suggesting that he who cries for peace "cries aloud in vain" and commending
the defensive forts that Britain had wisely erected in India (IV, lines 331–36).

"distant colonies" will find room for "The o'erflowings of a people, or your wrong'd / Brethren" (III, lines 389–91). Furthermore, they will (as the traders' defense of colonies went) provide "growing marts" for British manufactures (IV, line 538). In his most extreme claim for the universal benefits of the British wool trade, Dyer insists, in his peroration, that British domination of the seas is for the good of all: "Rejoice, ye nations, vindicate the sway / Ordained for common happiness" (IV, lines 654–55). Or in the blunt terms of Dyer's prose argument: "The naval power of Britain consistent with the welfare of all nations."

Wherever one looks, one finds evidence of Dyer's fundamental rhetorical strategy: to assert that there is no conflict of interest – between buyers and sellers of wool, between men and women, between proprietors and laborers, between immigrant weavers and native workers, between traditional weaving methods and new machines, between Britain's agricultural past and its commercial future, between the literary modes of pastoral and georgic. Because sheep-herding is the archetypal pastoral – as opposed to georgic – activity, Dyer has a means of imagining a nation that manages to marry the best of two worlds, quiet rural innocence that recalls the Golden Age, and bustling and industrious urban-centered manufacturing and trade that promises a new Golden Age of British power and prosperity. Or in the closing lines to Book III: "What bales, what wealth, what industry, what fleets! / Lo, from the simple fleece, how much proceeds." Dyer's quiet pun – fleets/fleece – makes his point.[46]

Like Thomson before him, Dyer knows that trading power is backed up by naval power, "the dreaded sound / Of Britain's thunder" (IV, lines 650–51). But he regards trade as superior to war, on both moral and practical grounds. An island nation can only extend its territory by means of war, and even if it prevails it will in some sense be overextended:

> What can avail to her, whose fertile earth
> By ocean's briny waves are circumscribed,
> The armed host, and murdering sword of war,
> And conquest of her neighbours?[47]

By contrast, a trading nation "ne'er breaks / Her solemn compacts, in the lust of rule: / Studious of arts and trade, she ne'er disturbs / The holy peace of states" (IV, lines 658–64). It is as if Dyer, a clergyman, had sensed (along with some contemporary observers) that a Christian patriotism

---

[46] Compare his wordplay with "empire" and "emporium."
[47] Cf. the denunciation of "ruinous war" (IV, line 328), and "War's horrid carnage" (II, line 337).

had to be based on benevolence rather than national supremacy. And by implication economic "sway" is sounder policy. Given this celebration of Britain as an economic empire, it is salutary to remember that during most of the period when Dyer was at work on *The Fleece* Britain was at war with France. Only between the Peace of Aix-la-Chapelle in 1748 and the outbreak of the Seven Years' War in 1756 were the two nations at peace. It was probably during these years that *The Fleece* took its final form. But by the time the poem appeared in print, the French had already taken Minorca from Admiral Byng; the day before the poem was published, on 15 March 1757, Byng was shot for failure to perform his duty. By the end of July a British army under the Duke of Cumberland, sent to relieve Frederick the Great, was defeated by a French force. It was an inauspicious time for a patriotic poem about peaceful trade to appear, and may in part account for the poem's contemporary neglect. By then the country's patriotic feelings had begun to focus on the war that would vastly enlarge the British territorial empire, and on Pitt, the "Patriot Minister."

By contrast, *The Fleece* is centered not on the soldier or the statesman or the merchant, not even on the gentleman. The landed gentleman, with leisure to consider the public weal, is perhaps Dyer's chief audience, but he plays less of a role in *The Fleece* than in *The Seasons*. The poet himself takes the Thomsonian "equal wide survey,"[48] inspecting, for example, the latest spinning machines ("We next are shown / A circular machine..." [III, lines 291 ff]):

> For this I wake the weary hours of rest;
> With this desire the merchant I attend;
> By this impelled the shepherd's hut I seek,
> And, as he tends his flocks, his lectures hear
> Attentive, pleased with pure simplicity,
> And rules divulged beneficent to sheep:
> Or turn the compass o'er the painted chart,
> To mark the ways of traffic.   (II, lines 503–10)

He is a man of labor rather than leisure: "those noble works, / Those high effects of civilising trade, / Employ me, sedulous of public weal" (lines 513–15). "Employ" suggests not that the poet is a speculative observer but a participant in the nation's work. He is "sedulous" (a recurrent term in the poem[49]), a word with strong georgic and Miltonic rather

---

[48] *Summer,* line 1617.   [49] III, lines 316, 560.

than gentlemanly associations.[50] Perhaps, so he hints, because the poet is sedulous of the public weal he will help his country escape the fate of Colchis, where Jason found none "To the public weal / Attentive" (II, lines 285–86).

MISGIVINGS

There seems to be no question that Dyer *designed* his poem as a patriotic celebration not so much of the British wool trade as of a fundamentally unified nation and of a British empire prepared to take its place as the world's dominant power. It seems idle to object that (with hindsight) we know only too well that the industrial revolution would shake Britain to its foundation, that "dark Satanic mills" loomed in the near future, and that more than thirty-five years of war with France lay ahead, never mind the loss of the American colonies. *The Fleece* expresses the ebullience of Britain at mid century. Furthermore, it seems to me wrong to suggest that Dyer lacks "awareness of any strain between the old and the new" or "any clear sense of being at a crossroads in human history."[51] Even while *The Fleece* declares harmony, unity, and mutual benefit, it intermittently reveals a sense that all is not well.

Misgivings emerge primarily around the traditional moral topics of luxury, idleness, and greed, and the relatively recent moral concern about slavery. Even as Dyer in his peroration imagines Britain's glorious commercial future, he worries about luxury goods being imported in exchange for woolens:

> Ye too rejoice, ye swains;
> Increasing commerce shall reward your cares.
> A day will come, if not too deep we drink
> The cup which luxury on careless wealth,
> Pernicious gift, bestows.   (IV, lines 669–73)

Luxury is much on Dyer's mind throughout *The Fleece*. Indian printed cottons are "feminine toys," designed for "the luxurious" (III, lines 375, 381). By contrast, "flavoured tea" and Chinese porcelain are "Things elegant, ill-titled luxuries," good so long as they are "In temperance used" (III, lines 378–80). And by implication sometimes used intemperately. European settlers in America who "for your crimes have fled your native land" are

---

[50] Cf. *Paradise Lost*, IX. 27.   [51] Feingold, *Nature and Society*, 93.

"intoxicated" by the "cup / Of luxury," and with their "nerveless arms" are "Unfit to cultivate Ohio's banks" (IV, lines 543–51).[52] Dyer censures too the "voluptuous idle" who imagine that they will find "easy habitations" in the New World (IV, line 544). It is odd to find such concern in a poem that confidently commends the value of labor. Perhaps Dyer's emphatic and recurrent praise of labor – " 'Tis art and toil / Gives Nature value" (II, lines 183–84), "man is born to care; / Fashioned, improved by labour" (III, lines 25–26), "Whate'er is excellent in art proceeds / From labour and endurance" (III, lines 349–50) – hints at his fear that Britons do not share his belief. Published at the same moment as John Brown's famously gloomy *Estimate*, Dyer's poem may share Brown's worries. The *Critical Review* thought Dyer's "recommendation of labor would almost invite the idle voluptuaries of our age to vigilance and activity."[53] "Greed" too makes Dyer nervous – the "greedy mariners" (perhaps recalling Thomson),[54] and the "greedy wretch" in "dusty towns" (I, lines 621, 663), though he elsewhere displaces his worry onto inanimate objects, the "greedy plough" (II, line 380) and the "greedy loom" (III, line 85).

Slavery, Dyer knows, is a "valued trade," and though the slaves are "wretched," little blame seems to fall on the British traders: the slaves are after all "by their tribes condemned," and if not sold into "life-long servitude" would be put to death (IV, lines 192–96). (Dyer here imagines not that a tribe sells enemies captured in war, but its own people.) Like many contemporaries, Dyer calls not for abolition but for "just humanity of heart" in the treatment of slaves on sugar and tobacco plantations, if only because slaves might one day revolt and take "vengeance" on "cruel" and "unrelenting" masters: "There are ills to come of crimes" (IV, lines 203–8). Dyer's closing words suggest that, like Thomson, he is troubled not just by cruelty but by the trade itself, and that in some way he fears Britain's commercial success in a crime that will one day be punished.

Warnings against luxury, greed, and slavery are common enough in the moral writing of the time, even among apologists for trade. Dyer's

---

52 In the 1750s France and Britain began to jockey for control of the as-yet unsettled Ohio country, a dispute which ripened into the *casus belli* of the Seven Years' War.

53 *Critical Review*, 3 (1757), 409. But the reviewer (Grainger) ultimately took the positive view: Dyer's poem is a "living testimony" of the "falsehood of Dr. Brown's dogmatical assertion concerning the dulness and depravity of the present age" (411).

54 Cf. Vasco da Gama in Thomson's *Summer*, led on by "bolder Thirst / Of Gold" (lines 1004–5), and the merchants in *Autumn*, who "brave the flood in quest of gain, . . . / Urged on by . . . hardened avarice" (lines 1278, 1285).

doubts go deeper, suggesting not that the pursuit of gain can be tempered, but that trade leads inevitably to cultural ruin. Taking a long view, he knows that Britain was not always dominant. Other nations once had a thriving wool trade – Egypt, Phoenicia, Venice, Flanders. "Our day arose / When Alva's tyranny the weaving arts / Drove from the fertile valleys of the Scheld" (III, lines 408–10). The plain implications of Dyer's metaphor are that "our day" will last but a day and will one day be over: some other nation will surpass us. What happens to a trading nation whose power has passed is plain as Dyer reviews the ruined ports of Rome, Alexandria, Sidon, Athens, Corinth, Rhodes (IV, lines 58–75).[55] The most famous of the trading nations of the past is Tyre, the model in the ancient world for commercial eminence and for corrupting luxury.[56] At the close of Book II, Dyer provides an extended description of Tyre, contrasting its days of prosperity ("stately towers" and crowded "marts") with its present-day desolation:

> Her lofty domes no more
> Not even the ruins of her pomp, remain;
> Not even the dust they sank in.

Nothing remains of her "ancient site" but a "solitary rock" (II, lines 650–52, 655–56). Like Milton's Satan, Tyre has been punished by an angry God, "by the breath / Of the Omnipotent offended hurled / Down to the bottom of the stormy deep" (lines 652–54). What gives this passage additional resonance is that since the seventeenth century proponents for Britain's trade had celebrated London as a modern Tyre, and moralists had held up Tyre as a warning of the wages of commercial pride.[57] Dyer's epitaph on Tyre – "a monument to those / Who toil and wealth exchange for sloth and pride" (II, lines 656–57) – only frames the fate that may await London.[58]

---

[55] Cf. "Where is the majesty of ancient Rome . . . / Where the Attic fleece, / . . . All in the solitude of ruin lost" (II, lines 331–37). Dyer, whose *Ruins of Rome* was published in 1740, is drawn to the image of ruins. Cf. I, line 345, where the "beauteous towers of Salem" are but "dust," I, lines 501–2, on "Pompeian towers, / And Herculanean," and I, line 526, on the "venerable ruins" of Athens.

[56] Cf. Young on Tyre, "Ancient of Empires!": "Great mart of nations – But she fell" (*Imperium Pelagi*, 2. 39, 43).

[57] As Louis Landa notes, "London's resemblance to the ancient city of Tyre is a constant refrain" in the homiletic and commercial writings of the early eighteenth century ("Pope's Belinda, The General Emporie of the World, and the Wondrous Worm," repr. in *Essays in Eighteenth-Century English Literature* [Princeton, 1980], 184–85).

[58] Cf. Dyer's pointed warning at the end of *The Ruins of Rome*: "O Britons, O my countrymen, beware, / Gird, gird your hearts; the Romans once were free, / Were brave, were virtuous" (lines 511–13).

Two other extended passages about heroic mariners suggest that Dyer worries not only about sloth but also about strenuous labor itself. The effect of the passages is to undercut the poem's patriotic pride. One comes from the ancient world: Jason and the Argonauts; the other from the present day: Commodore Anson's circumnavigation of the world in 1740–44. Ostensibly introduced to explain the rise of Greece as a wool producer, the tale of the Golden Fleece serves to invoke *The Golden Fleece* (1736), which had urged the value of Britain's wool trade and the threats from other wool-producing nations. It also has a topical resonance for Dyer, who is anxious that Britain's "golden fleece" (the soft and snow-white "comber's lock") not be stolen away by French smugglers (II, line 447). But Jason is no obvious paragon for a poet worried that Britain might lose its golden fleece, for his quest to "redemand the fleece" (II, line 222) from Aetes of Colchis suggests that its current possessor is not the rightful owner. Quite apart from the fact that the heroic Jason perhaps inadvertently serves as a figure for Britain's foreign commercial rivals, Dyer's use of the story is ambiguous. Jason is heroic in his journey, which Dyer describes at length (II, lines 218–77). Once arrived at Colchis, he finds an enervated city, sunk in luxury. However, instead of enduring the familiar series of trials (taming bulls, sowing dragon's teeth, etc.), he simply "grasps" the fleece, and flees (line 293) – Dyer disposes of this part of the story in twenty lines. The heroic tale is given a bathetic end. Is Jason now a figure for the foreign merchant's theft or for "grasping" avarice? Or, given the state of affairs in Colchis, is the moral for Britain that it must not rest on its laurels, must both avoid luxury and keep at its work in order not to lose the "fleece"? Or is it rather that preeminence in the wool trade will always be transient, that no nation can expect to maintain possession of the golden fleece?

Equally ambiguous is the narrative of Anson's voyage, which Dyer introduces as a model for "adventurous mariners" and as a warning to "His country's foes" if and when they try to interfere with British trade (IV, lines 598, 603). Even in Dyer's selective account, Anson's efforts are disproportionate to the results of his voyage. Sent to attack the Spanish in the Pacific, he rounds the Horn with great difficulty (Dyer does not mention that he lost one of seven ships), sacks the town of Paita, but does not dislodge the Spanish from their ports along the "far-stretched coast / Of Chili, and Peru, and Mexico" (lines 638–39). His force "unnerved" (line 642) by disease and heat (only 200 men survived of the original force of 961), and "[d]enied all hospitable land or port" (line 644), he sails west, where he meets and overcomes "the proud Iberian" (line 652). Dyer does not say that it is a treasure galleon, or that the chief result of the circumnavigation is not that Spanish power was broken but that Anson made it home – in a single ship – a rich man.[59]

Anson's exploit was made famous by the publication of the *Authentick Journal* of the voyage in 1745, and the flattering narrative of the authorized *Voyage Round the World*, published in 1748.[60] Dyer's account is oddly circumspect, perhaps because in 1751 Anson was made First Lord of the Admiralty, and Dyer may have not wanted to offend his political friends, who included Dyer's own patron.[61] Political writers had not hesitated to do so, however. As early as the week of Anson's triumphal return an anonymous poet sneered at the booty, "purchased at a treble cost" (of both treasure and blood).[62] Johnson's "Introduction to the Political State of Great Britain" (1756) openly regarded the voyage as a misconceived failure that only "excited our enemies to greater vigilance, and perhaps to stronger fortifications."[63] Dyer does not openly question the value of the voyage, but with the tools of a poet he subtly undermines its moral weight. Anson laboriously sailing around the Horn irresistibly recalls Milton's Satan sailing through Chaos, and arriving in Eden:

> all around
> Whirlwind, and snow, and hail, and horror . . .
> Yet on he fared . . .
>
> And reared his lofty masts, and spread his sails.
> . . .   no road he found
> To moor, no bottom in the abyss, whereon
> To drop the fastening anchor.
> (lines 604–5, 615, 632, 645–47)[64]

---

59 A contemporary print, *Englands Glory* (1744), provided "an exact View of the [32] Waggons Going into the Tower of London, with the Treasure taken from the Spaniards by Commodore Anson."

60 For a modern account, see Glyn Williams, *The Prize of all the Oceans: The Triumph and Tragedy of Anson's Voyage Round the World* (London, 1999).

61 Anson served in the Admiralty under the Duke of Bedford, and was married to a daughter of Lord Hardwicke (*DNB*).

62 "In this attempt, count o'er the numerous host / Of Albion's sons, unprofitably lost. / Then will your boastings into sorrow turn, / And injur'd Britons, Albion's fate shall mourn!" (*Daily Post*, 6 July 1744, cited in Williams, *Prize of all the Oceans*, 208.)

63 *Political Writings*, 146. Johnson later wrote that even if Anson and his men had performed all they claimed to have done – and Johnson clearly doubted it – "the consequence would yet have produced very little hurt to the Spaniards, and very little benefit to the English" ("Thoughts on Falkland's Islands," in *Political Writings*, 353).

64 Cf. *Paradise Lost*, II. 917, 927, 940, IV. 131–32. Cf. I. 250 ("Hail horrors, hail"). It has been argued that Milton's account of Satan's voyage was itself modeled on the account of Da Gama's epic voyage in Camoens' *Lusiad*, in Fanshawe's 1655 English translation (David Quint, *Epic and Empire: Politics and Generic Form from Virgil to Milton* [Princeton, 1993], 253–56).

There is little reason to suspect that Dyer is aiming at a mock-heroic effect; it would in no way serve his purpose. It seems more likely that Dyer is signaling – perhaps only half-consciously – his disquiet at the buccaneering Anson, whose adventure hardly squares with a vision of Britain as the peaceable mistress of the waves.

Finally, the well-known sheep-shearing idyll at the end of Book I suggests that in some respects Dyer, despite his commitment to Britain's future as a trading nation, half-wonders whether it might have been happier if it could somehow remain a purely pastoral society. Dense with echoes of Renaissance pastoral song-contests, and of the pastoral and Edenic Milton,[65] the scene explicitly creates an image of "the first happy garden" (line 617), and contrasts it with the present:

> Yet we abandon those Elysian walks,
> Then idly for the lost delight repine:
> As greedy mariners, whose desperate sails...
> Sigh a farewell to the sinking hills.
> (lines 619–21, 624)

"We" (Dyer and his readers) are like the "mariners," eagerly – even desperately – pursuing a commercial future, but fondly looking back at a pastoral past.[66] If only, says Dyer, I could "recall those notes which once the Muse / Heard" (625) – notes heard in his youth, but also in England's youth. Earlier, Dyer had envisaged a purely pastoral England, its lawns covered with sheep,

> Like flakes of gold illumining the green,
> What other paradise adorn but thine,
> Britannia! happy, if thy sons would know
> Their happiness.   (lines 169–72)

Again the lines echo Milton's tender address to the unfallen Adam and Eve: "Sleep on / Blest pair; and O yet happiest if ye seek / No happier state, and know to know no more" (*Paradise Lost*, IV. 773–75). Dyer knows there is no going back, but as he heads into Britain's commercial future

---

[65] Cf. Dyer's "light fantastic toe" (line 692) with "L'Allegro," line 34; his flower catalog ("Pale lilies, roses, violets, and pinks," I, line 695) and "taint-worm" (line 690) with "Lycidas," lines 44, 144–46; and his "early fruits / And those of frugal store, in husk or rind," and "dulcet cream / Soft tempered" with the meal in *Paradise Lost*, V. 324, 347.

[66] Mariners also appear in a faintly Satanic guise in the "trading bark with low contracted sail," lingering "among the reeds and copsy banks / To listen" (I. 718–20), half-recalling Satan, hiding in Eden and observing Eve, "abstracted... / From his own evil, and for the time... / Stupidly good" (*Paradise Lost*, IX. 463–65).

he more than half laments what he fears has been lost.[67] As patriot, he is "sedulous of the public weal,"[68] but as poet he wants to linger among the reeds and copsy banks, and at the poem's end, "with weary wing" after traveling "o'er ocean's wave" he returns to explore "Siluria's flowery vales, her old delight, the shepherd's haunts" (IV, lines 690–93).

---

[67] Cf. Barrell, who finds in Dyer's "Commercial Map" some hints of an "anti-imperial vision" that seeks to "limit and circumscribe . . . commercial possibilities" ("Afterword," 240–41).

[68] References to his "straying" or "raptured" muse (I, line 175, III, lines 554–55, cf. I. 552) recall Thomson, and suggest that Dyer is worried that he is not sedulous enough. Cf. *The Seasons, Summer*, lines 197, 586, 1101, 1409; *Autumn*, line 150.

CHAPTER 8

Oliver Goldsmith: "half a patriot"

Goldsmith's writing career – roughly from 1755 to 1774 – is bracketed by the Seven Years' War and the American Revolution, a period of intense patriotic fervor. During his years as a writer Britain, after early losses, emerged the victor in what was widely regarded as a great patriotic war against France, adding vast territory to its overseas empire. Many emigrated to the colonies in hopes of making their fortune, and others, having made it, returned home rich. Britons welcomed a new monarch, born and bred a Briton, a "patriot king." The new prime minister, the Scottish Lord Bute, laid claim to the title of "patriot minister" that had previously belonged to William Pitt, champion of the imperial war. But patriotism did not mean national unity: Britons divided against themselves – Scot against Englishman, "North Briton" against "South Briton" – in the vociferous struggle between Bute and his antagonists, John Wilkes and the renegade poet-priest, Charles Churchill, who positioned themselves as defenders of old English "Liberty." It is in this context of public displays of patriotism that I want to locate Goldsmith's two great political poems, *The Traveller* (1764) and *The Deserted Village* (1770).

Recognized more by his contemporaries than by critics today as a political writer, Goldsmith from his early published essays through the late poems hesitated to join in celebration of British victories, the acquisition of empire, or the robust health of traditional English political "liberty." On the contrary, he worried about the political and economic transformations he observed all around him. Though he is often portrayed as an idiosyncratic figure, out of step with contemporary political and economic thinking, he can be more accurately said to represent a branch of the loyal but doubting Opposition. During and after the Seven Years' War, when much of Britain, as Linda Colley has suggested,[1] was

---

[1] "[From 1763] until the American Revolution and beyond, the British were in the grip of collective agoraphobia, captivated by, but also adrift and at odds in a vast empire abroad and a new political world at home which few of them properly understood" (*Britons*, 105).

nervously coming to terms with victory, Goldsmith's essays and poems helped focus the widespread discussion about the country's new imperial identity, pressing his contemporaries to measure the difference between a "splendid" and a "happy" land.

He wrote not in order to dampen patriotic feeling, but to refine and to redirect it. An early reviewer of *The Traveller* remarked that in his account of England "the author has shewn a warm love for his country, without deviating into either bigotry or enthusiasm."[2] Goldsmith was hailed as a "Patriot" in Anthony King's *The Frequented Village* (1771), a poem offered to the world "as a Companion" to Goldsmith's *Deserted Village*.[3] In its own fashion *The Deserted Village* is a patriotic poem, though the England it celebrates is not the imperial England after the 1763 Peace of Paris. Goldsmith himself seemed to sense that his attachment to Britain was ambivalent: in a telling phrase from *The Traveller* (another patriotic poem, though not an uncritical one[4]), Goldsmith calls himself "half a patriot."

"Half a patriot" aptly describes his stance as a political writer in several respects.[5] The first has to do with national identity and local attachment, a particular problem for an Irishman who never returned to Ireland after he left it at age twenty-two in 1752, remembered it with fondness and dismissed that "unaccountable" fondness as a "maladie du Pays";[6] who never quite felt at "home" in his adopted England;[7] and who recurrently took up the stance of the "citizen of the world."[8] The early letters to the *Royal Magazine* on "A Comparative View of Races and Nations" (1759) provide an especially clear example of that ambivalence. The

---

[2] *Gentleman's Magazine*, 24 (December 1764), 594, repr. in George Rousseau, ed., *Goldsmith: The Critical Heritage* (London, 1974).

[3] *The Frequented Village* (1771) was "inscribed" to Goldsmith, "portray'd in whose inimitable page, / The Patriot glows, with more than common rage" (36). The "Advertisement" appeared in a "new edition" in Dublin in 1774. Its title is apparently inspired by Goldsmith's memory of "The smiling long-frequented village" in *The Traveller*, line 406.

[4] Cf. Ricardo Quintana, for whom the *Traveller* is "a patriotic poem, though the patriotism is of a different order from the uncritical nationalism of Addison's *Letter*" (*Oliver Goldsmith: A Georgian Study* [London, 1969], 130).

[5] Pace John Lucas, who suggests that Goldsmith sees patriotism as something of a trap into which he too ("half a patriot") has almost fallen. See his chapter on "Goldsmith and the Ambiguities of Patriotism," in *England and Englishness*, 58–59.

[6] In a 1757 letter from London to a friend in Ireland, *Collected Letters of Oliver Goldsmith*, ed. Katharine Balderstone (Folcroft, PA, 1928), 28.

[7] From London he wrote to an Irish friend of the "difficulties" he encountered "in a Country where my being born an Irishman was sufficient to keep me unemploy'd" (*Collected Letters*, 27).

[8] Cf. Macaulay: "Goldsmith's heart and genius were Irish; his wandering about in the world had given him a touch of cosmopolitan ease in his judgment of things and opinions, ... but in the form and matter of his writings he was purposely English" (repr. in Rousseau, ed., *Critical Heritage*, 356).

letter-writer identifies himself as an English traveler revisiting his "native country" after an absence of fifteen years (Goldsmith himself traveled in Europe from 1754 to 1756). Once more on "the happy island where I drew my first breath," he bursts out in a patriotic (and thoroughly conventional) apostrophe, familiar to readers at least since Thomson's day: "Hail Britain, happiest of countries! happy in thy climate, fertility, situation, and commerce; but still happier in the peculiar nature of thy laws and government." But within a few lines this British patriot turns critical observer and would-be teacher. He wishes that after his travels he might "enlarge one mind, and make the man who now boasts his patriotism, a citizen of the world; could I level those distinctions which separate mankind; could I mend that country in which I reside, by improvements from those which I have left behind."[9]

Second, as ambivalent patriot Goldsmith acknowledged his country's traditional political virtues – liberty and independence – but cautioned throughout his career against a Britain factious and avaricious at home, expansionist and triumphalist abroad. This is especially clear in another early essay "On Public Rejoicings for Victory" (1759). Even in that year of wonders, when the tide of battle had turned to promise a British victory in the Seven Years' War, Goldsmith takes pleasure in British military victories over France only to warn his contemporaries of the costs of winning.[10] He again begins with patriotic fervor, but quickly sets that fervor at an ironic distance, even in the opening sentence:

While our fleets and armies are earning laurels abroad, while victory courts us from every quarter, while our soldiers and sailors not only retrieve the fame of English valour, but raise our reputation from whatever history can shew; and mark the reign of George the Second, as the great period of British glory; our citizens and mechanics at home are by no means idle, but deal blow for blow, and once more slay the slain. (III, 16–17)

"Soldiers and sailors" retain Goldsmith's patriotic admiration,[11] but the "citizens and mechanics at home" cast a different light on British valor.

---

[9] *Collected Works*, III, 67–68.
[10] Cf. Goldsmith's remark on the death of Wolfe in 1763: "Perhaps the loss of such a man was greater to the nation than the conquering of all Canada was advantageous" (*An History of England, in a Series of Letters from a Nobleman to his Son*, 2 vols. [1764], II, 241); and a poem "On the Taking of QUEBEC," attributed to Goldsmith: "O WOLFE, to thee a streaming flood of woe, / Sighing we pay, and think e'en conquest dear, / QUEBEC in vain shall teach our breast to glow, / Whilst thy sad fate extorts the heart-wrung tear," in *Collected Works*, V, 413.
[11] Cf. "On the taking of QUEBEC": "Alive the foe thy dreadful vigour fled, / And saw thee fall with joy-pronouncing eyes; / Yet they shall know thou conquerest, tho' dead! / Since from thy tomb a thousand heroes rise," in *Collected Works*, V, 414.

Drunk with pride and with ale, they mimic and degrade British heroics. Like Dryden's Alexander, who under the influence of drink and song "Fought all his Battails o'er again" ("And thrice He routed all his Foes; and thrice he slew the slain"),[12] Goldsmith's homefront combatants "bravely become votaries for their country, and with true patriotism not disdained to fall dead – drunk in every house" (17). By the end of the short essay, whose tone is largely one of detached amusement, Goldsmith argues not for celebrations of national supremacy but for generous peace terms: "The only use of victory is peace . . . Now; now then is the time to offer terms of accommodation; and as we conquer our enemies in war, so let us excell them in generosity." Goldsmith's argument is based on practical as well as moral grounds. If a defeated enemy harbors undying resentment, and if the economic balance of power at home shifts (from "the industrious to the enterprizing"), "It is very possible for a country to be very victorious and very wretched" (21). A related argument on behalf of a generous peace is that, for Goldsmith as for other contemporary observers (including Johnson), a nation ought to be careful about acquiring a farflung overseas empire. More is sometimes less. In another early essay on "Some Thoughts preliminary to a general PEACE" (1759), Goldsmith reminds his readers of a familiar political maxim: "that an empire, by too great a foreign power may lessen its natural strength, and that dominion often becomes more feeble as it grows more extensive" (III, 32). An unthinking support for "patriotic" war may succeed in weakening rather than strengthening the very land one claims to love.

Finally, Goldsmith is "half a patriot" in a third and deeper sense. In answer to the questions that implicitly faced most of his literary predecessors in the century, "is there a place for the poet in modern *public* life? can a poet be an effective patriot, an instructor to his countrymen?", he offers a decidedly ambivalent response. Again, Goldsmith's characteristic doubleness is visible in his earliest discussions about authorship, from the *Enquiry into the Present State of Polite Learning in Europe* (1759) to the *Citizen of the World* papers (1760–62). The author of the *Enquiry* adopts the traditionally authoritative role of "man of taste," a gentleman qualified to speak to his countrymen on cultural and political matters. But in the crucial chapter 10 ("Of the Encouragement of Learning"), the typical modern author is cut off from the old ranks of "the Great" – the "link between patronage and learning . . . now seems entirely broken" – and

---

[12] *Alexander's Feast*, lines 67–68.

is now "kept pretty much at a distance" (311) from the world of power. As a result, he must turn to the bookseller and write "for bread."[13] In such circumstances, "the man, who under the protection of the Great, might have done honour to human nature, when only patronized by the bookseller, becomes a thing little superior to the fellow who works at the press" (I, 316). At moments such as these, Goldsmith seems resigned to the reduced status of the mercenary author; once the companion of ministers, the author is now fellow to a printer's devil. Even when he considers the contemporary claim that the modern author is happily freed from dependence on a patron, Goldsmith regards it with some skepticism. At the end of no. 84 of *The Citizen of the World* he observes that the author who writes for money and is rewarded by "the public" may "bravely assert the dignity of independence" (I, 313). But in the context of an essay that has surveyed the "indigence," the neglect, and the "sufferings" of poets, "bravely assert" may be little more than hollow bluster, and "independence" not the basis for fearless pride but an index of the poet's loss of connectedness.[14]

These early doubts about the loss of a "link" between poet and political or social community persist in his later political poems, where the leading common feature, apart from the horrors of forced emigration, is the poet's own sense of isolation and exile. But despite those doubts, Goldsmith does not abandon the ambition to speak out to an audience of his fellow Britons on matters of public moment: as one critic of *The Deserted Village* put it, Goldsmith "perceived, or thought he perceived, a national calamity; a calamity which he would willingly have been instrumental in redressing."[15] And yet in both that poem and in the earlier *Traveller* he reveals strong doubts about the poet's capacity to play a public and patriotic role, doubts that may literally have made it impossible for him to complete his two great political poems. His fears for his country are intimately tied up with his fears for the future of poetry and the poet.

To make the case for Goldsmith as a political writer, concerned to redefine the nature of British patriotism, we need to confront and displace two other images: Goldsmith the self-concerned fool, eager to shine, whose quick but shallow mind was even unable to talk intelligently about

---

[13] Cf. the foolish hack in "The Indigent Philosopher" (*Collected Works*, III, 181–84).
[14] Cf. the "Preface" to the collected *Citizen of the World* letters, in which the "Editor" views himself as neither poet nor philosopher, neither the inventor of "new political systems, or new plots for farces." Instead, he says, "I belong to no particular class" (II, 15).
[15] William Mudford, repr. in Rousseau, ed., *Critical Heritage*, 244.

his own work, an "idiot in the affairs of the world";[16] and Goldsmith the uninformed political naif, whose claims about depopulation and "deserted" villages were simply inconsistent with observable facts. These images were fostered initially by Boswell and Hawkins, who in their biographies of Johnson used Goldsmith as a kind of foil for their far greater – and more worldly – hero. Beginning in the nineteenth century, readers who accepted these images of Goldsmith have read his two major poems not as embodiments of "political thinking" (Goldsmith's own term for Addison's *Letter from Italy*) but as expressions of pastoral nostalgia and the lyric overflowings of a tender wounded sensibility.

In some respects modern readers are once again prepared to read Goldsmith as a political writer, and as a self-conscious patriot. By generously citing parallel passages in his earlier work, Goldsmith's modern editors have reminded us that in *The Traveller* Goldsmith was exploring a topic that he had first taken up in his 1760 series of essays in the *Royal Magazine* on "A Comparative View of Races and Nations." In *The Deserted Village* he was pursuing a political argument that had attracted his attention as early as his 1762 essay on "The Revolution in Low Life," described as a kind of "first prose draft" of the poem.[17] But the clearest evidence that Goldsmith's intentions were in large part political is found in the dedications to *The Traveller* and *The Deserted Village*, which emphasize the poet's determination to "illustrate" political "positions" and to make a case for one "side" of a much controverted argument. The responses of Goldsmith's first reviewers indicate that they took seriously these declarations of intention.

Those declarations were not identified, in the early reviews, with any political party. Modern critics have defined Goldsmith's politics as a consistent "Tory monarchism," animated by the fear that the power of a wealthy oligarchy was encroaching on that of the people, and convinced that the way to restore balance in England's "mixed" government was to restore or strengthen the power of the monarchy. Only the King, it was argued, could act as protector of the middle orders against the

---

[16] An image fostered by Hawkins and Boswell. See, for example, the famous anecdote about Goldsmith being asked to explain the opening line of his *Traveller* (*Life of Johnson*, III, 252–53), and Hawkins' account of Goldsmith's refusal of an offer of patronage from the Earl of Northumberland (*Life of Samuel Johnson* [London, 1787], 418–19. Cf. John Forster, *Life and Times of Oliver Goldsmith*, 2nd. edn., 2 vols. [London, 1854], I, 380).

[17] John Montague, "The Sentimental Prophecy: A Study of 'The Deserted Village'," in Andrew Swarbrick, ed., *The Art of Oliver Goldsmith* (London, 1984), 93. See also the notes in Lonsdale's and Friedman's editions.

depredations of a moneyed aristocracy. This is the politics that informs *The Citizen of the World* (1762), *The Traveller* (1764), *The Vicar of Wakefield* (1766), and the two versions of the *History of England* (1764, 1771), as parallel passages, provided by Goldsmith's recent editors, have made clear.[18]

But what is not yet clear is where this situates Goldsmith in the turbulent world of party politics in the 1760s, a world better understood by political historians than by literary critics, who still rely on simplistic and sometimes anachronistic "Whig" (progressive) vs. "Tory" (conservative) distinctions. A defender of the royal prerogative might well be a Tory, but the "King's Friends" included both Whigs and Tories. The very terms were challenged, by those who deplored the return of party spirit and by those who claimed to be *both* Whig and Tory, a supporter of English liberties, the traditional authority of the crown, and the church. Goldsmith nowhere identifies himself as a "Tory," or associates his political views about a strong monarchy with the Tory party at Westminster readmitted to politics at the accession of George III, with any of the ministers of the 1760s or 1770s, or even with the country squirearchy, traditionally a Tory group.[19] One of Goldsmith's well-wishing patrons, Hugh Smithson, Earl of Northumberland, was a Tory associated with Bute and the court.[20] But Robert Nugent, Viscount Clare, to whom Goldsmith addressed "The Haunch of Venison," was a long-time Whig MP who promoted the overseas mercantile interests of his Bristol constituents. In his youth Nugent had been something of a Patriot admirer of Pulteney, in his later years President of the Board of Trade.[21] He could have little sympathy with the prophecy, in *The Deserted Village*, that "Trade's proud empire hastes to swift decay." Goldsmith is sometimes linked with a vision of traditional Tory "paternalism," in which the local squire and clergyman look after

---

[18] See Donald Davie, "Notes on Goldsmith's Politics," in Swarbrick, ed., *The Art of Oliver Goldsmith*, 79–89.

[19] Ralph Wardle notes that Goldsmith "was not a party man" (*Oliver Goldsmith, the Poet* [Lawrence, KS, 1957], 220).

[20] Lord Lieutenant of Ireland from 1763 to 1765, he offered Goldsmith a position in Ireland (Forster, *Life of Goldsmith*, I, 379–81). Goldsmith was apparently introduced to Northumberland by Robert Nugent. He dedicated the ballad of *Edwin and Angelina* to the Countess of Northumberland in 1765.

[21] Robert Nugent (1702–88), created Viscount Clare and Baron Nugent in the Irish peerage (1766), Whig MP for Bristol, ally of Henry Fox in the 1750s, proponent of Bristol mercantile interests and an aggressive foreign policy, and President of the Board of Trade (1766–68). Goldsmith, who first met Nugent in 1765, was staying with him in late October 1770, five months after *The Deserted Village* was published. Nugent was also a minor poet, the author of an "Ode to Mankind" and an epistle "To Mr. Pulteney," later praised by Joseph Warton as a "Patriot" writer animated by a "great spirit of 'liberty'." See above, 54–55 and n.

contented (and docile) villagers. But it is striking that the lord of the manor is absent from the once-thriving Auburn. Goldsmith's idealized community is organized more as an integrated and harmonious union of yeomen than as a hierarchy of high and low.

If Goldsmith was a "monarchist," it was the office rather than its particular occupant that he celebrated. At a time when poets did not hesitate to address the King, Goldsmith in his discussion of royal authority in *The Traveller* conspicuously omits any reference to George III.[22] Johnson's "Tory" politics, by contrast, are rooted in a strong respect for the authority of a monarch with whom he once had a celebrated audience, and for whose government he wrote political pamphlets. Goldsmith's hesitation to identify himself with a party perhaps reflects the desire – shared by many of his contemporaries – to rise above party differences. But in the context of his hesitation to align himself with his king, Goldsmith may also signal his sense that the poet – even the patriotic poet – finds himself without allies, in a kind of internal exile.[23]

THE TRAVELLER

Addison's "Letter from Italy" (1701), one of the most admired poems of the century, was still well enough known in the 1760s for Goldsmith to include it in his *Beauties of English Poesy* (1767), an anthology of poems for young readers. He offered his own commendation: "Few poems have done more honour to English genius than this. There is in it a strain of political thinking that was, at that time, new in our poetry."[24] Addison's "Letter" initiated a series of poetic epistles from English travelers in continental Europe, reporting on local climate, manners, morals, and government, typically celebrating England's superiority in these respects to the countries on the continent. Goldsmith's contemporaries probably knew Addison's poem from Dodsley's *Collection* (1748, 1755, 1758), where they would also have found Lyttelton's verse epistles. The lead poem in the second volume was Lyttelton's "Epistle to Mr. Pope from Rome." It is typical of the genre in unfavorably comparing "unhappy Italy" to England, "which yet alone can boast / That Liberty corrupted Rome has lost" (37). Another poem, the "Epistle to Dr. Ayscough at Oxford

---

[22] Goldsmith rarely wrote of George III. His praise of George II in the early essays often has an ironical tinge. See the essay "On Public Rejoicings for Victory" (*Collected Works*, III, 17).

[23] For a different reading that questions Goldsmith's monarchism, see Lucas, who argues that *The Traveller* attacks the incipient tyranny of George III (*England and Englishness*, 57–59).

[24] *Beauties of English Poesy*, 2 vols. (1767), I, iii, quoted in *Collected Works*, V, 321.

Written from Paris in the year 1728," finds something to admire and to pity in French luxury and "arbitrary sway" (29). Inevitably, his mind turns homeward, to the land of mixed government and liberty:

> O native isle, fair Freedom's happiest seat!
> At thought of thee my bounding pulses beat.

At the same time his contemplation of "ev'ry state around" prompts some "doubt." As he contemplates European decline, "their lost rights, their ruin'd glories," he remembers that "These, like England, once were free" (30). His "Epistle" is an implicit warning to his countrymen. In a third epistle, "To My Lord —. In the Year 1730. From Worcestershire," the English traveler has at length returned "to his own native shore," and at last "has found that Happiness he sought in vain / On the fam'd banks of Tiber and of Seine" (39).

It seems clear that Goldsmith, in conceiving of his *Traveller*, bore in mind the genre to which Addison and Lyttelton had given distinctive form.[25] Once again an English traveler surveys European manners and morals before turning his mind to England.[26] But in place of the expected paean to English liberty, Goldsmith gives a soberly measured assessment of the advantages and disadvantages of the rough British spirit, and refuses to provide the conventional conclusion that English ways are best. In the context of the "epistle from abroad," *The Traveller* is plainly offered to eighteenth-century readers as a critique of uncritically patriotic assumptions.

That critique is launched early in the poem, when Goldsmith asks the philosophical traveler's traditional question – "where to find that happiest spot below?" (line 63) and offers an equally philosophical (but not patriotic) answer:

> if countries we compare,
> And estimate the blessings which they share;
> Though patriots flatter, still shall wisdom find
> An equal portion dealt to all mankind.
>
> (lines 75–78)

---

[25] A nineteenth-century editor, H. G. Bohn, first claimed in 1848 that Goldsmith was apparently indebted also to Blackmore's *The Nature of Man* (1711), which included a survey of the characters of European nations and "an episodical digression in praise of British liberty" as well as remarks on "the Briton's vices" (repr. in Rousseau, ed., *Critical Heritage*, 334).

[26] As Pat Rogers notes, Goldsmith's traveler does not move through the landscape, but sits motionless on an alpine peak, which provides the literal "prospect" from which he views the states of Europe. See his "The Dialectic of 'The Traveller'," in Swarbrick, ed., *The Art of Oliver Goldsmith*, 114.

It is always "the patriot's boast," wherever he lives, that "His first best country ever is at home" (line 74), but it is such vain and unthinking "boasts" that the half-a-patriot Goldsmith wants to chasten.[27] As he put it in the poem's dedication, "I have endeavoured to shew, that there may be equal happiness in states, that are differently governed from our own" (IV, 247). In our more politically skeptical and relativist times it is difficult to feel the shock that Goldsmith's poem would have administered to politically complacent Englishmen.

Goldsmith's purpose is in part the same that animated his "Comparative View of Races and Nations" (1760), to "teach the English to allow strangers to have their excellence," and to make "the man who now boasts his patriotism, a citizen of the world" (III, 68). But it is also, like Lyttelton before him, to warn his compatriots that the European nations may offer a picture of what England might one day be. Italy prompts not the conventional reminder that liberty, once won, can easily be lost – Goldsmith will later be more concerned about the excesses of liberty in England than their possible loss. Rather it is Italy's past commitment to "commerce" that feeds his worry about England's own implicit decision to become a commercial state.

> For wealth was theirs, nor far removed the date,
> When commerce proudly flourish'd through the state.

But foreign trade, as contemporary observers noted, is inherently unstable: customers may decide to buy goods elsewhere if the prices are lower. This had already happened to Italy:

> more unsteady than the southern gale,
> Commerce on other shores displayed her sail;
> While nought remain'd of all that riches gave,
> But towns unman'd, and lords without a slave.
> And late the nation found, with fruitless skill,
> Its former strength was but plethoric ill.
>
> (lines 139–44)

The medical term *plethoric* (an unhealthy repletion or excess) reminds us that Goldsmith commonly imagines the body politic of the imperial trading nation as "bloated."[28]

---

[27] In the first edition (1764) Goldsmith's dismissal of the unthinking patriot is sharper. After line 78 appears the couplet: "Find that the bliss of all is much the same, / And patriotic boasting reason's shame."

[28] Cf. *Citizen of the World*, no. 25 (*Collected Works*, II, 107) and *Deserted Village*, lines 389–94.

Holland offers reminders of other dangers that any commercial nation faces: the sacrifice of everything to the "love of gain." Everything is for sale: "even liberty itself is barter'd here" (line 306). And where riches are based on commerce, wealth will flow increasingly into the hands of the few who engage in foreign trade, and who in time will control the state:

> At gold's superior charms all freedom flies,
> The needy sell it, and the rich man buys:
> A land of tyrants, and a den of slaves.
>
> (lines 307–9)[29]

Switzerland stands as a warning of what can happen not if a nation sells its liberty but if it holds on to it with too fast a grip. Conventionally regarded as a vigorous race who inhabit the mountain home of freedom, and the model of a rough simplicity, the Swiss in Goldsmith's survey are narrowed and hardened by their penurious life. They possess the "sterner virtues" but not the tender ones: "love and friendship's finely pointed dart / Fall blunted from each indurated heart" (lines 231–32). Switzerland indeed proves to be a foretaste of Britain, where all the "claims that bind and sweeten life" (line 342) are disregarded, where "stern" reason (line 325) rules the heart.

As he mentally arrives in England, Goldsmith invokes the patriotic convention of British supremacy:

> Fir'd at the sound, my genius spreads her wing,
> And flies where Britain courts the western spring;
> Where lawns extend that scorn Arcadian pride,
> And brighter streams than fam'd Hydaspis glide,
> There all around the gentlest breezes stray,
> There gentle music melts on every spray;
> Creation's mildest charms are there combin'd.
>
> (lines 317–23)

The sudden intrusion of "poetic diction" ("western spring," "brighter streams," "gentlest breezes," "mildest charms") hints that he is setting up an idealized Britain only to subvert it. But we should not assume that Goldsmith is wholly immune to traditional patriotic celebration of

---

[29] Cf. "The Revolution in Low Life": "Wherever we turn we shall find those governments that have pursued foreign commerce with too much assiduity at length becoming Aristocratical; and the immense property, thus necessarily acquired by some, has swallowed up the liberties of all" (III, 197).

the British climate and landscape.[30] In the lines that immediately follow, the introduction of the British figure in the British landscape is initially heroic:

> Pride in their port, defiance in their eye,
> I see the lords of human kind pass by
> Intent on high designs, a thoughtful band,
> By forms unfashion'd, fresh from Nature's hand;
> Fierce in their native hardiness of soul,
> True to imagin'd right above controul,
> While even the peasant boasts these rights to scan,
> And learns to venerate himself as man.
>
> (lines 327–34)

Johnson apparently found these lines so moving that, as Lonsdale notes, when he recited them from memory in the Hebrides "the tear started into his eye."[31] Prior thought them a "noble and animated sketch of our countrymen," admired not only by Johnson but by "every good judge of poetry."[32] Goldsmith, so I have argued, is at least half a patriot.

"Freedom" is the great principle that governs the British heart. But like every other nation, Britain takes its ruling passion "to a mischievous excess." While the excesses of other nations occupy a decreasing proportion of Goldsmith's attention,[33] discussion of the defects of Britain occupy eighty-six lines, more than twice that of any other country. Freedom, as Goldsmith argues, fosters the spirit of "independence" – presumably the Briton's freedom to do what he wishes, to act "above controul," leads him to regard himself not as a member of a civic society but as an autonomous agent.[34] This "independence," which Britons "prize too high," has pernicious effects: it "Keeps man from man, and breaks the social tie" (line 340). The larger-than-life "lords of human kind" shrink to "self dependent lordlings" who, because "dependent" only on themselves, literally "stand alone," not so much proud and defiant as puny and

---

30 Cf. the praises of British landscape and climate in *Citizen of the World*, no. 114, where the clichéd phrases – "vernal softness of the air, . . . painted lawns and warbling groves" (*Collected Works*, II, 440–41) suggest a gentle irony.

31 *Life of Johnson*, V, 344, quoted in Lonsdale, ed., *Gray, Collins, and Goldsmith*, 649n.

32 In his *Life of Goldsmith* (1837), quoted in Rousseau, ed., *Critical Heritage*, 291.

33 The defects of each state take up progressively fewer lines, from Italy (42 lines), to Switzerland (32), to France (14), to Holland (8).

34 Hume refers to the "great liberty and independency, which every man [in England] enjoys" (*Essays Moral, Political, and Literary*, ed. Eugene Miner, rev. edn. [Indianapolis, 1987], 207). Goldsmith may have remembered Akenside's ode "To Curio," in which, addressing "England's sons," Akenside laments "that selfish fierceness through your blood" (st. 96).

isolated. Because the "bonds of nature" are broken,[35] British lordlings fall to quarreling among themselves, divide into factions,[36] and (like so many physical objects in a world no longer held together by Newtonian attraction) mutually "repel" each other, or erupt in tumultuous intestine "ferments." When the "motions" of "the general system" (lines 347–48) are stopped, not only social life but the cosmos itself has broken down.[37]

Had Goldsmith said no more to question the virtues of Freedom, that British darling, he would have done more than enough to discredit the patriot's boast. But he goes on to argue that the "bonds of nature" have been replaced by the unnatural (or "fictitious") "bonds of wealth and law." Wealth and law at first may seem opposites: the bonds of wealth may enable the rich to oppress the poor, but the rule of law will ensure that every man is treated alike. Yet the difference between these two "bonds" is only apparent: one of Goldsmith's favorite political themes is that "rich men rule the law" (line 386).[38]

It is a bleak prospect, prompting Goldsmith to foresee the decline of poetry itself. If all that ties men to each other is wealth and law, then there can be no hope for disinterested patronage: "talent sinks, and merit weeps unknown" (line 334). Goldsmith himself was set to benefit from the patronage system – it was the publication of *The Traveller* that brought him to the attention of Robert Nugent. And he had lamented what he regarded as the decline of patronage as early as 1759, when his *Enquiry into the State of Polite Learning* recalled the glory days under Lord Somers when "the link between patronage and learning was entire" and when "all who deserved fame were in a capacity of attaining it" (I, 310). In *The Traveller* Goldsmith sees the breaking of that "link" as a crucial instance of a more general shattering of "social tie" (line 340) and even the very "bonds of nature" (line 343). But the poet remains a central figure. In the country he imagines losing, the man of arts and the man of arms were allied, and poets and kings are inspired by the same goal:

> Time may come, when, stript of all her charms,
> The land of scholars, and the nurse of arms;

---

[35] In the earlier account of Switzerland, Goldsmith's language hints that patriotism itself is a kind of imprisoning bond. Because patriotism is a "passion," the torrent and whirlwind's roar "But bind [the patriot] to his native mountains more" (line 208). The patriot imagines that he makes a free choice, but his passion proves self-confining and ineradicable.

[36] Goldsmith's "imprison'd factions" suggests that the self-dependent Briton is in a sense not free but self-enslaved.

[37] Goldsmith here may have in mind "The gen'ral ORDER" in Pope's *Essay on Man*, a "system" that can break down if man presumes too high (I, 171, 250, 257).

[38] Cf. *Vicar of Wakefield*, chs. 19, 26.

Where noble stems transmit the patriot flame,
Where kings have toil'd, and poets wrote for fame;
One sink of level avarice shall lie,
And scholars, soldiers, kings unhonor'd die.

(lines 355–60)

Did this idealized Britain ever exist? Goldsmith's imperfect control of language – the metaphorical "stript" female turns into a "sink,"[39] and Miltonic "noble stems" act like eighteenth-century statesmen[40] – perhaps reveals his doubts. His revisions show that the link between poets and kings came to seem increasingly important: in the earliest version of the poem it is "statesmen" who have toiled and kings alone who died unhonored. The key idea – a self-gratifying one for a poet – seems to be that scholars are "level" with kings, both in life and in death. Goldsmith's prophecy also suggests that in a transformed Britain the poet will no longer play a public role.

But the poem does not end here, and in the ensuing verse paragraphs it is clear that Goldsmith has not abandoned his political – and ultimately patriotic – task. For it is now, in the expository language of eighteenth-century political discourse ("rabble" and "tyrant," "favour," "contending chiefs," "regal power," "proportion'd load," "depopulation") that Dr. Goldsmith offers his diagnosis of Britain's political "ills" – an ambitious aristocracy that seeks to contract royal authority, an economic policy that forces emigration, and his remedy for them – the regulation of a properly limited "freedom" and the strengthening of "the throne." (On remedying "depopulation," Goldsmith is oddly silent – as if he regards it as irreversible.)

The straightforward political analysis calling for a properly mixed government recalls the stance of Goldsmith's dedication, in which he quite explicitly announced that he had attempted to "illustrate" a set of political "positions," among which the last and most important was that Britain had carried the "principle" of freedom "to a mischievous excess." His argument that the cry of "freedom" was often little more than a mindless slogan or a cover for the interests of a "factious band" would have resonated instantly with those who were suspicious of the

---

39 Perhaps Goldsmith dimly remembered that Rochester in an obscene lyric ("On Mrs. Willis") had called a court whore a "common shore" (i.e., sewer).

40 "Noble Stems" (i.e., blueblooded scions) is from *Arcades*, line 82. Both "stem" and "nurse" are common in Shakespeare's history plays (*Henry V, Richard II, Henry VIII*). To "transmit" a family's name was the task of both the nobleman and the poet. "Patriot flame" is standard eighteenth-century political rhetoric, found in Patriots like Churchill ("The Patriot Poet," line 2) and in their opponents.

Patriots of the day, who as the poem appeared were still crying out for "Wilkes and Liberty!"[41] Implying that there is plainly a place for the poet on the political stage, Goldsmith adopts the public role of mediator: "Without espousing the cause of any party, I have attempted to moderate the rage of all."[42] But his apparently nonpartisan stance, a traditional rhetorical strategy in British politics, in fact coincided with the appeals of pro-ministerial writers such as Smollett, who in *The Briton* (1762–63) had recently been calling for his countrymen to rise above party in their support of the King and his ministers.[43] Goldsmith's political program might be fairly described as anti-Wilkesite and pro-crown.[44] As he hints in the "Dedication," he implicitly rises to speak against Wilkes' poetic ally, Charles Churchill, who until his death about six weeks before *The Traveller* appeared had served as chief propagandist for the anti-court party.[45]

In the end, however, Goldsmith raises doubts about whether the poet can still serve his king and country. As he imagines the emigrés in America, he sees in them an image of his own impotence:

> The pensive exile, bending with his woe,
> To stop too fearful, and too faint to go,
> Casts a long look where England's glories shine,
> And bids his bosom sympathize with mine.
>
> (lines 419–22)

Perhaps the poet too regards himself not, like Lyttelton, as safely restored to his native land, but as a kind of "pensive exile" in his own country.

It was apparently at this point that the first version of Goldsmith's poem ended. The story of Johnson's timely intervention to stiffen the

---

[41] Cf. *Citizen of the World*, no. 50, and the essay in *Public Ledger*, no. 4. Cf. also the "pretended champions for liberty" (like Mr. Wilkinson) who are tyrants in their hearts and families (*Vicar of Wakefield*, ch. 19).

[42] As Lonsdale notes ("'A Garden and A Grave': The Poetry of Oliver Goldsmith," in Louis Martz and Aubrey Williams, eds., *The Author in His Work* [New Haven, 1978], 11), Goldsmith writes not only to achieve a political end, but "is also concerned to create the conditions in which his own poetry would be appreciated."

[43] See *The Briton*, no. 1, which sought to "pluck the mask of patriotism from the face of faction," nos. 25 and 38, which sought to discredit the old "War words" Whig and Tory. It was of course Wilkes and Churchill who sneeringly called their anti-Bute journal *The North Briton*.

[44] Ministerial writers of the day were attempting to temper vocal English chauvinism, whether it was directed against the French (with whom Bute was negotiating an end to the Seven Years' War) or the Scottish (who were being appointed to key places by their fellow Scotsman). Like Smollett, Goldsmith (except at line 421) is careful to use the term "Britain" rather than "England."

[45] Ironically, Churchill, an outspoken critic of the ministry, can, like Goldsmith, be found complaining of the false patriotism that "Serves well the purposes of private fraud" ("The Conference," line 156), and of a "damned Aristocracy" that attempts to "seize the helm" of state and "rob the realm" ("The Farewell," lines 361–62).

moral backbone of Goldsmith's conclusion does not need retelling. Suffice it to say that the poem in one sense turns away from politics. Governments of "laws and kings" can finally do little to cause or cure human suffering: we make or find "our own felicity" (line 432). But in another sense the poem reaffirms its political lineage. Recasting a familiar trope, Lyttelton in his "Epistle" had remarked that the "restless" traveler in quest of happiness will search "in vain" until he discovers that contentment is only found within:

> In our own breasts the source of Pleasure lies
> Still open, and still flowing to the wise . . .
> Through various toils to seek Content we roam,
> Which but with *thinking right* were our's at home.

Goldsmith's conclusion – "Vain, very vain, my weary search to find /
That bliss that centers only in the mind" (lines 423–24) – often read as resignation or confession of defeat – apparently satisfied the stern moralist (and political writer) in Johnson, perhaps by sharpening the sense and the force of Lyttelton's conventional lines.

In this reading, I have sought to redress an imbalance in the contemporary view of Goldsmith by rearguing an older case that he is not the meditative and self-absorbed poet of sensibility, concerned primarily with subjective experience and with a kind of poetic failure, but is essentially a political poet. *The Traveller* is a work of "political thinking" concerned to redirect the turbulent current of English patriotism. But it would be more precise to say that what the poem expresses is ambivalence – the ambition and determination to speak out to his countrymen so as to "moderate" their party rage, and the difficulties that in modern Britain confront such a poetic program.

THE DESERTED VILLAGE (1770)

Ambivalence did not silence Goldsmith. Six years later, in *The Deserted Village*, he again took up the question of the condition of Britain. At least since the time of Johnson, it has been noted that the poem seems to grow out of the passage near the end of *The Traveller* in which Goldsmith reflects on the fall of the "smiling long-frequented village" and imagines the fate of its inhabitants, forced to emigrate to the new world (lines 397–422). Equally to the point, *The Deserted Village* continues to explore the fate of a poet who seeks but fails to find a homeland, and who sees in the "pensive exile" of *The Traveller*'s emigré an image of his own condition. Anthony

King's *Frequented Village* – which reimagines Goldsmith's deserted village in its heyday, and goes on to reaffirm the *Traveller's* conception of a proper freedom, "When King, and People's sentiments agree" (35) – in effect regards Goldsmith's two poems as parts of a single whole.

The language of the later poem too suggests that Goldsmith is still addressing the same interrelated set of topics that preoccupied him as early as the late 1750s: the imperial economy that encourages the exporting of men and the importing of mere "ore,"[46] the corruption that luxury brings in its train, the dangers of an overextended state, the loss of old England. Although the poem focuses on a deserted country village, Goldsmith sees that village as a symptom of deeper problems that Britain had been facing for years, and had not yet solved. Consider Goldsmith's use of two key images, *accumulation* and the *bloated* body, in which an apparent *increase* in wealth and power is actually a sign of fatal illness. The gross *accumulation* of opulence and splendor in a landscape emptied of its inhabitants – "wealth accumulates, and men decay" (line 52) – links *The Deserted Village* to the Rev. Mr. Primrose's dire account, in chapter 19 of *The Vicar of Wakefield*, of a state that has devoted itself to building wealth:

... if the circumstances of our state be such, as to favour the *accumulation* of wealth, and make the opulent still more rich, this will increase their ambition. An *accumulation* of wealth, however, must necessarily be the consequence, when at present more riches flow in from external commerce, than arise from internal industry ... For this reason, wealth in all commercial states is found to *accumulate*, and all such have hitherto in time become aristocratical. Again, the very laws of this country may contribute to the *accumulation* of wealth; as when by their means the natural ties that bind the rich and poor together are broken ... by these means ... riches will *accumulate*. Now the professor of *accumulated* wealth ... the polity abounding in *accumulated* wealth, may be compared to a Cartesian system ...

The "accumulation" of wealth is obsessively dwelt on until its cumulative weight seems an embarrassment or an obscenity. In *The Deserted Village* Goldsmith works by compression rather than repetition. Through a kind of fatal reciprocity, men waste away as (and because) wealth engorges. The "bloated mass" of the kingdom grown "to sickly greatness" (lines 389, 392) ties *The Deserted Village* to the comparison between the luxurious state and "one of those bodies bloated with disease, whose bulk

---

[46] The "laborious and enterprising" men who might be "serviceable to their country at home" are sent to people "the desarts of America," and in "exchange" the mother country imports "raw silk, hemp, and tobacco" (*Citizen of the World*, no. 17, in *Collected Works*, II, 75).

is only a symptom of its wretchedness" in *The Citizen of the World*, no. 25. Even after the terms of the Peace of Paris had added substantially to Britain's empire, Goldsmith continued to warn his countrymen about their appetite for territory. In the closing words of the *History of England* (1764) he warns that "There is ever a certain extent of empire which politics are able to wield; beyond this her magnificence is but easy pomp, and her size but corpulence" (II, 254). When a nation "shines brightest with conquest, it may then like a wasting temper, be only hastening to decay" (II, 234). *The Deserted Village* is a vision of that corpulence and that imminent decay.

Goldsmith's "Dedication" of *The Deserted Village* to Reynolds focuses, more than the dedication to *The Traveller*, on the poem's political purposes: to deplore "the depopulation of the country" and to "inveigh against the increase of our luxuries." He acknowledges that "several of our best and wisest friends" maintain that the depopulation lamented in the poem "is no where to be seen, and the disorders it laments are only to be found in the poet's own imagination." Goldsmith's response – that "I sincerely believe what I have written" – has too often been dismissed as nothing more than further evidence of political naiveté, or as defensiveness in the face of hostile critics. But Goldsmith's dedication was of course published *before* the reviewers read the poem, and makes clear that he knew he was entering a field of controversy where he would encounter "modern politicians" who would rise to challenge anyone who reflected unfavorably on modern Britain. It also makes clear that Goldsmith was not focusing narrowly on the single issue of rural depopulation: he links depopulation to the larger issue of luxury, and thus implicitly questions the underpinnings of the national economy. Again Goldsmith consciously challenges what had become the standard wisdom on the topic ("For twenty or thirty years past, it has been the fashion to consider luxury as one of the greatest national advantages . . ."). Following Goldsmith's own lead, we need to notice how *The Deserted Village* engages contemporary debates about luxury, enclosure, the rage for "improvement" (whether aimed at increased agricultural yields or at aesthetically redesigned pleasure parks), the decline of the small independent farmer into wage-earning laborer, and fears of rural dislocation.[47] In Goldsmith's mind an emptied village links the transformation of the English (and Irish) countryside with the transformation of England from traditional agricultural small island to modern commercial center of a world empire. England has become rich, but has been drained of its

---

[47] See R. S. Crane, ed., *New Essays by Oliver Goldsmith* (Chicago, 1927), xl.

lifeblood. The blooming "garden" of modern rural England it is in fact a flowery "grave."

When Goldsmith's first reviewers insisted that Goldsmith was wrong about rural depopulation, they were not simply correcting his misperceptions, but were continuing to sustain a contemporary debate. Goldsmith was not so much a naif as an able opponent whose views needed, so they felt, to be discredited. The *Critical Review* insisted that, *pace* Goldsmith's description in *The Deserted Village*, "England now wears a more smiling aspect than she ever did; and few ruined villages [a tactical concession] are to be met with except on poetical ground."[48] In a review printed in the *Monthly Review* and the *Gentleman's Magazine*, Hawkesworth conceded that luxury was an evil when it led to unemployment or to a decline in population. But – in a signally weak phrase – "we may perhaps be disposed to deny" that luxury is "at present depopulating our country, not only by preventing marriage, but driving our villagers over the Western Ocean."[49] Another early critic, John Scott of Amwell, thought Goldsmith's description was hyperbolic, and his account of the traditional village implicitly idealized. But he granted that Goldsmith's major political claim was in fact correct: "pleasure may be justly said to have encroached on cultivation, and the rich to have remotely abstracted from the provision of the poor." As a result of the "influx of foreign wealth," Scott agreed, "the little farmer has been annihilated, or at least metamorphosed into a labourer."[50] Goldsmith was clearly being taken seriously as a political observer.

But even as he engaged on what he regarded as the "right" side of the public debate about luxury, Goldsmith cast doubt on his own enterprise and on Reynolds' praise of him as a "Patriot." Even more than in *The Traveller*, he implied that the poet in Britain could no longer expect to influence the views of his readers on political topics. At the climax of *The Deserted Village*, the poet bids farewell to poetry itself. Foreshadowings of this symbolic gesture can be found as early as the dedication.

Consider first Goldsmith's defense of his thesis about depopulation. Although he insists that he has personally confirmed with his own eyes the truth of his allegations, he focuses rather on his own personal *belief* ("I sincerely believe what I have written") than on the objective *truth*.[51]

[48] *Critical Review*, 29 (June 1770), 435–43.
[49] *Monthly Review*, 42 (June 1770), 440–45. Cf. the language in *Gentleman's Magazine*, 40 (June 1770), 271–73.
[50] *Critical Essays* (1785), repr. in Rousseau, ed., *Critical Heritage*, 103.
[51] Lonsdale makes this point in "'A Garden and a Grave,'" 22.

Indeed, he declines to "enter into an enquiry, whether the country be depopulating, or not," virtually conceding that he would fail to make his case, and prove himself "an indifferent politician." This opens a gap between a *politician* who seeks to influence his listeners and a *poet* who only seeks the reader's "unfatigued attention to a long poem." As for the argument about luxury, Goldsmith, even as he states his "side of the question," manages to undermine his own authority. In resisting the fashionable modern defense of luxury, he regards himself "a professed ancient on that head," rather like the traditional moralist appealing to old truths today might say "Call me old-fashioned, but..." Such disingenuousness might allow readers to conclude that Goldsmith is out of touch with the modern world. Rather than earnestly insisting on the importance of his argument, Goldsmith closes with further self-directed irony: "Indeed so much has been poured out of late on the other side of the question, that, merely for the sake of novelty and variety, one would sometimes wish to be in the right." Mock self-deprecation? Goldsmith playing the fool? Or a hint that he is more concerned with being right than with convincing a reader? Thirty years earlier Pope, in forswearing further satire as ineffectual, took satisfaction from "the testimony of his own conscience." By contrast, Goldsmith's gesture suggests a loss of confidence in the poet's role.

Consider next the inconsistency in the language of the poem. Critics have long noted that the rhetoric oscillates between lyrical passages of nostalgic description ("Sweet smiling village, loveliest of the lawn...") and stern lines of sententious judgment ("... a bold peasantry, their country's pride, / When once destroyed, can never be supplied"). The latter imply that it is not too late for Britain to turn away from a ruinous course,[52] the former that the old Britain has been irrevocably lost. Goldsmith's use of the figure of *apostrophe* – a distinct feature of the poem – also suggests a divided aim. On some occasions the poet speaks to an imagined audience of political leaders – "Ye friends to truth, ye statesmen..." (line 265) – who are asked to "judge" and implicitly to take corrective action. But more commonly he addresses Auburn itself (lines 1, 35, 75, 337), "blest retirement" (line 97), "luxury" (line 385) – who are asked only to listen to the poet's lament.

That the poet has little hope for the success of his patriotic call is suggested too by his solitude. He walks through an almost-empty landscape,

[52] John Scott of Amwell regarded the "sentiment" of these lines as "noble" (*Critical Essays*, 1785, repr. in Rousseau, ed., *Critical Heritage*, 96).

conspicuously lacking the social function once performed by the village schoolmaster and preacher, a houseless wanderer hoping only to "die at home at last" (line 96). It is suggested too by the presence in the poem of a number of what might be called surrogates for the poet. Most of them are female, and each is weakened, nearly fatally, by circumstance or betrayal. The first is the "hollow sounding bittern," like the poet a "solitary guest" in the village, and singer of a dismal note commonly regarded as "the presage of some sad event."[53] It "guards its nest" – something the poet was in effect unable to do. Solitary too is the only human figure in the village:

> For all the bloomy flush of life is fled.
> All but yon widowed, solitary thing
> That feebly bends beside the plashy spring;
> She, wretched matron, forced, in age, for bread,
> To strip the brook with mantling cresses spread, . . .
> She only left of all the harmless train,
> The sad historian of the pensive plain.
>
> (lines 128–32, 135–36)

Like the poet, she is a "sad historian," her link with a protector broken. The odd detail whereby she is "forced" to find watercress "for bread" associates her, for Goldsmith's readers, with the figure of the hack poet, forced to write – in the clichéd phrase – "for bread."[54] The heavily punctuated line, with pauses after "wretched matron," "forced," and "in age," even invites us to imagine the sexual ravishing of an old woman.[55]

Literary hack work or selling one's talent – something Goldsmith worried about – may seem an inappropriate association for a village matron, but its very oddity suggests that some subterranean concern is forcing itself to the surface, and invites us to read *The Deserted Village* as a veiled allegory about the condition of authorship in modern Britain.[56] The fate

---

53 Cf. Goldsmith's description of the bittern in his *History of the Earth, and Animated Nature*, 8 vols. (London, 1774), VI, 4. In the poem Goldsmith also mentions the lapwing, known for its clamorous "whining" (*History of the Earth*, VI, 1–2) and for trying to lead intruders away from its nest.

54 "Hackney for bread" was already conventional by the time Fielding used it in *The Author's Farce* (1730), II. 3. Cf. George Primrose's account of his stint as a writer "for bread," *The Vicar of Wakefield*, ch. 20 (*Collected Works*, IV, 111), and the "Indigent Philosopher," who writes "in a News-Paper *for bread*" (*Collected Works*, III, 182). Goldsmith also echoes – perhaps inadvertently – his description in *The Traveller* of the Swiss, who "force a churlish soil for scanty bread" (line 168).

55 For the first meaning of "force" (vb.), *OED* gives "To use violence to, to violate (a woman)." Does Goldsmith perhaps remember the ravished "matrons" in *Macbeth* ("Your wives, your daughters, / Your matrons, and your maids, could not fill up / The cistern of my lust" [IV. iii. 61–63])?

56 As Lonsdale notes, "the threats to poetry, as outlined in the dedication, are also those which depopulate villages" ("'A Garden and a Grave,'" 18).

of the poet is plainly intertwined with the fate of the nation. "Bread" returns in connection with another broken female figure, the "poor houseless shivering female," once "modest" and "sweet" (lines 329–30), who now lies at the door of her "betrayer," asking "a little bread." She too is a surrogate for the poet, and for Goldsmith himself: like him she has left the village, apparently voluntarily, and has been betrayed into selling her talents "At proud men's doors."[57]

Betrayal is the recurrent threat in the poem, and it links the fate of the author and the fate of the nation through the mediating term of a venturing female sexuality.[58] The "land" of England is like "the fair female" who, when her "charms are past," "shines forth . . / In all the glaring impotence of dress," and is "by luxury betrayed" (lines 287–95).[59] Linked with both fallen women and with the poet, "Sweet Auburn" itself, her "charms" now "fled" (line 36) has in effect been seduced and abandoned by a "master" (line 39), a "spoiler" (line 49), a "tyrant" (line 37). When Goldsmith addresses "sweet Poetry," the pattern is complete. She too is a "Dear charming nymph" (line 411), "loveliest maid" (line 407),[60] but unlike the fallen female figures in the poem she flees sexuality, the "first to fly where sensual joys invade" (line 408).

The apostrophe to "sweet Poetry" introduces the strongest evidence in the poem that a patriotically engaged poetry in Britain is no longer possible "in these degenerate times of shame" (line 409), for Poetry itself joins the "rural virtues" in departing for the new world. In a striking reversal of the expected, Goldsmith's bids "farewell" to poetry not because he is taking leave of her, but because she is in effect taking leave of him. More to the point, she will continue to serve as "nurse of every virtue" and moral teacher of "erring man," but he is unwilling or unable to follow her. Pursuing the logic of the "progress poem" (like Gray's "Progress of Poesy," or Goldsmith's own *Traveller*) which traced the northward and westward course of liberty and poetry from Greece and Rome through Italy and France to England, Goldsmith now symbolically stands paralyzed, rooted in his British soil, and watches as Poetry moves westward

---

57 Cf. Lonsdale, who observes that both the poet and the "houseless shivering female" have "voluntarily left the country for the town . . . and the possibility emerges that his fate, involving some loss of innocence or prostitution of his talents, has been similar" ("'A Garden and a Grave,'" 25).

58 In contrast to an innocent sexuality, the "harmless love" of unfallen Auburn (line 362). But the "coy maid, half willing to be prest" (line 249) may already be inclining to her fall. Even the "bashful virgin's side-long looks of love" (line 29) are perhaps a prelude to a loss of innocence.

59 Cf. the "ravaged landscape" (line 358) of the New World.

60 Cf. the epithets for Auburn, "loveliest village" (line 1), "Loveliest of the lawn" (line 35).

to a fitter clime. It seems a judgment both on the failings of the nation and of a national poetry. Just as *The Traveller* implicitly demonstrates that the "letter from abroad" and the prospect poem can no longer perform their patriotic functions, so *The Deserted Village* demonstrates the obsolescence of several other "national" genres, not only the progress poem but the country-house poem (here the great house only oppresses the landscape), the topographical poem (like Denham's *Cooper's Hill*), and the Thomsonian celebration of English liberty:[61] in any event, the poet's words cannot save his country. Again the contrast with Pope is telling: for Pope in the "Epilogue to the Satires," "The last pen for freedom let me draw" are in effect his last words,[62] and if the words have no effect, it is not the fault of the poet. Goldsmith cannot say as much.

But he is unwilling to dismiss altogether the power of poetry to "prevail . . . over time" and to teach a nation – any nation – the source of its "native strength" (line 425).[63] By a kind of rhetorical sleight of hand, the final ten lines – in which Goldsmith petitions poetry to maintain its course – are a kind of abdication from the office of national poet and a simultaneous resumption of its power. "Teach erring man," says Goldsmith, apparently unable to perform the role himself,

> to spurn the rage of gain;
> Teach him that states of native strength possest,
> Tho' very poor, may still be very blest;
> That trade's proud empire hastes to swift decay,
> As ocean sweeps the labour'd mole away;
> While self-dependent power can time defy,
> As rocks resist the billows and the sky.
>
> (lines 424–30)

Aikin regarded the passage as a "dignified finishing to the work," a "noble address to the genius of poetry, in which is compressed the moral of the whole."[64] Although supplied by Johnson (suggesting Goldsmith's continuing uncertainty about the poet's authority), the last four lines grow

---

[61] Lonsdale comments pregnantly that the poem "enacts the collapse of the very poetic conventions in which it might have sought refuge," including (among others) the country house poem, the topographical poem, and the "panegyric of English commerce and liberty" (" 'A Garden and a Grave,' " 27).

[62] Pope is fond of the gesture: compare his Cobham, whose "last" words are "Save my country" ("Epistle to Cobham," line 265).

[63] Here I disagree with Lonsdale, who claims that if regarded as a piece of "political persuasion," *The Deserted Village* was "a striking rhetorical failure" (" 'A Garden and a Grave,' " 22).

[64] John Aikin, in his 1796 edition of Goldsmith's *Poetical Works*, I, 27–28, repr. in Rousseau, ed., *Critical Heritage*, 235. Aikin could have known from Boswell's 1791 *Life of Johnson* (II, 7) that the last four lines of the passage were written by Johnson.

out of Goldsmith's argument, and suggest that he has not completely abandoned his political hopes. The "self-dependent power" is at once the voice of poetry "prevailing over time" (line 421) and the "native strength" (line 425) of an agricultural nation that does not depend on foreign trade.

If we take a longer view of the poem's reception, we can even conclude that, far from failing, Goldsmith succeeded in creating a durable image of the old village England, an "imagined community" that never in fact existed, but (in Benedict Anderson's terms) stands as a measure of what has been lost and what still holds Britons together. Macaulay was no doubt right to observe that in Auburn Goldsmith "produced something which never was and never will be seen in any part of the world."[65] But as another critic remarked in 1808, Goldsmith describes an old England that we think we somehow always knew:

> Here almost all the imagery is familiar to our eyes, and all the sentiments to our hearts. We seem rather to remember what the poet describes, than to receive information from his lines; we acknowledge without hesitation the fidelity of his outline.[66]

We remember not because Goldsmith retails pastoral clichés, but because he in effect largely *invented* the world we think we lost. It is a small agricultural village whose inhabitants young and old are bound together by the rhythms of work and by traditional pastimes. As Aikin noted, it is "an imaginary state of England."[67] The happy villagers look up to their schoolmaster and their clergyman but in other respects they seem to live in what Aikin called "a kind of golden age of equality," when, as Goldsmith says, "every rood of ground maintained its man" (line 58). Implausibly enough, there is in happy Auburn no local lord of the manor, not even a colorful "squire,"[68] perhaps because Goldsmith wanted to maximize the contrast between idealized past and a present in which the the entire village has been swallowed up by a tyrannical "man of wealth and pride" (line 275). Auburn's "bold peasantry" are themselves the political center of the village, hardy, self-reliant, but – because viewed as a collective force – not divided into "self-dependent lordlings."

---

[65] "The village in its happy days is a true English village. The village in its decay is an Irish village" (repr. in Rousseau, ed., *Critical Heritage*, 351).

[66] Edward Mangin, in his *Essay on Light Reading* (1808), repr. in Rousseau, ed., *Critical Heritage*, 111.

[67] *Poetical Works of Goldsmith* (1796), repr. in Rousseau, ed., *Critical Heritage*, 234.

[68] As Scott noted, "that the domain of the ancient Feudal Lord, or Rural Squire, was less extensive than that of the modern Peer, Placeman, or Nabob, may be doubted" (*Critical Essays*, repr. in Rousseau, ed., *Critical Heritage*, 103).

In creating this "imaginary state," Goldsmith resists a contrary image of rural England that in his own day was gathering strength in both painting and poetry: the peaceful landscape of fields and hedgerows, in which contented and deferential yeomen and laborers blend into the scene, presided over by its "natural" rulers, the landed gentry, with the symbol of their rule, the country seat, in the distance. It is perhaps in part because the latter image prevailed, and still largely (despite the efforts of Raymond Williams and others) colors our idea of pre-industrial Britain, that we have difficulty reading Goldsmith as a national poet, a true patriot, who – albeit with considerable self-questioning – embodied for his countrymen an image of Britain's "native strength."

CHAPTER 9

Christopher Smart and William Cowper: "Christian patriots"

What happened to eighteenth-century poets when a patriotic commitment was infused with an even stronger Christian piety? The question
can perhaps best be answered by considering the apparently similar
cases of Christopher Smart and William Cowper. They are each best
known for having suffered a mental breakdown sufficient to require confinement, and for producing a substantial and diffuse body of religious
verse, colored by an Evangelical Anglicanism. They are conventionally
regarded as rather self-absorbed poets, preoccupied with the promise
or the problem of salvation. In fact, as is clear to their recent editors
and to readers who take the trouble to look beyond a handful of canonical poems – *Jubilate Agno* and the *Song to David* in the case of Smart,
The Task and "The Castaway" in the case of Cowper – both poets are
remarkably outward-looking, and wrote a considerable amount of secular verse. Both displayed keen and abiding interest in public life and in
the great political issues confronting their contemporaries. Both closely
followed the progress of a war against their great European rival, France –
for Smart, the Seven Years' War (1756–63), for Cowper, the American
Revolution (1776–83). Both celebrated military victories in verse, and
lamented military losses. More broadly, both offered, in poetry written
over several decades, a kind of running commentary on the condition
of Britain. Most important for my purposes, both poets self-consciously
regarded themselves as British "patriots," and although in one way or
other retired from public life, were concerned not only to declare a love
for the country but (again, self-consciously) to offer some public service
to the state. For both poets the patriotic impulse and the religious impulse are fused. But Smart, convinced of his own salvation, and confident
in national institutions of both church and state, is a largely uncritical
celebrant of his country in the halcyon years of the 1760s. By contrast
Cowper, convinced of his own damnation, dubious about the health
of church and state, was a severely critical patriot in the 1780s, in the

wake of Britain's loss of what he regarded as the jewel in the imperial crown.

Most readers of *Jubilate Agno* have followed Smart's own hints that the poem is a storehouse of curiosities and wonders, and furthermore that he himself is a "greater wonder" than anything in it. His declaration that, though confined in a madhouse, he will become the "Reviver of ADORATION amongst ENGLISH-MEN" (B332) is marked down as the wild claim of a man who insisted that people pray with him in the street, and his prophecy that "the English language [presumably with his assistance] shall be the Language of the West" (B127) the delusional fantasy of a man obsessed with the power of words.[1] The few critics who have focused on the fact that it is *"English-*MEN" and the *"English* language" that fascinate Smart have sketched the outlines of a "Christian patriotism" in his poems, not only *Jubilate Agno* but also the *Hymns and Spiritual Songs*. It is a patriotism based on the conviction of England's uniqueness, selected by God (as Smart himself was selected) to lead the nations. This conviction in turn stands on a set of foundational myths. Smart regards Englishmen as "God's selected sheep" (Hymn 5, line 11), the true descendants of the chosen people. According to his account, Christ and his apostles visited ancient Britain, and Christ himself is in effect not only the founder of the British state but the King of England,[2] the "God of patriot deeds" (Hymn 17), and the leading admiral at the helm of Britain's modern navy.[3] As the British empire expands, it will carry the true church, the Anglican religion, across the face of the earth.[4]

Smart's Oxford editors note that his assumptions are not all to be dismissed as lunatic ravings, or even as idiosyncratic mythologizing. Legend had placed both Joseph of Arimathea and Simon in ancient Britain, regarded St. Paul as founder of the English church,[5] and even claimed that Christ dedicated the church at Glastonbury. But by situating Smart's "Christian patriotism" in early British historiography, in the tradition of English hymnody, and in the context of the seventeenth-century idea

---

[1] Smart's poems are quoted from his *Poetical Works*, ed. Karina Williamson and Marcus Walsh, 6 vols. (Oxford: Clarendon, 1980–96).

[2] *Jubilate Agno*, B137, C87. [3] See Hymn 26.

[4] See the concise summary of Smart's "Christian patriotism" in *Poetical Works*, II, 21–23.

[5] *Jubilate Agno*, B225, 231, 232, 233, and notes, in *Poetical Works*.

that Britain was a new Israel,[6] they overlook the world of popular culture of the 1750s in which Smart began his career, the patriotic Protestant politics of the "Wilkes and Liberty" years of the 1760s in which Smart published eight volumes of verse, and Smart's lifelong celebration of his native tongue, land, and its political and military leaders. They also overlook the other poets at mid-century – from Thomson and Akenside to Collins, Gray, and Churchill – who in their several ways were asking how a poet might act as a patriot. In their company Smart emerges as the one with the greatest confidence – greater even than Akenside's in the legislative bard – that the poet can serve the state.

The one extended critical discussion of Smart's Christian patriotism, a New Critical exercise nearly forty years old, focuses narrowly on the text of *Jubilate Agno* and concludes that Smart offered himself as a "patriot of the Lord," a Davidic warrior who must "slay the Dragon" (B58), a martyr who must bear Christ's cross (B94), and a prophet sent to glorify God.[7] But in a broader reconsideration of Smart's patriotic poetry, what emerges is less the messianic figure of the poet, "the Lord's News-Writer – the scribe-evangelist" (B327), than the figure of a mighty Protestant nation and its established church. For whatever reason, in 1763 Smart seems to have emerged from years of confinement (during which he apparently suffered physical and mental abuse) not an embittered and alienated prophet, but a public-spirited poet committed to reforming and enhancing the liturgy of the national church.[8] *Jubilate Agno* – never published in Smart's lifetime – justly continues to attract our attention for its odd beauty,[9] but it is the underappreciated published work known to his contemporaries, and especially the *Hymns and Spiritual Songs for the Fasts and Festivals of the Church of England*, that best represents him as "Christian patriot." And when we take into account Smart's secular poems, both early and late, it becomes clear that his patriotic zeal extended beyond the Anglican church to his nation's language, land, and military and political leaders.

It is often forgotten that long before he was put away in a madhouse, Smart had established a reputation for himself as a versatile man of letters. Even as an undergraduate at Cambridge he was a precocious

---

[6] For a recent discussion of Britain's sense of affinity with ancient Israel, see Howard Weinbrot, *Britannia's Issue*, 405–74. But when he turns to Smart, Weinbrot considers only the *Song to David*.

[7] Albert J. Kuhn, "Christopher Smart: The Poet As Patriot of the Lord," *ELH*, 30 (1963), 121–36.

[8] As Arthur Sherbo notes, "Somehow Smart's pride in his Englishness was strengthened in his confinement and he tended more and more to lay great stress on the virtues and advantages of being a native of England" (*Christopher Smart: Scholar of the University* [East Lansing, 1982], 182).

[9] See for example Clement Hawes, ed., *Christopher Smart and the Enlightenment* (New York, 1999), in which four essays are devoted to *Jubilate Agno*, none to the *Hymns*.

poet. His address "To the King," included in the *Gratulatio Academicae Cantabrigiensis* published in 1748 at the end of the War of the Austrian Succession, suggests (like Collins' "Ode to Peace") that peace has been won in part because of England's military strength on land (William Duke of Cumberland's "formidable arm") and sea (the fleet "Swift as the eagle, as the lion strong"). After taking a degree at Cambridge in 1742, and staying on as a fellow for another seven years, Smart arrived in London in 1749 to make his way as a writer. He won success almost immediately, with the first of five prize-winning Seatonian poems on the attributes of "the Supreme Being." But he also took up the busy life of a bookseller's writer and editor, first for John Newbery's *Student, or Oxford and Cambridge Monthly Miscellany* (1750–51) and then for his *Midwife, or The Old Woman's Magazine* (1750–53) and *Lilliputian Magazine* (1751–53). Although the *Midwife* tended to view the world through a comic lens, its politics (largely left in the hands of Smart's co-writer, Richard Rolt) were broadly patriotic, and Smart presumably shared them. Rolt's recurring articles on "The Midwife's Politicks: or, Gossip's Chronicle of the Affairs of Europe" adopt the stance of the patriotic "true Briton."[10] In the 16 March 1751 number the magazine reprinted the prologue and epilogue to a recent performance of Thomson's *Alfred*. In the prologue, attributed to John Boyle, fifth Earl of Orrery, the playwright is said to appeal to an audience of "free BRITONS":

> True to his Country's, and to Honour's Cause
> He fixes, there, his Fame, and your Applause;
> Wishes no Failings from your Sight to hide,
> But, by free BRITONS, will be freely try'd.

In the epilogue, attributed to Rolt, two jolly soldiers cheer for "*England, old England*":

> 2nd. Should rebels within, or should Foes from without,
> Bring the Crown on his Head, or his Honor, in doubt;
> We are ready –
> 1st.   Still ready – and boldly foretell,
> That Conquest shall ever with Liberty dwell.[11]

Smart published his first volume of verse in 1752. One of the major pieces in the volume was a georgic poem, in the tradition of John Philips' *Cyder*, entitled *The Hop-Garden*, celebrating the hops grown in his native

---

[10] See *The Midwife*, 1:1 (1750), 46 and 1:2 (1750), 93.
[11] *The Midwife*, 1:6 (1750), 274–75. The attributions are Betty Rizzo's. Pierre Danchin, who concurs (*Prologues and Epilogues of the Eighteenth Century*, 5 vols. [Nancy, 1990–] V, 101), reports that the prologue was possibly spoken in a 1745 performance at Drury Lane.

Kent. Perhaps reasoning that British beer, no less than west-country cider, needed its bard, Smart followed in Philips' footsteps in the patriotic boast that, regardless of its reputation, French wine was far inferior to British drink:

> France
> Shall bow the neck to Cantium's peerless offspring,
> And as the oak reigns lordly o'er the shrub,
> So shall the hop have homage from the vine.
>
> (II, lines 301–4)

The topic of props (from ash, willow, or chestnut) to hold up the hop plants had earlier led Smart to think of sturdy oaks – and gratuitously (but inevitably) of British men o' war, commonly made of oak. Though "unfit" for use in the hop garden, the oak is reserved "for nobler ends" (I, line 310) – to build ships for "some British demi-god, / Vernon, or Warren," who "with rapid wing / Infuriate, like Jove's armour-bearing bird, / Fly on thy foes" (lines 312–15).[12] Another piece in the volume was his *Solemn Dirge, Sacred to the Memory of his Royal Highness Frederic Prince of Wales*. The Prince, a focus for the political ambitions of Patriot politicians and writers, died suddenly in 1751, at the age of forty-four, his death widely lamented (not only by Opposition elegists). Smart's *Solemn Dirge* addresses Frederick not as a Patriot leader of the Opposition, but as the fallen heir to the throne.[13] He was to address the new heir – the future George III – two years later.[14]

Also in the early 1750s Smart, drawing on the dramatic experience of his student days, joined a troupe of writers, musicians, and performers who put on a series of musical variety shows at the Haymarket Theatre under the running title of "Mrs. Midnight's Oratory." Beginning on 3 December 1751 and reappearing irregularly until 1761, "Mrs. Midnight's Oratory" – music and songs, parodies of "Orator" Henley's orations and of dramatic prologues and epilogues, and what Horace Walpole thought the "lowest buffoonery" – aimed to please a popular audience. Smart himself performed the role of Mrs. Midnight, and may have acted as one of the writers as well, in the years before his confinement in 1757.

---

[12] This is the earliest of Smart's many references to naval heroes. The much-celebrated Captain Edward Vernon had captured Porto Bello in 1739. Lesser known, Sir Peter Warren helped capture Louisburg in 1745.

[13] In *Jubilate Agno* Smart blesses a number of members of the political Opposition of the 1730s, including Chesterfield, Bolingbroke, Granville, and the Duke of Dorset (B607–12), but by the time he named them about 1760 they were dead, inactive, or supporting the administration.

[14] In a Latin translation of a tribute to the Prince of Wales "On St. David's Day 1753" (*Poetical Works*, IV, 261).

Although surviving evidence suggests the contents of the shows from the early 1750s were largely comic, it is clear that in later years they included lusty patriotic boasting about Britain's military success against France in 1759.[15] A 1763 printed collection of Mrs. Midnight's pieces, entitled *Mrs. Midnight's Orations*, possibly edited by Smart,[16] includes an "Epilogue" to a masque entitled *Britannia's Triumph*. The masque had apparently celebrated the victory at Agincourt, and the "Epilogue" – probably presented in 1759 or 1760 – celebrates another such victory over France in 1759, Britain's great "year of victories." Although it is unlikely that Smart wrote the "Epilogue," its language suggests the kind of popular patriotism that probably colored "Mrs. Midnight's Oratory." The British Lion is "rous'd by *Gallia's* restless boundless Pride, / And bold Encroachments," and resolves to bear such insults and assaults no longer: "The Sons of BRITAIN caught the genial Sound, / They fought, they conquer'd, were in Arms renown'd; / Reviv'd the fading lustre of their Name, / And shew'd the World, they were not lost to Fame."[17] The closing lines turn to Smart's favorite force, the British navy, and its triumph over the French:

> The historic Pen
> Shall dwell with Rapture on each sacred Name
> And *Britain* from this Aera date her fame.
> Th'admiring World with Wonder shall survey,
> In ev'ry Clime her Ensigns boldly play:
> And *FRANCE* now humbl'd, shall behold with Pain,
> Another conquering GOD-LIKE MONMOUTH REIGN.
>
> (28)

Another dramatic "Prologue" in the printed collection sings likewise a song of triumph over the "trembling Foe." As Britain extends "her wide Domain" over earth and sea, her Genius, "Elate with Hope, foresees the rising Dawn, / Of Patriot Glories in a Race unborn" (37). Several other pieces, including "Mrs. Midnight's Loyal Oration," celebrate the upcoming coronation of George III, "a truly Patriot *British* King." A "Dramatic Interlude" entitled *The Gifts* opens with a dialogue between Liberty and Britannia, mourning the death of George II, and beholding with pleasure

---

[15] Playbills indicate that the performance on 14 February 1760 included a "Rhapsody on the Death of a Late Noble Commander by Mrs. Midnight." See Sherbo, *Christopher Smart*, 270. The late commander was probably Wolfe, word of whose death in September 1759 would not have arrived in London before November.

[16] According to Betty Rizzo and Robert Mahony, *Christopher Smart: An Annotated Bibliography, 1743–1983* (New York, 1984), 245.

[17] *Mrs. Midnight's Orations* (London, 1763), 27.

the new "Patriot King." Gifts from the gods are offered – laurel wreath, scepter, and mace – and the interlude closes with tribute to "*Britain*'s darling Patriot King" (67). Such patriotic rhetoric was commonplace in the years around 1760, the same years in which Smart himself, confined to bedlam, was blessing God for English victories and asking that grace be given to "the Young King." Although the patriotic words of *Jubilate Agno* were never read by his contemporaries, they would not have sounded unfamiliar to the audiences at "Mrs. Midnight's Oratory" who would have remembered Kit Smart's stage performances.[18]

Another of Smart's literary projects in the 1750s suggests the culture of popular patriotism in which he and his readers were steeped. From January through March 1756 Smart was writing for the *Universal Visiter*, yet another short-lived magazine, this one founded by Smart himself and his friend Rolt. Like many magazines of the day, it aimed to treat both literature and politics, printing new poems and brief essays as well as a "Monthly Register" of political and military news from home and abroad. Particularly for the first five monthly issues the magazine seems intent on stirring the interest of its readers in an imminent and necessary war with France. The tone is consistently ebullient, displaying robust confidence in the condition of the nation at a time when many observers, notably John Brown in his famous *Estimate*, published the following year, worried that Britain was corrupted by foreign influence.[19] Rolt and Smart signed many of the pieces themselves, and may well have written some of the unsigned ones, though they also printed unsigned contributions from other writers, including Johnson. As with their previous collaboration, Rolt generally took responsibility for the political pieces, including a "Dissertation on Liberty of Government" (January), in which the familiar history of "English Liberty" leads up to Magna Charta, "the *foundation* of the *English* LIBERTIES, and the *bulwark* of the *British* CONSTITUTION," and then to the Bill of Rights of 1689, "declaratory of those LIBERTIES to which *Englishmen* are intitled; and, God grant that they may never be violated!"[20]

Rolt also signed a four-part "Dissertation on British Colonies in America" (which explained to readers why the colonies were an essential source of wealth to the mother country – and in effect why it was in the

[18] Sherbo even speculates that Smart may have been let out from confinement in Potter's madhouse in 1760 to take part in a revival of "Mrs. Midnight's Concert and Oratory" (*Christopher Smart*, 270–71). But other Smart scholars (notably Betty Rizzo) find this extremely unlikely.
[19] Rolt's "Some Thoughts on Agriculture" (February) concludes that "ENGLAND is the *happiest spot* in the universe for all the *principal kinds* of Agriculture" (63).
[20] *Universal Visiter* (January 1756), 22.

national interest to protect them), and in April the "Thoughts on the Necessity of a War," which offered assurances of the undying support of "*Britons*, whose souls glow with liberty, and whose last drop of blood is ready to be shed in its defence" (183).[21] The May issue contains both "Some Observations relating to England and France," observing that "France has always been the natural enemy of England" (223), and the text of "His Majesty's Declaration of War Against the French King" on 17 May. In June readers found a brief dissertation "On Naval Power" and another containing "Remarkable Instances of British Bravery." It is plain enough that the magazine's political agenda was to build sentiment for the war – at a time when some Britons (including Johnson and Goldsmith) had real doubts – and to promote patriotic feeling of a rather traditional but crude sort.

Smart seems to have been responsible for the literary side of the magazine, but as coeditor he probably worked in close coordination with Rolt and shared his political views. Although the magazine printed a variety of light verse, a number of the poems have a distinctly patriotic design, including "On the War with France" (May) by Rolt, "A New Song" (June), a rollicking piece of military enthusiasm, ending with

> Huzza for *Old England*, whose strong-pointed Lance
> Shall humble the pride and the glory of France.

In the July number "An Ode, written by a Young Lady" sighs about early French victories but prophesies that Britannia will ultimately prevail,[22] and in October a "Prologue" to *Eliza* (a new opera by Rolt on the defeat of the Spanish Armada) celebrates a great English victory.[23]

Smart's own contributions included several original poems on recent public events. One offers compliments "To the Right Honourable Earl of Darlington," just named successor to Pitt as Paymaster of the nation's armed forces – as the nation prepared for war. Another, "Stanzas, occasioned by the Generosity of the English, to the Distressed Portuguese" (who had endured the Lisbon earthquake of 1 November 1755), proclaims that "charity" is part of English national identity: "Without her, Virtue barren wou'd remain, / And ENGLISHMEN, be ENGLISHMEN in vain." Finally, the February issue included a loose translation by Smart

---

[21] Also in April, Rolt contributed "An Account of the Island of Minorca" (183–86), explaining the importance of the island and of French intentions to seize it.

[22] In September appeared "A Song. To the Tune of, God Save Great George our King" (432), denouncing Admiral Byng (who had been accused of negligence in the recent loss of Minorca) and praising General Blakeney, who had attempted to defend the fort at Port Mahon.

[23] *Eliza* was produced at Drury Lane on 20 January 1757.

of the famous "Callistratus ode" that had attracted the notice of both Akenside and Collins before him. Although Athenian patriots died in their struggle, Smart writes, in a striking phrase that recalls his "Stanzas" in the previous issue, "They gave th'Athenians to themselves again." The poem hints that the spirit of [H]armodius and Aristogiton lives still in British patriots prepared to wield the "sword of liberty" in the imminent struggle with France, and thus to be "themselves again."

In the *Universal Visiter* arts and arms are allied. Just as Rolt had celebrated English "Liberty," Smart celebrated England's literary heroes. The frontispiece to the collected edition shows the pantheon of writers – Chaucer, Spenser, Shakespeare, Milton, Waller, and Dryden – who had invented and perfected England's literary language, suggesting that its writers were among England's most valuable resources. Smart himself wrote "Literary Observations" on Chaucer, Spenser, and Shakespeare, as well as "Some Thoughts on the English Language," a patriotic essay anticipating the delight in his native tongue displayed later in *Jubilate Agno*. English, he boasts, clearly displays its "superiority over all the modern languages at least." English prose is "admirably adapted to express the sentiments of a brave, sensible, sincere people in a resolute, determinate, and open manner" (8). Appended to the essay is Smart's own poetic tribute, "Hail, Energeia! hail, my native tongue," in which the English language, "concisely full and musically strong," has the sound and surge of an advancing army, arrayed in "thunders,"

> Now piercing loud, and as the clarion clear,
> And now resounding rough to rouse the ear:
> Now quick as light'ning in its rapid flow,
> Now, in its stately march, magnificently slow.

Engaged in "glorious strife" with "the pencil" (i.e., the traditional rivalry of word and image, poetry and painting), Smart's "native tongue" evokes from him the admiration he accorded to imperial military power.

It is unclear what hand Smart had in other essays or poems. Three months later, in the April issue, appeared "Some Thoughts on a National Militia," signed by "C." It has been attributed to Smart, though it is probably not by him.[24] The essay supports Pitt's Militia bill, which passed the Commons in March and was now before the Lords, to supplement (if not replace) the regular standing army, whose numbers were feared to be insufficient to fight a continental war. Like Smart, the essayist is roused by the image of a strong and free nation: "A *national militia* is

---

[24] Rizzo and Mahony (*Bibliography*, 26, 40, 662) regard it as probably written by Rolt.

the natural, strongest, and most proper defence of free countries...Is it not necessary to trust the sword in the hands of a free, loyal, brave, and generous people, who will chearfully die in the defence of their excellent sovereign, and his happy dominions?"[25] Whether or not Smart was directly involved, as writer, in other unsigned pieces in the *Universal Visiter*, we can reasonably conclude that he participated fully in the patriotic project of the magazine, and that his own pieces, even though less marked by nationalist fervor than Rolt's, took coloration from the context in which they appeared. When Smart's direct involvement in the magazine declined after April, it was apparently not because of political differences with Rolt but because of his own ill health and mental instability.

Up until the time of his confinement in 1757, Smart's public literary work identifies him as a man of rather miscellaneous letters, associated with collaborators who took a largely humorous view of contemporary politics, but prepared to present himself, when the occasion called for it, as a patriotic pro-Pitt Englishman (though not attached to any particular faction). Kuhn and others who have focused on Smart's later career have concluded that the fervent "Christian patriotism" of his later religious writings is of a different order. While granting that Smart in the 1760s is more ardent than before, I would argue for a fundamental continuity of patriotic impulse, and that his writings of the mid 1750s can provide clues for the frame of mind in which he wrote *Jubilate Agno* (wr. 1758–63) and the *Hymns and Spiritual Songs*, which Smart's Oxford editors believe were composed between June 1762 and January 1763.[26] Smart's career after his release from Potter's madhouse in 1763 suggests too that he continued to participate in the generalized patriotic championing of a Protestant England against a Catholic France.

One piece of evidence that argues for continuity between Smart of the pre-confinement and post-confinement years is his continuing relation with John Wilkes. Wilkes was the most famous "Patriot" in the early 1760s, and a variety of evidence links Smart with him, not the Wilkes of radical and anti-administration politics but the Wilkes of popular

---

[25] The similarity between the rhetorical flourish ("chearfully die in the defence of their excellent sovereign") and the close of "Thoughts on the Necessity of a War" in the same issue (Britons are ready to shed the "last drop" of blood to guard the "sacred person and throne" of the King) suggests that Smart may have had a hand in the latter essay as well – or in neither.

[26] Sherbo had earlier argued (in *JEGP*, 55 [1956], 41–57) that they were composed between March 1759 and August 1760.

Protestant English patriotism whom Linda Colley has emphasized.[27] Smart apparently met Wilkes soon after his arrival in London. An "Anecdote" published in 1771, after Smart's death, reported that he once composed an extempore epigram on Wilkes' squint at a party at Vauxhall Gardens. Editors date the poem about 1750.[28] The relationship lasted for the rest of Smart's life. Years later he composed an "ODE in commemoration of the Birthday of John Wilkes, Esq.," publicly performed on 31 October 1769.[29] In 1765 Wilkes had subscribed to Smart's 1765 volume containing his translation of the Psalms and his *Hymns and Spiritual Songs*. Wilkes himself makes no appearance in Smart's poems, although Wilkes' ally, Churchill, is blessed in *Jubilate Agno* (B295). As Sherbo has noted, Smart and Wilkes had several other common acquaintances. The printer Dryden Leach was responsible for both Churchill's 1763 *Poems* and Smart's 1765 *Psalms of David*. Smart's volume was sold by the same bookseller, William Flexney, named in *Jubilate Agno* (D62), who had published Churchill's 1761 *Rosciad*. Other friends in common included a number of members of the Sublime Society of Beef Steaks, which Wilkes joined in 1754.

Nowhere does Smart align himself with the famous "Wilkes and Liberty" slogan, though in *Jubilate Agno* oddly enough he declares that he "stood up" for "Liberty, Property, and No Excise" (B107) – a slogan from the rather distant days of the controversy in 1733 over Walpole's proposal for an excise tax, which sent many of his Whig supporters into opposition. "Liberty and Property" remained an all-purpose opposition shibboleth through the century, of the sort that Goldsmith regarded as mindlessly patriotic.[30] In 1759 "No Excise" was perhaps still a rallying cry for the trading interests with which both Smart and Wilkes were allied.[31] Smart does not appear to have shared Wilkes' opposition to the ministries of the 1760s,[32] though he apparently joined with him in a readiness to scorn

---

[27] See her discussion of Wilkes and "Little English patriotism" in *Britons*, 105–17.

[28] *Poetical Works*, IV, 479–80. See also Sherbo, *Christopher Smart*, 250–51.

[29] According to an announcement in the *Public Advertiser* (30 October 1769). The ode itself is lost. See Rizzo and Mahony, *Bibliography*, 10–11.

[30] See his 1760 account of the crippled veteran who declares huzza for "Liberty, property, and Old England" (*Citizen of the World*, no. 109, in *Collected Works*, II, 465).

[31] Smart seems to have been familiar with the rhetoric of popular demonstrations, such as the celebration at Newcastle in 1733 of those who "made so glorious a STAND against the Increase of Excise Laws" (see Rogers, *Whigs and Cities*, 274).

[32] Smart has a kind word for the Duke of Newcastle in 1762 (*Jubilate Agno*, D62), perhaps because he was for a time allied with Pitt in the prosecution of the Seven Years' War, or because one of his patrons, Henry Vane, Earl of Darlington, was a Lord of the Treasury (1749–55) and a political ally.

the Scots who flooded south to London in 1760, when Lord Bute became prime minister.

A tinge of patriotic English Scottophobia would explain Smart's curious translation of "The 100th Psalm, for a Scotch Tune," published (while he was still confined) in Newbery's *Christian's Magazine* in 1761, a poem which has escaped all critical notice. Smart's psalm seems innocent enough, except for his ironic interpolation of a sentiment not found in the King James version:

> His gates are not too straight nor strong
> To keep out sicke a lively song,
> And sicke a menceful sight. (lines 16–18)

"Menceful" puns on "menaceful" (i.e., threatening)[33] and the Scottish *menseful* ("well-behaved, polite")[34] – and suggests that the Scottish psalm-singer is made to confess to being a "menace" to good Christians. Likewise, for "his mercy is everlasting" Smart gives "Sith by his merits we are blest, / And rescued from our crimes" (lines 20–21). "Crimes" might pass as a poeticism for "sins," but in the context of anti-Scots prejudice in 1761 it probably suggests a range of villainies, from Jacobitism to the "theft" of places and pensions that once went to Englishmen. When Smart returned to Psalm 100 to translate it for his 1765 collection, his two separate versions have no equivalent for the "menceful sight" or "crimes." The "Scotch" version of Psalm 100 is a trifle, and in any case its Scottophobia is mild. But it suggests that Smart continued to think like an "English patriot." Like Wilkes, he usually preferred to use the old term "England" instead of the politically correct new *Great Britain* (encompassing both England and Scotland).[35]

A popular patriotism also marks Smart's secular poems published in the 1760s. The 1763 *Poems on Several Occasions* included an "Ode To Admiral Sir George Pocock" and another "To General Draper." In 1764 appeared an "Ode to the Right Honourable the Earl of Northumberland." It has been suggested that the odes celebrate a "Christian"

---

33 *OED* gives a 1746 citation ("a Menaceful mob of Macedonians").

34 Williamson, who suspects no irony, glosses "menceful" only as the Scottish dialect word, but acknowledges that its meanings are "scarcely appropriate here" (*Poetical Works*, IV, 462). Did Smart perhaps remember Pope's parody in "A Roman Catholic Version of the First Psalm"?

35 One exception to the pattern of popular English patriotism is the poetic fable, "The English Bull Dog, Dutch Mastiff, and Quail," written in 1755 and published in the *Gentleman's Magazine* in 1758, a poem which seems to laugh at the English bulldog and Dutch mastiff, who each boast of national superiority. Although one suspects continuous irony, the prologue urges that national "prejudices" be abandoned: "let's be patriots of mankind" (line 20). The sentiment is not characteristic of Smart. In *Jubilate Agno* bull and dog are built into the very structure of the English language itself (B643–47).

patriotism and martyrdom – Smart himself refers to *"Christian* Patriots" in the Pocock ode. Without denying that Smart's heroes are Christians, I would argue that he puts equal emphasis on their *Englishness*. What he salutes is not their endurance and martyrdom – Christian virtues that Smart himself was called upon to exercise in confinement – but their victories and their fame. Pocock was already "renown'd" for victories over the French "in either India" (line 14), but gained his greatest fame by the capture of Havana from the Spanish on 13 August 1762, reported in the *London Gazette* on 30 September. Smart apparently read the daily papers even in the madhouse: he saw the report, and thanked God "for the taking the Havannah. Septr 30th 1762" (*Jubilate Agno*, D112). But Pocock was already well known to those who followed the navy, such as George Cockings, who names Pocock (among many other naval offi-cers) in his *War: An Heroic Poem* (1760) and in a reprinted and expanded section of the poem entitled "Britannia's Call to her Brave Troops, and hardy Tars" (1762).[36] Although he shows no evidence of knowing Cock-ings' poem, Smart, like Cockings, ranks Pocock with other great English naval heroes of past wars: Howard, Frobisher, Drake, Vernon,[37] and Blake. In celebrating an English naval victory, Smart joined a large cho-rus of journalistic and poetic voices.[38]

But his ode, unlike Cockings' "Heroic Poem," suggests that for a Christian hero the victory is always God's, and heroic fame is not a plant that grows on mortal soil. Smart reflects this deferral of the hero's reward in his own encomiastic practice. He sings first not of the hero, but of an earlier "seaman," Christ himself, whose ship, long before Pocock sailed into *The Havana*, "gain'd *the Haven*" (line 4) – typically under-stated Smartian wordplay. Before the poet can "make the point in view" (another complex pun that links him with both Pocock and Christ),[39] the "Muse" must first "humble [herself]" – i.e., make obeisance to God. It is then that she "mounts the skies / And in *New Salem* vindicates her seat," where she hoists an "ENGLISH FLAG" on the "topmost spire" (line 12) of the

---

[36] Pocock is named in Cockings' preface (v) and in the poem itself (5).

[37] Smart had first written of Vernon in *The Hop-Garden*, where "Vernon, or Warren [Sir Peter Warren, commander of a squadron at the taking of Louisburg in 1745], shall with rapid wing... Fly on thy foes" (I, 313–15).

[38] Cockings declares that he "design'd the poem for the honour of my King and Country" (*War: An Heroic Poem*, xiii).

[39] "Make the point" combines (1) navigation: to reach the point of land which marks the destination – as Pocock the sailor made his landfall, (2) falconry: a hawk rises vertically in the air to "make her point" – as Smart "at one spring mounts the skies", and (3) archery: the pointblank is the white bull's eye at the center of the target (cf. Christ "Swift as an arrow to the *White*" [line 2]). It may also encompass Masonic ritual: the candidate for the "Second Degree" displays (makes?) three "points of entrance" (cf. *Jubilate Agno* B129, where Smart himself has "the blessing of God in the three POINTS of manhood, of the pen, of the sword, and of chivalry").

heavenly temple, implicitly to match the English flag that Pocock hoisted above the citadel in La Havana. For Pocock too the hero's triumphant welcome must await the time when a higher master will commend the actions of the good and faithful servant.

> And yet how silent his return
>   With scarce a welcome to his place –
> Stupidity and unconcern,
>   Were settled in each voice and on each face.
> As private as myself he walk'd along,
> Unfavour'd by a friend, unfollow'd by the throng.
>
> Thy triumph, therefore, is not here,
> Thy glories for a while postpon'd.   (lines 37–44)

It has been suggested that Smart was drawn to the idea of the hero unhonored in his own land, victim of ingratitude, a Christian martyr not unlike himself.[40] But this is to overlook the fact that, thanks to Smart's ode, Pocock's "NAME" will be "acknowledged and rever'd . . . Whene'er thy tale is read or heard" (lines 61–63), and, thanks to grateful beneficiaries of Pocock's charity, remembered in daily prayers made in "TEN THOUSAND CHURCHES" (line 66). In holding out the promise that the hero will be rewarded at last by "God's applauses" Smart by no means dismisses the world in which Pocock has the honor of "the consul's robe" (i.e., he served in Parliament), "connubial bliss and homefelt joy, / And ev'ry social praise" (lines 67–68).

General William Draper is another military leader saluted by Smart as a "CHRISTIAN HERO" (line 37). Again Smart emphasizes his victory – Draper led the expedition that captured Manila from the Spanish in 1762 – and his Englishness. Having as a Etonian schoolboy written a poem on Achilles, Draper exceeds his classical model as a "CHRISTIAN HERO" who

> prefers a higher claim
> To God's applause, his country's and his own;
> Than those, who, tho' the mirrour of their days,
> Nor knew the Prince of Worth, nor principle of praise.
>   (lines 39–42)

(Note that in this ode a "Christian Hero" may properly aspire to self-esteem and to the applause of his country.) But Draper has mounted

---

[40] See Kuhn, "The Poet as Patriot of the Lord," 121–22. Four years after the taking of Havana, Pocock resigned his commission, perhaps because he was passed over when a new First Lord was named in September 1766. But when Smart's poem appeared, in 1763, Pocock was still a famous peacetime admiral. Note that while Smart's account of Pocock's return to England does not match the welcome accorded to the conquering hero, it accords with another heroic pattern – the return of Odysseus to Ithaca, incognito.

"a little higher still": he has served to "Advance...Th'Ideas of an Englishman" (lines 43–44) by combining the "strength" of the warrior who "shakes his lance" with the "skill" of the poet who "grasps his pen." Even his sturdy no-nonsense name (far simpler than "Marlbro'" – an aristocratic name shared by England's greatest general and his grandson, Draper's former superior officer) proclaims his Englishness:

> O ENGLISH aspect name and soul,
> All ENGLISH to our joyful ears and eyes!

Even when he advances to take a place in the archangel Michael's celestial ranks, Draper and his seed will "carry God's applauses in their heart" but – in the poem's final patriotic flourish – will "shew an ENGLISH face, and act an ENGLISH part" (line 120). The Englishman is by no means lost in the Christian hero.

Again, critics have observed that Draper is presented as another hero insufficiently recognized in his own land, but have not sufficiently noticed that his victory at Manila was gazetted (so Smart's note reads) on "the 16th of April, 1763," and that the "song of all thy deeds" (line 57) – Smart's own "rough unbidden verse" (line 108) – will serve to inspire children to "active prowess" (line 58). The four stanzas devoted to the honors that Draper does *not* receive probably allude to the unprecedented popular celebration a generation earlier of Admiral Vernon, whose name and image were diffused throughout the nation after his capture of Porto Bello.[41] Smart clearly admired Vernon's "fam'd *Herculean* deed" ("Pocock," line 50), knew that English forces had won many equally great victories in the Seven Years' War, and perhaps sought a stylized and not completely serious way of deterring any odious comparisons between the famous Vernon and his lesser-known friend and patron (and fellow Cambridge-man) Draper.[42]

In a collection of poems published the following year Smart addressed an ode to yet another Christian (and English) hero, the Earl of Northumberland, "on his being appointed Lord Lieutenant of Ireland." This is the same Northumberland to whom Goldsmith was introduced, also in 1764, on the same occasion. Goldsmith saw only a great man; Smart saw a Protestant Englishman who would maintain firm control of Ireland's

---

[41] Vernon's birthday was celebrated for several years after 1740 with bonfires and ballads; London gave him "freedom" of the city. See earlier, 36, and Rogers, *Whigs and Cities*, 235–40.

[42] Draper's exploits were well-enough known to appear in Cockings' *War*, where he is twice named (xi, 23) with other naval heroes. It was only after Smart's poem appeared that Draper had grounds for disappointment, when his published *Colonel Draper's Answer* (1764) was unsuccessful in persuading the government to press for ransom from the Spanish.

papist majority. In the "Advertisement" to the poem he honors Northumberland for displaying "the true spirit of an Englishman, born to encounter opposition and triumph over difficulty." He had earlier praised the previous Lord Lieutenant (Hartington) on his appointment, and now links Northumberland with other previous Lords Lieutenant (Stanhope and Halifax, both descended from political English families) and with two Protestant English heroes (his son Lord Warkworth, the Marquis of Granby, who because he risked his life "for his country" [at the Battle of Minden in 1759] deserves "his country's voice," and the Duke of Somerset, who blocked the admission to the English court in 1687 of the emissary of the pope [the "Babylonian Whore"]).

Northumberland himself is honored for his "genuine patriotic zeal, / Which stedfast to the common-weal / By loyalty adheres" (lines 49–51). Smart's "moral Muse" will now offer a "Song of Triumph" for another of England's "distinguish'd patriots" (line 1). His "humble muse" will presume to join with Northumberland "to counter-work the mines of Rome" (line 74) – that is, to expose the "insidious arts" of every "lurking priest" (lines 82, 106). At least one contemporary reviewer, the poet John Langhorne, acknowledged Smart's own patriotic accomplishment, and implicitly identified the poet himself as the hero of the poem: "For this ode ... he merits the thanks of every true Protestant, for he fights with a truely British spirit against the Whore of Babylon."[43]

In the context of Smart's tributes to secular heroes, his volume of *Hymns and Spiritual Songs* in 1765 comes into focus as an extension of his efforts as English poet-patriot. As editors have noted, several of the hymns (nos. 17, 21, 26) display Smart's patriotic interest in the Royal Navy; two of the hymns (nos. 17, 21) share an ABABCC stanza form with the "Ode to Pocock." Hymn 15, for Whitsunday, when the apostles received the gift of tongues, is animated by Smart's delight in the English language:

> O thou God of truth and pow'r
> Bless all Englishmen this hour;
> That their language may suffice
> To make nations good and wise.
> (lines 21–24)

---

43 *Monthly Review*, 31 (1764), 231. Also in the 1764 volume is a tribute to another Protestant English soldier, Major-General William Kingsley, who had fought to victory at the Battle of Minden in 1759 ("On being asked by Colonel Hall to make Verses upon KINGSLEY at MINDEN"). Again Smart deploys the tropes of human silence and the inadequacy of human praise: "GOD himself ... / Must give th'applause alone" (lines 23–24). Cf. also Smart's dedication of his *Works of Horace* (1767) to Sir Francis Blake Delaval, "who thought it no dishonour to be incorporated in the foremost ranks of British Grenadiers, who was one of the first to set his foot upon the shore of the common enemy [at St. Malo in 1758]" (from Smart's dedication, *Poetical Works*, IV, 3).

In the hymns (see nos. 5, 17) the enemy, as in the "Ode to Northumberland," is a militant Roman Catholicism. England is "The land of God's selected sheep" (Hymn 5, line 11).

For Smart the reform of the liturgy of the national church was a patriotic work. It was not merely a private obsession. At least since Robert Nelson's *Companion for the Festivals and Fasts of the Church of England* (1704, and still being reprinted at mid-century) and Bishop Ken's collection of *Hymns for all the Festivals of the Year* (1721), High Churchmen had urged that observation of festivals, fasts, and saints' days be restored, and that the language of the liturgy be brought closer to that of the Scriptures (rather than the Book of Common Prayer).[44] This campaign attracted wide attention in Smart's own day.[45]

To strengthen the established church was itself a work of patriotism, especially since church, state, and monarchy were so thoroughly intertwined. This is made clearest in the four "Solemn Days" included among the annual cycle of festivals and fasts in the Book of Common Prayer: 30 January (the anniversary of "the Martyrdom of King *Charles* I"), 29 April (the anniversary of the Restoration – "the Day of the Return of King *Charles* II"), Accession Day (accession to the throne of the ruling monarch), and 5 November (the anniversary of the Gunpowder Plot – "the Papists Conspiracy" – of 1605).[46] Each of these civil fasts or feasts focuses on the monarch as the head of both church and state, joins Elizabethan and Civil War past with imperial present, and reaffirms English Protestantism as the state religion, whether led by a Stuart or a Hanoverian.

Smart's Hymn 5, "King Charles the Martyr," links the executed King with Smart's military heroes. Like them, Charles performs "Great acts" that will shine in "human annals." And like theirs, his "Great sufferings claim applause divine" (lines 23–24). But even in this sorrowful memory of martyrdom, Smart feels obliged to make the political point that Charles was "ill-advis'd" (line 15) to marry a Frenchwoman and a Roman Catholic, still regarded, more than a hundred years later, as enemies of England. He may even hint that, in the language of the Prayer Book, it was in part Charles' own sin (of marrying a Moabite) that provoked God to deliver him "into the hands of cruel and unreasonable Men."

[44] See the comments of the editors of the *Hymns*, in *Poetical Works*, II, 7, 13–14.

[45] For example, in the pages of the *Monthly Review* for 1762 is a long review of a new work entitled *The Liturgy of the Church of England, in its ordinary Service, reduced nearer to the Standard of Scripture* (*Monthly Review*, 27 [Oct. 1762], 298–308).

[46] The Prayer Book makes clear that the stability of the government is a chief concern.

Hymn 17, "The King's Restoration," at 120 lines (twenty six-line stanzas) by far the longest hymn in the collection, is a kind of companion piece to Hymn 5. Indeed, the twenty-second stanza looks back to the moment when the health of the nation's constitution "Was broke, and ruin'd by the general shock" of the execution of Charles I, and then to the moment ("THIS DAY") when his heir was "acknowldg'd and restor'd." Except for this line, and a brief reference to "the royal oak" (still worn on 29 May, Oak Apple Day, to commemorate his escape after the Battle of Worcester), Charles II is elided in the poem, in favor of his niece, Queen Anne (who gets three stanzas), and his father, whose "Remember" (uttered on the scaffold) provides the rhetorical shape of the last four stanzas.[47] The rest of the hymn is devoted to a history of English "heroic actions past," especially against Catholic enemies, under the guidance of "the God of patriot deeds" (lines 3–4). Not surprisingly, Smart gives the usual roll call of famous English victories ("Cressey's field," Poitiers, Agincourt, the Armada). He also assumes that his readers will remember an array of naval heroes – "Howard, Forbisher,[48] and glorious Drake" (line 28) from the Armada years, "Forest, Suckling, Langdon" (line 35) from the Seven Years' War, "A Russel, Shovel, Rook, a Benbow, and a Byng" (line 66) from the War of the Spanish Succession, most of whom he had celebrated in his secular odes.[49] Smart brings English heroism into the imperial present by thanking God

> for the naval sway
> Which o'er the subject seas we claim;
> And for the homage nations pay,
> Submissive to the great Britannic fame.
>
> (lines 19–22)

Naval sway after the Peace of Paris links the Restoration hymn to Hymn 26, "The Accession of King George III." Under George

> Our gallant fleets have won success,
> Christ Jesus at the helm,
> And let us therefore kneel and bless
> The sovereign of the realm.
>
> (lines 9–12)

---

[47] Charles' last words on the scaffold were kept in English memory by Royalist apologists and historians, including Hume, in his *History of England*, vol. I (1754), where Charles' "Remember" is prominent in ch. 59.

[48] Smart uses the older spelling of "Frobisher."

[49] For identification, see *Poetical Works*, II, 401–3.

At a time when Goldsmith worried that the increased extent of its over-seas lands was more than Britain could manage, Smart delights in the enlargement of empire:

> Where neither Philip's son was sped,
>   Nor Roman eagles flew,
> The English standard rears its head,
>   To storm and to subdue.
> . . . .
>
> His eastern, western bounds enlarge,
>   Which swarms in vain contest,
> And keep the people of his charge
>   In wealth and godly rest.
>   (lines 5–8, 29–32)

As Williamson and Walsh note (*Poetical Works*, IV, 417), in his Accession Day hymn Smart differs from contemporary hymnists in putting more emphasis on the King's role as head of the state than as spiritual head of the church.

Finally, in his Hymn 29, for "The Fifth of November," Smart returns to the vigorous denunciation of "Papists" that marked the "Ode to Northumberland." Some anti-Catholic sentiment is of course appropriate for the occasion, the discovery of the so-called Gunpowder Plot to blow up parliament in 1605, but Smart gives full vent to his Anglican prejudice. The conspirators are "the children of evasion," guilty of "the most flagitious crimes":

> There is no such great perdition
>   In the story of mankind,
> Not by craft and superstition,
>   Yea, and cruelty combined.
>   (lines 21–24)

But Smart was not notably more virulent in his anti-Romanism than contemporary hymnists, or than the language of the Prayer Book.[50] Even in "God Save the King" Englishmen deplored the "knavish tricks" of the King's "enemies." As the Oxford editors note, Smart ignores the *other* dimension of 5 November, anniversary of the landing of William of Orange at Torbay in 1688. He is unusual among eighteenth-century English "patriots" in never once – throughout his works in verse or prose – honoring (or even mentioning) the Protestant hero who delivered England from popery and secured its liberties at the Revolution. Were

---

[50] As Williamson and Walsh note, in *Poetical Works*, IV, 421. They also observe that Smart was not unusual in regarding the plot as a punishment for English inattention to religious duties.

it not for his thoroughgoing anti-Romanism, it would be enough to make one wonder whether Smart harbored some lurking fondness for the Stuart family.

Patriotic sentiment is most evident in the hymns for the four civil "Solemn Days," where it is licensed by the Book of Common Prayer, and rarely intrudes inappropriately into the hymns for the religious feasts and fasts. But Smart's hymns are designed for an *English* church. A "glorious English cross" flies from the steeple in the hymn for Easter Day – not the Union jack but the old cross of St. George, symbol both of Christ's triumph and of England, the "ENGLISH FLAG" that Smart hoists on "the topmost spire" of the temple in New Salem in the "Ode to Pocock" (line 12). The deity Smart addresses is himself an honorary Englishman: "God of heartiness and strength, / God of English pray'r and laud" (Hymn 21, lines 43–44). It is the Anglican faith that will be carried across the seas by English ships and missionaries:

> Farther yet, and farther east,
> English sails shall be unfurl'd,
> Wafting many a pious priest
> To protest against the world.
>
> Farther yet, and farther west,
> We shall send the faith abroad,
> Against nations to protest,
> That are still by Christ unaw'd.
> (Hymn 27, lines 25–32)

In his hymns for the established Church of England, Smart continues to deploy the patriotic language of *Mrs. Midnight's Orations* and *The Universal Visiter.*

COWPER

Near the end of *The Task* Cowper, after summing up the life of leisure and contemplation, makes the remarkable claim that the retired poet "serves his country; recompenses well / The state beneath the shadow of whose vine / He sits secure, and in the scale of life / Holds no ignoble, though a slighted place" (VI, lines 968–71).[51] In so doing, he boldly insists that the poet may indeed be a patriot, one who not only loves his country – "England, with all thy faults, I love thee still," Cowper had earlier

---

[51] Cowper's poems are quoted from his *Poems*, ed. John Baird and Charles Ryskamp, 3 vols. (Oxford: Clarendon, 1980).

proclaimed (*The Task*, II, line 206) – but one who serves her. He knew that his poetic predecessors had made such claims; Horace had ironically assured Augustus that poets are of use to the state,[52] and Churchill had vowed that "With all her faults [England] is my Country still."[53] But Cowper's explicit and insistent language suggests that he had made the relationship of patriotism and poetry a central problem.

Cowper is best remembered now as a celebrant of the private pleasures of rural retirement, or as the tortured Calvinist obsessed with the damnation that he knew his God had foreordained for him. It is sometimes recalled that despite his withdrawal to the country, he fed avidly on news of the great world, but not enough remarked that his poems and letters offer observations on the chief events in the great world, a kind of running commentary on the condition of the nation. As Donald Davie once remarked, Cowper provides "the fullest image in poetry of the public life of his times."[54] He writes about the American war, ministerial politics, the debates about public schools, the controversy over the slave trade, and the impeachment of Warren Hastings. In 1779 and 1780 alone he published poems on the trial of Admirals Keppel and Palliser, on Admiral Rodney's victory over a Spanish fleet, on the promotion of Lord Thurlow to be Lord Chancellor, and on the burning of Lord Mansfield's library in the course of the Gordon riots.[55] In later years he wrote "On the Loss of the Royal George" (a shocking accident in which 400 sailors lost their lives).

Furthermore, Cowper self-consciously beheld the world with the eyes of a patriot, a habit he developed as a boy.

I learn'd when I was a Boy, being the Son of a staunch Whig and a man that lov'd his country, to flow with that patriotic Enthusiasm which is apt to break forth into poetry, or at least prompt a person if he has any inclination that way, to poetical endeavors. (*Letters and Prose Writings*, I, 551)

As a young man at the Inner Temple, he took pleasure in "enumerating victories and acquisitions that seemed to follow each other almost in a continued series" in 1759: when he heard news of the victories of Admiral

---

[52] "Epistle to Augustus," *Epistles*, II. 1. 124.   [53] "The Farewell" (1764), lines 27–28.

[54] *The Late Augustans* (London, 1958), xxvii. Cf. Kenneth MacLean, who noted over fifty years ago that Cowper's 1782 *Poems* provides "splendid picture of the England of that day" (*The Age of Johnson*, ed. F. W. Hilles [New Haven, 1949], 284).

[55] "On the Trial of Admiral Keppel," "An Address to the Mob on Occasion of the Late Riot at the House of Sir Hugh Palliser," "On the Victory Gained by Sir George Rodney over the Spanish Fleet off Gibralter in 1780." Cf., from the same years, poems on the war with France: "Επινικιον" and "A Present for the Queen of France."

Boscawen at Lagos, Admiral Hawke at Quiberon Bay, and General Wolfe at Quebec, "how did I leap for joy!" (II, 12).

What especially provoked him as he grew older (as it did earlier retired poets like Pope) was what he regarded as the spectacle of a declining empire. But he did not look on as an "unconcerned Spectator." In the dark days of 1782 he does not regard himself as "destitute of true Patriotism, but the course of public events has of late afforded me no opportunity to exert it. I cannot rejoice, because I see no reason, and I will not murmur, because for that, I can find no good one" (II, 12). Bad news does not call him back to town from his retirement in the country, but it induces him to worry about how, in the words of a minor mid-century poet on a similar occasion, he might "save sinking Britain."[56]

Unlike Smart, Cowper regarded England's condition as perilous, and if Smart ignored John Brown's dire *Estimate*, Cowper took the view that Brown's assessment was correct even if resounding victory in the Seven Years' War seemed to prove him wrong. What Brown saw around him in 1757, Cowper saw in the 1780s:

> his judgment was not fram'd amiss,
> Its error, if it err'd, was merely this –
> He thought the dying hour already come,
> And a complete recovery struck him dumb.
>   But that effeminacy, folly, lust,
> Enervate and enfeeble, and needs must,
> And that a nation shamefully debas'd,
> Will be despis'd and trampl'd on at last,
> Unless sweet penitence her pow'rs renew,
> Is truth, if history itself be true.
>   ("Table Talk," lines 390–99)

Particularly in the poems in his 1782 volume Cowper offers himself as a latter-day Brown. Although these couplet poems are often called Cowper's "moral satires," as if he were following in Pope's footsteps, they show rather that Cowper is uncomfortable with the stance of censorious and ridiculing satirist, and wants to think of himself as a kind of secular preacher, attempting to induce a sinful nation to recognize its sins, repent, and reform. He assumes that Britain was once a great nation, and that is has fallen: "Compare what then thou wast, with what thou art" ("Expostulation," line 557). Worse, he assumes that Britons

---

[56] See Isaac Hawkins Browne, "The Fire Side" (1746), repr. in Lonsdale, ed., *The New Oxford Book of Eighteenth-Century Verse*, 404. Cf. another mid-century retired poet, Sneyd Davies, who looks back from retirement at a world of vice and folly, e.g., his verse epistle to Thomas Taylor, and his "Voyage to Tintern Abbey."

were once God's chosen people, but that a "vindictive God" (line 407) has withdrawn his favor. The task he assigns to his readers is to understand why, and he asks of them a series of disingenuous rhetorical questions: "Why weeps the muse for England? . . . What ails thee [Britain]?" ("Expostulation," lines 1, 272).

The central element in Cowper's stance is a conscious patriotism. Like Smart he enthusiastically supports Britain's war against France, takes pride and delight in her military victories, and deploys the conventional language of patriotic pride. A 1779 verse epistle "To Sir Joshua Reynolds," apparently designed for newspaper publication, offers prophecy in the form of instructions to a painter for a canvas depicting British victory over European foes:

> Iberia trembling from afar
> Renounces the confed'rate war:
> Her Efforts and her Arts o'ercome,
> France calls her shatter'd navies home . . .
> Astonishment and Awe profound
> Are stamp'd upon the Nations round:
> Without one Friend, above all Foes,
> Britannia gives the World Repose.
>
> (*Poems*, 1, 219, lines 33–36, 39–42)

In a private note on the poem, Cowper regards himself as a "Volunteer" laureate who will "sing poor Britannia a Song of Encouragement" at "a time of so much national Distress."[57] Keppel and Palliser, he reminds his readers, were "Bold in Britain's Cause" and deserve the thanks of their countrymen rather than their ungrateful contempt.[58] France's aid to the rebellious American colonists is denounced as an attempt to "Pick a Gem from England's Crown."[59] Because of its wise and honorable king, Britain is a "Blest country! where these kingly glories shine" ("Table Talk," line 81). A poem entitled "Heroism" develops this traditional patriotic theme: "Oh place me in some heav'n-protected isle, / where peace and equity and freedom smile . . . / A land that distant tyrants hate in vain, / In Britain's isle, beneath a George's reign"(*Poems*, 1, 434–35, lines 83–84, 89–90).[60]

---

[57] See *Poems*, 1, 494–95. A canceled passage at the opening of "Table Talk" establishes that poem's occasion as the war, in which perfidious Europeans and rebellious colonists defy "my gallant Country" (*Poems*, 1, 241).

[58] "An Address to the Mob on Occasion of the Late Riot at the House of Sir Hugh Palliser," *Poems*, 1, 212, line 16.

[59] "Επινικιον," *Poems*, 1, 217, line 11.

[60] Feingold dismisses Cowper's patriotism: "For all his patriotism Cowper [finds] no way to express his public themes in a celebrative mode" (*Nature and Society*, 143).

Such language does not distinguish Cowper from many other voices of his day. He seems to have sensed as much, and (again like many contemporaries) sought to distance himself from a false patriotism, declaiming against those who hid their selfish ambitions in the cloak of patriotism. One early poem, "The Modern Patriot" (1782), is devoted to British politicians who encouraged the American colonists. Cowper, sharing Smart's view of the value of the colonies but not of motives of professed patriots, regarded this as the promotion of civil broils, lawlessness, and rebellion. "Patriots" in "Table Talk" aim only to "catch at popular applause" (line 144) and "love good places at their hearts" (line 190). The recurring figure of the false patriot haunts *The Task*: he is "bursting with heroic rage" (IV, line 48), "burns with most intense and flagrant zeal / To serve his country" but is then bought off with "money from the public chest" (III, lines 795–96), calls himself – here Cowper has in mind the privately debauched Charles James Fox – the "nation's friend" but is "in truth, the friend of no man there" (V, lines 504–5). In an age of "cold pretence," "Patriots are grown too shrewd to be sincere," loudly declaiming "on the part / Of liberty, themselves the slaves of lust" (V, lines 494–95, 98–99).

In contrast to the false patriot stands the true one, but Cowper can find few examples in his own day. Chatham, who died in 1778, was such a one:

> In him, Demosthenes was heard again,
> Liberty taught him her Athenian strain;
> She cloath'd him with authority and awe,
> Spoke from his lips, and in his looks, gave law.
> His speech, his form, his action, full of grace,
> And all his country beaming in his face,
> He stood...
> Once Chatham sav'd thee, but who saves thee next?
> ("Table Talk," lines 342–48, 367)

Another was Captain Cook, also recently dead, who "Steer'd Britain's oak into a world unknown, / And in his country's glory sought his own" ("Charity," lines 25–26). For other examples Cowper goes back to the Civil War, when "Albion's sons / Were sons indeed. They felt a filial heart / Beat high within them at a mother's wrongs, / And shining each in his domestic sphere, / Shone brighter still once call'd to public view" (*The Task*, V, lines 517–21).[61] But (in a phrase that Burke may have

---

[61] In a 1782 letter Cowper notes that the "Tyrant" Cromwell was "mistaken for a true Patriot" and that "true Patriots, (such were the long Parliament)" were "abhorred as tyrants" (*Letters and Prose Writings*, II, 31).

borrowed) "th'age of virtuous politics is past" (v, line 493). The "suns" of Chatham and of Wolfe are "set" (ii, line 252).

At a key moment in "Table Talk" Cowper denies that true patriotism has disappeared ("the virtue still adorns our age" – line 340), but he can in fact name no living exemplar of it, though he will know him when he sees him:

> Such men are rais'd to station and command,
> When providence means mercy to a land.
> He speaks, and they appear; to him they owe
> Skill to direct, and strength to strike the blow,
> To manage with address, to seize with pow'r
> The crisis of a dark decisive hour.
> So Gideon earn'd a vict'ry not his own.
>
> (lines 354–60)

Providence has the power to send such a man (if only it will), as Cowper knew from the story of Gideon in Judges 6, a story to which he was often drawn.[62] He puts emphasis not on Gideon's soldiery but on his *speech*, his "skill" in directing other men and in providing them "strength." For a poet, it is a fantasy of "command" that Cowper pretends to disavow.[63] As he puts it in *The Task*, "To shake thy senate, and from the heights sublime / Of patriot eloquence to flash down fire / Upon thy foes, was never meant my task" (ii, lines 216–18). And yet, in the name of "the land I love" he "can feel thy fortunes, and partake / Thy joys and sorrows with as true a heart / As any thund'rer there" (lines 219–21, 224). Although he implies that his true "task" is found elsewhere, he dreams that the poet might possess political authority.

What service then, what task, can the patriotic poet realistically hope to perform? "Table Talk" in effect asks this question. The poet is ill-equipped to advise on taxes and "the nation's debt" (line 177),[64] and does better "to pitch the key of rhyme / To themes more pertinent, if less sublime" – "ministerial arts," timorous admirals "extoll'd for standing still" and "Generals who will not conquer when they may" (lines 188–190, 192, 194). "When [satiric] themes like these employ the poet's

---

[62] He alludes to it at least five times in his poems.

[63] Cf. the poet's commanding eye in *The Task*: "Now roves the eye, / And posted on this speculative height / Exults in its command" (i, lines 288–90).

[64] In a 1782 letter Cowper remarks that "The political world affords us no very agreeable Subjects at present, nor am I sufficiently conversant with it to do justice to so magnificent a theme if it did," and resolves to leave the "mysteries of Government" to those better qualified (*Letters and Prose Writings*, ii, 12).

tongue" (line 198), the nation will perhaps listen. Reflecting Cowper's ambivalence, the poem is scored for two voices, the more skeptical "A." generally serving to deflate the patriotic "rant" (line 299) of "B." When B. preaches penitence but warns of a "reprobated race" that risks the curse of an angry God, A. drily inquires whether he means "to prophecy, or but to preach" (line 479). Cowper is evidently hesitant to set up for a modern-day Jeremiah.[65] He is stirred by indignation and foresight of "distant storms" (line 495), but then turns away from prophecy: "But no prophetic fires to me belong, / I play with syllables, and sport in song" (lines 504–5). This Horatian mood only lasts a moment, and Cowper wonders aloud whether a poet might now serve the cause of "Religion," acting as her "skilful guide into poetic ground" (line 717). Anything less would be a misapplication of "the powers of genius" (line 749). Cowper, still ambivalent, senses the gravity of the theme, but also the narrowness of its appeal. As the poem ends, A. ironically welcomes the return of Sternhold and Hopkins, but B. doesn't back down.

In "Expostulation" Cowper wonders whether a mere poet can hope to bring about national repentance: "How shall a verse impress thee? by what name / Shall I adjure thee not to court thy shame?" (lines 654–55). As self-appointed scourge of the nation, he suspects that his "warning song is sung in vain, / That few will hear, and fewer heed the strain" (lines 724–25). Perhaps he should adopt "a sweeter voice, and one de-signed / A blessing to my country and mankind" (lines 726–27). Not a satirist's curse or a preacher's warning of damnation, but a blessing – perhaps in place of the divine blessing that he fears has been withheld. By such means the patriotic poet, acting now as Good Shepherd, may perhaps hope to "Reclaim the wand'ring thousands, and bring home/ A flock so scatter'd and so wont to roam" (lines 728–29). As editors sug-gest, the ending of "Expostulation" looks ahead to the gentler tone of the remaining poems in the 1782 volume – "Hope," "Charity," "Conversa-tion," "Retirement" – and to *The Task* of 1785. In those poems Cowper perhaps finds the more modest role that he aims to play, a bard who seeks to unite "the faithful monitor's and poet's part" ("Hope," line 757). *Monitor* is a complex term. It carries more than its weakened present-day meaning – one who watches over or keeps track. For Cowper it probably included the root sense of "one who warns or admonishes," but hinted archly that he was acting not even as authoritative schoolmaster but

---

[65] In "Expostulation" Cowper implicitly compares himself to Jeremiah, "the prophet who wept for Israel" (line 33).

as a sort of head boy commissioned by the absent master to look after the younger scholars – Cowper commonly addresses Britain familiarly as "thou."[66] But *monitor* was also a well-established metaphor for the conscience.[67] A poet who acted as "monitor" might serve as conscience of the nation. Some readers, if they remembered the pro-Pitt *Monitor* of the Seven Years' War, might have sensed a political and patriotic resonance. Cowper's apparent modesty – he aspires to "A monitor's, though not a poet's praise" ("Retirement," line 806) – may conceal a lofty moral mission.

It was in his function as "monitor" that Cowper sought to trouble the nation's conscience about the slave trade ("Charity," lines 137–243)[68] or about India: "Hast thou, though suckl'd at fair freedom's breast, / Exported slav'ry to the conquer'd East, / Pull'd down the tyrants India serv'd with dread, / And rais'd thyself, a greater, in their stead" ("Expostulation," lines 364–67).[69] But by the time of *The Task*, Cowper jokes that nobody listens to the "monitors that mother church supplies." "In George's days" the only effective "monitor" is the wooden back brace that improves one's posture. Grimly remembering the moral significance of man's erect stance (and his *recta ratio*), Cowper notes that, "admonish'd" by a modern "monitor" – as it was colloquially called[70] – "we can walk erect" (II, lines 576, 580, 593). Rectitude has given way to standing up straight.

With his moral mission in question, he nervously worries that the retired poet does not have sufficient "employment."[71] It is perhaps because he himself is plagued with doubt that Cowper assures his reader (and himself) that the poet "serves his country; recompenses well / The state." But the standard by which he asks to be measured has been reduced: "if his country stand not by his skill, / At least his follies have not wrought

---

[66] Johnson's *Dictionary*: "Monitor: One who warns of faults, or informs of duty; one who gives useful hints. It is used of an upper scholar in a school commissioned by the master to look to the boys in his absence."

[67] Johnson cites Bishop South, who speaks of the monitor that Adam carried in his bosom. Boswell speaks of having "no better monitor" than one's "own good sense" (*Boswell's London Journal 1762–1763*, ed. Frederick Pottle [New Haven, 1950], 82). For Goldsmith on authors as "monitors" of "fashions, follies, and vices," see above, 70.

[68] Cf. "Canst thou, and honour'd with a Christian name, / Buy what is woman-born, and feel no shame" ("Charity," lines 180–81). Cowper's "The Negro's Complaint" was written in response to a request for a ballad "to be sung in the streets to assist the movement to abolish the slave trade" (*Poems*, III, 283).

[69] Cf. *The Task*: "Is India free, or do we grind her still?" (IV, line 30).

[70] See *OED*, "monitor," sb. 4. The earliest citation is Cowper's line.

[71] I have developed this point in "Redefining Georgic: Cowper's *Task*," *ELH*, 57 (1990), 865–79.

her fall" (v, lines 968–69, 975–76). As he was writing *The Task*, Cowper read Knox's *Essays*,[72] perhaps pausing over Knox's idea that he is a true patriot who "secretly serves his country in the retired and unobserved walks of private life."[73] In *The Task* he sees himself in the "gentle savage," Omai:

> I see thee weep, and thine are honest tears,
> A patriot's for his country. Thou art sad
> At thought of her forlorn and abject state,
> From which no power of thine can raise her up.
>
> (I, lines 657–60)

A number of signs suggest that Cowper's faith in his role as patriot was always shaky. Although born into a great Whig family, he declined to associate himself with any Whig faction or with any minister but the elder Pitt.[74] He offered nominal support to the King and Lord North in the 1780s, but not to the rest of the ministry or to parliament. He displays little confidence in the moral health of an empire that tolerates the slave trade in the Atlantic and rapacity in India. He seems to lack Smart's sense of continuity between past British glory and the present, perhaps because where Smart saw triumph he saw decline. In Cowper's ode on "Boadicea," apparently written in 1781 before the British surrender at Yorktown,[75] a Druid bard assures the mighty "British warrior queen" that Rome's victory will be temporary. But his prophetic vaunt that "empire is on us bestow'd" sounds hollow, since Cowper supplies none of the conventional signs of British imperial might – Agincourt, Armada, Blenheim, or even Porto Bello and Quebec – that might have provided some substance to the prophecy, or linked ancient Britons to their descendants.[76]

---

[72] See his 30 October 1784 letter to Newton (*Letters and Prose Writings*, II, 290–91).

[73] See above, 31–32.

[74] W. B. Hutchings attempts to align Cowper's politics with those of the Rockingham Whigs. See "William Cowper and 1789," *Yearbook of English Studies*, 19 (1989), 71–93. Martin Priestman's claim that the "basis" of Cowper's "political outlook was eighteenth-century Whig mercantilism: that is, that the interests of trade were the fundamental interests of the country" (*Cowper's Task: Structure and Influence* [Cambridge, 1983], 36) does not take into account Cowper's opposition to the slave trade and the East India Company.

[75] Cornwallis surrendered on 19 October 1781. Shortly after hearing of it, Cowper wrote to Joseph Hill on 9 December: "I consider the loss of America as the ruin of England" (*Letters and Prose Writings*, I, 555. See also I, 546, 549–50, 557, 568, 569–70).

[76] Ignoring Cowper's ahistoricity, Vincent Newey sees only "armed imperialism" and "expansionist patriotism" (*Cowper's Poetry* [Liverpool, 1982], 239), and Peter Faulkner "one of the most forceful and effective Imperialist poems of the late eighteenth century" ("William Cowper and the Poetry of Empire," *Durham University Journal*, 83 [1991], 165).

All of the institutions in which patriotic Britons of Cowper's day took pride are seen as having failed:[77] parliament ("a scene of civil jar"),[78] the landed gentry (unlike Thomson, Cowper praises no country seats), the aristocracy who devote themselves to pleasure; the "Associations" and "Leagues" that Linda Colley has argued form a prominent part of the patriotic establishment in the later eighteenth century.[79] (Like Goldsmith, Cowper finds something unnatural in legal "bonds.") Even the established church, which with the royal navy served for Smart as the backbone of empire, is for Cowper a bankrupt institution.[80] While Smart's hymns aimed to reform the liturgy that united a nation of Anglicans in common worship, Cowper's *Olney Hymns* are based not on the cycle of feats and fasts in the Book of Common Prayer but on passages of scripture, are concerned not with the common body of the church but with the "Rise, Progress, Changes, and Comforts of the Spiritual Life,"[81] and are addressed not to the founder of the church and nation but to a personal savior.

In the closing books of *The Task* Cowper looks beyond political life and even beyond patriotism. To be sure, Britain, because it unlike France preserves liberty, is still "the chief / Among the nations, seeing thou art free" (v, lines 460–61). And like Goldsmith before him Cowper clings still to "My native nook of earth" (line 462), despite its defects of climate and culture.[82] But even more important than political liberty is a higher kind, a "liberty unsung / By poets" (lines 538–39), a "liberty of heart, deriv'd from heav'n, / Bought with HIS blood who gave it to mankind" (lines 545–46). By the same token, there is something higher than patriotism:

> Patriots have toiled, and in their country's cause
> Bled nobly, and their deeds, as they deserve,
> Receive proud recompense . . .
> But fairer wreathes are due, though never paid,
> To those who posted at the shrine of truth,

---

[77] *Pace* Maurice Quinlan's remark that Cowper evinces a "love of liberty within the framework of traditional British institutions" (*William Cowper: A Critical Life* [Minneapolis, 1953], 106).

[78] "Expostulation," line 294.

[79] See *The Task*, IV, lines 663–75, where Cowper inveighs against "man associated and leagued with man / By regal warrant, or self-joined by bond / For interest-sake." For an account of voluntary patriotic societies such as the Association of Anti-Gallicans, the Society of Arts, and the Marine Society, see Colley, *Britons*, 88–98. Feingold observes that Cowper lacks faith in "political incorporation" (*Nature and Society*, 151).

[80] See his comments on modern preaching (*The Task*, II, lines 326–573).

[81] The title to Book III of *Olney Hymns*, in *Poems*, I, 172.

[82] Cowper's unfavorable comparison of British "roughness" and blunt "unadult'rate manners" (v, lines 465–88) with French "humane address / And sweetness" (lines 469–70) recalls Goldsmith's dislike of British "independence." See above, 216–17.

Have fall'n in her defence. A patriot's blood
Well spent in such a strife may earn indeed
And for a time insure to his loved land
The sweets of liberty and equal laws;
But martyrs struggle for a brighter prize,
And win it with more pain.

(v, lines 704–6, 712–19)

Cowper may be thinking of such Greek patriots as Harmodius and Aristogiton, whose death in the name of "liberty and equal laws" was remembered by Akenside, Collins, and Smart. He also reflects ideas current in contemporary sermons, such as Archibald Bruce's *True Patriotism* (1685), that a patriot's highest duty is to God. Curiously, however, Cowper does not devote his poetic powers to commemorate martyrs (on his terms, a high task for a Christian patriot), and develops rather, for some 160 lines, the idea of the man made truly free (of sin) by God's grace. It is one of Cowper's loftiest strains, climaxing in the parting of a "veil opaque" to reveal the "author" of nature (lines 892–93). The irony, of course, is that Cowper, bravely offering the promise of religious freedom to his readers, was privately convinced that he himself would never taste it.

The ecstatic vision at the end of Book v forms the climax of the poem, but there remain the more than 1000 lines of Book vi ("The Winter Walk at Noon") to suggest that Cowper has not abandoned politics. In them he revisits the topic of patriotic service, first by declining to join in the public celebration of the "statesman of the day" (vi, line 696) who is wildly greeted by the "rabble" in the streets: "Hath he saved the state? / No. Doth he purpose its salvation? No" (lines 704–5). Cowper is probably thinking of the younger Pitt, rapidly ascending to fame and given the freedom of the City of London in February 1784. He thought no better of Pitt than of Charles James Fox, another acclaimed "Patriot."[83] But his questions suggest that a patriot who saves the state would deserve honor. Even though as poet he refuses to provide "panegyric" (line 720), he is not without his public uses if he offers a "taste of comfort in a world of woe":

He serves his country; recompenses well
The state beneath the shadow of whose vine
He sits secure, and in the scale of life
Holds no ignoble, though a slighted place.
... if his country stand not by his skill,
At least his follies have not wrought her fall.

(lines 968–71, 975–76)

---

[83] "The Son of Lord Chatham seems to me to have abandoned his father's principles. I admire neither his measures nor his temper" (*Letters and Prose Writings*, ii, 215–16).

In dark times when a nation has been brought low by the follies of its leaders, a humble poet might, by a modest standard, be a true patriot.[84]

Even though *The Task* seems to signal that Cowper has largely withdrawn from public life, his letters show that he had not lost his fascination with parliamentary politics[85] or his enthusiasm for "British liberty,"[86] and that he followed closely "the News from Paris" about the French Revolution. (Like many of his contemporaries, he was at first cautiously hopeful, then deplored the Terror.) He took the trouble in 1793 to explain to Lady Hesketh the principles of a "*true* Whig" – commitment to a balance among King, Lords, and Commons.[87] He continued to send poems protesting the slave trade, and rallying support for the royal family, to London and provincial newspapers,[88] as if he regarded himself as a sort of volunteer laureate whose views on matters of public moment would be eagerly followed.[89] And the final phase of his literary career shows that he still aspired to be his country's poet, not by celebrating its greatness but by embellishing its poetry. Taking on the translation of Homer's epics meant matching himself not only against Homer but also against Pope, "whose writings have done immortal honour to his country."[90] Cowper too sought implicitly to do "honour to his country" and to its language, supplanting Pope's couplet version by rendering the *Iliad* and *Odyssey* into Miltonic blank verse, demonstrating anew that "no subject, however important, however sublime, can demand greater force of expression than is within the compass of the English language" (VI, 64). As he was finishing the Homer and preparing to take up a translation of Milton's Latin and Italian poems, Cowper began a poem on "Yardley Oak," which he would not live to finish, that marks perhaps the coda to his life as a poetic patriot. In the poem Cowper broods on the

---

[84] But even here the biblical vine under which he sits secure (cf. 1 Kings 2:25) hints that Cowper's real allegiance lies elsewhere. For more on this point, see Griffin, "Redefining Georgic," 875–76.

[85] See letters commenting on the rivalry between Pitt and Fox in 1788 and 1789 (*Letters and Prose Writings*, III, 256, 258, 263–64).

[86] In 1784 he worried that "Stuartism" – i.e., a tendency to royal absolutism – was the characteristic of the reign of George III, and "having always been somewhat of an Enthusiast on the subject of British liberty, I am not able to withold my reverence and good wishes from the man whoever he be, that exerts himself in a constitutional way to oppose it" (*Letters and Prose Writings*, II, 215).

[87] *Letters and Prose Writings*, IV, 332.

[88] Three poems on the slave trade appeared in 1788, three more on the royal family in 1789. For details, see *Poems*, vol. III.

[89] In 1792 he felt obliged to correct a rumor by informing the printers of the *Northampton Mercury* that his opposition to the slave trade had not weakened, enclosing a "Sonnet Addressed to William Wilberforce, Esq."

[90] Cowper's Preface to the first edition (1791) of his Homer, in *Letters and Prose Writings*, V, 61.

durability of a great tree that was once "King of the woods" and is now but "a cave / For owls to roost in." Like the nation itself – and the oak tree was an established emblem of England[91] – Yardley Oak, once in "a state / Of matchless grandeur," has declined into "magnificent decay":

> Embowell'd now, and of thy antient self
> Possessing nought but the scoop'd rind that seems
> An huge throat calling to the clouds for drink . . .
> Yet is thy root sincere, sound as the rock,
> A quarry of stout spurs and knotted fangs
> Which crook'd into a thousand whimsies, clasp
> The stubborn soil, and hold thee still erect.
> So stands a Kingdom whose foundations yet
> Fail not, in virtue and in wisdom lay'd,
> Though all the superstructure by the tooth,
> Pulverized of venality, a shell
> Stands now, and semblance only of itself.
>   (lines 110–12, 116–24)

England too, so the poem hints, is only a shell of its former self, and has become like Yardley Oak "a thing / Forgotten as the foliage of thy youth" unless the poet's "verse rescue thee awhile" by praising the soundness of its "foundations."

[91] One recalls that the druid bard in "Boadicea" sits "beneath a spreading oak" (line 5).

CHAPTER 10

Ann Yearsley: "the female Patriot"

As late as the 1770s it was relatively rare for a woman poet to step forward as a patriot. Still regarded with suspicion in some quarters if she published at all, the female poet was typically limited (or self-limited) to private or domestic topics, the only matters with which she was thought to be sufficiently familiar. Earlier in the century women writers had found a way to present themselves as public-spirited citizens, but as the example of Lady Mary Wortley Montagu suggests, they did so with some self-protective hesitation. Ambitious for literary fame (so her latest biographer argues), as an aristocrat she was reluctant to publish. Bold enough not to limit herself in her poems to "female" topics – she was fully as effective as Pope in her satiric exchanges with him – she shied away, in her poetry, from public themes, despite the fact that she was brought up in one active Whig political family and married into another, and despite her close connections with several of Walpole's political allies. But she did find an alternate means to take up a stance as a political and even a patriotic writer: the famous series of letters she sent back from Turkey to a network of correspondents in 1716–18, the so-called "Embassy Letters," later copied, collected, and circulated more widely in manuscript, and finally published shortly after her death, apparently with her encouragement.[1] Although she discreetly avoided any mention of her husband's diplomatic mission, or any suggestion that she was herself engaged in international diplomacy, Lady Mary self-consciously traveled, and wrote, as an Englishwoman on a foreign tour of inspection.

---

[1] She also wrote (anonymously) nine essays for her brief-lived periodical, *The Nonsense of Common-Sense*, from December 1737 to March 1738. Posing as a male author, avoiding any open declaration of her political affiliation, and claiming to write only "short essays of Morality," she obliquely defended Walpole's ministry against criticism from "the pretended patrons of Liberty," denying that the Excise Law or the Stage Licensing Act threatened English liberties, and arguing that reducing interest on the national debt (a measure supported by the ministry) was "the real patriot scheme" (*Essays and Poems and Simplicity: A Comedy*, ed. R. Halsband and Isobel Grundy [Oxford: Clarendon, 1977, rev. 1993], 109, 135, 141).

In Lady Mary's day the English travel writer commonly produced patriotic credentials, reporting on foreign ways so as to confirm English superiority, or to bring back some useful idea or invention that might improve English life, and carefully assuring the reader that loyalty to his native land makes him happy to return home. Traveling through France and Italy in the 1760s, Smollett, perhaps the best known of the British travelers on the continent, sturdily declared himself "attached to my country because it is the land of liberty, cleanliness, and convenience."[2] Even though Lady Mary took unusual delight not only in the "perpetual spring" of Turkey's climate, but in the surprising degree of freedom that its women enjoyed, she includes such patriotic assurances herself. Professing "the loyalty of my heart," she facetiously wishes that the British parliament would send to Turkey "a ship load of your passive-obedient men, that they might see arbitrary government in its clearest strongest light."[3] Writing to the Princess of Wales (daughter-in-law of the reigning King), she remembers her Hanoverian principles: "this climate, happy as it seems, can never be preferred to England with all its frosts and snows, while we are blessed with an easy government, under a King, who makes his own happiness consist in the liberty of his people" (*Letters*, I, 155).

But as every reader remarks, she more commonly seems open to the subversive idea that her native land is not in every way superior. The pavements in Dutch streets are cleaner than those in London (I, 3), Turkish law is in many respects "better designed, and better executed than ours" (II, 143), and Turkish customs often strike her as more sensible than those in England.[4] In a pointed challenge to the patriotic assumption that Britons, above all others, are a free people, she deliberately notes that Turkish women, though confined (as all travelers knew) by veils, in practice "enjoy more liberty than we have" (II, 33). Even when she arrives back in Dover and declares that she "cannot help looking with partial Eyes on my Native Land," she distances herself from the comfortable patriotic commonplaces:

After having seen part of Asia and Africa and almost made the tour of Europe, I think the honest English squire more happy, who verily beleives the Greek wines less delicious than March beer, that the African fruits have not so fine a

[2] *Travels Through France and Italy*, ed. Frank Felsenstein (Oxford, 1979), 341.
[3] *Letters of the Right Honourable Lady M—y W—y M—e*, 3 vols. (London, 1763), II, 19–20. Cf. another letter in French, published without her permission in *Le Nouveau Mercure* in 1718: "Je fais tous les jours des voeux pour revoir mon Roy, ma patrie, & mes amis" (*Complete Letters of Lady Mary Wortley Montagu*, ed. Robert Halsband [Oxford, 1965], I, 404).
[4] Cf. her discussion of lying in for childbirth (II, 146–47), adoption and inheritance (III, 38–39), and the pursuit of pleasure (III, 52).

flavour as golden pippins, that the *Beca figuas* of Italy are not so well tasted as a rump of beef, and that in short there is no perfect enjoyment of this life out of Old England.

The "honest English squire" may still believe, but the citizen of the world cannot. Travel has spoiled her, by arousing an "Ambitious thirst after knowledge which we are not form'd to enjoy. All we get by it is a fruitless desire of mixing the different pleasures and conveniences which are given to Different parts of the World and cannot meet in any one of them." Still, she must make the effort to accept her English fate: "I pray God I may think so [i.e., as the English squire does] for the rest of my life; and since I must be contented with our scanty allowance of day-light, that I may forget the enlivening sun of Constantinople" (III, 129–30).

In the conventional view, Lady Mary is too much of a free spirit, or too much of a citizen of the world, to be confined by narrow preference for her homeland. By another reading, it is not only her intelligence and her habitual irony which hold her back from a frankly patriotic stance, but some sense that the role of patriot is not one for which she, as a woman, would be regarded as qualified. While the typical male patriotic traveler reported in detail on the fortifications that still defended many European cities (such reports might give Britain an advantage in the next siege), Lady Mary demurs: "This is also a fortified town, but I avoid ever mentioning fortifications, being sensible that I know not how to speak of them" (I, 89–90, cf. I, 9). The best-known example of her patriotic attachment to her native land is her determination to introduce into England the Turkish practice of inoculation against smallpox. But even here she holds back from setting up as a patriot: "I am patriot enough to take pains to bring this useful invention into fashion in England" (II, 62). "Patriot enough" to take pains, but self-mocking enough to dramatize the resistance she expects to meet from English physicians: "Perhaps, if I live to return, I may, however, have courage to war with them. Upon this occasion, admire the heroism in the heart of, Your Freind" (II, 63).[5]

A second example suggests how, as with Lady Mary's "heroism," aspiration to female patriotism was deflected into irony or playfulness, perhaps because such aspirations threatened to trespass onto male territory.

---

[5] Compare the facetious profession of patriotism in a March 1724 letter to her sister, Lady Mar, after sending an account of the "Galantrys" of the Duke of Wharton and the Schemers' Club: "I consider the duty of a true English Woman is to do what Honnour she can to her native Country, and that it would be a Sin against the pious Love I bear the Land of my Nativity to confine the renown due to the Schemers within the small extent of this little Isleland, which ought to be spread where ever Men can sigh or Women wish" (*Complete Letters*, II, 39–40).

Cultural anxiety about the idea of female heroism, or of women competing with men, lies behind the reappearance of old amazonian figures
such as Thalestris in Pope's *Rape of the Lock*, and in contemporary ballads about women who dressed as soldiers to follow their men into war,
whether for love or for glory.[6] One very real female warrior – and female
patriot – was much publicized: the famous Jenny Cameron, who fought
for the Pretender in the Jacobite rebellion of 1745–46: "At the Battle of
Preston-pans, *Falkirk*, and *Culloden*, she was seen at the head of her Party,
leading them on thro' Fire and Smoak to the very Muzzles of the Enemies
Guns, never flinching from Danger, but, like another Amazon, with the
most undaunted Bravery, inspiriting her Men with Courage by her own
Example, leading them on to the Attack, and doing all the Parts of an
experienced and consummate General."[7] Another female contemporary, perhaps with the example of Jenny Cameron in mind, swore equal
devotion, but proffered her service as a poet:

> I on no other Terms a Man would be,
> But to defend thy glorious Cause and thee;
> For both my Life to lose I'd bravely chuse,
> I now can only serve thee with my Muse;
> But were my Pen a Sword, thy Foes I'd meet,
> And lay the conquer'd World beneath thy Feet.[8]

Reports filtering back to London of loyal English troops fleeing at
Falkirk prompted some playful public speculation about the role that
a patriotic woman might perform in defense of her king. For example,
an epilogue to a 1746 London production of Otway's *Venice Preserv'd* is
addressed to the ladies in the audience:

> To you, ye FAIR, your Country flies for Aid,
> Deserted by her Sons, who once were brave,
> She begs of You to conquer and to save.

The ladies are not asked to serve as amazonian soldiers themselves, but
to emulate the part of Otway's Belvidera, who reclaimed "the Traytor's
Heart":

---

[6] For a study of popular ballads about warrior women, see Diane Dugaw, *Warrior Women and Popular Balladry* (Cambridge, 1989).

[7] "Appendix" to *The Life of Dr. Archibald Cameron* (London, 1753). Her story was well known as early as 1746, when there appeared a proposal to print "Memoirs of the remarkable Life and surprizing Adventures of Miss Jenny Cameron" (BL shelfmark 1850C10).

[8] "POEM by a Lady on seeing His Royal Highness the Prince Regent" (Edinburgh?, 1745), BL shelfmark 11621.h.1(8). There is another copy at C.115.i.3(76).

'Tis yours to triumph; but by milder ways,
Let *Belvidera* be your guide to Praise...
Rouse the quick Sense of Shame, by Sloth suppresst.
The Female Patriot's glorious Steps pursue:
Britain shall owe her Peace, her fame to you.[9]

In another contemporary epilogue after the defeat at Falkirk, Peg
Woffington (famous for playing breeches parts) steps forth as a "Female
Volunteer," smiling with sexual innuendo:

Well, if 'tis so, and that our *Men* can't *stand*,
'Tis Time we Women take the *Thing in Hand*.
  Thus, in my Country's Cause I now appear,
A bold smart *Kevenhuller'd*[10] Volunteer.

But she won't actually turn soldier: she'll maul the rebels, she swears,
with her eyes.[11] Turning serious, she advises women to inspire men to
do their duty:

In Freedom's Cause, ye Patriot-Fair, arise,
Exert the sacred Influence of your Eyes;
On valiant Merit deign alone to smile,
And vindicate the Glory of our Isle;
To no base Coward prostitute your Charms
Disband the Lover who deserts his Arms:
So shall you fire each Hero to his Duty,
And *British* rights be sav'd by *British* Beauty.[12]

A few women saw no occasion for playfulness or wit, and found their
patriotic role as poets. One contributed verses "On the Signal Victory
at Gladsmuir. By a Lady," celebrating "our brave Successful HERO [the
Duke of Cumberland]," but lamenting that "*British* Blood / Must flow

---

9 Printed in *The Museum*, no. 4 (10 May 1746), repr. in *The Museum*, 3 vols. (1746), I, 134–35. In the
   next issue of *The Museum* appeared another poem about female heroism. "An Ode to the People
   of Great Britain" recalls the response of Queen Elizabeth to an earlier papist threat (the Spanish
   Armada) when England was freed from papal yoke and power "by the Woman-Hero's Hand"
   (no. 5, 24 May 1746, repr. I, 179).
10 Wearing a broad-brimmed high-cocked hat "of extravagant proportions" made fashionable for
   military men "or bullies about town" by Andreas von Kevenhuller, general in the Austrian army
   (see F. W. Fairholt, *Costume in England*, 2nd. edn., rev. H. A. Dillon, 2 vols. [London, 1885], I,
   368).
11 Perhaps recalling Pope's *Rape of the Lock*, in which, "A mournful glance Sir Fopling upwards cast, /
   'Those eyes are made so killing' – was his last" (v, lines 63–64), and "When bold Sir Plume had
   drawn Clarissa down, / Chloe stepped in, and killed him with a frown" (v, lines 67–68).
12 *The Female Volunteer: or, an Attempt to Make our Men Stand* (London, 1746). The broadside also
   appeared in another form as "An Epilogue Design'd to be spoken by Mrs. Woffington, in the
   Character of a Volunteer," in a collection of ballads and broadsheets in the British Library
   (shelfmark 1850c10), misprinting "your charms" as "pour charms."

t'exalt the public Good."[13] When troops loyal to George II had put down the Jacobite threat, another female poet appealed that mercy be shown to the rebels.[14]

Lady Mary's "Embassy Letters" appeared in print in 1763 to great acclaim. After 1763 women writers begin to take up political and patriotic topics with increased frequency, not only in letters and tracts[15] but in poems as well. Elizabeth Griffith's *Amana* (1764), while dramatizing the tale of an Egyptian tyrant, seizes the occasion to celebrate British "Liberty." In her preface Griffith contrasts "the miseries of those nations which are subject to despotic power" and the "exulting sense of the peculiar blessings of liberty that we enjoy in these thrice happy kingdoms." And in the final lines of the play the heroine's father breaks the Egyptian illusion by directly addressing a British audience, and complimenting a British king who has just presided over a happy conclusion to the Seven Years' War:

> Let those who dwell in Albion's happy land,
> Grateful acknowledge heaven's most bounteous hand:
> Its choicest boon in freedom is bestowed,
> And their best praise to its protector owed;
> Who not in Britain's cause alone sustains
> The toils of council, and of hostile plains:
> The world's great champion, born for all mankind,
> In whom the oppressed a certain refuge find.[16]

Other women writers similarly found opportunities to celebrate British liberty. The lead poem, for example, in Anna Barbauld's *Poems* (1777) is "Corsica," a rapturous address to the gallant little island fighting for its independence from Italy and France:

> Hail generous Corsica! unconquer'd isle!
> The fort of freedom; that amidst the waves
> Stands like a rock of adamant . . .
>
> (lines 1–3)[17]

---

[13] British Library, "Tracts on the Rebellions of 1715, 1745," shelfmark C.38.g.14(12).

[14] "An Ode, Addressed to His Royal Highness William Duke of Cumberland, by a Lady," British Library, shelfmark 11602.i.5(6). Its "postscript" reads: "O sway the King to Mercy, LORD, / Whilst Thou preserv'st his Throne! / Let his illustrious Clemency, / Unite all Hearts in one."

[15] C.f. Ann Mellor, *Mothers of the Nation: Women Political Writers in England, 1780–1830* (Bloomington, 2000).

[16] *Amana. A Dramatic Poem*, "by a Lady" (London, 1764), iv, 54. My attention was drawn to this play by Betty Rizzo, now completing a biography of Griffith.

[17] Quoted from the *Poems of Anna Letitia Barbauld*, ed. William McCarthy and Elizabeth Kraft (Athens, GA, 1994).

Corsica, where "the flame of LIBERTY glows strong," served European observers, from Rousseau to Boswell, as a mirror in which they might regard their own devotion to "freedom," and urge themselves to remain true to that ideal:

> What then should BRITONS feel? should they not catch
> The warm contagion of heroic ardour,
> And kindle at a fire so like their own?   (lines 15–17)

Boswell, she notes, had (in his *Account of Corsica*, 1768) found in Corsica "animated forms of patriot zeal." She too voyages to Corsica, but as a mental traveler: "while warm in thought / I trace the pictur'd landscape" (lines 31–32). And like Boswell she hails General Paoli (in 1777 in exile in England):

> Success to your fair hopes! a British Muse,
> Tho' weak and powerless, lifts her fervent voice,
> And breathes a prayer for your success.
>
> (lines 133–35)

She imagines both that Paoli will return to free his country, and that she (or some patriot-poet like her) will record his fame:

> thy sacred name
> Endear'd to long posterity, some muse,
> More worthy of the theme, shall consecrate
> To after ages, and applauding worlds
> Shall bless the godlike man who sav'd his country.
>
> (lines 179–83)

But Paoli has failed, and Barbauld links his failure as a leader with hers as a patriot-poet: "So vainly wish'd, so fondly hop'd the Muse: / Too fondly hop'd. The iron fates prevail" (lines 184–85). But even so, "th'attempt is praise" (line 196). Like Paoli, the poem hints, she has made an "attempt." And even if she has not succeeded in writing a heroic poem about modern political liberty, the "freedom of the mind" is undestroyed (line 201).

By the time Barbauld published her poem on "Corsica," her own country was at war with the American colonies. The Peace of Paris (1783), which prompted Cowper and other lovers of their country to self-examination, was also marked by the attempt by another woman poet to put the best face on what had been for many Britons a disastrous defeat. The twenty-one-year-old Helen Maria Williams, who was later to celebrate the early stages of the French Revolution, regarded the return of peace with the newly independent colonies in the same mood that

Collins evoked in his "Ode to Peace" at the conclusion of an earlier war. Her ambitious "Ode on the Peace," extending to thirty-two stanzas, first published in the *Gentleman's Magazine* in 1783, finds the peace consistent with the interests of the true British "patriot":

> Bless, all ye powers! the patriot name
> That courts fair Peace, thy gentle stay;
> Ah! Gild with glory's light, his fame,
> And glad his life with pleasure's ray.

Like patriot-poets before her, Williams offers herself as "Th'historic Muse" whose "tablet still records the deeds of fame / And wakes the patriot's, and the hero's flame." In her view, the Peace of Paris, like the peace which Collins had celebrated, preserves both England's "honour" and "glory":

> While Albion on her parent deep
> Shall rest, may glory light her shore,
> May honour there his vigils keep
> Till time shall wings its way no more.[18]

In another poem in her 1786 volume, "An Epistle to Dr. [John] Moore," she addressed the "Author of a View of Society and Manners in France, Switzerland, and Germany," whose book enabled her, like Barbauld before her, to become a mental traveler: "In your light Frenchman pleas'd I see, / His nation's gay epitome" (II, 8). With the help of Moore's accounts, she provides brief sketches of the standard stops on the Grand Tour, and of such Enlightenment heroes as Voltaire and Frederick the Great. But her poem makes no comparison between continental states and her native England, and avoids explicitly political topics. This is not the case with her second epistle "To Dr. Moore" (1792), this time addressed to Moore at home in Wales from her "exile" in Revolutionary France. She consciously writes as a Briton: in a poetical epistle to her, he had, she says, traced "The landscapes of my native isle." In reply, she surveys the valley of the Loire, now a "Delightful land" where happy peasants, no longer slaves, enjoy a "bounteous harvest":

> For now on Gallia's plains the peasant knows
> Those equal rights impartial heaven bestows.

---

[18] "An Ode on the Peace," in *Poems*, 2 vols. (London, 1786), I, 45, 53–54, 56. Johnson and Boswell, neither of them friends to the American colonists, admired the ode, perhaps because it praised a peace negotiated by a government they supported. Boswell noted in 1791 that the Peace of Paris "may fairly be considered as the foundation of all the prosperity of Great Britain since that time" (*Life of Johnson*, IV, 282n).

He now, by freedom's ray illumined, taught
Some self-respect, some energy of thought,
Discerns the blessings that to all belong,
And lives to guard his humble shed from wrong.

Williams' rhetoric, celebrating "Auspicious Liberty," is thick with the early claims of the Revolution. And she turns the light of liberty back on her native land, where enemies of the Revolution are constructing a defense of feudal "precedent." Where Burke sees the English constitution as a "Gothic pile," consecrated by age, she sees "The lonely dungeon in the caverned ground; / The sullen dome above those central caves, / Where lives one despot and a host of slaves."[19]

In a later poem, "On the Death of the Rev. Dr. [Andrew] Kippis" (1796), written after the rise of Robespierre, she remembers and honors the dissenting minister who had early befriended her and promoted her career. She contrasts the earlier era of "Gallic Freedom" with the present, when "Th'ignoble Tyrant of his Country stood, / And bathed his scaffold's in the patriot's blood." Williams fears that as an early and enthusiastic celebrant of liberty she too is "Destined the patriot's fate in all to share" – she had been briefly imprisoned by Robespierre in October 1793. Now she has fled to take refuge in Switzerland, a "weeping exile" both from her adopted home in France and her native land – where she is regarded by many with political suspicion. Standing in implicit contrast to Robespierre is Dr. Kippis, for whom, in death, "his Country twines her civic palm." She honors him for his benevolent concern "for the general weal, / The Christian's meekness and the Christian's zeal."[20]

Charlotte Smith is another such patriotic writer in exile, sympathetic to the early promise of the French Revolution, critical of a corrupt British court, but devoted to liberty. Her long poem, *The Emigrants* (1793), takes up the plight of the French anti-revolutionary *émigrés* then in exile in England and longing to return to their "dear native land" (Book I, line 219) and to "regain / Their native country" (II, lines 438–39), as an occasion to reflect on a much broader desire to regain one's native country: Smith herself (then in "unvoluntary exile" [I, line 155] in France), like Helen Maria Williams, longs for an England of true liberty and equality.

Smith had initially greeted the French Revolution as "the noblest cause that ever warm'd / The heart of Patriot Virtue" (I, lines 346–47), but now

<hr />

[19] In *Letters from France*, 2nd. edn. (1792), II, 10–13, cited from Roger Lonsdale, ed., *Eighteenth-Century Women Poets* (Oxford, 1990), 416–17.
[20] *Gentleman's Magazine* (1796), cited from Lonsdale, ed., *Eighteenth-Century Women Poets*, 419–20.

laments that the revolutionaries have disgraced the name of liberty (I, line 350); Marat wears the "Patriot's specious mask" (II, line 124). But she deplores those Britons who dismiss the Revolution as a fraud, and carry on a war against France "to keep Europe's wavering balance even" (II, line 322). Meanwhile, in Britain, the "land of highly vaunted Freedom" (I, line 245), the "venal, worthless hirelings of a Court" disregard the condition of the poor, but may live to regret it:

> learn, that if oppress'd too long,
> The raging multitude, to madness stung,
> Will turn on their oppressors; and, no more
> By sounding titles and parading forms
> Bound like tame victims, will redress themselves!

Smith plainly warns that the revolutionary flame may well spread from France to Britain, but she faces that prospect not with the enthusiasm of the radical but the alarm of the reform-minded defender of "Order":

> Then swept away by the resistless torrent,
> Not only all your pomp may disappear,
> But, in the tempest lost, fair Order sink
> Her decent head, and lawless Anarchy
> O'erturn celestial Freedom's radiant throne.
> (I, lines 333–42)

The driving force behind Smith's poem is not the spectacle of revolution in France, but the scene of "Pride, Oppression, Avarice, and Revenge" (II, line 427) that she finds in Britain. To some extent that force, as Smith herself acknowledges, derives from personal grievance, from "the o'erwhelming wrongs / That have for ten long years been heap'd on me!," the "fearful spectres of chicane and fraud" to which the law has "lent its plausible disguise" (II, lines 353–55, 357). Challenging Britain's flattering image as a land of laws, Smith, like Goldsmith who lamented that "Laws grind the poor, and rich men rule the law" (*The Traveller*, line 386), speaks darkly of "legal crimes":

> For such are in this Land, where the vain boast
> Of equal Law is mockery, while the cost
> Of seeking for redress is sure to plunge
> Th'already injur'd to more certain ruin
> And the wretch starves, before his Counsel pleads.
> (I, lines 36–41)

As her editor suggests, Smith is probably referring to her efforts to gain for her disenfranchised children their rightful share of a trust that had been established for their benefit: they too have in effect lost their share of their own dear country.

Helen Maria Williams' poem on Kippis was published in the *Gentleman's Magazine* in 1796. In the same year there appeared in England a volume of poems entitled *The Rural Lyre*, by Ann Yearsley.[21] It presents, as if in response to Williams' radicalism, a British patriotism that celebrates both liberty and order, both Britain's remote past and her present. By 1796 much of Britain, not just the Burkean conservatives, regarded Revolutionary France as deeply unsettling, if not demonic. Most of the radicals such as Wordsworth who had initially declared their enthusiasm were having second thoughts. Britain, which had prided itself as the home of liberty, saw French *liberté* as a threatening parody. For some fearful Britons, so Charlotte Smith regretted in 1793, "the very name of Liberty has not only lost the charm it used to have in British ears, but many, who have written, or spoken in its defence, have been stigmatized as promoters of Anarchy, and enemies to the prosperity of their country."[22] The patriotic British response to France, to fearful Britons who shrank from talk of "Liberty," and to those others like Helen Maria Williams who continued to declare their admiration for the Revolution, was to re-argue the case for the British understanding of liberty as self-discipline and a respect for law, and to denounce the French version as mere license and mob rule. Yearsley's patriotic verse in *The Rural Lyre* is part of this British response.

Yearsley was already well known for two volumes of verse – *Poems on Several Occasions* had appeared in 1785, *Poems on Various Subjects* in 1787 – and for her much-publicized quarrel with her one-time patron, Hannah More, who was disappointed to discover that the so-called "rustic muse" whose poems she corrected and whose career she sought to promote was not content to defer to More's judgment about matters literary and economic. In those two volumes Yearsley had largely limited herself to domestic genres – brief epistles and epitaphs, an address "to Sensibility," a poem "To Indifference," or "a Tale for the Ladies" – and had with a few exceptions avoided political topics or national affairs.[23] But in 1788 she

---

[21] Among her subscribers were the Duke and Duchess of Devonshire.

[22] Dedication of *The Emigrants* to the poet William Cowper (*Poems of Charlotte Smith*, ed. Stuart Curran [Oxford, 1993], 134).

[23] Exceptions include the poem "To the Bristol Marine Society" in her 1787 volume, a poem in praise of marine commerce, and "To Mr. R[obert Raikes]," on Sunday schools. "On Mrs. Montagu" takes pleasure in Montagu's patriotic answer to Voltaire's remarks on Shakespeare. A "Song" in praise of Chloe's music in the 1787 volume casually names "Wolfe, and Manners."

found a public topic on which she could speak: the slave trade, then the matter of vigorous debate in parliament between its defenders and those, like Wilberforce, who sought to abolish it in Britain. This is a subject on which her former patron, Hannah More, had written: her *Slavery, a Poem* appeared earlier that year. So too had Helen Maria Williams, whose *Poem . . . on the Slave Bill* was also published in 1788, and may well have prompted the poems by More and Yearsley.

More's poem is addressed to "Liberty", but

> Not that mad Liberty, in whose wild praise
> Too oft he trims his prostituted bays;
> Not that unlicens'd monster of the crowd,
> Whose roar terrific bursts in peals so loud,
> Deaf'ning the ear of Peace; fierce Faction's tool,
> Of rash Sedition born, and mad misrule.

More's own footnote makes clear that by unlicensed mad liberty she has in mind the anti-Catholic Gordon riots of 1780. The poem goes on to hold Britain to its own high ideals:

> Shall Britain, where the soul of Freedom reigns,
> Forge chains for others she herself disdains!
> Forbid it, Heaven! O let the nations know
> The liberty she loves, she will bestow.[24]

Yearsley's *Poem on the Inhumanity of the Slave-Trade* is dedicated to her new patron, Frederick, Earl of Bristol and Bishop of Derry, but like More's is directed primarily at the members of parliament, the "few / Who fill Britannia's senate, and are deem'd / The fathers of your country" (27). Instead of appealing directly to Britain's political principles, it invokes "social love" (25, 28, 29) and the benevolence and mercy that Christian slavers forget:

> Is this your piety? Are these your laws,
> Whereby the glory of the Godhead spreads
> O'er barbarous climes! Ye hypocrites, disown
> The Christian name, nor shame its cause. (22)

She rejects the claims of Burkean "custom": "Custom, thou hast undone us! Led us far / From God-like probity, from truth, and heaven" (3). In her

---

Robert Manners, killed in naval action in 1782, had been elegized as a fallen hero in Crabbe's *The Village* (1783). In 1788 she composed a poem "To the King: On His Majesty's Arrival at Cheltenham 1788," sent it to court to be forwarded to the King, and transcribed it into a copy of her *Poems* (1785). See Moira Ferguson, "The Unpublished Poems of Ann Yearsley," *Tulsa Studies in Women's Literature*, 12 (1993), 20.

[24] *Works*, 2 vols. (New York, 1846–47), II, 27, 29. More's slaves have "active patriot fires" (27, line 86).

angriest passage, she denies the claim that the slave trade, even if vicious, serves to benefit the country by enriching it:

> I scorn
> The cry of Av'rice, or the trade that drains
> A fellow-creature's blood: bid Commerce plead
> Her publick good, her nation's many wants,
> Her sons thrown idly on the beach, forbade
> To seize the image of their God and sell it: –
> I'll hear her voice, and Virtue's hundred tongues
> Shall sound against her. Hath our public good
> Fell rapine for its basis? Must our wants
> Find their supply in murder? Shall the sons
> Of Commerce shiv'ring stand, if not employ'd
> Worse than the midnight robber? Curses fall
> On the destructive system that shall need
> Such base supports! Doth England need them? No.
> (26)

By arguing on behalf of a better understanding of the "public good," Yearsley implicitly offers herself as a patriot. But the position she stakes out is a relatively conservative one. In anticipation of British horror at the disorder of the French Revolution, and of her own later poems, she sings "the strain / Of Heav'n-born Liberty" (2) but finds it compatible with social "order": "Hail, social love! true soul of *order*, hail!" (28).[25]

As news of the Terror reached London, Yearsley again responded with poems deploring the anarchic violence. Her "Reflections on the Death of Louis XVI" appeared soon after the King's execution in 1793, as did her "Sequel" to the former poem. And an "Elegy on Marie Antoinette" followed the next year. All three poems, cast in elegiac quatrains, were published as brief pamphlets, "printed for and sold by the author at her public-library" – that is, at the circulating library she had established in Bristol in January 1793. Yearsley's poems have struck some modern critics as a tactical retreat from liberal principles and a careful advertisement of loyalty to the British government, but they are in fact wholly consistent with her poem on the slave trade and with her later poems. They do not so much mark her as a "royalist" (much less a Burkean) as underline her commitment to the "Order" and "Social Love" that has been disrupted, and that will one day, she hopes, be restored. The revolutionaries have

---

[25] Suvir Kaul has argued (*Poems of Nation, Anthems of Empire*, 233) that anti-slavery poems of the 1790s are typically built on "nationalist foundations," are designed to secure Britain's global dominance on ethical and material grounds, and are generally consistent with "conservative" politics.

been deluded by "fancied Liberty" (5).[26] Louis is even bid to "breathe / Forgiveness thro' thy Murd'rer's Soul" (8). His queen is urged to "reconcile" herself to the hope of "happier Prospects." The poet promises to record the "Truth" of the event (6).[27]

Neither these poems on the royal executions in Paris nor her poem on the slave trade was reprinted in *The Rural Lyre*, perhaps suggesting some ambivalence about having implicitly staked out public positions on topics of national concern. But the contents of Yearsley's third collection of poems suggest that she was not about to forswear politics. (The title may have been chosen not to signal subject matter but firmly to revise More's dismissive "rustic muse."[28]) Most of the poems in the volume restrict themselves to traditionally female topics and forms ("To Mira, on the Care of her Infant," "The Captive Linnet"),[29] but four are notable for their ambitious dimensions and their political topics. One is an "Elegy Sacred to the Memory of Lord William Russell." Why her thoughts turned to Russell in 1796 is not clear, though it is not unlikely that the spectacle of the public beheading of Louis XVI in 1793 sent her mind back to the events leading up to the English "Revolution" of 1688 and to the beheading of Russell in the aftermath of the so-called "Rye House Plot" against Charles II in 1683. Russell stood high in the Whig pantheon of heroic resistance to Stuart "tyranny,"[30] and his descendant, the fifth Duke of Bedford, was well known in the 1790s for his radical sympathies. In Yearsley's retelling of what she calls the "tragic tale," Charles II is a "wasted monarch," "enervated," "sunk in voluptuousness" (in this respect perhaps an image of what his critics saw as Louis XVI's devotion to pleasure). Charles is too ready to listen to Roman Catholic priests who convince him to break his promises and to pledge "fair Albion to yon

---

[26] It is perhaps notable that Yearsley does not take up the opportunity to commend liberty "in *Britannia*'s Vale": "joyous Liberty" is found only with "poor Fancy" (5).

[27] In a poem "on the last interview between the King of Poland and Loraski" (published with the "Elegy" on Marie Antoinette), Yearsley's patriotic hero is moved to a "Recital of his Country's Woe" (13), and laments her "*Loss of Liberty*" (14).

[28] For "rustick" Johnson gives "rural," "artless," and "plain" but also "rude; untaught; inelegant" and "brutal; savage."

[29] "Prayer and Resignation," in which the poet seems to disavow any interest in whether the nation humbly prays "for War and noble PITT" or whether "yon noisy Gallicans conspire / To steal our gold," is read by Mary Waldron as a "rather testy and derisive repudiation" of political discourse (*Lactilla, Milkwoman of Clifton: The Life and Writings of Ann Yearsley, 1753–1806* [Athens, GA, 1996], 268). But Yearsley may be working within a familiar subgenre of poems, many of them by women, inspired by Frances Greville's "A Prayer for Indifference" (1759).

[30] Thomson commends him in *The Seasons*: "Let me strew / The grave where Russel lies; whose temper'd Blood, / With calmest Chearfulness for thee [i.e., for "Britannia"] resign'd, / Stain'd the sad Annals of a giddy Reign, / Aiming at lawless Power, / Tho' meanly sunk in loose inglorious Luxury" (*Summer*, lines 1522–27).

Gallic lord" (in the secret Treaty of Dover) in return for what Yearsley's footnote calls "money to pursue his pleasures." Russell is the "dauntless" patriot, distressed at "Thy country's wrongs, the hopeless peasant's woe." Once he is imprisoned and sentenced to death, focus shifts to Russell's father, the old Earl (and later Duke) of Bedford, loyal political ally of the King's father, who pleads that the King restore to him "my deserving child." But Charles will not relent, and the poem comes to a grisly end at the scaffold, as Yearsley sees Russell's "shade" fly back to its "native sky" and "the axe display'd – / Too near the throne – I saw the visage roll." Not "his visage" but "*the* visage." But whose visage is it? Yearsley's calculated withholding ("near the throne") allows us to blend the scene of Russell's execution with the recent executions in Paris – and perhaps with the imagined revenge against a long-dead Stuart tyrant.

What political meaning does such a poem carry in 1796? Surely not the fantasized execution of George III – there is no reason to think Yearsley anything but a loyal subject.[31] Perhaps, at a time when the correct meaning of the English Revolution was being debated – was it, as Burke thought, a reaffirmation of traditional English freedoms, or, as Richard Price insisted, a radical break with the past? – Yearsley's poem reaffirms Price's view, and expresses patriotic British reverence for a Whig hero and martyr. Perhaps, at a time when violence had just put an end to the French monarchy, it deplores the use of judicial murder for political ends.

Another elegy in Yearsley's volume mourns a more recent event: the killing by British soldiers in 1793 of some twenty "inhabitants of the ancient city of Bristol" (Yearsley's home town) who had gathered – or perhaps rioted – to protest the breaking of a promise that a hated bridge-toll would be lifted. Writing some time after the event, Yearsley does not hesitate to call it "murder" – the word appears three times in the poem's 120 lines – and "massacre" by cold "assassins." And her footnotes provide chilling chapter and verse to document the event: one victim was "The Father of seven Children," another a stranger "just arrived" in town was "shot through the heart," a third a young pregnant woman "stabbed with a bayonet," her body thrown into the river by the soldiers, "who opposed the removal of the bodies." But Yearsley claims she does not seek to inflame passions: the poem urges the families of the victims not

---

[31] For contemporary debate over the meaning of the old statute defining treason "when a man doth compass or imagine the death of our Lord the King," leading to the passage of the Treasonable Practice Act in December 1795, see John Barrell, *Imagining the King's Death: Figurative Treason, Fantasies of Regicide, 1793–1796* (Oxford, 2000).

to "nurse . . . dark revenge" and, as with her elegy on Louis XVI, urges
the "lamented victims" themselves in a Christian spirit to "pardon all
who wrong'd you."

As with the poems on the slave trade, on the French monarchs, and
on Russell, Yearsley regards shocking public events from the point of
view of private mourners, the weeping "little brothers" and the "fond
mother" of the "gentle" African Luco, sold into slavery, the father of the
condemned Russell.[32] Her sentimentality softens the edge of political
criticism. As with the poem on Russell, its political weight is difficult to
gauge. The prose "Advertisement" (dated "30th September 1793") which
introduces the poem to her readers in 1796, presumed to be unfamiliar
with the riot three years earlier, seems just as deeply ambivalent as the
poem itself. On the one hand it suggests that time has already begun its
healing work, has "softened the frowning jealousy of power on one part,
and the sense of misfortune on the part of those who lost their children,
their friends, and fathers." On the other, Yearsley seems to speak with
barely concealed sarcasm, pretending to disclaim all "presumption of
judging" and to show the proper deference to those who are wealthier
and wiser than she:

The Author disclaims the presumption of judging rich men or wise men: Wealth
must be adored in a becoming manner: Wisdom is so beloved – hem – Wisdom
ought to be so beloved in Bristol, and every where else, that the man or the woman who possesses it is as a consecrated vessel suffered to lie by for sacred purposes. Full of These gentle considerations necessary to well-doing, the Author
only begs leave to say – [and her bare statement of the facts follows]. (100)

One recent critic finds the advertisement "defiant," but implies that in
the poem itself Yearsley disappointingly pulled her punches, perhaps
because she "kept her eye on the market," i.e., because she was anxious
not to offend potential readers.[33] But in fact the poem is consistent
with Yearsley's support, both in the poem on the slave trade and in
other poems in *The Rural Lyre*, for social "order" and with the concern,
widespread among her contemporaries, about the spread of the French
contagion. The ironic final lines of the advertisement – "as every poet
who has hitherto sung in [Bristol's] shade has been rewarded, the Author
expects her civic wreath" – suggest that Yearsley's public politics are
mixed up with more personal resentments.

[32] Harriet Guest has recently argued (*Small Change*, 252–67) that Anna Seward's *Monody on Major
André* (1781) and *Elegy on Captain Cook* (1780) display a new and "distinctively female" patriotism
(255), identified with the notions of loss and bereavement.
[33] Waldron, *Lactilla*, 265.

"Civic wreath" suggests the "reward" – whether gratitude or something more solid – that she has learned not to expect. But it may also hint at her aspiration to be acknowledged as a "civic" writer. If the "civic wreath" is the traditional "civil crown" of oak-leaves, granted for civil as opposed to military honors, such as those granted to Cicero recognizing him as "Father of his Country,"[34] or the wreath offered by Britannia to the Duchess of Devonshire in Rowlandson's "Liberty and Fame Introducing Female Patriotism to Britannia," Yearsley here not only identifies herself as citizen of Bristol rather than British soldier, but also makes a claim to be regarded as a Ciceronian patriot, whose chief care is for her "Country." This is a claim she substantiates more clearly with two other poems in *The Rural Lyre*, "The Genius of England" and (the lead poem, and the longest one in the volume) "Brutus." They suggest that although she was clearly troubled by unjust violence in Britain's past and present, she tried to defuse discontent, and articulate a patriotic celebration of her native land, summoning her fellow citizens to the defense of both "Liberty" and "Order." They also suggest that an older form of literary patriotism is still found in the 1790s, and that women poets of the day are not limited to a patriotism based on elegiac feeling.

"The Genius of England" has no specific historical occasion such as the Bristol riot of 1793, but because the poem appears "at this dread hour" (95) Yearsley suggests some urgency. It is prompted by "murm'ring" (95) and "complaining spirits" (99) of England's "rebellious children" (94), such murmuring as the agitation by the radical London Corresponding Society for universal male suffrage, Paine's complaints that Britain's "hereditary system" divided the nation into those with power and wealth and those without, and continuing demands for the abolition of the slave trade. Yearsley's response is a stern speech to the "children," delivered by a paternal "Genius of England," imagined to be standing (according to the poem's title) "On the Rock of Ages, Recommending Order, Commerce and Union to the Britons." "Rock of Ages" suggests both the "rocks of Albion" (99) on which Britain is soundly founded, and the scriptural "Rock" of revealed "Religion" (95),[35] whose authority is invoked to prompt submission. But the spokesman of the poem, England's

---

34 "A garland of oak-leaves and acorns bestowed upon one that saved the life of a fellow citizen in war" (*OED*). Pope uses the term in *The Temple of Fame*, lines 242–43, in his account of Cicero, honored by his fellow citizens as "the Great Father of his Country" after exposing the conspiracy of Catiline. For "civick," Johnson, citing Pope, gives "Relating to civil honours or practices; not military."

35 Yearsley apparently alludes to the first line ("Rock of Ages,...") of Toplady's famous hymn, "A Living and Dying Prayer for the Holiest Believer in the World," first published in 1776.

"Genius," is plainly a secular figure, concerned to promote "Order, Commerce and Union." Yearsley appeals to what she imagines to be both a protector and an inborn national spirit, a common figure in eighteenth-century poems, especially those that addressed the state of the nation.[36] She aligns her poem with patriotic verses of an earlier happier day – when a united Britain humbled French pride. At the triumphal end of the Seven Years' War, one patriotic poet addressed "The Genius of Britain" to Pitt, whose breast, the poet says, "Glows ardent with the Patriot's sacred fire" (the former "Patriot Minister" was then out of office). The poet's "British spirit, emulating thine,"

> Could ne'er burn incense at Corruption's shrine;
> Who far from courts maintains superior state,
> And thinks that to be free is to be great.

That poem's title alluded to an earlier "The Genius of Britain. An Iambick Ode. Written in MDCCLVI," in which the "Genius" surveys British history – the glories of Crécy, Agincourt, Alfred, Edward, Henry V, and Elizabeth – and urges Britons to defend themselves against the French threat: "Britons, exert your own unconquer'd might, / A Freeman but defends a Freeman's right."[37] Yearsley implicitly tries to call back such days of unity and strength, but she betrays doubts that she can ever succeed. Her poem rises to no compelling Popean vision of "Order," and no articulation of the relationships among "Order," "Commerce," and "Union." It remains something of a harangue, an obsessive insistence on "Order" (the word appears eight times in its 107 lines; "Liberty" or "Freedom" appear, equally mechanically, but four times). The great fear is "Anarchy's furious and disloyal brood" (99), a clear reference to, and dismissal of, French-inspired Jacobin protest. The assassins of her "Bristol Elegy" now reappear as cannibalistic enemies of the nation: "Away, / Assassins, to the feast where Murder smiles / Triumphant o'er her bleeding victims." Familial grief for the Bristol victims is now England's own "Paternal anguish . . . / Whilst froward tempers wearied me" (95). Even the praise of "Commerce," after a century of similar tributes, seems perfunctory. Yearsley makes no effort to make the case anew, for she cannot imagine objection: "Who / . . . hails not Britannia's commerce?" She is apparently more concerned at the danger that the French navy poses to

---

[36] Cf. the end of Pope's first "Epilogue to the Satires," where "Old *England*'s Genius, rough with many a Scar," is imagined as a defeated soldier in the triumphal procession of Vice: "Dragg'd in the Dust! His Arms hang idly round, / His Flag inverted trails along the ground!" (lines 152–54).

[37] *Poetical Calendar*, 6 (1763), 102, 106.

British maritime trade: "This is the pow'r my rival's hate would lure /
From you and me" (97).

On the whole the poem shows more aspiration than accomplishment.
One feature perhaps points to a distinctive element of her version of patriotism. The poem is initially addressed to England's "rebellious children"
(94), later to her "Sons" (97), but finally to "Women and men, my family of Britons" (99), as if Yearsley is explicitly, if awkwardly, including
women readers in her patriotic appeal. No writer before her, save Mary
Wollstonecraft, had appealed specifically to women as fellow members
of the "family of Britons." Not "Men and women" but "Women and
men," as if to signal clearly that women, even if they had no political
rights,[38] were to be addressed as citizens.

The major work in Yearsley's *The Rural Lyre*, and the poem that most
fully lays out and embodies her aspirations as a patriotic poet, is "Brutus:
A Fragment," a narrative poem of 524 lines, in heroic couplets, that en-
compasses the history of the founding of Britain by its eponymous first
king, Brutus. To call it a "Fragment" is perhaps disingenuous, a piece of
self-protective modesty, or a sign that Yearsley shares contemporaries' interest in the aesthetic form of the fragment.[39] More likely she is imitating
the practice of her friend Joseph Cottle, whose "War: A Fragment" was
published in Bristol in 1795.[40] In the prose "Argument" she more aptly
offers the poem as a "humble specimen" of a full-length epic poem. It is
as if she were presenting a *proposal* for such a poem in hopes of arousing
interest among subscribers. Still affecting modesty, she suggests that she
herself is not the poet to attempt the greater work: from her little "spark"
she wishes that "a body of fire may arise in the imagination of some
more able Poet." This was almost a conventional gesture for the female
poet venturing onto heroic ground, recalling Barbauld's expression of
diffidence about the theme of Paoli, or even Lady Mary's reluctance to
write about fortifications. Why "Brutus"? Perhaps because in 1796 the
name has some currency in contemporary political pemphlets.[41] In fact,

---

[38] According to *The Laws Respecting Women as they Regard their Natural Rights* (1777), "By marriage the
very being or legal existence of a woman is suspended" (65). Whether married or unmarried, a
woman could neither vote nor hold any public office.

[39] For discussion of the late-eighteenth-century aesthetic of the fragment, see Marjorie Levinson,
The Romantic Fragment Poem (Chapel Hill, 1986) and Elizabeth W. Harries, *The Unfinished Manner:
Essays on the Fragment in the Later Eighteenth Century* (Charlottesville, 1994).

[40] Cottle's note informs the reader that the poem "was extracted from a didactic poem of some
extent on HAPPINESS. If the specimen given should be approved of, the remainder of the piece
will probably appear in a second edition" (*Poems* [Bristol, 1795], xvi).

[41] Cf. *The Letters of Brutus to Certain Celebrated Political Characters* (1791), attributed to Henry Mackenzie;
A Letter to the Right Honourable H. G-tt-n (1795), signed by "Brutus"; and a sonnet in the *Morning
Post* for 9 February 1795, attributed to "Brutus."

of course, the story of Brutus had already inspired the poets, most notably Pope. Yearsley could not have read Pope's eight-line "Fragment of Brutus, an Epic," not published until it appeared in the Twickenham Edition in 1954, but she could have read a full account of the projected poem in Owen Ruffhead's *Life of Alexander Pope* (1769). Like Yearsley, Ruffhead had offered the "sketch" of the poem on Brutus "as a model to employ some genius, if any there be, or shall hereafter arise, equal to the execution of such an arduous task" (410). She was obviously well acquainted with the old story of Brutus, first told by Geoffrey of Monmouth, and could have drawn her knowledge from Milton's *History of Britain*[42] or Aaron Thompson's *The British History, Translated into English from the Latin of Jeffrey of Monmouth* (1718), which included Brutus' prayer to Diana rendered in English couplets by Pope.[43]

A comparison of Thompson's and Pope's Brutus in fact suggests that Yearsley may have taken her inspiration from Pope, who puts his emphasis not on Brutus the warrior but Brutus the benevolent legislator. Geoffrey's Brutus is primarily an Achillean figure: he and his wandering band of soldiers repeatedly engage in bloody battle, and after conquering typically slaughter their enemies. They ravage the country of Mauretania from end to end. After a victory in Aquitaine, they sack and burn the cities, and plan to exterminate the people. Upon landing in Albion, near the end of Geoffrey's account, Brutus kills all the giants (the only native inhabitants), and gives the land a new name: Britain. In the final two paragraphs he builds the capital city of Troia Nova (later London), and presents it to the citizens, giving them also a code of laws. Pope's Brutus, whose story begins as he prepares to set sail for Britain from the Pillars of Hercules, is a new Aeneas: his mission is not to conquer or to found an empire (or give it a name), but to civilize, and to introduce among the people arts, true religion, and "a just form of government" (line 410). In what is already "Britain" he finds friendly native "Britons" (the Druids), and helps them defeat the giants. He restrains his young warlike kinsman ("an Achilles") who is eager to conquer the Druids, and defeats the forces of "superstition, anarchy, and tyranny," whereupon "the whole island submits to good government" (line 421). Like Pope, Yearsley focuses on the last stage in Brutus' history. Her hero

---

[42] The story of Brutus is told at length. See *Complete Prose Works*, v, Pt. 1, 8–17. She is less likely to have known Hildebrand Jacob's *Brutus the Trojan: Founder of the British Empire*, of which the first five books were published in 1735 but apparently soon sank out of sight. Cf. also *A New and Complete History of England, from the first settlement of Brutus... to the year 1793* (London, 1791–94).

[43] Neither Ruffhead nor Thompson appear in the catalogue of Yearsley's circulating library, though she did have a nine-volume edition of Pope's *Works*, apparently one of Warburton's. But it is clear that her reading was not limited to the books in her library collection.

encounters people already called "Britons." She is concerned above all with good government rather than military conquest, with order and its antitheses violence and anarchy.

The story of Brutus offers some difficulties to the patriot poet who would use it as the founding myth for a nation of law and liberty, for Brutus landed on an island already inhabited by native Britons. Yearsley's solution, like Pope's, is to focus on Brutus as peacemaker and legislator and to split the Britons into two groups, savages who are furious and violent, and those who prove tractable. Brutus is also a problematic figure for the celebrant of British liberty. Like a later foreign invader, William I, he might easily be regarded as the enemy of native liberty. Yearsley's solution, at a time when the cries of liberty from France seemed to challenge Britain's much-advertised devotion to liberty, is to try to reconcile liberty and order. It is as if, like Collins and Goldsmith before her, she seeks to refine the spirit of English liberty so as to temper its excess and to bring about greater social harmony. She deploys the story in order to commend the same political principles that animate her other patriotic poems – the danger of civil strife, anarchy, and licentiousness, the importance of "order."

Her narrative begins not at the Pillars of Hercules but in Brutus' native Italy, where he has been "driven by a storm," and where, despite the urging of an oracle to sail west beyond Gaul, he has lingered with his countrymen. Venus prays to Jove for pity on her Trojans, and asks that they be granted "some narrow realm" where Brutus may "by some gen'rous nation blest, / Wear down a virtuous life." Jove consents, swearing that "Brutus should hail him on Britannia's shore." The scene quickly shifts to the "venerable cliffs" of England, where Venus asks that Neptune befriend Brutus, who then safely lands amid calm seas. Brutus thanks Jove:

> Thou hast preserv'd us from the dreary main,
> Grant that we may here in social bands remain;
> In peace, and war, beneath thy awful shield
> May Britons learn to conquer, and to yield;
> Adore thy laws, near thy eternal shrine
> Hang high the shield of Liberty divine!
>
> (*The Rural Lyre*, 7)

"Social" – a recurrent word in her poems – carries the same value for Yearsley as it does for Thomson and Goldsmith. And her conception of "Liberty" involves knowing both how (and when) to "conquer", and how (and when) to "yield." The scene shifts again (as if Yearsley were fast-forwarding through her story), and Brutus encounters a heavenly figure dressed like Diana the huntress. She proves to be Liberty, "the goddess of this isle," whose charge is "To guard these shores, and bless the Britons' line." She says little of liberty, much of "union" ("union is my Britons' strongest boast"), and declares herself enemy of "The hydra Anarchy" and "Licentiousness" (which "usurps my name"). For reasons that Yearsley does not make clear in her "Fragment," Liberty warns the invader that a "warlike host" is preparing to attack him, and in effect adopts his cause. The allegorical meaning is apparently that there is something in native British liberty, or something in Brutus himself, or both, that harbors some licentiousness or anarchy and needs to be tamed.

On the way back to his men, Brutus spies a band of "Gigantic mortals, painted red and green" with images of animals and warfare. These are evidently the tribe of Geoffrey's Gogmagog whose pagan bloodlust Yearsley perhaps intended to develop into a full episode if she were to expand her "specimen" into a full-length epic. Inspired by Brutus' return, the Trojans give battle not to giants but to what seem to be British tribes of mortal size, in a condensed version of pitched battle (complete with single combat) in classical epic. But Brutus, as if remembering Liberty's words about the power of union, "Lamented war, stern foe to social good, / Mourn'd Britain early soil'd with Britons' blood." He already seems to regard war with the Britons not as conquest but as civil strife – suggesting again that Yearsley has in mind the potential for revolutionary violence in the Britain of her own day. Brutus signals retreat, and thinks how he might win the Britons over through some means other than violence. To help him (and Yearsley) out of this difficulty, Venus appears to deflect a deadly spear, and Liberty reappears to remind him that the true king is the one who knows that you can win by declining to use force: "To yield is to deserve a throne. / Let fall thy spear: my Britons are not slaves: / There lives no conqueror but the man who saves." Yearsley's Britons offer an image of themselves to her readers: they are avatars of those eighteenth-century Britons who "never will be slaves." So too do her Trojans, who serve as a figure for the Britons, powerful and paternalistic, called on in contemporary abolitionist poems to act with benevolence toward savage races. Like African slaves, the "savage" Britons are "Untaught" and "unpolish'd," but capable of "firm . . . friendship," and ready to learn "refinement" from "instruction."

Brutus obeys the voice of Venus, and dramatically lays his shield and helmet on the ground. Instantly (if improbably), the enemy is won over:

> Dissolving influence thrill'd the Britons' hearts,
> They clasp'd the chief, resign'd their dreadful darts.

"Peace" and "Plenty" – perhaps echoing Pope's *Windsor Forest*[44] – with equal speed bless the entire island:

> To arts or commerce turn'd each kindred host,
> Liberty fix'd her bulwarks round the coast:
> Beneath her feet old Neptune wander'd slow,
> To waft her navies o'er the rocks below.

Brutus' Britain, replete with "arts," "commerce," and "navies," is an image of Yearsley's own Britain, her lines in part recycled from "The Genius of England," where under the influence of order Britons view "Arts, sciences; those bulwarks of your isle, / Triumphant navies, rising o'er the scene" (98).

The scene again shifts suddenly to the quiet forest, where Brutus comes upon a "rustic altar," adorned with shield, corslet, and spear, which reminds him of his own father, and which turns out to be devoted to the memory of the father of a "beauteous maid" who steps forth, armed with a spear, to challenge him. She is Hermia, not a Briton but "Trojan born," daughter of one of Brutus' fellow sailors, shipwrecked with her father on the British coast. Hermia seems to be Yearsley's own invention: she appears neither in Pope nor in Geoffrey, where Brutus before his arrival in Britain has married Greek Ignoge, who eventually bears him three sons. Yearsley's Brutus arrives unmarried, and in Hermia meets a figure who combines the chaste Diana (she has "bow and quiver o'er her shoulder," and a "vestal robe" over her virgin form), the goddess Liberty (Hermia declares that she "is and will be free"), and Aeneas-like filial piety. Perhaps Yearsley makes her a Trojan so as to make her a female version of her hero. Brutus again symbolically drops his arms, as does Hermia, in mutual recognition that love conquers all. She turns over her arrows and bow, and agrees to "follow" him: "Where'er thou bidd'st, I'll go." Yearsley condenses the rest of their story into some twenty lines: she bears him three sons (who initiate "a long race of kings") but continues

---

[44] Yearsley may combine the dramatic arrival of peace when "great Anna" says "Let Discord cease!" (line 327) with the early picture of Windsor Forest, where "peace and plenty tell, a STUART reigns" (line 42). Cf. Pope's "blushing Flora" (line 38), "smiling" Industry (line 41), and the "blessings" of the gods (line 36) with Yearsley's "beauteous Flora," and "Plenty," who "brought forth her blessings with a smile" (18).

to tend her father's altar, and dies in Brutus' arms. He soon joins her and "Slept with his Hermia in the grassy tomb, / Beneath the oak that yearly lost its bloom."

In the poem's closing paragraph Liberty retires to the tomb to ask Jove's protection for the pair, and receives the ambiguous answer that "Not all shall die who love thy sacred charms," perhaps a disturbing reminder that the love and defense of liberty carries a heavy cost. Yearsley's hasty ending, encompassing future British glory, is equally ambiguous: after a poem in celebration of the forswearing of violence, Liberty with "hair dishevell'd" stands on the cliffs as her "sons arose, and call'd for arms," and in challenge to Neptune himself, "seiz'd the trident of the world."

> Venus and Jove smil'd from their brightest sphere,
> AND GODLIKE ORDER FIX'D HER STANDARD HERE.

Perhaps Yearsley refers here to the future British empire's control of the seas as the basis of its global power, a power she now seems to regard as wholly benign, blessed by the gods, and consistent with the establishment of "Order."

Whether Yearsley, in a full-length epic, would have worked out the tensions between victory through yielding and victory through armed seizure of the "trident of the world" is impossible to say. It seems clear that she hoped to find a way to reconcile "Liberty" and "Order" so as to convey to her readers a message both anti-revolutionary and patriotic. That she may have harbored some doubts about the reconciliation is perhaps suggested in the frontispiece to *The Rural Lyre*, an engraving entitled "British Liberty" (see figure 7), which represents a partially clothed female figure, her long thick hair dishevelled, with a "Liberty cap" set on the the end of her staff (or spear?), seated beneath a spreading oak (symbol of Britain) and beside a classical grave monument marked with the name of Brutus, and adorned with sword, shield, helmet, and an anchor. She is named "British Liberty" to distinguish her clearly from the contemporary French version, which Yearsley and many of her contemporaries associated with licentiousness. With her right hand Liberty gestures toward a scene in the background, and with her left she seems to make an appeal to heaven. The engraving appears to represent simultaneously three different scenes in the poem: (1) the arrival of Brutus on the British shore in the Trojan ships, visible in the harbor in the distance; (2) a council of peace, in which a seated Brutus meets the representatives of the Britons with sword downturned; and (3) Liberty at the grave of Brutus

Figure 7. "British Liberty," frontispiece to Ann Yearsley, *The Rural Lyre* (1796). BL shelfmark 11641.h.6.(1)

and Hermia, appealing to Jove to keep them in his care.[45] The sculpture on the monument suggests both Brutus' martial virtues (sword, shield, and helmet) and the importance of British sea power (anchor), both in the past and future.[46] The plaintive expression on Liberty's face is perhaps designed to reflect the text of the poem ("Here Liberty to breathe her woes retir'd . . . "), perhaps, like her dishevelled hair,[47] to present her in formal mourning for the dead.[48] But it remains striking that in a volume whose lead poem is apparently intended to found in Britain's origins a patriotic politics of "Liberty" and "Order," the frontispiece focuses on the death of the founder and on the felt need for heavenly protection.

It is notable that the frontispiece focuses not on the male hero but on the figure of a woman. Liberty (goddess of the isle, a kind of "Genius" figure) is not the only woman to play a prominent role in a poem that begins with Venus' prayer to Jove to "Pity my Brutus . . ." and closes with Liberty's prayer to Jove for eternal care. (By contrast, Ruffhead's sketch of Pope's plans suggests that women would only play minor supporting roles; no women are named in the list of eleven dramatis personae.) In the course of the narrative Yearsley finds room, almost arbitrarily, for a number of other female figures.[49] A British warrior is associated not with his father but with his mother ("Zaunus came next, of swarthy Lara born"), a Trojan warrior wears a "spangled collar . . . / Gift of his mother." The giants Brutus encounters come in both sexes, and the "young females of the giant train" are given more lengthy description than their male counterparts:

> Their flaxen hair fell low beneath the waist,
> The tawny hide their fairer bodies grac'd – . . .
> Or variegated plumage, to adorn
> Her head, and raise less happy rivals' scorn. –
> To dignify, deface, or hide her charms.

Yearsley's female giant is no amazon, shunning the company of men. She is both warrior and "beauteous maid" who paints her body, and a

---

[45] Beneath the engraving of "British Liberty" appears the legend, " 'Eternal Jove,' she cried, 'be these thy care'."

[46] Perhaps too the anchor (commonly found on graves) suggests, anachronistically, Christian hope.

[47] "Dishevelled" hair is a conventional sign of female mourning, as Johnson's *Dictionary* suggests with illustrations from *The Faerie Queene* and Dryden's translation of the *Aeneid*.

[48] Yearsley perhaps recalls Collins' "1746" ode, in memory of those who died to preserve liberty, where "Freedom" repairs for "awhile" to "dwell a weeping hermit."

[49] In her tragedy, *Earl Goodwin* (performed in Bristol and Bath in 1789, printed in London in 1791), Yearsley assigned prominent roles to Editha and Emma, wife and mother of Edward the Confessor.

"pious" maiden who scoops out a skull to form a votive bowl, and calls on Thor, "Her god of love – her father's god of war." The most prominent female figure in the poem is of course Hermia, Yearsley's invention. The effect of her martial appearance and subsequent marriage with Brutus is not, as with Virgil's Lavinia, to suggest the blending of the invaders with natives, but as it were to make the Trojan hero of her poem both male and female. The final female figure is Yearsley herself, who makes no appearance in the poem, but her name is signed to the volume's dedication and her portrait occupies the title's facing page, in effect a second frontispiece. This portrait, reprinted from her 1787 volume, show-ing a soberly clad, coiffed, and hatted Ann Yearsley, "the Bristol Milk Woman & Poetess" whose facial features resemble those of the repre-sentation of "British Liberty."[50] By juxtaposing the two portraits, Years-ley implies that the female patriot-poet too serves the cause of British liberty.[51]

"Brutus" in combination with "The Genius of England" suggests a broadly Whiggish poet determined to champion "British Liberty," a form of liberty consistent with "Order" and best promoted by "Union" and "Commerce." This is not inconsistent with the "Elegy to the Memory of the Lord William Russell" and the "Bristol Elegy," which assert British liberties and warn against domestic tyranny and violence. In the latter, Yearsley worries more about governmental repression, in the former more about the excesses of liberty. There is no reason to suppose that "Brutus" is designed to provide patriotic cover for a radical-leaning poet's subversive tendencies.[52] Her politics, while they may disappoint some contemporary critics looking for a working-class ideology of resistance to authority, reflect the reformist beliefs of the broad political middle ground, neither radical nor high-flying Tory, in the 1790s.

Yearsley's loyalist politics did not prevent her from being attacked. In Richard Polwhele's *The Unsex'd Females* (London, 1798) she is grouped somewhat indiscriminately with a number of women writers of the decade, including Charlotte Smith, Helen Maria Williams, and Mary

---

[50] Donna Landry (*Muses of Resistance: Laboring-Class Women's Poetry in Britain, 1739–1796* [Cambridge, 1990], 173) imagines "British Liberty" to be a representation of Yearsley herself; Waldron (*Lactilla*, 311 n) sees "some physiological resemblance." As Tompkins notes, the portrait presents Yearsley in traditional milkwoman's dress, cloak, kerchief, and large flat hat worn over a cap (J. M. S. Tompkins, *The Polite Marriage* [Cambridge, 1938], 60).

[51] Of Yearsley's 128 subscribers, their names ranked in the "List of Subscribers" that precedes her dedication, fifty-four are women.

[52] As Waldron supposes (*Lactilla*, 255).

Wollstonecraft. Polwhele took his title from a phrase in Thomas Henry Mathias' *The Pursuits of Literature*, a much-reprinted compendium in verse (and prose footnotes) which links women writers and an enthusiasm for the French Revolution: "Our unsex'd female writers now instruct, or confuse, us and themselves, in the labyrinth of politics, or turn us wild with Gallic frenzy."[53] Polwhele, like Mathias before him, was a firmly anti-Jacobinical writer who disapproved of any sympathy for the French Revolution. More than that, he regarded women who ventured into the "labyrinth of politics" (regardless of their principles) as unnatural. It is perhaps this conviction that induces Polwhele to lump Yearsley with Williams, "fir'd by freedom" (18) and "an intemperate advocate for Gallic licentiousness" (19n), with Smith, "infected with the Gallic mania" (18n), and with Wollstonecraft, "the Arch-priestess of female Libertinism" (20n). Polwhele declares that his "business . . . with Mrs. Yearsley is to recall her, if possible, from her Gallic wanderings – if an appeal to native ingenuousness be not too late" (20n).

Yearsley, unlike Polwhele's other "unsex'd females," was never a radical and never an admirer of the Revolution. But as she made clear in "The Genius of England" and in "Brutus" she was convinced that women were competent to discuss national politics and were to be regarded as citizens. This is what she most clearly shares with Wollstonecraft, whose *Vindication of the Rights of Women* (1792) drew the fire of Polwhele and other conservatives. Wollstonecraft insisted that it is women's "first duty" to "find themselves as rational creatures, and the next in point of importance, as citizens, is that, which includes so many, of a mother." To be a good citizen, a woman must be a good wife and mother: "the wife . . . who neither suckles nor educates her children, scarcely deserves the name of a wife, and has no right to that of a citizen"(264). To be a good mother, a woman must be a citizen: "if children are to be educated to understand the true principles of patriotism, their mother must be a patriot" (87). Women will best perform their traditional roles if they also perform the roles traditionally assigned to men: "Make women rational creatures and free citizens, and they will quickly become good wives and mothers" (306). Polwhele would have none of it: ignoring Wollstonecraft's nexus of motherhood and citizenship, he insisted that she was both "unsex'd" and inflamed with lust.

---

[53] Thomas Henry Mathias, *The Pursuits of Literature*, 11th. edn. (London, 1801), 244. The book began appearing in 1794, and its first edition was complete in 1797. Mathias' sentence (quoted from the 7th. edition) appears as the epigraph on Polwhele's title page.

Polwhele's diatribe is one sign that female patriot-poets continued
to meet resistance. But his poem did not succeed in silencing his adversaries. In 1798 appeared Mary Robinson's "The Progress of Liberty." The
Norwich poet, Elizabeth Bentley, lesser known today, extended her series
of poems occasioned by signal events in the political world, commending the patriotic spirit of the country's leaders: "On the Bill for Preventing the Exportation of British Wool. 1788,"[54] "On his Majesty's Happy
Recovery. March 1789,"[55] "On the Abolition of the African Slave-Trade.
July, 1789,"[56] "Ode to Peace, June, 1790," "On the Victory over the Dutch
Fleet, October 11th, 1797," and "Song. The Briton's Resolution. August
1800."[57] As the new century opened, women poets continued to take up
public and political topics once assumed the sole property of men. Anna
Barbauld, who had written an "Epistle to William Wilberforce, Esq. On
the Rejection of the Bill for Abolishing the Slave Trade" (1791) and "On
the Expected General Rising of the French Nation in 1792" (1793), went
on to publish "Eighteen Hundred and Eleven" (1812), a poem written in
one of the darker hours of the Napoleonic wars. Like *The Deserted Village*,
it fears that Britain's greatness has passed, and laments the emigration of
empire to the new world. Although attacked by contemporary reviewers
(who disliked her politics) as unladylike and "unpatriotic," the poem was
plainly offered as a patriotic prayer on behalf of

> my Country, named beloved, revered,
> By every tie that binds the soul endeared,
> Whose image to my infant senses came
> Mixt with Religion's light and Freedom's holy flame![58]

As the examples of Barbauld, Bentley, and Yearsley show, it is dramatically clear that in a little over a generation since Montagu's letters
were published, women poets now regarded themselves as competent to
write on topics once left to men. Rather than deploring the "jingoistic

---

54 Parliament, "fir'd with noblest zeal," is said to have "Stood forth and acted for their country's
    weal." As a result, "each true patriot's name / Shall stand recorded in the book of fame" (*Genuine
    Poetical Compositions* [Norwich, 1791], 11).
55 George is hailed as "The best of patriots and of kings" (*Genuine Poetical Compositions*, 19).
56 The "patriot sons of Liberty" are urged to "proceed, / Dare to complete the gen'rous God like
    deed" (22).
57 The last two poems were published in her *Poems* (Norwich, 1821).
58 *The Poems of Anna Letitia Barbauld*, 154. The poem remembers "the patriot's prayer" at Runnymede
    (134) and praises William Roscoe's "patriot breast" (147). Croker sneered that "the empire might
    have been saved without the intervention of a lady-author." For his and other contemporary
    reviews, see *Poems*, 309–10.

strain"[59] in these poems, critics would do well to consider further the increasing confidence that Yearsley and others displayed, and their increasing readiness to step forward, as patriots. For in so doing she and other women poets joined a succession of mainstream poets, from Thomson to Cowper, who did not hesitate to offer their services to their country or to recognize its signal accomplishments both in war and in peace.

[59] Like Moira Ferguson, Landry would prefer to find that women poets of the eighteenth century shared her radical politics and does not examine the poetic patriotism of the age on its own terms. Even Waldron, who recognizes that Yearsley was neither working class nor radical, observes that her "didactic" and "jingoistic" poems are "not attractive to the twentieth-century mind" (*Lactilla*, 271).

Conclusion

What can be concluded from this survey of poetry and patriotism in eighteenth-century Britain? First, the prominence of the "Patriot" opposition to Walpole in the 1730s has obscured the more or less continuous discussion of patriotism throughout the eighteenth century in pamphlets, broadside ballads, and more serious verse. The contemporary discourse of patriotism – much of it controversial – might be expected to have deterred serious poets from taking up the topic, for fear of associating themselves with the crude drum-beating xenophobia of the popular press; with a facile and sycophantic praise of the ministry; or with the "false" patriotism that was denounced by many pro-government writers as a cover for self-interest. But patriotism continued to make its appeal after the leader of the Patriots of the 1730s had discredited himself, perhaps because war with France resumed, in the 1740s, after some thirty years of peace; or because of the internal threat of Jacobitism, which encouraged or frightened many into a more vocal loyalty to the Hanoverians; or because of the self-conscious and confident "Britishness" that Linda Colley and others have charted.

Second, that poets of the mid and late century clearly do not turn their backs on contemporary history and politics. Even when the poet retires to a country churchyard or rural Olney, or regards the world from Hagley Park or from Clifton Hill, he or she adopts an implicitly (and sometimes explicitly) political and patriotic stance. The major figures – Thomson, Collins, Gray, Goldsmith, Smart, Cowper – and several of those we usually regard as minor – Akenside, Dyer, Yearsley, and others – all display eager engagement, sometimes quite explicitly, with the public discussion of national issues: war and peace, commerce, empire. Not only that, they aspire to the role of "my country's poet."

Third, the range of response is broader and more nuanced than suggested by conventional accounts in literary histories of "Whig panegyric"

and "Tory satire." (Nor do the poets fall neatly into enthusiastic supporters of the government and a critical Opposition.) Between those extremes
is a great variety of patriotic poetry, some of it frankly celebratory, some
of it hortatory. Much might be called loyal critique; some expresses anxious misgivings on the part of poets who love their country but worry
about its future. Fourth, public-spirited and patriotic verse attracted the
attention of both poets and critics. The classical Greek lyric poets –
Pindar, Alcaeus, and Tyrtaeus – retained a reputation, throughout the
eighteenth century, as "patriots." British poets were aware of the patriotic
poetry of their predecessors and contemporaries: Collins knew the
patriotic poems of Thomson, Gray those of Tickell, Cowper those of
Pope, Barbauld those of Collins. Readers (or at least reviewers) remarked
on their patriotism.

These conclusions compel us to revise and perhaps even lay to rest
the lingering idea that the literary history of the eighteenth century falls
into two halves – an "Augustan age" ending in the 1740s and an "age
of sensibility" beginning in that decade and extending to the beginning
of the "Romantic" period. To be sure, it has long been acknowledged
that an "Augustan" or Popean tradition continues into the second half
of the eighteenth century, especially in the work of Johnson, Goldsmith,
Crabbe, and others. It is now clear that the old distinction between a
"public" Augustan poetry and a "private" poetry of late century cannot
be sustained. This study has focused on the poems from the 1740s to the
1790s, but it has looked back to poems published during the War of the
Spanish Succession (1704–13), and has established virtually continuous
interest in the poetry of patriotism until at least the end of the century.
The production of such poems may well be attributable to the virtually
continuous warfare between Britain and continental adversaries and
to the highly visible expansion (and contraction after 1783) of Britain's
commercial and territorial empire.

Within this fundamental continuity, can we identify distinct stages or
trends? The answer is no. Thomson in the 1740s is no more (or less)
engaged by and moved by the state of the nation than is Cowper in the
1780s or Ann Yearsley in the 1790s. Pope's impulse to retire from the
world into Windsor Forest and his ambivalent attraction to the glories
of London and of overseas commerce is very similar to Cowper's withdrawal to Olney and his anxious survey of empire. Even though Pope
writes at the conclusion of a war in which Britain emerged victorious and
Cowper in the aftermath of the loss of the American colonies, *Windsor
Forest* and *The Task* share a political stance.

I find no evidence to support the conclusion that patriotic poetry declined after 1783, as if reflecting a loss of national self-confidence. Nor does the evidence support the argument that the nature of patriotism itself changed. Even if more women were stepping forward as patriots, it would not be accurate to say that patriotism itself became feminized, associated with the "private, sentimental, and impassioned."[1] Ann Yearsley's patriotic poems differ markedly from those of Anna Seward. But the focus for patriotism may be said to change over the decades. In retrospect, one can see that about 1714 patriotic poets were helping the nation to negotiate the transition from a Stuart to a Hanoverian monarchy. In the 1730s patriotism took the form of the "Patriot" opposition to Walpole. In the 1790s British patriots were preoccupied with the political energy released, both abroad and at home, by the French Revolution.

Did the poets' view of their own public role change significantly over the century? It was once assumed that the poets of Pope's age confidently assumed that their voices would be heard and the sting of their satire felt, and that poets in the "age of sensibility" felt that they had lost a social function. That assumption now seems questionable. What has been called "vocational anxiety"[2] can de discovered throughout the century, even in the poems of Pope and Swift, who sometimes worry that they are dismissed by those who wield the power in the state. And the poets in the generation after Pope are not ready to concede that the poet no longer has a social function. Some firmly insist that they perform a public role. Some clearly want to find a public role, but anxiously worry that there *may* no longer be one, or if so that its responsibilities are much reduced. Each of the poets who offers himself or herself as a patriot – one who loves the country, and one who would serve it – implicitly asks what form that service might now take. Some reaffirm the old idea that the poet, in part by recording virtuous deeds and conferring fame, can inspire men and women to virtuous action. Some aspire to shape public opinion on specific political issues, others to forge an inspiring vision of what the country is or could be, a national myth, or seek to foster the spread of "social" love. Some monitor the falling away from British ideals, or hint at the dark side of the very thing they celebrate – British power, British commerce, or the spirit of British independence.

Readers of eighteenth-century poetry today have not been much drawn to the poetry I have considered in this book. But by averting their eyes from the poetry of patriotism, they blind themselves to a significant part of the literary culture of the day. After remarking on Prior's "Carmen

---

[1] Guest, *Small Change*, 267.
[2] Kaul's term in *Poems of Nation, Anthems of Empire*.

Seculare" (1700) and his poems on Marlborough's victories at Blenheim
and Ramillies, Johnson observed that "Through the reigns of William
and Anne no prosperous event passed undignified by poetry" (*Lives*, II,
186). The patriotic devotion to "my country" was at the heart of one of
the most popular plays on the eighteenth-century stage, Addison's *Cato*,
first performed in the spring of 1713. When Cato declared that "What
Pity is it that we can but die once to serve our country" (Act IV, scene
4) and weeps for the loss of "my country," British audiences, both Whig
and Tory, although divided over the merits of the just-concluded Peace
of Utrecht, joined – or rather competed – to applaud and weep. "Here
tears shall flow," wrote Pope in his epilogue to the play, "Such tears, as
Patriots shed for dying Laws." As late as 1759 *Cato* was still being celebrated for "the spirit of liberty and patriotism which it breathes."[3] Beginning
in 1748 Dodsley's *Collection* continuously kept the patriotic poems of the
first half of the century before new generations of readers. British successes later in the century prompted odes of celebration from Collins, Smart,
and others.[4] And in the closing decades, when Britons flocked to view
Benjamin West's *Death of General Wolfe* and to subscribe to the many patriotic societies, the best-known poet of the day was Cowper, self-identified
patriot and anxious for his country's fate. Among the selections included
in Vicesimus Knox's *Elegant Extracts* (1789), perhaps the best known of the
late-century anthologies, was a passage from Dyer's *Fleece* ("Hail, noble
Albion! . . . ") which Knox entitled "Praise of England," and an Oxford
University prize poem by the Reverend Christopher Butson "On the
Love of our Country."[5]

If we are to arrive at more comprehensive, balanced, and historically
accurate accounts of the poetry of this period, we need to find room
for the poetry of patriotism – broadside ballads, odes and panegyrics,
anxious laments and stirring exhortations, or surveys of the condition of
Britain[6] – that engaged poets and their readers throughout the century.

---

3 Thomas Wilkes, *General View of the Stage* (London, 1759), 31–33.
4 Johnson's claim that during and after the Seven Years' War, "when France was disgraced and
overpowered in every quarter of the globe, when Spain, coming to her assistance, only shared
her calamities, and the name of an Englishman was reverenced through Europe, no poet was
heard amidst the general acclamation" ("Life of Prior," *Lives*, II, 186–87) is probably colored by
his political and moral disapproval of the 1756–63 war and his sense, in 1779, that the American
war was going badly.
5 *Elegant Extracts* (London, 1789), 300–1. The Dyer passage is from Book I, lines 153–76.
6 A bound volume of separately published mid-eighteenth-century poems in the New York Public
Library (NAC. p.v. 1+) suggests that some eighteenth-century readers/collectors may have regarded condition-of-Britain poems as a distinguishable group. The fourteen items include three
by Akenside (the "Epistle to Curio," the "Ode to Huntingdon," and a book of odes), two by
Goldsmith (*The Deserted Village* and *The Traveller*), and Dyer's *Fleece*.

Bibliography

PRIMARY WORKS

A. ANONYMOUS WORKS

The Analysis of Patriotism; or, an inquiry whether opposition to Government, in the present state of affairs, is consistent with the principles of a patriot (London, 1778).

An Authentick ACCOUNT of the BATTLE fought . . . near Culloden (n.p., 1746).

A Ballad. To the Tune of Chevy Chase (London, 1749).

A Coalition of Patriots Delineated (London, 1735).

The Consequences of Trade (London, 1740).

Considerations on the Conduct of the Dutch (London, 1745).

On the Duke of Cumberland's Late Defeat of the Rebels. By a West-Country Gentleman; An Ode on the Birth-day of His Royal Highness William Duke of Cumberland (n.p., 1746).

An Elegy Inscribed to the Duke of Cumberland (Edinburgh, 1746).

An Epilogue on the Birth-Day of His Royal Highness the Duke of Cumberland (n.p., 1746).

Essay on Patriotism, and on the character and conduct of some late pretenders to that virtue, particularly of the late popular gentleman (London, 1768).

An Essay on Patriotism, in the Style and Manner of Mr. Pope's Essay on Man (n.p., 1766).

The Female Patriot. An Epistle from C–t–M-c–y to the Reverend W–l–n On Her Late Marriage (London, 1779).

The Female Volunteer: or, an Attempt to Make our Men Stand (London, 1746).

Fontenoy: A New Satiric Ballad (London, 1745).

The Fourth Ode of the Fourth Book of Horace Imitated and Applied to His Royal Highness the Duke of Cumberland (London, 1746).

The Golden Fleece (London, 1736).

History of the Westminster Election, 2nd. edn. (London, 1785).

Io Triumphe! A POEM upon Admiral VERNON (London, 1741).

A Joyful Ode: Inscribed to the King, on the late Victory at Dettingen (London, 1743).

Liberty and Patriotism: A Miscellaneous Ode (London, 1778).

Liberty: An Ode, Occasion'd by the Happy Victory obtain'd by His Royal Highness the Duke of Cumberland (n.p., 1746).

The Life of Dr. Archibald Cameron (London, 1753).

Ministerial Patriotism Detected; Or the Present Opposition Proved to be Founded on Truly, just and laudable Principles (London, 1763).

Modern Patriotism. A Poem (London, 1734).

Mrs. Midnight's Orations (London, 1763).
National Gratitude Due for National Mercies (London, 1746).
New Ballad on the Battle of Drummossie-Muir, near Inverness (Edinburgh, 1746).
A New Ballad on the Taking of Porto-Bello, by Admiral Vernon (London, 1740).
An Ode, Addressed to his Royal Highness William Duke of Cumberland, by a Lady (n.p., 1746?).
The Patriot, or A Call to Glory; A poem, In Two Books (Edinburgh, 1757).
The Patriot and the Minister Review'd: by Way of Dialogue (London, 1743).
The Patriot Muse, or Poems on Some of the Principal Events of the Late War; Together with a Poem on the Peace (London, 1764).
The Patriots Guide. A Poem Inscribed to the Earl of C–M, Junius, and John Wilkes (London, 1773).
Patriotism! A Farce (London, 1764).
A Poem on the Battle of DETTINGEN. Inscrib'd to the King (London, 1743).
POEM by a Lady on seeing His Royal Highness the Prince Regent (Edinburgh? 1745).
Poetical Calendar, vol. 6 (London, 1763).
Power and Patriotism: A Poetical Epistle Humbly Inscribed to the Right Honourable H. P. Esq. (London, 1746).
The Progress of Glory: An Irregular Ode, Address'd to His Majesty, on the Happy Suppression of the REBELLION (London, 1746).
A Religious Ode, Occasion'd by the Present Rebellion. Written Oct. 11, 1745. By a Clergyman (London, 1745).
Report of the Proceedings and Opinion of the Board of General Officers on their Examination into the conduct, behaviour, and proceedings of Sir John Cope . . . &C (London, 1749).
To his Royal Highness Charles, Prince of Wales, Regent of the Kingdoms of Scotland, England, France, and Ireland (n.p., 1745).
A Scheme for rewarding the Heroic Actions of His Royal Highness the Duke of Cumberland (Edinburgh, 1746).
Sedition and Defamation Display'd (London, 1731).
On the Signal Victory at Gladsmuir. By a Lady (n.p., 1745?).
The Three Politicians: or, a Dialogue in Verse Between a Patriot, A Courtier, and their Friend. Concluding with an Exhortation to Admiral Vernon (London, 1741).
Verses to his Royal Highness the Duke of Cumberland: on His being wounded, at the Repulse of the French near Dettingen (London, 1743).

B. ATTRIBUTED WORKS

Akenside, Mark, *Poetical Works*, ed. Alexander Dyce (London, 1857).
    Poetical Works, ed. Robin Dix (Madison, NJ, 1996).
Alexander, William, *History of Women*, 2 vols. (London, 1779).
Anderson, Robert, ed., *The Poets of Great Britain*, 14 vols. (London, 1795).
Arnall, William, *Opposition No Proof of Patriotism; with Some Observations and Advice Concerning Party-Writings* (London, 1735).
Barbauld, Anna Letitia, *Poems*, ed. William McCarthy and Elizabeth Kraft (Athens, GA, 1994).

Bentley, Elizabeth, *Genuine Poetical Compositions* (Norwich, 1791).
   Poems (Norwich, 1821).
Bentley, Richard, *Patriotism, a Mock-Heroic*, 2nd. edn. (London, 1765).
Bessborough, Earl of, ed., *Georgiana: Extracts from the Correspondence of Georgiana, Duchess of Devonshire* (London, 1955).
Blackstone, Sir William, *Commentaries on the Laws of England*, 7th. edn., 4 vols. (London, 1775).
Blackwell, Thomas, *Letters Concerning Mythology* (London, 1748).
Bolingbroke, Henry St. John, Viscount, *Political Writing: The Conservative Enlightenment*, ed. Bernard Cottret (New York, 1997).
Boswell, James, *Life of Johnson*, ed. G. B. Hill, rev. L. F. Powell, 6 vols. (Oxford: Clarendon, 1934–50).
   Boswell's London Journal 1762–1763, ed. Frederick Pottle (New Haven, 1950).
Brown, John, *Estimate of the Manners and Principles of the Times* (London, 1757).
   Dissertation on the Rise, Union, &c. Of Poetry and Music (London, 1763).
Bruce, Archibald, *True Patriotism; or, a Public Spirit for God and Religion Recommended, and the Want of It Reprehended* (Edinburgh, 1785).
Burke, Edmund, *Writings and Speeches of Edmund Burke*, gen. ed. Paul Langford, 8 vols. to date (Oxford: Clarendon, 1980–).
Carew, Richard, *A Survey of Cornwall* (1602; new edition, London, 1723).
Carte, Thomas, *General History of England* (London, 1750).
Chalmers, Alexander, *Works of the English Poets*, 21 vols. (London, 1810).
Churchill, Charles, *Poetical Works*, ed. Douglas Grant (Oxford: Clarendon, 1956).
Cicero, *On Duties*, tr. M. T. Griffin and E. M. Atkins (Cambridge, 1991).
Cockings, George, *War: An Heroic Poem*, 2nd. edn. (Boston, 1762).
Collins, William, *Poetical Works of William Collins*, ed. Anna Barbauld (London, 1797).
   Poetical Works of Collins, ed. John Langhorne (London, 1804).
   Works, ed. Richard Wendorf and Charles Ryskamp (Oxford, 1979).
Conybeare, John, *True Patriotism* (London, 1749).
Cottle, Joseph, *Poems* (Bristol, 1795).
Cowper, William, *Letters and Prose Writings*, ed. James King and Charles Ryskamp, 5 vols. (Oxford: Clarendon, 1979).
   Poems, ed. John Baird and Charles Ryskamp, 3 vols. (Oxford: Clarendon, 1980).
Defoe, Daniel, *A Brief Deduction of the Original, Progress, and Immense Greatness of the British Woollen Manufacture* (London, 1727).
   A Tour Through the Whole Island of Great Britain, ed. Pat Rogers (Harmondsworth, 1971).
Dodsley, Robert, *A Collection of Poems*, 6 vols. (London, 1748–63).
   A Collection of Poems by Several Hands (1782), intro., notes, and indices by Michael F. Suarez, SJ (London, 1997).
Drayton, Michael, *Poems*, ed. John Buxton, 2 vols. (London, 1953).
Dryden, John, *Works*, gen. eds. E. N. Hooker and H. T. Swedenberg, Jr., 18 vols. to date (Berkeley and Los Angeles, 1961–).

Duck, Stephen, *An Ode on the Battle of Dettingen* (London, 1743).

Duncombe, John, *Letters by Several Eminent Persons Deceased*, 3 vols. (London, 1773).

Dyer, John, *The Ruins of Rome* (London, 1740).

The Fleece, in *Minor Poets of the Eighteenth Century*, Everyman Library (London, 1930).

Ellis, William, *The Modern Husbandman*, 3 vols. (London, 1744).

Fielding, Henry, *The Author's Farce* (1730), ed. Charles Wood (Lincoln, NE, 1966).

The True Patriot and Related Writings, ed. W. B. Coley (Middletown, 1987).

Fordyce, James, *Sermons to Young Women*, 14th. edn., 2 vols. (London, 1814).

Gay, John, *Poetry and Prose*, ed. Vinton Dearing, 2 vols. (Oxford: Clarendon, 1974).

Gee, Joseph, *Impartial Inquiry into the Importance and Present State of the Woollen Manufactories of Great Britain* (Gainsborough, 1742).

Gibbon, Edward, *The History of the Decline and Fall of the Roman Empire*, ed. David Womersley, 3 vols. (London, 1994).

Goldsmith, Oliver, *An History of England, in a Series of Letters from a Nobleman to his Son*, 2 vols. (London, 1764).

History of the Earth, and Animated Nature, 8 vols. (London, 1774).

New Essays by Oliver Goldsmith, ed. R. S. Crane (Chicago, 1927).

Collected Letters of Oliver Goldsmith, ed. Katharine Balderstone (Folcroft, PA, 1928).

Collected Works, ed. Arthur Friedman, 5 vols. (Oxford: Clarendon, 1966).

Gray, Thomas, *Poems of Mr. Gray. To which are prefixed Memoirs of his Life and Writings*, ed. William Mason (London, 1775).

Poems of Mr. Gray. With Notes by Gilbert Wakefield (London, 1786).

Works of Gray, ed. John Mitford, 5 vols. (London, 1835–43).

Works of Thomas Gray, in Prose and Verse, ed. Sir Edmund Gosse, 4 vols. (London, 1884).

Gray's English Poems, ed. D. C. Tovey (Cambridge, 1898).

Correspondence, ed. Paget Toynbee and Leonard Whibley, 3 vols. (Oxford: Clarendon, 1935).

[Griffith, Elizabeth], *Amanna. A Dramatic Poem* (London, 1764).

Hawkins, Sir John, *Life of Samuel Johnson, LL. D.* (London, 1787).

Hervey, John Lord, *The Conduct of the Opposition, and the Tendency of Modern Patriotism* (Edinburgh, 1734).

Holt-White, Rashleigh, ed., *Letters to Gilbert White* (London, 1907).

Horace, *Satires, Epistles, and Ars Poetica*, tr. H. R. Fairclough (London, 1970).

Hughes, John, *Poems on Several Occasions*, 2 vols. (London, 1735).

Hume, David, *Essays Moral, Political, and Literary*, ed. Eugene Miller, rev. edn. (Indianapolis, 1987).

Hurd, Richard, *Hurd's Letters on Chivalry and Romance*, ed. Edith Morley (London, 1911; repr. New York, 1976).

Isocrates, tr. George Norlin, 2 vols. (Cambridge, MA, 1929).

Johnson, Samuel, *Lives of the English Poets*, ed. G. B. Hill, 3 vols. (Oxford: Clarendon, 1905).

Journey to the Western Islands of Scotland, ed. Mary Lascelles (New Haven, 1971).
Political Writings, ed. Donald Greene (New Haven, 1977).
A Dictionary of the English Language, 4th. edn., 2 vols. (London, 1773, repr. Beirut, 1978).
Letters of Samuel Johnson, ed. Bruce Redford, 4 vols. (Princeton, 1992–94).
"Junius," *Letters of Junius*, ed. John Cannon (Oxford: Clarendon, 1978).
Kames, Henry Home, Lord, *Sketches of the History of Man*, 2 vols. (Edinburgh, 1774).
The Gentleman Farmer (London, 1779).
Kennett, Basil, *The Lives and Characters of the Ancient Grecian Poets* (London, 1697).
King, Anthony, *The Frequented Village* (London, 1771).
Knox, Vicesimus, *Essays Moral and Literary*, 6th. edn., 2 vols. (London, 1785).
Elegant Extracts (London, 1789).
Lambard, William, *A Perambulation of Kent* (London, 1576).
Lockman, John, *An Ode, on the Crushing of the Rebellion anno MDCCLXVI* (London, 1746).
Lonsdale, Roger, ed., *The Poems of Gray, Collins, and Goldsmith* (London, 1969).
ed., *The New Oxford Book of Eighteenth-Century Verse* (Oxford, 1984).
ed. *Eighteenth-Century Women Poets* (Oxford, 1990).
Lowth, Benjamin, *Lectures on the Sacred Poetry of the Hebrews*, tr. G. Gregory (London, 1787).
Lyttelton, George, *Epistle to Mr. Pope* (London, 1730).
Macaulay, Catharine, *History of England from the Accession of James I to the Elevation of the House of Hanover*, 3rd. edn., 8 vols. (London, 1763–83).
Martyn, Benjamin, *Timoleon*, 2nd. edn. (London, 1730).
Mason, William, *Works*, 4 vols. (London, 1811).
Mathias, Thomas Henry, *The Pursuits of Literature*, 11th. edn. (London, 1801).
McCann, Timothy, ed., *The Correspondence of the Dukes of Richmond and Newcastle, 1724–1750* (Lewes, 1984).
Milton, John, *Complete Prose Works*, gen. ed. Don Wolfe, 8 vols. in 10 (New Haven, 1953–82).
Complete Poems and Major Prose, ed. Merritt Hughes (New York, 1958).
Mitchell, Joseph, *Poems on Several Occasions*, 2 vols. (London, 1729).
Montagu, Elizabeth, *Essay on the Writings and Genius of Shakespeare* (London, 1769).
Montagu, Lady Mary Wortley, *Letters of the Right Honourable Lady M–y W–y M–e*, 3 vols. (London, 1763).
Complete Letters of Lady Mary Wortley Montagu, ed. Robert Halsband, 3 vols. (Oxford, 1965).
Essays and Poems and Simplicity: A Comedy, ed. Robert Halsband and Isobel Grundy (Oxford: Clarendon, 1977).
More, Hannah, *Slavery, a Poem* (London, 1788).
Works, 2 vols. (New York, 1846–47).
Newcomb, Thomas, "An Ode, presented to His Royal Highness the Duke of Cumberland, on his return from Scotland" (London, 1746).
Newman, Charles Christian, *The Love of our Country* (London, 1783).

Ogilvie, John, *Essay on the Lyric Poetry of the Ancients* (1762, repr. Los Angeles, 1970).
Paine, Thomas, *The Rights of Man* (New York, 1984).
Pindar, *Odes of Pindar*, ed. Francis Lee (London, 1810).
Playfair, John, *Works*, 4 vols. (Edinburgh, 1822).
Polwhele, Richard, *The Unsex'd Females* (London, 1798).
Pope, Alexander, *Poems*, gen. ed. John Butt, 11 vols. (New Haven, 1938–68).
  Correspondence, ed. George Sherburn, 5 vols. (Oxford: Clarendon, 1955).
  Selected Prose, ed. Paul Hammond (Cambridge, 1987).
Price, Richard, *Political Writings*, ed. D. O. Thomas (Cambridge, 1991).
Ralph, James, *The Case of Authors by Profession or Trade* (London, 1758).
Ruffhead, Owen, *Life of Alexander Pope* (London, 1769).
Russell, William, *Essay on the Character, Manners, and Genius of Women*, 2 vols. (Philadelphia, 1774).
Shakespeare, William, *The Complete Works*, ed. G. B. Harrison (New York, 1948).
Smart, Christopher, *Poetical Works*, ed. Karina Williamson and Marcus Walsh, 6 vols. (Oxford: Clarendon, 1980–96).
Smith, Adam, *The Wealth of Nations*, 2 vols. (London, 1776).
Smith, Charlotte, *Poems*, ed. Stuart Curran (Oxford, 1993).
Smith, John, *The Grasiers Advocate: or, Free thoughts of wool, and the woollen trade* (London, 1742).
  Chronicon Rusticum-Commerciale, or Memoirs of Wool, Woollen Manufactures, and Trade, (Particularly in England) From the Earliest to the Present Times, 2 vols. (London, 1747, 2nd. edn., 1756–57).
Smollett, Tobias, *Complete History of England*, 8 vols. (London, 1791).
  Travels Through France and Italy, ed. Frank Felsenstein (Oxford, 1979).
  Poems, Plays, and "The Briton", intro. Byron Gassman, ed. O. M. Brack, Jr. (Athens, GA, 1993).
Spence, Joseph, *Observations, Anecdotes, and Characters of Books and Men*, ed. James Osborn, 2 vols. (Oxford: Clarendon, 1966).
Spingarn, Joel, ed., *Critical Essays of the Seventeenth Century*, 3 vols. (New York, 1908–9).
Stockdale, Percival, *Churchill Defended, a Poem Addressed to the Minority* (London, 1765).
Thompson, Aaron, *The British History, Translated into English from the Latin of Jeffrey of Monmouth* (London, 1718).
Thomson, James, *The Castle of Indolence and Other Poems*, ed. A. D. McKillop (Lawrence, KS, 1961).
  Letters and Documents, ed. A. D. McKillop (Lawrence, KS, 1958).
Walpole, Horace, *Correspondence*, gen. ed. Wilmarth S. Lewis, 48 vols. in 49 (New Haven, 1937–83).
  Walpoliana, 2 vols. (London, 1800).
Warton, Joseph, *Essay on the Genius and Writings of Pope*, 2 vols. (London, 1756, 1757).
  ed., *Works of Alexander Pope*, 9 vols. (London, 1797).
Wilkes, Thomas, *General View of the Stage* (London, 1759).

Williams, Sir Hanbury, *Works*, 3 vols. (London, 1822).
Williams, Helen Maria, *Poems*, 2 vols. (London, 1786).
Poem on the Bill lately passed for regulating the Slave Trade (London, 1788).
Wollstonecraft, Mary, *Vindication of the Rights of Woman* (1792), ed. Miriam Kramnick (Harmondsworth, 1978).
Yearsley, Ann, *Poems on Several Occasions* (London, 1785).
Poems on Various Subjects (London, 1787).
Poem on the Inhumanity of the Slave-Trade (London, 1788).
Earl Goodwin (London, 1791).
An Elegy on Marie Antoinette, . . . Queen of France. With a poem on the last interview between the King of Poland and Loraski (Bristol, 1795).
The Rural Lyre (London, 1796).
Young, Edward, *Poetical Works*, 2 vols. (London, 1866).

C. MAGAZINES

British Magazine.
Critical Review.
Daily Advertiser.
Gentleman's Magazine.
Literary Magazine.
London Magazine.
The Midwife.
Monthly Review.
The Museum.
Universal Visiter.

SECONDARY WORKS

Anderson, Benedict, *Imagined Communities: Reflections on the Origin and Spread of Nationalism*, rev. edn. (London, 1991).
Atherton, Herbert, *Political Prints in the Age of Hogarth: A Study of the Iconographic Representation of Politics* (Oxford: Clarendon, 1974).
Barrell, John, *English Literature in History, 1730–1780: An Equal, Wide Survey* (London, 1983).
"Afterword," in Gerald Maclean, Donna Landry, and Joseph P. Ward, eds., *The Country and the City Revisited: England and the Politics of Culture, 1550–1850* (Cambridge, 1999), 231–50.
Imagining the King's Death: Figurative Treason, Fantasies of Regicide, 1793–1796 (Oxford, 2000).
Bate, W. Jackson, *From Classic to Romantic: Premises of Taste in Eighteenth-Century England* (Cambridge, MA, 1946).
The Burden of the Past and the English Poet (Cambridge, MA, 1970).
Bloom, Harold, *The Anxiety of Influence* (New York, 1973).

Bogel, Fredric, *Literature and Insubstantiality in Late Eighteenth-Century England* (Princeton, 1984).

Brewer, John, *The Common People and Politics, 1750s–1790s* (Cambridge, 1986).

Buck, Howard S., "Smollett and Dr. Akenside," *JEGP*, 31 (1932), 10–26.

Bucke, Charles, *On the Life, Writings, and Genius of Akenside* (London, 1832).

Cannon, John, *Samuel Johnson and the Politics of Hanoverian England* (Oxford, 1994).

Carver, P. L., *The Life of a Poet: A Biographical Sketch of William Collins* (London, 1967).

Coleridge, Samuel Taylor, *Table Talk*, ed. Carl Woodring, 2 vols. (Princeton, 1990).

Colley, Linda, *Britons: Forging the Nation, 1707–1837* (New Haven, 1992).

Courthope, W. J., *History of English Poetry*, 6 vols. (London, 1895–1909).

Danchin, Pierre, ed., *Prologues and Epilogues of the Eighteenth Century*, 5 vols. (Nancy, 1990–).

Davie, Donald, ed., *The Late Augustans* (London, 1958).

"The Language of the Eighteenth-Century Hymn," in Donald Davie and Robert Stevenson, eds., *English Hymnology in the Eighteenth Century* (Los Angeles, 1980), 1–19.

Davis, Leigh, *Acts of Union: Scotland and the Literary Negotiation of the British Nation, 1707–1830* (Stanford, 1998).

Dix, Robin, "The Literary Relationship of Mark Akenside and David Fordyce," *Scottish Literary Journal*, 23 (1996), 13–20.

Dobrée, Bonamy, "The Theme of Patriotism in the Poetry of the Early Eighteenth Century," *Proceedings of the British Academy*, 35 (1949), 49–65.

English Literature in the Early Eighteenth Century, 1700–1740 (Oxford, 1959).

Doob, Leonard, *Patriotism and Nationalism* (New Haven, 1964).

Dowling, William, *The Epistolary Moment: The Poetics of the Eighteenth-Century Verse Epistle* (Princeton, 1991).

"Ideology and the Flight from History in Eighteenth-Century Poetry," in Leopold Damrosch, ed., *The Profession of Eighteenth-Century Literature* (Madison, 1992), 135–53.

Downey, James, and Ben Jones, eds., *Fearful Joy: Papers from the Thomas Gray Bicentenary Conference at Carleton University* (Montreal, 1974).

Duffy, Michael, *The Englishman and the Foreigner* (Cambridge, 1986).

Dugaw, Diane, *Warrior Women and Popular Balladry* (Cambridge, 1989).

Dussinger, John A., ed., *Questions of Literary Property in Eighteenth-Century England (Studies in the Literary Imagination*, 34: 1 [2001]).

Empson, William, *Some Versions of Pastoral*, rev. edn. (Harmondsworth, 1965).

Erskine-Hill, Howard, *The Poetry of Opposition and Revolution: Dryden to Wordsworth* (Oxford, 1996).

Fairholt, F. W., *Costume in England*, 3rd. edn., rev. H. A. Dillon, 2 vols. (London, 1885).

Faulkner, Peter, "William Cowper and the Poetry of Empire," *Durham University Journal*, 83 (1991), 165–73.

Feingold, Richard, *Nature and Society: Later Eighteenth-Century Uses of the Pastoral and the Georgic* (New Brunswick, 1977).

Ferguson, Moira, "The Unpublished Poems of Ann Yearsley," *Tulsa Studies in Women's Literature*, 12 (1993), 13–46.

Foreman, Amanda, *Georgiana, Duchess of Devonshire* (London, 1998).

Forster, John, *Life and Times of Oliver Goldsmith*, 2nd. edn., 2 vols. (London, 1854).

Foxon, David, *English Verse, 1701–1750* (London, 1975).

Fulford, Tim, *Landscape, Liberty, and Authority: Poetry, Criticism, and Politics from Thomson to Wordsworth* (Cambridge, 1996).

Garrod, H. W., *Collins* (Oxford, 1928).

Gerrard, Christine, "*The Castle of Indolence* and the Opposition to Walpole," *Review of English Studies*, 41 (1990), 45–64.

 The Patriot Opposition to Walpole: Politics, Poetry, and National Myth, 1725–1742 (Oxford, 1994).

Goldgar, Bertrand, *Walpole and the Wits: The Relation of Politics to Literature, 1722–1742* (Lincoln, NE, 1976).

Goldstein, Lawrence, *Ruins and Empire: The Evolution of a Theme in Augustan and Romantic Literature* (Pittsburg, 1977).

Goodridge, John, *Rural Life in Eighteenth-Century English Poetry* (Cambridge, 1995).

Greenfeld, Liah, *Nationalism: Five Roads to Modernity* (Cambridge, MA, 1992).

Griffin, Dustin, "Redefining Georgic: Cowper's *Task*," *ELH*, 57 (1990), 865–79.

 "Akenside's Political Muse," in Robin Dix, ed., *Mark Akenside: A Reassessment* (London, 2000), 19–50.

Guest, Harriet, *Small Change: Women, Learning, Patriotism, 1750–1810* (Chicago, 2000).

Harries, Elizabeth, *The Unfinished Manner: Essays on the Fragment in the Later Eighteenth Century* (Charlottesville, 1994).

Harris, Robert, *A Patriot Press: National Politics and the London Press in the 1740s* (Oxford: Clarendon, 1994).

Hart, Jeffrey, "Akenside's Revision of *The Pleasures of Imagination*," *PMLA*, 74 (1959), 67–74.

Hawes, Clement, ed., *Christopher Smart and the Enlightenment* (New York, 1999).

Helgerson, Richard, *Forms of Nationhood: The Elizabethan Writing of England* (Chicago, 1992).

Hill, Bridget, *Republican Virago: The Life and Times of Catharine Macaulay, Historian* (Oxford: Clarendon, 1992).

Hobsbawm, Eric, *Nations and Nationalism since 1780: Programme, Myth, Reality* (Cambridge, 1990).

Houpt, Charles T., *Mark Akenside: A Biographical and Critical Study* (Philadelphia, 1944).

Hutchings, W. B., "William Cowper and 1789," *Yearbook of English Studies*, 19 (1989), 71–93.

Irlam, Shaun, "Gerrymandered Geographies: Exoticism in Thomson and Chateaubriand," *Modern Language Notes*, 108 (Dec. 1993), 891–912.

Jackson, Wallace, "Thomas Gray and the Dedicatory Muse," *ELH*, 54 (1987), 277–98.

Jones, W. Powell, "The Contemporary Readers of Gray's Odes," *Modern Philology*, 28 (1930–31), 61–82.

Thomas Gray, Scholar (New York, 1937).

Jordan, Gerald, and Nicholas Rogers, "Admirals as Heroes: Patriotism and Liberty in Hanoverian England," *Journal of British Studies*, 28 (1989), 201–44.

Jump, Harriet, "Akenside's Other Epistle," *Notes and Queries*, n.s. 33 (1986), 508–12.

"High Sentiments of Liberty: Coleridge's Unacknowledged Debt to Akenside," *Studies in Romanticism*, 28 (1989), 207–24.

Kaul, Suvir, *Thomas Gray and Literary Authority: A Study in Ideology and Poetics* (Stanford, 1992).

Poems of Nation, Anthems of Empire: English Verse in the Long Eighteenth Century (Charlottesville, 2000).

Kidd, Colin, *Subverting Scotland's Past: Scottish Whig Historians and the Creation of an Anglo-British Identity* (Cambridge, 1993).

British Identities Before Nationalism: Ethnicity and Nationhood in the Atlantic World, 1600–1800 (Cambridge, 1999).

Kippis, Andrew, ed., *Biographia Britannica*, 2nd. edn., 5 vols. (London, 1778–93).

Knight, Charles, "The Images of Nations in Eighteenth-Century Satire," *ECS*, 22:4 (1989), 489–511.

Kramnick, Jonathan, *Making the English Canon: Print-Capitalism and the Cultural Past, 1700–1770* (Cambridge, 1998).

Kuhn, Albert, "Christopher Smart: The Poet as Patriot of the Lord," *ELH*, 30 (1963), 121–36.

Landa, Louis, *Essays in Eighteenth-Century English Literature* (Princeton, 1980).

Landry, Donna, *The Muses of Resistance: Laboring-Class Women's Poetry in Britain, 1739–1796* (Cambridge, 1990).

Langford, Paul, *Walpole and the Robinocracy* (Cambridge, 1986).

Lemire, Beverly, *Fashion's Favourite: The Cotton Trade and the Consumer in Britain, 1600–1800* (Oxford, 1991).

Leranbaum, Miriam, *Alexander Pope's "Opus Magnum" 1729–1744* (Oxford: Clarendon, 1977).

Levine, William, "Collins, Thomson, and the Whig Progress of Liberty," *SEL*, 34 (1994), 553–78.

"'Beyond the Limits of a Vulgar Fate': The Renegotiation of Public and Private Concerns in the Career of Gray and other Mid-Eighteenth-Century Poets," *Studies in Eighteenth-Century Culture*, 24 (1995), 223–42.

Levinson, Marjorie, *The Romantic Fragment Poem* (Chapel Hill, 1986).

Lipking, Lawrence, "The Genius of the Shore: Lycidas, Adamastor, and the Poetics of Nationalism," *PMLA*, 111 (1996), 205–21.

"The Gods of Poetry: Mythology and the Eighteenth-Century Tradition," in Albert Rivero, ed., *Augustan Subjects* (Newark, DE, 1997).

Lonsdale, Roger, "The Poetry of Thomas Gray: Versions of the Self," *Proceedings of the British Academy* (1973), 105–23.

"'A Garden and a Grave': The Poetry of Oliver Goldsmith," in Louis Martz and Aubrey Williams, eds., *The Author in His Work* (New Haven, 1978).

Lucas, John, *England and Englishness: Ideas of Nationhood in English Poetry, 1688–1900* (London, 1990).

Mack, Maynard, *Alexander Pope: A Life* (New York, 1985).

Maclean, Gerald, Donna Landry, and Joseph P. Ward, eds., *The Country and the City Revisited: England and the Politics of Culture, 1550–1850* (Cambridge, 1999).

MacLean, Kenneth, "William Cowper," in F. W. Hiles, ed., *The Age of Johnson* (New Haven, 1949), 257–67.

Mahony, John, "Mark Akenside," in *Dictionary of Literary Biography*, vol. 109, *Eighteenth-Century British Poets: Second Series*, ed. John Sitter (Detroit, 1991).

McKillop, A. D., "The Background of Thomson's *Liberty*," *Rice Institute Pamphlets*, 38, no. 2 (1951).

"The Reception of Thomson's 'Liberty,' '" *Notes and Queries*, 198 (1953), 112–13.

McNairn, Alan, *Behold the Hero: General Wolfe and the Arts in the Eighteenth Century* (Montreal, 1997).

Meehan, Michael, *Liberty and Poetics in Eighteenth-Century England* (London, 1986).

Mellor, Anne, *Mothers of the Nation: Women Political Writers in England, 1780–1830* (Bloomington, 2000).

Moore, Cecil, *Backgrounds of English Literature, 1700–1760* (Minneapolis, 1953).

Musgrove, S., "The Theme of Collins's Odes," *Notes and Queries*, 185 (1943), 214–17, 253–55.

Newey, Vincent, *Cowper's Poetry* (Liverpool, 1982).

Newman, Gerald, *The Rise of English Nationalism: A Cultural History, 1740–1830* (New York, 1987).

Nichols, John, *Literary Anecdotes of the Eighteenth Century*, 9 vols. (London, 1812–15).

Odney, Paul, "Thomas Gray's 'Daring Spirit': Forging the Poetics of an Alternative Nationalism," *Clio*, 28:3 (1999), 247–60.

Pittock, Murray, *Poetry and Jacobite Politics in Eighteenth-Century Britain and Ireland* (Cambridge, 1994).

Inventing and Resisting Britain: Cultural Identities in Britain and Ireland, 1685–1789 (Basingstoke, 1997).

Priestman, Martin, *Cowper's Task: Structure and Influence* (Cambridge, 1983).

Quinlan, Maurice, *William Cowper: A Critical Life* (Minneapolis, 1953).

Quint, David, *Epic and Empire: Politics and Generic Form from Virgil to Milton* (Princeton, 1993).

Quintana, Ricardo, "The Scheme of Collins' *Odes on Several . . . Subjects*," in Carroll Camden, ed., *Restoration and Eighteenth-Century Literature* (Chicago, 1963), 371–80.

Oliver Goldsmith: A Georgian Study (London, 1969).

Radcliffe, Evan, "Burke, Radical Cosmopolitanism, and the Debate on Patriotism in the 1790s," *Studies in Eighteenth-Century Culture*, 28 (1999), 311–39.

Richmond, Sir Herbert William, *The Navy in the War of 1739–48*, 3 vols. (Cambridge, 1920).

Rizzo, Betty, and Robert Mahony, *Christopher Smart: An Annotated Bibliography, 1743–1983* (New York, 1984).

Robertson, William, *Elements of the Philosophy of the Human Mind*, 3 vols. (London, 1829).

Rodger, N. A. M., *The Wooden World: An Anatomy of the Georgian Navy* (Annapolis, 1986).

Rogers, Nicholas, *Whigs and Cities: Popular Politics in the Age of Walpole and Pitt* (Oxford, 1989).

Rousseau, George, ed., *Goldsmith: The Critical Heritage* (London, 1974).

The Perilous Enlightenment: Pre- and Post-Modern Discourses (Manchester, 1991).

Saintsbury, George, *Peace of the Augustans* (London, 1916).

Salmon, Thomas, *Modern History*, 3rd. edn., 3 vols. (London, 1744–46).

Sambrook, James, *James Thomson 1700–1748: A Life* (Oxford: Clarendon, 1991).

"'A Just Balance between Patronage and the Press': The Case of James Thomson," in John A. Dussinger, ed., *Questions of Literary Property in Eighteenth-Century England* (*Studies in the Literary Imagination*, 34:1 [2001]), 137–53.

Scott, Mary Jane W., *James Thomson, Anglo-Scot* (Athens, GA, 1988).

Sha, Richard, "Gray's Political *Elegy*: Poetry as the Burial of History," *Philological Quarterly*, 69 (1990), 337–57.

Shankman, Steven, "The Pindaric Tradition and the Quest for Pure Poetry," *Comparative Literature*, 34 (1988), 219–44.

Sherbo, Arthur, "The Probable Time of Composition of Smart's 'Song,' 'Psalms,' and 'Hymns and Spiritual Songs,'" *JEGP*, 55 (1956), 41–57.

Christopher Smart: Scholar of the University (East Lansing, 1967).

Sitter, John, *Literary Loneliness in Mid-Eighteenth-Century England* (Ithaca, 1982).

Steele, James, "Thomas Gray and the Season for Triumph," in James Downey and Ben Jones, eds., *Fearful Joy: Papers from the Thomas Gray Bicentenary Conference at Carleton University* (Montreal, 1974), 198–240.

Stewart, Mary Margaret, "William Collins' Ode on the Death of Charles Ross: The Search for Audience and Patronage," *Age of Johnson*, 8 (1997), 209–22.

Stone, Lawrence, ed., *An Imperial State at War: Britain from 1689 to 1815* (London, 1994).

Suarez, Michael, "Trafficking in the Muse: Dodsley's *Collection* and the Question of Canon," in Alvaro Ribeiro and James Basker, eds., *Tradition in Transition* (Oxford: Clarendon, 1996), 297–313.

Swarbrick, Andrew, ed., *The Art of Oliver Goldsmith* (London, 1984).

Tompkins, J. M. S., *The Polite Marriage* (Cambridge, 1938).

Urstal, Tone, *Sir Robert Walpole's Poets: The Use of Literature as Pro-Government Propaganda, 1721–1742* (Newark, DE, 1999).

Wagstaffe, W. H. D., "Notes Respecting the Life and Family of John Dyer, the Poet," *The Patrician*, 5 (1848), 78–81.

Waldron, Mary, *Lactilla, Milkwoman of Clifton: The Life and Writings of Ann Yearsley, 1753–1806* (Athens, GA, 1996).

Wardle, Ralph, *Oliver Goldsmith, the Poet* (Lawrence, KS, 1957).

Weinbrot, Howard, "William Collins and the Mid-Century Ode: Poetry, Patriotism, and the Influence of Context," in Howard Weinbrot and Martin Price, *Context, Influence, and Mid-Eighteenth-Century Poetry* (Los Angeles, 1990), 1–39.

   Britannia's Issue: The Rise of British Literature from Dryden to Ossian (Cambridge, 1993).

Wendorf, Richard, *William Collins and Eighteenth-Century English Poetry* (Minneapolis, 1981).

Williams, Anne, *Prophetic Strain: The Greater Lyric in the Eighteenth Century* (Chicago, 1984).

Williams, Glyn, *The Prize of all the Oceans: The Triumph and Tragedy of Anson's Voyage Round the World* (London, 1999).

Williams, Ralph, *Poet, Painter, and Parson: The Life of John Dyer* (New York, 1956).

Williams, Raymond, *The Country and the City* (Oxford, 1973).

Wilson, Kathleen, *The Sense of the People: Politics, Culture, and Imperialism in England, 1715–1785* (Cambridge, 1995).

Wimsatt, W. K., *The Portraits of Alexander Pope* (New Haven, 1965).

Zionkowski, Linda, "Bridging the Gulf between the Poet and the Audience in the Work of Gray," *ELH*, 58 (1991), 331–50.

Index